ACADEMIA LUNARE

That Very Witch

Fear, Feminism, and the American Witch Film

Payton McCarty-Simas

Cover Image © Stephanie Monohan 2025

Text © Payton McCarty-Simas 2025

First published by Luna Press Publishing, Edinburgh, 2025

The right of Payton McCarty-Simas to be identified as the Author of the Work has been asserted by them in accordance with the Copyright, Designs and Patents Act 1988.

That Very Witch: Fear, Feminism, and the American Witch Film © 2024. All rights reserved. No part of this book may be used or reproduced in any manner for the purpose of training artificial intelligence technologies or systems. No part of this publication may be reproduced, stored in a retrieval system, or transmitted in any form or by any means, electronic, mechanical, photocopy, recording or otherwise, without prior written permission of the copyright owners. Nor can it be circulated in any form of binding or cover other than that in which it is published and without similar condition including this condition being imposed on a subsequent purchaser. The views and opinions expressed in this book are those of the author and do not necessarily reflect the opinions or beliefs of the publisher and its affiliates. Luna Press Publishing disclaims any responsibility for the materials contained in any third party website referenced in this work.

www.lunapresspublishing.com

ISBN-13: 978-1-915556-60-8

A CIP catalogue record is available from the British Library

CONTENT WARNING

At the core of this research are horror witch movies in their historical context: this book will discuss themes of a sexual nature, violence, threat, suicide, drug use, racism.

Contains mature language and movie spoilers.

For rebellion is as the sin of witchcraft.
—Samuel 15:23

If the Devil has PR, then it's cinema.
—Mike Warnke, "The Devil Worshippers" (1985)

Contents

Introduction   1
"Something Wicked This Way Comes"

Chapter One   4
Good Witch or Bad Witch: The Paradox of Womanhood

Chapter Two   13
The Cinematic Witch as Anxiety of the Feminine

PART ONE: Season of the Witch   21
The Countercultural Witch Films of the Long Sixties

Chapter Three   23
Setting the Stage for the Countercultural Witch Film (1960-1964)

Chapter Four   40
The Countercultural Witch Is Born (1965-1967)

Chapter Five   69
The Countercultural Witch as Feminist Symbol (1968-1973)

Chapter Six   98
The End of the Countercultural Witch Horror Cycle

PART TWO: Unpleasant Dreams   115
Feminism, Satanic Panic and the Witch Films of the 1980s

Chapter Seven   117
Look What's Happened to Rosemary's Baby

Chapter Eight   124
The Roots of Satanic Panic (1977-1983)

Chapter Nine   140
Backlash, Comedy, and the Witch Film

Chapter Ten   172
Witch Films, Satanic Panic Specials, and "Morale-Boosting Entertainment"

INTERLUDE 181
Notes on the Postfeminist Witch Film (1990-2013)

Chapter Eleven 183
Riot Grrrls, Girl Power, and the Bitchification of the Witch

Chapter Twelve 207
Fantasy, Franchising, Fracture, and the "Girlboss" Witch

PART THREE 221
Gender, Genre, Psychedelics, and Abjection in the 2010s "Witch" Horror Cycle

Chapter Thirteen 223
Defining the 2010s Witch Horror Cycle

Chapter Fourteen 232
Genre and the 2010s "Witch Film"

Chapter Fifteen 243
Dancing with the Devil: Psychedelics and Altered States

Chapter Sixteen 248
Witchcraft as Abject Transcendence

Chapter Seventeen 251
The Tragedy of The Love Witch

Epilogue 261
Disenchanted?

Acknowledgements 273
Works Cited 274
Film/Mediography 298

Introduction

"Something Wicked This Way Comes"[1]

This book began five years ago, as I was preparing to write my undergraduate senior thesis. An avid horror fan and a child of haunted New England, I filled the troglodyte summer months of the pandemic on Cape Cod watching my comfort movies—things like *Rosemary's Baby* (1968), *The Blair Witch Project* (1999), *The Craft* (1996), and *Suspiria* (1977) Somewhere between rewatching *The Witch* (2015) for the millionth time and watching *Suspiria* (2018) for the first, I noticed a pattern. The sorceresses of the 2010s *weren't dying* at the ends of their movies. They were laughing. I was fascinated.

That summer, I looked into the witch films of the 2010s, tracking this alongside the rise of Donald Trump (and what he called his own "witch hunt"),[2] the birth of #MeToo, and the renewed popularity of the occult and New Age spirituality. I searched for meaning in this sudden transfiguration of my favorite horror monster from burned at the stake to burning up the screen and was delighted to find her reveling in the destruction of systems of oppression, dissolving boundaries, and making mayhem. I decided to write about it.

As this investigation would indicate, my interest in film comes from a fascination with its power to serve as a cultural record, a broad-ranging sociological id born out of competing commercial and artistic interests. Growing up at a time when many of my friends were forbidden to read *Harry Potter* because it supposedly denigrated Christianity and encouraged the real-life practice of witchcraft, I quickly understood that the media I so eagerly devoured held meaning in the obscure world of adults beyond my personal entertainment. Books and films soaked up political significance often far beyond what their creators intended. I view movies as a highly collectivized commercial product, crafted by studios and individuals alike to respond to trends (real or perceived) in the culture (subcultural, aesthetic, generic, etc.) to make as much money as possible. Upon their release, they continue to evolve and change as audiences and critics watch them, discuss them, and recontextualize them over and over again. That's not to say that writers and directors don't exert significant control on the meanings of their films, of course as I recount the stories of the witch films in this

---

1. *Macbeth*, Shakespeare.
2. Markham-Cantor 2019.

book, I combine the stated impulses of their creators, shaped by their films' development history, with the political and social histories into which their creations arrive. This way, I present each film as a product of its time and place, individual examples of what Robin Wood once called our culture's "collective nightmares."[3] As such, they become cracked mirrors not quite of the culture as it is, but of what individuals, companies, and audiences either believe, desire, or *fear* it might or might not be.

In my undergraduate thesis, I explored the history of the witch as a feminist archetype and a source of masculine anxieties, and I began tracing her evolution on screen in those terms. I quickly realized, though, that to understand why *The Witch* resonated so strongly with women in 2015, I needed to understand the impact *Rosemary's Baby* had in 1968, and how that differed from earlier films like *Black Sunday* (1960) or *Bell, Book and Candle* (1958). *The Craft* can't be fully legible as a text without *Elvira, Mistress of the Dark* (1988), and none of these films truly come to life without an understanding of the state of women at the time of their release.

To say that witches are a feminist symbol may not come as a surprise at this point in history. As horror scholar Barbara Creed points out in her 1993 book *The Monstrous-Feminine*, witches are the only predominantly female classic horror monster, and unlike vampires or werewolves, this particular monster is burned into our cultural psyche by very *real* ghost stories and tales of femicide that have marred our history since before our nation's founding.[4] Witches have always been deeply political symbols of women's oppression, as well as women's power to resist it. But since the mid-2010s, witches have been in vogue, alongside other feminist antiheroes, "feral" women, and "unlikable female characters" in our pop culture. Over the past decade, this icon of dark femininity has become omnipresent: you might have noticed a New Age section at the local Barnes and Nobles stocked with the *Modern Witch Tarot Deck*[5] (sold as a youthful, stylish, all-female celebration of womanhood) and explicitly feminist Wicca-for-beginners guides with titles like *Witch Please.*[6] This mainstream wave of witchery and New Age belief—from your friend's dedication to the Co-Star astrology app to the remake of *Wicked* (2024) with Ariana Grande—is part of a longer history of this much loved (and deeply feared) archetype of the monstrous feminine. All of which led me to wonder: how did we get here? Why are we seeing this now? What about the witch has become so appealing to the feminists of the past decade, as opposed to, say, the feminists of the 2000s? Or the 1980s? What can we learn from the pop cultural feminist (or the merely feminist-coded) witch? *Are* these witches feminist?

---

3. Wood, 2003, pp. 30.
4. Creed, 1993, 73.
5. Sterle, 2019.
6. Maxwell, 2022.

The chapters that follow take on these questions, spanning seven decades, thirteen presidential administrations, and hundreds of films. Each chapter is a miniature cultural history (and historiography), telling the story of an era through its movies. As I work to answer the questions "what was the state of feminism at this point in American history?" and "how do the witch films of this era illustrate this era's feminist struggles?" the films I highlight vary wildly in style and substance, quality and ambition. Each era takes up this "monster" and imbues her with the concerns *du jour*, transforming her from housewife to homewrecker, hippie to mall goth, and, fascinatingly, back again. Some of the films I explore aren't horror films at all, but nevertheless speak to the political projects of feminists and anti-feminists alike, while others were produced outside the US but hold significant ties to American culture and American concerns. And though the witch on film is as old as film itself, my focus really begins with the birth of New Hollywood, the point in history at which the moving image and feminist politics for me converge, beginning around the time President Kennedy trounced Nixon not on the issues but on the TV set.[7] As far as television goes, let me note, too, that while I will reference the most popular witch TV shows of each era as points of comparison, this is a work centered on film and film history. While it would be possible to examine such texts as *Bewitched* (1964-1972), *Charmed* (1998-2006), or *The Mayfair Witches* (2023-present) to explore this archetype's pop cultural evolution, that project is better left to historians of that medium.

Most of this book was written while staring down the barrel of the 2024 presidential election, in a moment when conservative judges already felt empowered to suggest that women incur the wrath of God when they seek reproductive healthcare, when the rise of AI has blended real life and our media simulacra of it goes far beyond what even Jean Baudrillard or Marshall McLuhan would have believed possible. In the aftermath of Trump's decisive victory, I view this project in part as a look at how we got here as a nation.[8] What kinds of stories we tell to give each other the creeps provide a window into what—and *whom*—we fear. Following those scary stories through history, finding them over and over again across time and genre, seeing them told everywhere—from the grindhouse and the arthouse to the multiplex and the video store, and eventually on streaming platforms—we can begin to learn *why* we fear what they represent. And what it means when those stories *lose* their power to scare and become something else.

---

7. The first Nixon-Kennedy presidential debate was the first of its kind to be televised. Whether or not Nixon managed to hold his own on the issues was immaterial: he appeared sweaty, disheveled, and nervous while the highly telegenic, handsome younger candidate solidified his status as the political equivalent of Elvis Presley for voters.
8. Smith and Stanley, 2024.

Chapter One

Good Witch or Bad Witch: The Paradox of Womanhood

Witches appear as frightening figures in almost every culture, and cinemas across the globe depict this archetype differently, from the ghostly, vengeful witches of Japan and Latin America to the vampiric, seductress witches of Eastern Europe. The most familiar version of the American witch—the one with the pointy hat and the broom—can trace its origins through a polyglot history of Western European paganism (and Christianity's fears about it), the feverish paranoia of Colonial New England, and the very real witch hunts that plagued them both.

The story of the witch in the context of Western culture and cinema, particularly in America and Britain, is also intractably linked to a history of racism and institutional misogyny that shapes the characters in this book, most of whom are white (often blonde) and attractive. Along with their European mythological origins, many cinematic witch-tales reflect our culture's deep-seated miscegenation fears. These fears, steeped in bigotry, characterize myriad non-white cultures as primitive, superstitious, and devilish, implicitly capable of corrupting pure, vulnerable white women. Take Tituba, the first woman to confess to the crime of witchcraft during the Salem trials. Enslaved by the Rev. Parris, Tituba, who was either Afro-Caribbean or Native American (accounts vary), confessed, under the obvious threat of physical abuse by her enslavers,[1][2] to having signed the Devil's book and ridden on a broom. Forced testimonials from others accused, presented Tituba as a malevolent practitioner of a dark religion and represent the second most familiar American witch archetype, the Afro-Caribbean "voodoo queen."[3] Tituba has subsequently been mythologized as a sort of supernatural instigator, telling the young white women of Salem about witchcraft practices in Barbados and even performing spells for their entertainment, thus planting the seeds of their demonic delusions. Over time, as more attention has been paid to this historical scapegoating, depictions of

---
1. Schettino, 2019.
2. Karlsen, 1998, 36-7.
3. While no books have yet been written on the subject of the Black witch in American cinema, "Black Magic Women: How Racial and Gender Stereotypes Shaped Witch Archetypes in U.S. Popular Culture in the Long Sixties" by Jade Connolly-Cepurac offers an excellent introduction to this topic.

Tituba have evolved, but the pattern of vilification is fundamental to many cinematic narratives about white witches, who learn their craft from people of color who rarely appear on screen.

Much as mainstream American feminism has historically sidelined the struggles of women of color, witch films have largely overlooked or scapegoated them while appropriating their cultures' folklore, religion, and history to titillate white audiences. Thus, the white witch icon of American horror films exists in tense conversation with these other archetypes, representing a particular set of hegemonic patriarchal anxieties. This chapter will briefly probe the historical origins of those fears around women and power, beginning with the European witch crazes (or hunts) of the Middle Ages.[4]

Witch crazes spread across Europe repeatedly between the 1300s and the mid-1700s, leading to the deaths of thousands of people, mostly women, many of whom were hanged or burned at the stake. This brutality was deeply related to the way femininity was then understood and constructed: the Medieval European conception of femininity hinged on notions of excess and what philosopher Julia Kristeva defines as "the abject" in her book *Powers of Horror* (1982). The abject, or that which is unincorporated, ambiguous, archaic, or pre-symbolic, Kristeva says, has been historically associated with the female body and the processes of birth and bodily excretion (i.e. vomiting, defecation, menstruation, labor) as a site of pre-social, natural, yet-to-be-pathologized consciousness.[5] At this point in history, women were considered to be overly sexual and overly feeling, in need of a rational male protector. This same excessive perception of female sexuality, barely restrained by the men around them, undergirded accusations of witchcraft among neighbors that sent entire regions into the states of panic that led to systematic torture and public executions. The Catholic church actively encouraged these witch hunts, publishing the *Malleus Maleficarum* (the "Hammer of Witches") in Germany in 1486, a virulently misogynistic text that offered advice for identifying and exterminating witches. Through the early-mid 18th century, legal systems in France, England, Germany, and Colonial New England, among others, supported these murders as well.[6]

---

4. In this book, I will be using the term "witch craze" to connote broad periods of time during which witchcraft panics occurred, though not as a substitute for any particular series of witch trials. This was once the preferred term for what we currently call "witch hunts", another term I will use to suggest its current meaning. I've chosen to incorporate "witch craze" because as a term it conveys a heightened community affect, an atmosphere that shares certain elements with other, less harmful "crazes" or fads. Thus, the term is useful as a means of linking periods of witch paranoia to cultural trends in other contexts.
5. Kristeva, 1982, 4, 14.
6. For more on the legal system and witch hunting, see *The Last Witches of England* by John Callow, 2021.

For the purposes of this book, the literal, bloody history of the witch is less significant than the fact that she *is* a historical figure, and one with whom political and aesthetic valances have been associated. Scholars, philosophers, and feminists alike have written deeply political work on this topic. Silvia Federici, for example, compellingly argues that by the 1600s, the Medieval construction of femininity as abject—outside of a man's control, steeped in Christianity—was promulgated as witch lore in order to shore up European societies as they converted to capitalism. For Federici, the fact that the power of women in pre-capitalist communities was systematically undercut during this period, and that "the devil [was] being conjured up" as a reason for these women's behavior...

> ...remains baffling unless we assume that only through their demonization could forms of behavior that in the past had been tolerated or viewed as normal be rendered odious and frightening in the eyes of a broader population of women to whom the death of the witch served as a lesson of what to expect should they follow her path.[7]

Interpretations of witch crazes and their origins have evolved, and each permutation of the witch as a pop cultural figure is significant. The hypersexual construction of femininity during the 13th-century European witch craze, in addition to functioning as a later tool of capitalist resocialization, has, separately, been tied by feminist scholars to Christendom's early desire to eradicate European paganism, many forms of which foregrounded female or feminine deities with the power both to create and destroy life.[8] As Federici points out, the superstitions of medieval Europe included shamanism and witchcraft as a natural part of the world.[9] In the 1970s (see chapter 5), feminist theologian Merlin Stone argued that much of Christian femininity is constructed in opposition to this older pagan femininity, which survived covertly. She points out that pagan goddesses, "associated with sexual pleasure, reproduction, [and] prophecy", allowed more religious power for women than did Christianity.[10] Scholar Nel Noddings has pointed out that Stone's suggestion that some goddesses were specifically associated with serpents and fig trees as symbols of "wisdom (magic), immortality, and fertility", and that because snake bites "contributed... to the hallucinogenic states in which priestesses prophesied 'out of their own heads'," the description of "the serpent speaking to Eve" prior to the Fall could be viewed as part of the Bible's delegitimization of pagan practice and female religious and sexual agency.[11]

---

7. Federici, 2018, 20.
8. Noddings, 1989, 12-13.
9. Federici, 2018, 27.
10. Stone, 1976, 211.
11. Noddings, 1989, 53-4.

This argument, suggesting that literal pagan fertility cults of women pervaded Europe throughout the Middle Ages, worshiping the Horned God and the Great Mother in secret, was popularized by Margaret Murray in her wildly influential 1921 book *The Witch-Cult in Western Europe*, one of the earliest and most influential feminist studies of witchcraft. Though its research was quickly discredited, Murray's 1929 entry for "witchcraft" in the *Encyclopedia Britannica*, espousing these views, was reprinted in updated editions until 1969.[12] Her argument for a "joyous", woman-focused witch cult that worshipped nature in covens of thirteen has resonated through to the present in sentiment if not in historical understanding, shaping occult practice to this day. Nel Noddings' 1989 *Women and Evil* posits that in pagan tradition, femininity and sexuality were celebrated as divine, thus attractive to men and women alike; therefore, the church concluded that "this religion had to be stamped out, and all of its accomplishments to be tabooed or forbidden under the law",[13] leading to the demonization of female sexuality—a conclusion Kristeva echoes in her construction of the abject as, among other things, "religious abominations".[14] "If anyone personifies abjection without assurance of purification," Kristeva says, "it is a woman."[15]

Whether directly tied to the witch-cult hypothesis or not, this mythical narrative speaks to a shift in pre-modern European conceptions of femininity that inexorably constructed the power of the witch as an anti-feminine signifier. Women's sexuality became a violent supernatural force as men accused witches of erotically invading their dreams and satanically seducing them—or worse, rendering them impotent with black magic. For Federici, the women who resisted their subjugation were cast as witches as part of a "a massive, internationally organized, legally approved, religiously blessed assault on their bodies" in the name of capitalist reformation.[16] For Noddings, this reorganization was culturally imposed by the Church for more strictly religious reasons.

As the witch is constructed cinematically, these two historical frames are often used in tandem, and thus understanding both as resonant with each other is useful. In order to constrain female sexuality, rendering it abject and taboo while simultaneously celebrating woman's role as mother, Christianity creates what Noddings describes as the paradoxical nature of womanhood. Flesh becomes sinful when Eve succumbs to temptation and eats the Forbidden Fruit, redeemed only through the asexual, divine birth of Jesus to Mary. By positing that women alone (as represented by Eve) are weak-willed and require masculine protection (the divinely guided Mary), Christian men

---

12. Simpson, 1994, 89.
13. Noddings, 1989, 53.
14. Kristeva in Creed, 1999, 252.
15. Kristeva, 1982, 85.
16. Federici, 2018, 31.

were able to regulate female sexuality. In Noddings' words, "Confined to the home and subject to men's rule, the obedient woman has been an angel... loose in the world or rebellious toward male domination, she becomes 'the devil's gateway,' an ambiguous evil indeed."[17] Kristeva suggests that in order for this construction to function as an effective mechanism of taboo, the notion of sin had to be *internalized* by women as well as men in the Augustinian Catholic idea that sin occurs in thought as well as deed.[18] Within this construction, by regulating minds in addition to actions, the paradox of womanhood becomes foundational to the Christian feminine consciousness. It holds women accountable for their own repression while simultaneously promoting the idea that unconstrained femininity is dangerous to society. Eve's role in the Fall, even as it demonizes womanhood, also maintains many of the powerful connections drawn from paganism between women, nature, and power. In Federici's words:

> The witch hunt instituted a regime of terror on all women, from which emerged the new model of femininity to which women have to conform to be socially accepted... sexless, obedient, submissive, resigned to subordination to the male world, accepting as natural the confinement to a sphere of activities that in capitalism has been completely devalued.[19]

These interlocking understandings of the witch as a religious and economic threat to masculine domination goes back even further. In his 1862 book, *Satanism and Witchcraft*, 19th-century French historian Jules Michelet connects this paradox and its implicit feminine power to the figure of the witch in Medieval Europe. The book, which caused a tremendous scandal upon its release, argues that witches were traditionally understood to be morally bereft, prideful, wrathful women (generally either women past reproductive age or adolescent girls) who give their souls to Satan and have sex with him in order to gain power.[20] They were thought to make potions ("flying ointment" being the most famous) and perform magic that allowed them, among additional "unnatural" powers, to control or harm others, seduce people, fly, and transform themselves into animals.[21] Rather than calling them morally bereft as the Church did, Michelet asserts that, in tandem with the social and economic hardships of the Middle Ages, the witch was a direct product of the Church's oppression of women, sexuality, and paganism. "From when does the Sorceress date?" Michelet asks in the introduction of his book. "I answer unhesitatingly, 'From the ages of despair' [or the Middle Ages]. From the profound despair the world owed to the

---

17. Noddings, 1989, 60.
18. Kristeva, 1982, 112-13.
19. Federici, 2018, 32.
20. Michelet, 1998, 88.
21. Karlsen, 1998, 10, 47, 130.

Church... 'The sorceress is the Church's crime.'"[22] His argument combines a rejection of notoriously corrupt Medieval Christianity with an understanding of the foothold paganism and superstition maintained.

The book's bioessentialist understanding of womanhood as close to nature draws from the same pagan mythos, rendering explicit more contemporary assessments of the connection between paganism and the feminine such as those posited by Kristeva and Noddings. Michelet concludes,

> By a monstrous perversion of ideas the Middle Ages regarded the flesh, in its representative, woman (accursed since Eve), as radically impure. The virgin, exalted as a virgin and not as Our Lady, far from raising actual womanhood to a higher level, had degraded it, starting men on the path of the barren, scholastic ideal of purity.[23]

Meanwhile, he claims, woman "carries shut within her breast a fond remembrance of the poor ancient gods ... now fallen to the estate of spirits, and a feeling of compassion for them."[24]

Michelet also strives to re-naturalize the relationship between the feminine and the natural, returning to a pagan understanding of women as possessing mysterious divine powers: "'Nature makes them Sorceresses'—the genius peculiar to woman and her temperament."[25] He also suggests that rather than view witches as victims of seduction by the Devil—either ignorant of the circumstances of their possession or irredeemably evil—they should be viewed as products of their harsh circumstances who knowingly chose witchcraft.[26] Women are outlaws of the church, he says, and "Is not Satan the outlaw of outlaws? And he gives his followers the joy and wild liberty of all free things of Nature, the rude delight of being a world apart, all-sufficient unto itself."[27] By "signing the Devil's book", or swearing allegiance to the Devil and becoming witches, women not only gain freedom from sexual and moral oppression, but return to what Michelet views as an older, more natural state that exists out of time and reinstates the woman's role in religious practice. "The Black Mass," he says,

> "would seem to be this redemption of Eve from the curse of Christianity had laid upon her. At the Witch's Sabbath woman fulfills every office. She is priest, and altar, and consecrated host, whereof all the people communicate."[28]

---

22. Michelet, 1998, xiv.
23. *Ibid*, 87.
24. *Ibid*, 27.
25. *Ibid*, viii.
26. *Ibid*, 42.
27. *Ibid*, 70.
28. *Ibid*, 102.

Thus, the witch can be viewed as an amalgam figure of the Christian anxiety surrounding the allure of paganism as well as the threat of feminine religious and sexual power in that context; this leads to the association between the feminine and the abject. As Kristeva writes, by associating maleness with order and societal control, "that other sex, the feminine, becomes synonymous with a radical evil that is to be suppressed."[29]

As feminist scholars have noted, witches in the Medieval context were also associated with the threat of lower-class women's medical autonomy under Feudalism—itself fundamental to their economic security—as well as a continuation of the association between women and altered states of consciousness (beginning with the figure of the pagan priestess/female oracle). Women were (as now) stereotypically believed to be more empathetic as well as overly emotional and instinctual, leading to their being seen as both more collective than men (the parallel to the witches' coven can be drawn here) and naturally suited to practice medicine and midwifery.[30] Simultaneously, however, women with knowledge of medicinal herbs and curative practices were viewed with suspicion by those who lacked it, particularly in tandem with their image as naturally treacherous outside of male control—a conception actively proffered by the Church in treatises on witch hunting such as the infamous *Malleus Maleficarum*: it calls women "a foe to friendship, an inescapable punishment, a necessary evil, a natural temptation, a desirable calamity, a domestic danger, a delectable detriment, an evil of nature, painted with fair colors!"[31] [32] Midwives in particular drew the ire of the *Malleus*, which describes them as "surpass[ing] all others in wickedness."[33] As Barbara Ehrenreich and Deirdre English point out in their influential 1973 feminist pamphlet "Witches, Midwives, and Nurses: A History of Women Healers", because the cures proffered by healers and wise-women did not rely on confession to function, they were viewed as a threat to Catholic doctrine in addition to a usurpation of God's power.[34] Moreover, many remedies used by lay healers were derived from poisonous and hallucinogenic plants such as belladonna and ergot, heightening the sense of the potential subversive power of witches: like the pagan goddesses the Church feared before them, they held the powers of life and death in a way that their male contemporaries did not.[35] Thus, the *Malleus*' image of witches' powers as all sinfully, sexually derived, were part of a broader campaign to

---

29. Kristeva, 1982, 70.
30. Noddings, 1989, 129.
31. Kreimer and Sprenger, 1971, 43.
32. The *Malleus*, it has been pointed out, becomes in retrospect more an anthropological treatise on the Church's view of women than on witches: the two words, "woman" and "witch" are in fact frequently used interchangeably.
33. Kreimer and Sprenger, 1971, 43, 269.
34. Ehrenreich and English, 1973, 20, 46.
35. *Ibid*, 47.

paint witches as unfeminine: "The common belief that witches engage in infanticide and cannibalism," for example, or that Satanic midwives offer the souls of newborns to Satan, "perverted the idea of the woman as nurturing mother."[36]

In Colonial New England, these same threats to the social order were brought to the fore in many accusations of witchcraft—even prior to the height of the witch craze and the Salem Witch Trials. According to Caren Karlsen, New England's accused witches had one thing in common: they were "rowdy women who stood out," often expressing "dissatisfaction with the material conditions of their lives." That could mean wanting to own private property, hold religious office or influence, or make decisions about their sexual autonomy regardless of age.[37] Many women were exiled as witches in the 1630s and 40s as a result of their desire for a more direct role in religious practice.[38] The same form of anti-feminine inversion visible in the image of the witch in Medieval Europe can be seen in the claims made about witches in Colonial New England: assertions that they caused failed harvests, prevented animals from giving milk or laying eggs, and caused women to miscarry were common—all signs of an anti-maternal, nonreproductive femininity viewed as unnatural and against Christian womanhood.[39] Witch crazes and witch hunts across the Western world (most of which took place during times of major social change, as Ehrenreich and English point out) are related to Christian fears of feminine power.[40] Nel Noddings' paradox can be resolved "with the realization that the dichotomous view of woman as evil (because of her attraction to matters of the flesh) and good (because of her compassion and nurturing) served as a means of control."[41]

Much as the witch crazes took place in moments of social upheaval, so too has witchcraft captured the public imagination during more recent turbulent times. The relationship between witchcraft, the occult, and feminism has a well-documented history. In the 19th century, interest in witchcraft blossomed as industrialization changed the social landscape across Europe and the United States and Spiritualism gained popularity in the wake of World War I. At this time, feminists and other political radicals took up the witch as a symbol of resistance, in part inspired by the cultural impact of Michelet's book and its rhetorical framework.[42] According to Per Faxneld in his book *Satanic Feminism* (2014), arguments that used witches as symbols of embattled resistance "became widespread" in the late 1870s when "the persecutions of witches [were] likened to the 'recent slaughter of

---

36. Schimmelpfennig, 2013, 29.
37. Karlsen, 1998, 127.
38. *Ibid.*
39. *Ibid*, 7.
40. Ehrenreich and English, 1973, 35.
41. Noddings, 1989, 3.
42. Faxneld, 2014, 206-7.

Communists in Paris.'"[43] In the United States, radical suffragette Matilda Joslyn Gage embraced this framework at the turn of the last century, arguing in well-read feminist publications that witchcraft in the Middle Ages served as a form of satanic resistance to patriarchal domination as perpetuated by the church.[44] At the same time, a link between witchcraft and diagnoses of hysteria (themselves believed by feminists to be a tool of misogynist oppression), was popularized in medical literature, with some patients turning to mediumship and beginning to call themselves "latter-day witches".[45] Both the suffragette and the medium represent distinctly feminine centers of power and autonomy, different though they may appear on the surface. These last two examples, women seizing on the overtly political, vilified witch (witch as symbol of resistance) or gravitating towards the more individualistic, overtly mystical witch (here tied to notions of bioessentialist "femininity" in medicine), are representative of related but often distinct strains in the cultural imaginary around this figure. Both continue as the broader pattern of witches' deification and vilification evolves in tandem with feminism over time, most notably in the 1960s and early 1970s, again in the 1990s, and once more in the mid-late 2010s and early 2020s. Suffice it to say, then, from the Middle Ages to the present, broader constructions of the feminine—and its subversive counterpart, the witch—"seem to represent at bottom an emptying of male consciousness about the feminine" rather than a representation of women's experiences.[46] For this reason, the witch as a figure in pop culture—and particularly the horror film, the genre which film critic Robin Wood once called "the struggle for recognition of all that our civilization represses or oppresses"—continues to hold sway.[47]

---

43. Faxneld, 2014, 206-7.
44. *Ibid*, 198.
45. *Ibid*, 210.
46. Noddings, 1989, 70.
47. Wood, 2003, 28.

Chapter Two

The Cinematic Witch as Anxiety of the Feminine

> "The presence of the monstrous-feminine in the popular horror film speaks to us more about male fears than about female desire or feminine subjectivity."
> -Barbara Creed, *The Monstrous-Feminine*[1]

> "Thou shalt not suffer a witch to live"
> -*Exodus* 22:18
> -Mrs. White, *Carrie*

Horror movies have always been strongly associated with women, both on-screen (in the 2010s women had more speaking and on-screen time in horror films than in any other genre) and off (studies have shown that the films of the early slasher cycles such as *Halloween* and *Friday the 13th* were marketed primarily to women).[2] [3] But, as Barbara Creed points out, there is only "one incontestably monstrous role in the horror film that belongs to the woman—that of the witch."[4] Witches taunted and terrified men on screen as early as 1896, in Georges Méliès' silent film *Le Manoir du diable*. In the 6-minute film, a young beauty conjured by the Devil dazzles a hapless young man before transforming into a crone and encircling him with a crowd of her dancing, broomstick-wielding sisters, pointing and shaking with laughter at his fright before disappearing again just before the Devil is banished by the man's crucifix. This early example is in many ways emblematic of the way this movie monster is depicted, as allowed her fun only to suffer punishment at the film's close. Unlike most other supernatural horror monsters (vampires, werewolves, etc.), though, witches are characters based on a reality of historical trauma. While Europeans commonly believed in both vampires and werewolves contemporaneously with the witch crazes of the Middle Ages, witchcraft was an oft-punished offense comparable to heresy for centuries, based in the violent assertion of Christian morality onto the female body.[5] While vampires and other monsters in the horror film represent a more ambiguous threat of "otherness" (be it sexual, gendered, or racial difference), the witch represents in plain terms a fear of female agency and power.

---

1. In Kristeva, 1982, 4, 14.
2. "Using Technology to Address Gender Bias in Film", 2017.
3. Nowell, 2011, 115.
4. Creed, 1993, 73.
5. Karlsen, 1998, 121.

As Stephen King suggests in his overview of the horror genre in TV, film, and literature, *Danse Macabre* (2010), horror cycles typically coincide with "periods of fairly serious economic and/or political strain" (he uses the studio horror of the Great Depression and the B-films of the Cold War '50s as examples); for this reason, he suggests, these horror cycles become reflections of the "free-floating anxieties" and "moral dislocations" of those periods.[6] This same principle could, as with historical spikes in popular interest in witchcraft, be applied more specifically to periods of social and political tensions over feminism. In *Satanic Feminism*, Per Faxneld, who describes the witch as "a partly floating signifier... double-edged and... filled to the brim with conflicting resonance," points to the spike in representations of witches in the 1910s and '20s during the movement for women's suffrage, a period that coincided with a renewed popular interest in the occult, from the teachings of Alistair Crowley to a rise in spiritualism.[7] One film, *Häxan* (1922), addressed these parallels directly, historicizing the links between Medieval clerical hypocrisy and witchcraft accusations and then-contemporary medical hypocrisy and hysteria diagnoses. An experimental proto-essay film featuring lavish, hallucinatory historical reenactments and folkloric fantasy sequences, *Häxan* was inspired by Danish director Benjamin Christensen's research on witchcraft in the mid-1910s (including Michelet's *Satanism and Witchcraft*). It takes an unabashedly feminist stance, comparing forms of heteropatriarchal subjugation without compromise, showing for example an inquisitor violently restraining a "witch" and a doctor violently restraining a "hysteric", declaring "Poor little hysterical witch! In the Middle Ages you were in conflict with the church, now it is the law." This message, in addition to the film's explicitly anti-religious themes, proved too controversial for American censors, and Häxan was only released in revised form in 1929.[8]

Witch films are uniquely flexible. They have no set of generic conventions the way that, say, vampire or zombie films do. There are recurring motifs and themes, particularly within some periods' witch cycles. But fundamentally the narrative structures or aesthetic signifiers of the Blair Witch have little in common with those of Carrie White or Elvira. Some of cinema's most famous witches do not come from horror films at all. Rather, they are often products of children's films (Disney's animated witches rivaling only the Wicked Witch herself in fame) or romantic comedies, such as *Practical Magic* (1998) (see chapter 12). Because of this range, the witch film proves itself an excellent sponge for cultural anxiety, soaking up the style of the day and transforming, like a witches' glamor, to serve the needs of its creators.

In her article, "The Monster as Woman: Two Generations of Cat People", Karen Hollinger discusses sexually threatening women in horror, comparing

---

6. King, 2010, 29.
7. Faxneld, 2014, 214.
8. Hollinger, 2015, 356.

the two versions of *Cat People* (Jacques Tourneur's 1942 film and Paul Schrader's 1982 remake) to explore how horror films reflect the politics of their eras. For Hollinger, these two films represent "a complex formulation related not only to the psychic needs of [the film's] male spectators… but also to the social conditions under which the films were made."[9] Although this is not mentioned in Hollinger's analysis, Irena (Simone Simon), Tourneur's titular cat person—one of the more iconic and unquestionably most autonomous female monsters of this period—is a product of witchcraft and Satan-worship. In both versions of the film, Irena states that her tribe first gained the ability to transform into leopards after selling their souls to the Devil and becoming witches. This fact makes Hollinger's suggestion that these two films are a response to "the threat of the potency of non-phallic sexuality … controlled only by the woman's internalization of patriarchal standards" even more compelling in this context: this assertion echoes the function of the witch as an abject symbol of control and fear as defined by Kristeva and Noddings.[10] [11]

An analysis of Tourneur's *Cat People*, Hollinger says, "makes it tempting to see the female monster as defying the usual filmic avenues of disavowal and expressing a threat beyond narrative control."[12] This is not entirely true of *Cat People* because Irena is murdered at the end in a graphic display of phallically charged power (i.e. stabbed through the middle on a long pole). But the original *Cat People* does allow Irena more power and sexual agency than the film's 1982 remake. Hollinger notes that America's patriarchal grasp on women shifted significantly from 1942, before the Women's Movement, to the 1980s. Nevertheless, women's roles were still in flux in the 1940s, when wartime feminist gains, such as women's acceptance in the workforce, were viewed as societally advantageous. Even if women were depicted as somewhat more autonomous in some genres like the screwball comedy (in which many women were fast-talking and employed) or the film noir (in which women's sexual desire was depicted as practically overwhelming), *Cat People*'s leniency towards Irena's power—followed by its violent suppression—suggests a more ambivalent stance. By 1982 however, for Hollinger, following the Women's Liberation movement of the 1960s and '70s, too many gains had been made for the same forms of leniency to be acceptable: "the patriarchal assumption of women's internalization of its cultural standards and codes," Noddings' paradox of womanhood, "could no longer be confidently entertained."[13] Consequently, in the remake, Irena (Nastassja Kinski, who, in this version, kills chickens rather than people)

---

9. Hollinger, 2015, 356.
10. *Ibid.*
11. *Ibid*, 350, 353.
12. *Ibid*, 353.
13. *Ibid*, 356.

is given a brother (Malcolm McDowell), a male cat-person whose power is unquestionably stronger than hers. He dominates her sexually even before her violent death, denying her any modicum of gendered power.

Strangely, the witch *as such* rarely appeared in 1940s horror films. While a few do exist and deal with witchcraft as central subject matter, (the B-horror pictures *The Seventh Victim* (1943) and *I Walked with a Zombie* (1943), are notable examples), the most famous witch films of the decade are far more lighthearted. *The Wizard of Oz* (1939), the Ur-text of the fantasy witch film, was released August 1939, introducing the movie-going public to the green face and pointy hat that would come to define a particular branch of caricatured witch imagery forever. Tellingly, though, the original character design, proposed by the film's producer, Mervyn LeRoy, was far less grotesque and far more overtly sexual. Academy-Award-winning actress Gale Sondergaard was initially cast for the part, and as she described later in life, in the film's original design, "I would wear sequins everywhere—a tight black sequined dress, a black sequined hat. The makeup would be very glamorous and thus, subtly, very wicked."[14] Wardrobe test photos for this version of the witch attest to this abandoned direction, with heavy cupid's bow lipstick and dark penciled eyebrows that evoke the femme fatales of the decade to come. The idea was scrapped when other key members of the film's creative team insisted that, rather than "a glamorous witch… children need that wicked, hateful… ugly witch"[15] to be frightened, eliding some of the fundamental basis for the witch's frightening mythos in the process, streamlining the misogynist fears around women's power. Sondergaard quit the film as a result. The film, of course, has two witches—one good, one bad. While the Wicked Witch did ultimately terrify generations of children with her green skin and warty chin, Glinda the Good Witch is depicted more as a fairy godmother than as a witch, with her sparkly pink wings, princess dress, and long star-tipped wand. Thus, "witchcraft" remains the purview of evil while "magic" conjures bubbles, musical numbers, and home sweet home.

The other iconic witch film of the decade, *I Married a Witch* (1942), combines the two archetypes in the explicitly sexualized Jennifer Broome (Veronica Lake), the film's titular bride, as LeRoy had hoped *The Wizard of Oz* would. *The Chicago Tribune* called the film "a story of modern witchcraft, the like of which has not been seen on any screen"[16] and *I Married a Witch* can be viewed as the birth of the modern cinematic witch as we understand her today, the kind who will appear most often throughout this book. By synthesizing the good and bad witches into a single character, this screwball comedy subtly gestures towards the conservatively-inflected psychodrama at the heart of witch lore that will continue to play out for decades to come.

---

14. Harmetz, 2013, 122.
15. Munn, 2018, 122.
16. Tinee, 1943, 19.

Marketed with glamor shots of Lake in a tall pointy hat or riding a broom, the film's playful treatment of its subject leans into the iconography of the witch as a Halloween costume. As such, witchcraft *per se* is treated as unilaterally evil in this film, associated with mischief, murder, spoiled crops, and male sexual dysfunction. After a priest burns Jennifer at the stake during the Salem witch trials, she curses his descendants to be unlucky in love, dooming them to frigid marriages or lives of solitude—a highly feminized and sexualized form of punishment in keeping with the archetype's historical roots. Once her spirit is accidentally freed from her tomb in the 1940s present, she plans to continue her reign of terror on the men sired by the family that killed her by erotically subjugating their latest heir; that is, until her love spell goes awry, enchanting her instead of him, and reinstating the paradox of womanhood within her. Only then can witchcraft be used for good as she loosens him up, cleans his house, and gets him elected governor of Massachusetts. Even then, however, her insecure husband asks her never to use her magic, a goal she works towards throughout the latter half of the film. Once she takes the love potion, like Eve, she senses something inherently sinful in her magic, begging her husband not to have children for fear of the power her baby girls might have. *I Married a Witch* ends with the image of the happy couple's two lovely little girls, their mother scolding them violently for playing with a broom. This "comical" conclusion projects a future of repression for the next generation of witch-wives, a portent of conflicts to come in American homes as well as on American screens.

Interestingly, the film's source material was not so lightly shaded—the novel, *The Passionate Witch* (1941), finds the bride bewitching her husband into a life of sordid sex and orgiastic black magic. As described in an essay by experimental filmmaker Guy Maddin, in the book upon which the film is based, Jennifer "sneaks from the nuptial bed at night to ride a goat and slits the throat of a rooster in the bathroom. And things turn even more ghastly from there…"[17] Whether or not Jennifer's untamed sexual powers proved too much for the Hays Office or the screenwriters, this choice to adapt the material from dime store pulp to screwball sap at the height of the film noir femme fatale's prominence suggests that open erotic power and black magic in the same female character were still a bridge too far—and this pattern continues. The tension at the heart of this dynamic can be found in each witch cycle that coincides with periods of feminist activism. *I Married a Witch* serves as a reminder that while the boom-and-bust film cycles may initially seem linear (female empowerment = witches *with* power), things aren't nearly that simple.

The witch remained elusive on American screens until Christmas day, 1958, when another witch-comedy was born, tying the mainstream cinematic witch to the nascent counterculture for the first time and presaging the witch

---

17. Maddin, 2017.

cycle to come in the next decade.[18] Our story begins in earnest with Richard Quine's *Bell, Book and Candle* (1958), which earned nominations for two Oscars in 1959, a year some historians have argued marks the beginning of the decade we call the sixties. Kim Novak, the film's sultry star, appeared on the November cover of *Life Magazine* holding her character's familiar, Pyewacket the Siamese cat. Novak's upturned eyes are rimmed with cat-eye makeup and she wears a sleek black turtleneck. The photo spread inside, shows Gillian (Novak) brooding in her stylishly disheveled Greenwich Village studio apartment. In the film, Gillian, a dealer of "primitive art", and her brother (Jack Lemmon) and aunt (Elsa Lanchester, aka the Bride of Frankenstein), live a bohemian life at the heart of the city's thriving beatnik scene.

About a year before the film's release, Jack Kerouac's *On the Road* (1957) became a bestselling novel and Allen Ginsberg's peyote-fueled, *Howl* (1956) was confiscated in San Francisco, leading to a banner obscenity trial that thrust The Beats into the national spotlight. The film, based on a 1950 play devoid of these subcultural trappings, takes advantage of this coalescing scene, transforming the blonde bombshell witch of the '40s into a perennially barefoot beatnik intellectual, casting spells cross-legged and trading sardonic witticisms at a jazz club called the Zodiac while her brother plays the bongos. The witch had become "hip". The beatnik scene parodically depicted in *Bell, Book and Candle*, with its emphasis on consciousness expansion in various artistic and synthetic forms from action painting to cut-up poetry, is the essential precursor to the countercultural witch films of the decade to come—to the point of being characterized by some historians as a form of "proto-hippie"-ism[19]: this was the era of William Burroughs' *Naked Lunch* (1959), Aldous Huxley's *At the Doors of Perception* (1954), and Simone DeBeauvoir's feminist *The Second Sex* (1949)—and *Bell, Book and Candle* capitalizes on the off-beat avant-garde scene coalescing amidst these intellectual influences in its plot as well as its style: Gillian's romantic interest, Shep Henderson (Jimmy Stewart), is a successful publisher looking for the latest trends. When he hears the author of occult paperbacks with kitschy titles like *Magic in Mexico* is looking for a new publisher, he's ecstatic: his last book "sold like the Kinsey Report!... There's always a big market for the supernatural."

Underneath it all, though, as *Life* informed its readers of the film, even in this "fun-loving family of witches and wizards who... give free reign to their every whimsical whigmaleerie... [Gillian] vaguely disapproves of it all and secretly yearns for normalcy."[20] Like Jennifer in *I Married a Witch*,

---

18. This isn't to say that the witch disappeared from pop culture, however—Arthur Miller's *The Crucible*, originally performed in 1953, took the Salem Witch Trials as a metaphor for Cold War era McCarthyism. Meanwhile, Jade Connolly-Cepurac compellingly argues that a cycle of racist "voodoo" films occasionally featured Black witches in the mid-1950s as the civil rights movement began, though not with regularity.
19. Turner, 2006, 35-6.
20. "Bewitching Tale About Witches", 1958, 67.

Gillian wants love, stability, and a man to be "boring" with—and this time, it doesn't even take a spell to convince her that her life of cool is fundamentally hollow. It was her idea all along. The film's message is repressive, using exploitation film structures under its air of big-budget prestige to suggest, as the *Malleus Maleficarum* does, that "when a woman thinks alone, she thinks evil."[21] Looking back on the film in *The New Yorker* five decades later, Michael Sragow wrote: "there's an undeniable frisson to the way the movie's magic subculture echoes the closeted gay world of the fifties: it's easy to view the Zodiac Club as a gay bar."[22] This connection isn't subtle, nor is its negativity: Shep suggests that both Kinsey's bestselling 1953 report——which suggested that over a third of American men had at least some "homosexual experience" and queer women were more likely to have orgasms than heterosexual ones—as well as the witch books he's so eager to sell are "fake tourist stuff." In the film, witches are incapable of love, and the independent life Gillian leads is shown alongside what she sees as the cat-owning spinsterhood of her Aunt Queenie.[23] Gillian needs Shep in order to experience "real" deep emotions.

Ultimately, in *Bell, Book and Candle*, Gillian wants no part in magic or the counterculture, though the film's creators and viewers are still able to enjoy their subversive (if parodied) pleasures for much of the film's runtime. By the film's conclusion, she's lost her magic abilities and sports high heels, trading in her red and black wardrobe for pastel corals and yellows and her "strange" African art collection for seashell bouquets (a symbolic exorcism of "primitive influences"). While magical antics are fun when leveled against a romantic competitor and college nemesis (who, in a very McCarthyist move, sent a letter informing on Gillian to the dean for not wearing shoes, adding a different Cold War valence to the term "witch hunt"), when used to bewitch a man or to subvert the values of the system more broadly, magic can only lead to a lonely life.

According to her creator, *Bell, Book and Candle* and *I Married a Witch* directly inspired one of the most popular witches of the 1960s—Samantha, the star of *Bewitched*, which ran from 1964 until 1972, enemy to feminists like Betty Friedan.[24] But this strain of domesticated, conservative magic embodied by Jennifer, Gillian, and eventually Samantha would soon find itself at odds with another, much more far-out strain of the craft already semi-visible in the milieu to which Gillian so desperately feels she doesn't belong. By the mid-late 1960s, a rash of "witchsploitation" films would come together in America across a range of genres and contexts, indirectly

---

21. Kreimer and Sprenger, 1971.
22. Sragow, 2012.
23. Casting Lanchester in this role also adds to the queer subtext—Lanchester, a politically active bohemian, was married to famously queer actor and director Charles Laughton, and her role in *Bride of Frankenstein* (1935) is a touchstone of Code-era lesbian film to this day.
24. McLellan, 2011.

placing this "double-edged signifier" at the heart of some of the era's most powerful debates around feminism, sexuality, and the counterculture. In Part 1, I will explore the true birth of this cycle in the early 1960s, situating it within the rapidly evolving subcultures of the moment that would draw from the scientific worlds of the Cold War laboratory and college campus to bring psychedelia and protest to the white middle-class mainstream. The results would prove tantalizing, divisive, and deeply anxiety-inducing.

PART ONE

Season of the Witch:
The Countercultural Witch Films of the Long Sixties

Chapter Three

Setting the Stage for the Countercultural Witch Film (1960-1964)

> "When she stopped conforming to the conventional picture of femininity, she finally began to enjoy being a woman."
> -Betty Friedan, *Television and the Feminine Mystique*[1]

During the 1960s, as hippies superseded beatniks and Americans clamored for greater individual freedom, the witch appeared everywhere in the movies, transforming herself from a hysterical victim to an avenging angel, from an ugly crone to a sexy swinger, from a matronly medium to a hip chick casting heavy spells.[2] Within these aesthetic shifts came an equally dramatic shift in political sensibility. As the decade progressed, the way the witch was depicted on screen evolved alongside questions of sex, gender, and the politics of both. In this era, belief in the paranormal slowly gained currency across the country, with advertisements for tarot and astrology classes appearing, in the underground press, alongside listings for upcoming protests and abortion helplines—and in mainstream magazines like *Cosmopolitan* next to recipes and advice columns. The witch's relationship to questions of faith, politics, and identity, particularly for women, makes her a compelling microcosm by which to understand debates that roiled the nation from affluent suburbs to college campuses to rural communes. The fears she conjures are elemental.

During this period, witchcraft in the popular imaginary was a fractured signifier. It suggested both sexual empowerment and sexual enslavement; collectivist naturalism and individualistic consumerism; science and superstition; intellectual control and hedonistic abandon. But how could this character come to be a feminist icon, a misogynist boogeyman, a harbinger of religious decline, a sex symbol, a trend, and a joke all at once? Using a number of films from a wide range of different contexts (from studio blockbusters to auteurist art films to pornography to exploitation movies), Part I will trace the history of the countercultural witch film cycle, looking at this figure across her various contexts to suggest that in a decade haunted by questions of *belief*—in alternative communities and more equitable futures

---

1. Friedan, 1998, 465.
2. Periodizing the 1960s is a complicated task, and different historians take different approaches. Here, I will be covering the "long sixties", typically understood to end in 1973.

on the one hand and conservative religious and patriotic ideals on the other—the witch's evolution as a symbol of mysterious and arcane power reflects these shifting landscapes, particularly in the Women's Liberation Movement. As Jon Lewis put it in his book, *Road Trip to Nowhere*,

> [t]oday the movies from the counterculture era that continue to matter were in their day aberrations, movies that got made despite industry policy, movies made elsewhere (overseas, in the B-industry, by independent contractors working on some half-baked deal with a studio)—movies nobody with money and clout at the time gave half a chance at success.[3]

While some of the films in this chapter were more commercially successful than others (and some of these films were barely seen at all), when taken together, they paint a vivid, politically salient picture of a culture in flux, full of dead ends, weird vibrations, and experiments that mostly failed.

"The place: anywhere in the USA," a man's voice cheerfully announces as light music twinkles in the background. "The time: any day, at any season of the year." A mother and father sit by a fireplace in an affluent living room, watching their young children play. Soon, the camera pans to a blonde teenager with rosy cheeks and a light pink sweater, sitting to the side, apart from her family. "She has entered her teens," the narrator tells us. The girl stands, watching her parents talk, oblivious to her. She leaves the room.

The 1963 industrial film *The Age of Curiosity*, directed by Gerald Weiler, made to promote *Seventeen Magazine*, presents an idealized image of American youth culture—an image of how the country was trying to market itself in an age increasingly defined by mass communications. This America had watched Kennedy and Nixon debate on live television in 1960, and later joined First Lady Jackie Kennedy for a televised tour of the White House. The America being sold was the one sending westerns like *How the West Was Won* (1962), shot in Cinerama, to the top of the box office alongside musicals like *Bye Bye Birdie* (1963) and epics like *Lawrence of Arabia* (1962). It was prosperous, white, "modern", and well-informed.

Reflecting this kind prosperity, the teens *The Age of Curiosity* depicts are wholesome and well rounded, with newly significant cultural and financial autonomy: "The teenager for the first time in history is fully involved in the cultural life of the nation," the narrator announces, because "by 1965 half the population of the US will be 25 and under. 40 percent will be under twenty." Groups of teen girls are shown in blazers and skirts cheerfully entering a high school with large glass windows. The advertisers highlight

---

3. Lewis, 2022, 3.

burgeoning independence: "Being bright is very *in* these days," the narrator tells us we see teenage girls working intently on science projects, listening to classical music, and performing "service in the community". The emphasis on education and self-actualization in these vignettes accurately reflects one of the most dramatic increases in higher learning in American history: by 1961, 38% of American youths would attend college (up from 14% before WWII), rising to over half by the decade's end, almost tripling from 3 million to almost 9 million American college students from 1959 to 1973, with a noticeable increase in women's enrollment.[4]

Yet while teenage girls are described in positive intellectual terms as "living breathing question marks interested in just about everything—they may well be the most inquisitive creatures on earth!" much of their curiosity is re-directed here towards makeup ("They want to know all about looking their prettiest!") and China patterns for their weddings ("more girls get married at eighteen than at any other age!"). Building on this sense of purity and domesticity, the film also highlights an interest in religion among the women of the Baby Boom, and in a manner that inadvertently captures one of the tensions building in a country transforming itself in ways these advertisers are working to elide: while the narrator describes how teenage girls' "need to understand also leads many to probe religious faith," the young blonde woman from the film's opening passages reappears, fresh-faced and smiling in a white hat and gloves, to shake a priest's hand outside a large church on a sunny day. It's Mia Farrow in her first credited film role, just five years before her star turn in *Rosemary's Baby* (1968).

In retrospect, with this casting choice, cracks begin to form in the apple-pie image being projected, like an episode of *The Twilight Zone*: in 1961, Time complained about "delinquent" youth engaging in violent rebellion "for its own sake."[5] Church attendance and Sunday School enrollment were beginning a noticeable decline.[6] JFK's Commission on the Status of Women reported that the average woman "earn[ed] up to 40 percent less than men, on the same job."[7] Even as businessmen watching *The Age of Curiosity* were deciding whether to feature *Seventeen* in their stores, the young women they hoped to draw could read **Sylvia Plath's *The Bell Jar* (released in January 1963), a text that gives credence to their struggles with mental illness, alienation, and misogynist violence, vividly breaking taboo by describing the fear that what every man "secretly wanted when the wedding service ended was for [women] to flatten out underneath his feet like [a] kitchen mat"**[8]; as if to prove this fear correct, young wives and mothers being lauded in the film

---

4. Turner, 2006, 30.
5. "For Its Own Sake" 1961.
6. McLeod, 2007, 61.
7. Lear, 1968.
8. Plath, 2005, 85.

as angelic homemakers were driving Betty Friedan's *The Feminine Mystique* (released in February) to the top of the bestseller list, feeling recognized by one of the era's leading feminist voices' describing "the problem with no name."[9] At the same time, Helen Gurley's wildly bestselling title *Sex and the Single Girl* (1962) was promising an alternative—ringing in the sexual revolution by telling prospective wives in their teens and twenties that "marriage [was] 'insurance for the *worst* years of your life. During the best years, you don't need a husband'" because sex alone is a "powerful weapon" to use on any man a woman may want.[10][11] This assertion, previously espoused by any number of Marilyn Monroe's bombshell blondes only to be disavowed by true love at the films' conclusions, was here being presented in earnest: Singles' bars were springing up around the country to accommodate the growing class of unmarried women in the workforce—with rapidly expanding access to FDA approved, federally legalized, birth control—ready to use their newfound economic power for their own benefit and live on independently, to boycott companies that discriminated against women, and not necessarily to buy *Seventeen*.

American political life was similarly in flux. In November '63, only a few short months after the film's release President John F. Kennedy would be shot to death in Dallas, a tragedy whose aftermath was viewed by 96% of America's homes with televisions;[12] Prime Minister Ngô Đình Diệm's assassination would lead to a massive increase in America's presence in Vietnam's civil war. The March on Washington would demonstrate the sincerity of young activists' "service to their community", a commitment whose implications were notably vague in *The Age of Curiosity*'s all-white classrooms. Groups like Students for a Democratic Society (SDS) and Student Nonviolent Coordinating Committee (SNCC) were ballooning as a wave of newly empowered college students educated itself about racism, classism, misogyny, and political power. While these graduates would have access to a hot job market, affordable homes, and a broad range of potential spouses, the hopeful economic situation was a sharp contrast to the suspicion that hung over the political and cultural mainstream like a cloud. In its founding document, the Port Huron Statement, SDS leaders described the prevailing mood of college activists thusly: "Our work… is guided by the sense that we

---

9. Plath, 2005, 85.
10. D'Emilio and Freedman, 2012, 303, 304.
11. The 1964 film based on *Sex and the Single Girl* (directed by *Bell, Book and Candle*'s Richard Quine) reimagines its hotshot author in conservative terms, as lonely and, quite possibly, a virgin. Ultimately, sexual freedom only causes confusion for these characters (played mostly by Hollywood elder statesmen such as Henry Fonda, Lauren Bacall, and Tony Curtis, though Natalie Wood plays the central role) all of whom end up monogamously pairing off with each other (the women of course forgiving their men). The film was extremely successful, suggesting that while the sexual revolution was certainly a hot subject, the social mores Dr. Gurley's book rejects were still firmly in place on American screens and endorsed in American living rooms.
12. Hoberman, 2005, 37, 87.

may be the last generation in the experiment with living."[13] As one young woman put it at the time, "There are models of marriage and adult life, but… they don't work… how do you be an adult in this world?"[14]

Some were already seeking answers outside the realm of political action, building on an ethos the Beats had cultivated in the arts, this time in the lab. At Harvard, Timothy Leary, then an up-and-coming psychology professor, was seeking "the most effective way to cut through the game structure of western life."[15] Like Ginsberg and the Beats before him, the answer he found was taking drugs to "expand consciousness"—specifically then-legal hallucinogens like psilocybin and LSD which were being investigated by the US government as mind-control tools. Leary's and others' experiments were initially covered with breathless, if nervous, fascination by outlets like *Time*. In a March, 1960 story, "The Psyche in 3-D" described LSD as "one of the most potent drugs known to man", taken up by the likes of Cary Grant as a combination therapeutic aid and party game. Beyond this association with Hollywood stars, the drug's mind-altering effects were described in flashy cinematic terms: LSD provided "visions in wide screen, full color… 'it is as though a 3-D tape were being run off in the visual field'… Family conflicts may be projected onto the LSD screen in puppet shows, acted out by Disney characters." Framed as a tool for stepping outside one's own psychodramas, the drug's effects were also already associated with the cosmic, supernatural, and decidedly spiritual. In one prescient section, the author describes "fantasies of seeing God and the Devil 'locked in mortal cosmic combat'" "symbolic of emotional disturbances" played out by archetypal figures like, among others, "witches".[16]

This kind of magical thinking had also spread to what would eventually be known as the head scene. While it would take several years for the mainstream to catch up, in February 1962, Astrologer Samael Aun Weor declared the 1960s "the Age of Aquarius", divining from the stars that the next phase of human consciousness would be defined by peace, harmony, human agency, and enlightenment. That same spring, Leary decided to facilitate a mass mystical experience in a campus chapel, giving his graduate students large doses of hallucinogens and was soon fired. Coverage about LSD started to change, even at *Time*. A 1963 article decried researchers "slipping LSD to unqualified buddies, who were using the drug for kicks."[17] One such "buddy" was Ken Kesey, who, after a first run-in with CIA mind control experiments, began passing out huge quantities of LSD, which he called "instant nirvana", to his hip houseguests in Menlo Park. Paired with the already-

---

13. Turner, 2006, 34, 28, emphasis added.
14. *Ibid*, 31.
15. Stephens, 1987, 158.
16. "The Psyche in 3-D", 1960, 2.
17. "LSD", 1963.

psychedelicized artistic scene of the "proto-hippie" beatnik movement, the stakes of the social, sexual, and creative shifts these artists believed LSD had the potential to create were perceived as existential, with a need for change and a dismissal of conventional orthodoxy that was correspondingly dire.[18] Rather than seek solutions from without, these individuals and their followers were beginning to search within.

With this in mind, the kind of adulthood—indeed the kind of world—that *Seventeen*'s advertisers aimed to project was being rapidly supplanted by a new, uncertain reality that led many of America's young people to look beyond the Cold War consensus for answers to their insatiable curiosity. This cultural transformation, cultivated with cinematic hallucinogens and the media theory of figures like Marshall McLuhan (who posited that new technologies like television functioned as extensions of humanity, fundamentally altering the human consciousness) as well as eastern philosophy, used the movies as a central reference point in an era when Hollywood was undergoing a massive transformation. Viewed in retrospect, Mia Farrow's first performance, a wordless starring role in *The Age of Curiosity*, can be viewed as a sort of prequel to the strange cultural era that was about to begin, a season of the witch in which she'd be set to star.

Before this could happen though, the cinematic landscape would have to undergo a similar series of crises. In the early 1960s, before the counterculture had truly begun to consolidate itself, box office returns were in freefall, as creaky studio vehicles failed to adapt to a rapidly evolving American culture. The fifties had been, as one writer put it in a prescient 1957 *Life* piece, a "horrible decade" for the movie business:

> In one fell decade Hollywood was knocked down by TV, kicked in the jaw by a court order that broke up the profitable, monopolistic alliance between the theater chains and the studios [Paramount v US, 1948], and at last all but destroyed by an upheaval in America's recreational habits. Movies had once been the entertainment resource for the entire country, but after the war... hi-fi sets, bowling balls, fishing tackle, golf clubs, do-it-yourself kits and 10,000 other consumer items flooded the U.S. As postwar automobiles, bedazzling with chromium, re-emerged from Detroit, movie theaters, suddenly discovered to be shabby and obsolete, began to close their doors. "No-body said, 'Let's go to the movies,' anymore,'" one producer explains.[19]

The slow decline of a studio system that favored what the article called "million-dollar mediocrities" continued in the early '60s. Even critically successful films like *Cleopatra* (1963) and *Mutiny on the Bounty* (1962) regularly pushed past three-hour runtimes, coming in catastrophically over

---

18. "LSD", 1963.
19. "Amid Ruins of an Empire, a New Hollywood Arises", 1957.

budget and behind schedule. As a means of compensation (and survival), more emphasis was put on smaller, cheaper independent productions and B-pictures with riskier subject matter and more adventurous styles. This shift allowed directors, writers, and stars to seize more power from the producer-focused studio system, and auteur directors like Sidney Lumet and Alfred Hitchcock were helping to tear down the already crumbling facade of strict studio self-censorship with sexually explicit films like *The Pawnbroker* (1964) and *Psycho* (1960). By 1963, Jack Valenti, head of the MPAA, was working to establish talks with the Kennedy administration about redesigning Hollywood censorship rules in the face of a youth culture opening itself up to sexual expression.[20] As *Life* put it, "'Creative people'... have taken over the actual making of movies"—a "New Hollywood" was beginning to emerge, growing out of the low-budget, youth-oriented genre product that studios viewed as a regrettable necessity.[21]

The story of the witch film begins with these kinds of youth films. American International Pictures (AIP), an independent production company, had set the standard for the low-budget "quickie" genre film of the 1950s. Primarily releasing films by the likes of (in)famous exploitationeer Roger Corman, they specialized in disreputable sci-fi and horror films designed to appeal to "the 8-to-21 groups" with "teen-age stories" whose "titles, monsters, and gimmicks are the stars," as Samuel Z. Arkoff, one of AIP's founders said in a 1958 interview.[22] Shooting films in under two weeks on shoestring budgets and packaging them as drive-in double bills had been wildly successful throughout the '50s. AIP's profits lay in their cynical approach to their material: as Arkoff put it, "basically we're merchandisers"[23], identifying a trend (hot rods, rock n roll, etc.) and delivering countless variations on the theme. In retrospect that tactic transforms their filmography into a veritable catalog of the era's youth culture. On this score, AIP was also a sort of proving ground for some of the biggest stars and directors of New Hollywood and the counterculture (Jack Nicholson, Peter Fonda, and Dennis Hopper, etc.) speaking to a symbiotic relationship with youth culture. By the early sixties, AIP had built up its coffers sufficiently to expand into international co-productions with bigger budgets, in addition to partnering with overseas production companies to distribute their films in the American domestic market. After years of giant monsters, beach parties, and alien robots, the studio turned to another subject: the occult.

The first two major witch films of the 1960s both came to the US from Europe courtesy of the AIP imprimatur, a fact that speaks to the lack of precedent for the subgenre in the US market at the time. The first of these

---

20. D'Emilio and Freedman, 2012, 136.
21. "Amid Ruins of an Empire, a New Hollywood Arises", 1957.
22. Scheuer, 1958.
23. *Ibid.*

was *Black Sunday* (1960), the directorial debut of Italian *giallo* director Mario Bava.[24] This film, like the occult itself in the early '60s, was singled out in the press for its status as a "curious product of internationalism."[25] Based on a short story by Russian novelist Nikolai Gogol, *Black Sunday*, set in Moldova, stars British soon-to-be horror icon Barbara Steele. In AIP's hands, the film was also re-dubbed in English by a cast of American actors, making it a blend of cultures that would become more familiar as the decade wore on and foreign art-film imports (and exploitation shockers) became central pillars of the youth cinephile scene.

Black Sunday tells the story of Asa (Barbara Steele), a witch who is burned at the stake during the 17th-century inquisition as punishment for her "infernal love" of Satan. She casts a curse on her brother who accused her, dooming him and his descendants to her eternal wrath. Hundreds of years later, a doctor and his student accidentally free her from the curse that binds her spirit. The witch's ghost then stalks her innocent young relatives, Katia (also Steele) and her brother, hypnotizing their friends and servants, turning them into her minions. Asa drinks their blood to gather strength and beauty (literally regrowing flesh and blood in a series of excellent body-horror sequences) before capturing Katia and attempting to steal her life-force. But Katia's chaste paramour, the medical student, stabs Asa to death once more.

The film's deliberate doubling of its two female characters, the beautiful, innocent young woman and the sexually voracious, mutilated witch, is notable for the way it highlights the dual nature of witch-lore once deliberately elided by films like *The Wizard of Oz* (1939). Katia, the victim, is almost sexually attracted to Asa, the witch, an identical double of herself whose portrait she gazes into and dreams of constantly. Here, the slippage between the ugly crone witch, Asa, (whose face is still marred by her execution) and the alluring maiden into which she so often transforms is flattened: related by blood and physically identical but for the ravages of age and torture, the two are opposite sides of the same person. The sexual nature of this supernatural duality is made explicit when the men finally locate Asa's crypt inside the family castle, hidden behind a chaste portrait from her life before the Inquisition, the image used to establish Katia's striking physical resemblance. Her coffin, though, they discover, is hidden by yet another portrait, this one a nude of Asa with a serpent and a crystal ball in her hands. This nude portrait, directly behind the clothed one, literalizes the erotic threat both women pose as vectors for supernatural, sinful sexual power—the fear that Katia will literally "become" Asa is so strongly sexual that the witch impersonates the virgin, attempting to seduce her love interest. The only give-away is that Asa

---

24. *Giallo* is a popular Italian genre, born in the 1960s, which blends psychological thriller, mystery, and slasher elements. Bava is one of its most famous pioneers, alongside Lucio Fulci and, most notably, Dario Argento whose witch film, *Suspiria* (1977), is to this day one of the most renowned witch films of the era.
25. Eichelbaum, 1961, 26.

has only a ribcage where her heart (and breasts) should be, revealing her to be a sterile, anti-feminine threat, both antierotic and, literally, heartless. Asa's death at the end of the film represents the exorcism of these qualities in Katia—a return to traditional femininity.

The film was a tremendous financial success—upon its release it immediately became the most profitable AIP film in the company's history—and the way it was received signaled a broader shift in the American horror landscape. While some critics dismissed it as a stiff exercise in the "grotesque", more suggested that it represented a return to an older tradition of atmospheric genre filmmaking after years of schlock. *Black Sunday*, according to the *Hollywood Reporter*, was "a serious horror story, not made for laughs or satire but with the same care and purpose of any other kind of film story. This is the way they used to be made, during the great period of motion picture horror films."[26] Another critic took this periodizing impulse further, musing that "ever since the decline and fall of *Dracula*, we've been treated to a series of outer-space monsters. It's nice to be back on earth again."[27] This "fine old fashioned horror film", became an early sign that the horror genre was looking elsewhere for inspiration—in this case, back to horrors in the Victorian horror/sci-fi tradition that opted for a modicum of seriousness over the ironic kitsch of *Attack of the Crab Monsters* (1957) or even the comedy-witch of *Bell, Book and Candle* a year later. The witch film will prove central to the horror film as a potentially "serious" genre in this decade, even as it becomes a pillar of what one critic called the 1960s "sex and sadism market" brought about by AIP's more typical output.

Alongside this recognition of the film's artistic bonafides, critics observed a contrasting, but equally significant impulse—its barely suppressed monstrous femininity in the form of overt sexuality paired with overt violence. The same critic who praised the film's seriousness complained that Bava's cinematography of his undead star was "considerably too imaginative for the very young, bordering on necrophilia."[28] This comment is particularly notable given the lengths AIP went to in trimming the film to avoid this precise characterization.[29] As critics' interest in the film's "seriousness" attests, this witch film had arrived into what was still Eisenhower's America, where female villains and their female victims were largely distinct. Even as the Hays Code was crumbling, on-screen sexuality of any kind was still suspect enough that AIP felt the need to defend (however disingenuously) its string of innocuously voyeuristic "beach bikini" films from charges of salaciousness, calling them "the epitome of morality" because "there are no overtly sexy sequences and no sex talk among the kids… the stars of AIP's beach pictures are always

---

26. Powers 1961, 3.
27. *Ibid.*
28. *Ibid.*
29. Koteki, 2021.

talking about getting married."³⁰ By this token, it is unsurprising that Arkoff viewed Asa's sexuality in *Black Sunday* with extreme skepticism: "anything that was suggestive of playing around—*fornicating* a corpse, you know what I'm saying?—we wouldn't stand for it."³¹ While sexually alluring female monsters had been common to the classic horror films of the 40s, AIP and its competitors had been selling creature features for almost a decade.³² When female monsters did appear in the AIP films of the '50s, they were obviously distinguishable from their womanly counterparts, either attractive "aliens" with ray guns and shiny suits (*Cat Women of the Moon, The Astounding She-Monster* [both 1957]), marked as literally inhuman and often described as "not women", or beautiful human women who then transformed into ugly creatures (*Cat Girl* [1957], *The Wasp Woman* [1959]), a similar distancing that binaristically separates the "good" beauty from the "evil" beast.

Critics recognized that *Black Sunday* delivered a different, more liminal kind of female horror monster, one who threatens to replace her victim without her lover's knowledge. A *Variety* critic appeared particularly uncomfortable with the "necrophile" tendencies of Steele's doubled character, even treating them as a mistake: Steele, he says, "manages to be attractive in both parts, which may not have been the original intention."³³ Treating the sexualization of Steele's witch as a mistake, as opposed to a deliberate thematic choice in keeping with the narrative doubling of her two characters, highlights another shift in the image of this particular horror archetype since the '40s—the assumption that "bad" witches must be ugly as the *Oz* team had insisted the Wicked Witch be. Asa's physical rejuvenation from marred corpse to beautiful witch reflects a broader transition in the witch films to come: soon, this assumption of ugliness would be matched by its opposite, leading to a schism in witch lore, where the line between innocent victim and evil sorceress would become blurred. These concerns were also tied to questions of age-appropriateness: another critic called the film a "sortie in satanism and sadism," noting that the prints playing at drive-ins featured a preface warning audiences (in fine Corman fashion) that the film should be "restricted to those over fourteen."³⁴ This combination of erotics and violence would continue to define the witch films of the era as the entire cinematic landscape became more explicit.

Another curiously international film, this one closer to home, established some of the other fundamental thematic dynamics of the witch cycle to come, namely by playing out paranoid narratives revolving around questions

---

30. McGee, 1996 in Heffernan 2015, 3.
31. Lucas, 2013, 310.
32. Exploitation films did feature attractive female villains in non-supernatural and non-horror exploitation films like those of the women's prison or juvenile delinquent pictures of the '50s, who actively play on femme fatale tropes.
33. Tube. 1961.
34. Beckley, 1961, 15.

of *belief*—in the supernatural, in one's identity, and in the institutions to which one belongs—in a modern setting. These questions, so fundamental to science fiction, become notably gendered in the witch films of this era, drawing on a history of women's pictures in the process. *Night of the Eagle* (1962) was written by American science fiction writers Charles Beaumont and Richard Matheson. Both successful novelists and screenwriters in their own rights, both men had also already written highly successful episodes of the *Twilight Zone* as well as screenplays for Roger Corman's cycle of Edgar Allan Poe adaptations (Matheson: *House of Usher*, *The Pit and the Pendulum*; Beaumont: *Premature Burial*, *The Masque of the Red Death*). The two men collaborated on *Night of the Eagle* (released as *Burn, Witch, Burn* in the US), adapting it from Fritz Leiber's 1943 novel *Conjure Wife*, and offered the finished script to AIP. The same channels of international collaboration that had led to *Black Sunday*'s American release led AIP to co-produce the film with Anglo-Amalgamated in England, to lower shooting costs.[35]

The film, like the novel from which it was adapted, plumbs the psychological underbelly of a marriage between a rationalist psychology professor, Norman (Peter Wyngarde), and his wife, Tansy (Janet Blair). The story begins with Norman, who specializes in the psychology of superstition, giving a lecture. With the phrase "I do not believe" scrawled in enormous letters on the board, he argues that in a world threatened by the possibility of nuclear war "reality is vital", and superstition is a dangerous product of what he calls "a morbid desire to escape reality." This rationalism is tested when Norman, who is up for a promotion, discovers that Tansy, his charming, well-educated wife, is a witch. She has been using "conjure magic" she learned in Jamaica to help his career for years, while other faculty wives are casting spells against him so their husbands will win promotions instead. Norman works to convince Tansy her magic is a neurosis, a hysterical reaction to stress unbecoming of "a woman of [her] intelligence." Yet, after he destroys her good-luck spells, his life descends into escalating disarray: a smitten student accuses him of rape—a narrative choice that renders the "innocent" Norman sexually disempowered while the previously "harmless" female student is made sexually threatening. In a jealous rage, her boyfriend tries to murder him as revenge. Soon, the phone is ringing at odd hours and the doors rattle on their hinges; Tansy becomes distant, telling him that another faculty wife, Flora (Margaret Johnson), is attempting to possess her body. Though Norman strains to dissuade her, the audience's perspective is split between both characters, lending credibility to Tansy's point of view through hyper-subjective shooting and giving the film a paranoid quality reminiscent of films like *Rebecca* (1940). Norman's rationalism is stretched to the breaking point when Tansy is compelled, seemingly by hypnosis, to the ocean and

---

35. Dixon, 2019.

attempts to drown herself. Norman, apparently convinced, reads up on magic and attempts to recast a protection charm. When the pair returns to campus, Flora and Norman meet in her office, where she taunts him with his own disbelief: in a particularly arresting sequence, Flora sets a house of cards on fire, asking him whether he believes his house is in fact on fire with Tansy inside or whether she's "just a silly woman." Norman, after rushing from the room, erases the "not" on his blackboard, leaving "I do believe." At the film's conclusion, the couple's house has in fact burned down, though the police say the cause was a leak in the gas stove. The couple are reunited, but Norman's doubt remains. It is left unclear whether the magic was real or hallucination,

At base, the film uses racialized fears as a vector for gendered anxieties even more explicitly than *Bell Book and Candle*. Magic in *Night of the Eagle* is inflected by a racist primitivism that paints Afro-Caribbean religious practices (Obeah, the "conjure magic" the wives use) as, in Norman's words, "stupid", "phony", and "irrational", though ultimately paternalistically benign and abstractly worthy of study in its distanced Caribbean context. When used by white women, though, these practices become overtly threatening, a means by which ostensibly subservient wives surreptitiously exert control over their lives, their homes, and their unsuspecting husbands. A product of the 1940s' incipient interest in the Crowleyan occult that produced *I Married a Witch* (1942) and *Cat People* (1942), the novel is explicit in its racist conflation of the feminine supernatural and highly othered "primitive" superstition in a manner that speaks to many of the films of this cycle.[36] In one scene, as the faculty play bridge at a party, the novel literalizes its philosophy: Norman plays a mental game he calls "spot the primitive… pretend[ing] the people around [him] were members of a savage race."[37] Picturing them with brown skin, "frizzy" hair, tribal tattoos and piercings, Norman finds "nothing unusual about the men," whom he categorizes as chiefs and craftsmen, "but the women!" Watching them play cards (which he now pictures as a tarot deck), he finds he can all too easily envision them using the second sight and casting spells that would make "even the bravest warrior… nervous."[38] Norman's conclusions in this scene are the heart of both the book and the film's view of femininity and women in general:

> Maybe all women were the same. Guardians of mankind's ancient customs and traditions—including the practice of witchcraft. Fighting their husband's battles from behind the scenes, by sorcery. Keeping it a secret; and, on those occasions when they were discovered, conveniently explaining it as feminine susceptibility to superstitious fads. Half of the human race still actively practicing sorcery. Why not?[39]

---

36. Bansak, 2003, 511.
37. Leiber, 1977, 76-7.
38. *Ibid*, 78.
39. *Ibid*, 81.

In this context, white women become dangerous, racialized Others, secretly more powerful than their husbands, easily dismissed by men's own naive sense of modern rationalism. Where *Bell, Book and Candle* kept this association loose, *Night of the Eagle* literalizes and internalizes it. This racist use of primitive stereotype contrasts the white supremacist stereotypes around "pure" white femininity that create the witch in the first place: the powerfully abject "witch woman" is antithetical to the domesticated Christian feminine ideal, turning the "intelligent" faculty wives into warrior-castrating monsters. The fact that the two are identical, one hidden away inside the other in the same way Asa can pass herself off as Katia in *Black Sunday*, is the real threat these women pose for Norman.

At this juncture in 1962, the threat this monstrous femininity represents, then, is a form of dangerous, unconstrained ambiguity as-of-yet unmoored from *direct* associations with feminism, but still playing with many of the central fears that will come to shape perceptions of the women's movement. As sociologist Margaret Mead argued when describing the witch's enduring appeal as a horrific figure across cultures, men harbor the anxiety that "the woman who yields in a man's arms has only lent herself to him for her own dangerous purposes or that the woman sleeping by a man's side is really somewhere else in mind and spirit, leaving behind only an empty shell."[40] The film plays on this masculine fear that women are fundamentally unknowable—uncontrollable even after they have been rendered "safe" by the multilayered "protections" of modernity, marriage (Sylvia Plath's "door mat"), and institutionalized rationalist humanism—and does so in the same way Jules Michelet suggested that sterile Christianity sequestered women's sexual identity. Both texts ultimately suggest that woman "carries shut within her breast a fond remembrance of the poor ancient gods,"[41] threatening to escape and wreak havoc on the patriarchal world. Here however, rather than present witches as downtrodden, as Michelet does, Norman fears the witches may *already* secretly control the world.

Night of the Eagle was inadvertently prescient by placing these fears on the college campus of the early 1960s, couching modern concerns about sexual harassment allegations and the bomb in fears of black magic and matriarchy: the Cold War consensus, a mindset characterized by historian Elaine Tyler May as one of "containment" in which "men and women sought to constrain their emotions, maintain their marriages, and build safe, secure, and independent homes" as a protective measure, was coming under threat from individuals who actively sought to disrupt reality (chemically, magically, or otherwise) and reshape it to better their lives, patriarchs' needs

---

40. Mead, 1971, 54.
41. Michelet, 1998, 27.

be damned. In this context, Norman's binaristic insistence that "reality is vital" undoubtedly resonated with male viewers.⁴²

Night of the Eagle's atmospheric approach to its psychological premise was, like *Black Sunday*'s morbid eroticism, ahead of the mood of early '60s horror churned out by AIP. Even as some audiences were given protective bags of salt and a slip with a protective incantation, critics praised *Night of the Eagle*'s style and tone as a throwback to a more serious era of horror.⁴³ *The New York Times* called it "the best outright goose-pimpler dealing specifically with witchcraft since 'I Walked With a Zombie,'" a comparison that evokes both Lewton's influence on atmospheric woman-focused horror and the racist roots of the genre (the critic loved this film's "superb Caribbean flavoring").⁴⁴

Yet in this period before witchcraft was in vogue, reviews almost unanimously wrestled with the question of the film's "believability" in a manner that anticipated broader cultural shifts. The *Times* review argued that the film's supernatural climax was, "we maintain, entirely logical within the context," an interestingly assertive, yet oddly cagey phrase on its own, clarified by other reviews that insisted the film "takes wild flights of fancy by suggesting that it's possible to delude professional psychiatrists with black magic."⁴⁵ Another critic derisively insisted that "it is impossible to accept the situation of two presumably intelligent women succumbing to black magic," in an interesting echo of Norman's own phrasing near the beginning of the film.⁴⁶ In this context, the film's explorations of modern belief in superstition are reflected out again by critics who appear almost entirely unwilling to entertain the supernatural in a modern context, preferring, like Corman's marketing, to present it as a cheesy gimmick: in one review, Tansy is described as "gripped by hysteria" before the characters "belatedly realize that the supernatural happenings merely existed in their imagination."⁴⁷ This pat summary dismisses the film's complex attempts to unpack the relationship between gendered conceptions of hysteria and neurosis, sexist paternalism, superstition and belief, before summarily rejecting the film's ambiguous ending in its entirety, a dismissal that parallels the assumption that the doubling in *Black Sunday* was accidental. Interestingly, the same review calls attention to the film's "slight feminine slant" as a potential point of audience appeal, indicating an understanding of the film's status as a quasi-women's picture with a proto-feminist perspective and nuanced female characters. As the decade wore on and the cultural climate became more mystical, these sorts of assumptions, like Norman's own, would begin to transform.

42. May, in Turner, 2006, 30.
43. Weldon, 1983.
44. Thompson, 1962.
45. "Night of the Eagle." *Kine Weekly* 1962.
46. "Night of the Eagle", *Monthly Film Bulletin*, 1962.
47. *Ibid.*

Taken together, AIP's first forays into the witch film demonstrate some of the basic elements with which the witch cycle will build: these films were simultaneously more serious than typical B horror films and, in *Black Sunday*'s case, more grotesque. In both films, the violence on display heightens a sense of gendered anxiety around women's uncontrollable internality (in both cases, an evil that is defeated, if only just). *Night of the Eagle* reappropriates the tropes of the women's picture (its "feminine slant"). This film also establishes one of the subgenre's central conflicts, namely, masculine rationality/science vs feminine irrationality/superstition in a modern setting, concluding—though critics refused to accept it—that the two, like Asa and Katia's identities, are more connected than they appear.

In the fall of 1964, a year largely devoid of witch films, a competing image of witchcraft would appear in American households: ABC's *Bewitched* would air for the first time. The show tracks another marriage, this one between a mortal man, Darrin (Dick York) and a witch named Samantha (Elizabeth Montgomery), who promises not to use magic at Darrin's request. Directly inspired by the witch romantic comedies of the '40s and '50s, the show was the most visible piece of the decade's witch pop culture until *Rosemary's Baby* launched the witch horror cycle's explosion in earnest. *Bewitched* was immediately contentious for feminists and their opponents. In her 1964 *TV Guide* essay "Television and the Feminine Mystique", Betty Friedan highlights a marked absence of dynamic female characters on the networks over decades—including shows like *Bewitched*:

> [T]he most puzzling thing about the image of woman on television today is an eerie Twilight Zone sense that it is fading before one's eyes. In the bulk of television programs today, and even, increasingly, in commercials, one literally sees no image of woman at all. She isn't there... Put the two [contrasting] images together—the woman on the screen and the one watching it—and you see how television has trapped itself in the feminine mystique.[48]

As television historian Walter Metz points out in his book on *Bewitched*, Samantha has been accused since her creation of "personif[ying] mass culture's ideal wife", particularly from a historical perspective in which she represents such an ideal on screen "in that last moment before mass culture tried to encompass the women's movement."[49] Similarly, Darrin represents "the most ideologically committed sexist of them all" by enforcing a "puritanical order" in his home in his quest to stamp out her magic.[50] From this perspective, shared by feminists like Friedan, "*Bewitched* was as anti-feminist, anti-sexual, and pro-centrist as a sit-com could be."[51]

---

48. Friedan, 1998, 59-60.
49. Metz, 2007, 94.
50. *Ibid.*
51. *Ibid.*

Metz also notes that the show's reception was genuinely ambivalent, using Isaac Asimov's satirical 1969 *TV Guide* essay "Husbands Beware!" with "its assault on the reductive progressive-versus-conservative argument about *Bewitched*" as his central point of analysis.[52] This essay—the same one to which I refer in my aside on television in the introduction to this book—is crafted as a cheeky, fictional conversation between Asimov (as patriarch) and his teenage daughter (as feminist). It plays out the same kinds of anxieties already on display in *Night of the Eagle* and its incredulous reception—as well as in the film to which I will turn next. The essay begins with a cartoon of a cowering Darrin, boxed into a corner by Samantha, here portrayed as a cat with a ghoulish, alligator-like face, blonde tresses, and a pointy black hat. The caption reads: "'Bewitched' is destroying all that is most holy and wonderful in marriage—'wifely terror.'"[53] Asimov adopts the perspective of a bloviating misogynist, praising shows like *I Love Lucy* for their depictions of "unpolluted husbandhood" in which the man is the dominant force in the American family, primarily through the enforcement of fear (quoth Lucy in nearly every episode: "Ricky's going to *kill* me!"): "To keep the family stable," Asimov's character argues, "the husband must keep his wife in a condition of abject terror." In *Bewitched*, however, Samantha's power changes these dynamics and Asimov's character moans, "[h]ow can I bring myself to tell you the mind-shattering nature of the result. The *husband* is terrified... revolting!"[54] The primary example he uses of Darrin's humiliation on the show is his inability to cheat on Samantha with a "young lady of surpassing beauty" for fear that Samantha, in cat form, is watching him, making manifest the sexual threat of this empowered feminine archetype even in its weakest form. Asimov's "beautiful, blonde" teenage daughter, though, is unimpressed:

> "Oh, Daddy, don't you see that *Bewitched* is just another example of the degradation of womanhood? Here's a woman with un-imaginable magical power and she uses it entirely to shore up her husband's ego... Has she no life of her own?" [to which Asmiov replies] "See what harm the program has been doing? She wasn't even aware of the disgrace of Darrin's terror. The toxin of *Bewitched* is pouring into the veins of innocent Americans and I must fight it."[55]

While it is truly hard to argue for a purely reclamatory reading of *Bewitched* from a modern perspective, Asimov's satirical essay serves as an excellent reminder that even the most milquetoast depictions of this archetype, largely created to sell cereal to mothers stuck at home, is heavily

---

52. Metz, 2007, 98.
53. Asimov, 1969, 7.
54. *Ibid*, 10.
55. *Ibid*.

invested with political significance at the dawn of the Second Wave feminist movement, and *was being discussed on those terms*—suddenly, jokingly or not, men find themselves nervous, even terrified.

Chapter Four

The Countercultural Witch Is Born (1965-1967)

"Perhaps today, the Christian can do no better than echo the prayer of the worried father who pleaded with Christ to heal his spirit-possessed son: 'I believe; help my unbelief.'"
-John T. Elson, "Is God Dead?"[1]

The focus of this chapter is a witch film most notable for the way it inadvertently captured a series of pop-cultural shifts in real time. While the film, as one historian put it, "died instantly at the box office,"[2] its deeply troubled production, which stretched over almost three years, would, in an almost cosmic manner, absorb and reflect many of the transitions taking place. Originally announced in 1965 as *Day of the Arrow* (but eventually retitled and released in 1966 as *Eye of the Devil*), this MGM film was based on a book by British author Robin Estridge. The novel speaks to the same impulses undergirding Norman's rationalist crisis of faith in *Night of the Eagle* (1962), as well as critics' response to it: *New York Times* columnist Anthony Boucher praised Estridge's *Day of the Arrow* in somewhat tortured terms for its "masculinity", complaining that the gothic novels of Daphne Du Maurier are "addressed primarily to a feminine audience. Oh, to be sure, men can enjoy them and very much indeed," but that in doing so, "we feel somewhat like intruders, in danger of profaning a rite by our alien presence," a framing that adopts the gendered, conspiratorial/ritualistic language of *Night of the Eagle*'s coven of conjure-wives. Thus, Estridge's novel "which tells very much the same kind of... story", is *"comforting"* for its "male viewpoint... with a mind working in a completely masculine", i.e. rationalist, "manner."[3]

The novel's plot presages *The Wicker Man* (1973) in many ways, telling the story of Phillipe, a French marquis who believes his community's crops will fail unless (with the help of a heretic priest, a sadistic hunter, and a young witch named Odile) he sacrifices himself to the pagan gods. Phillipe's wife, Catherine, must try to convince him that his superstition is false and that witches and the Devil aren't real. In an interesting echo of *Bell, Book*

---

1. Elson, *Time*, 1966.
2. Capua, 2010, 149.
3. Boucher, 1964, 144, emphasis added.

and Candle (1958), Kim Novak was cast as Catherine in the film, while David Niven took the role of Phillipe.

With Niven and Novak in the leading roles, the film, though still a B-horror picture, was initially marketed as a relatively respectable one. Narratively, it reverses the polarities of *Night of the Eagle*, with Catherine attempting to solve the mystery of her husband's strange behavior, protecting him and their two children with saintly forbearance. The roles of the film's witch, Odile, and her brother, Christian, were cast with relative unknowns, further emphasizing Catherine's centrality to the story. Set in the present, the majority of the film's runtime is dedicated to the mystery of the marquis' desire to return to his birthplace in France, a town organized around folkloric traditions and festivals. Once there, Catherine and the children are kept from Phillipe by a priest, Père Dominic (Donald Pleasence), Odile, and Christian, who exhibit strange and violent behavior. As Catherine seeks to uncover the reasons for Phillipe's evasiveness, she finds that these three, along with her husband, believe themselves to possess supernatural powers.

Odile, like Asa in *Black Sunday* (1960), is a sexual threat and, in some sense, the film's true antagonist. Though she appears in a relatively small number of scenes compared to Père Dominic, Odile is presented as Catherine's binary opposite, the sensuous id of the community and the only one who demonstrates genuinely supernatural ability. Catherine fears that Phillipe is sleeping with this younger woman—styled as a Beatnik/proto-hippie in a black turtleneck with long blonde hair—a concern Odile uses to manipulate her. In a climactic scene, Odile lures the children to play on a crumbling roof, evoking the classic association between witches and infanticide. When Catherine comes running, she tells Odile that she was only allowed to play on the roof as a child because "no one cared enough" to stop her, adding to the subtle characterization of this witch as a beautiful, overgrown wild child delinquent—a common characterization for the youthful counterculture on the rise at the time. Odile then hypnotizes Catherine when the older woman tries to confront her about the children's safety: "Did [Phillipe] say he would [chastise me]? Did he lie to you?" she asks in medium closeup, the lens gauzy, giving her a delicate sensual look in contrast with Catherine's flat wide shot and disheveled appearance. "Men always lie. Personally, I have no use for them..." she murmurs, casting strange reflections in Catherine's eyes with a necklace that belonged to Phillipe's ancestors. The editing becomes associative and subjective as reeling shots of the precipice flash across the screen, like a premonition or a curse. "You are getting very tired," she continues in the same blank tone, drawing Catherine closer to the edge of the roof. Just as *Night of the Eagle* troubles the relationship between a married couple by suggesting that women's inner lives are mysterious to their husbands, here Odile emphasizes a more mundane threat, infidelity, to the same effect, using it as a wedge into which the supernatural can creep, like a devil on Catherine's shoulder, and suggesting that women can exist without men. Of course, the reality Catherine soon finds is that Phillipe's physical relationship with Odile is more ritualistic than carnal: they do have sex, it is implied, though only in the context of a Black Mass, an alienating discovery that divorces sex from love or even pleasure. Her hypnotic spell on Catherine is also sexually tinged, characterized by sensuous closeups on her eyes and lips as she instructs Catherine to come closer and hold her hand.

Eye of the Devil, unlike *Night of the Eagle*, ends on a tragic note for the heterosexual nuclear family. Catherine is unable to save Phillipe, who goes through with the ritual to save the town's crops. He is led into the woods by the entire village before being shot with an arrow by Christian. Though Catherine vows to never return to the castle, her young son is drawn to it, returning in secret to retrieve the necklace Odile had been wearing and tell Père Dominic he will return. While this closing beat, as well as Phillipe's central role in the titular deadly ritual, would appear to frame the film's magic as a patriarchal tradition, the emphasis on the conflict between Catherine and Odile contradicts this: as the remainder of the family drives off in the closing shot, they speed by Odile, sitting in the rain, watching; her enigmatic eyes fill the frame before the screen fades to black. While the existence of the supernatural is never made explicit, left off as a nagging doubt in Catherine's mind and a promise of future pain for her son, whatever power does exist, be it psychological or paranormal, belongs to Odile. The nurturing mother, the representative of the continued functioning of the family, has failed to protect her husband or her son from this young witch's power.

Eye of the Devil has been described as a "jinxed" production for a number of reasons, and this aura of mystical calamity itself serves as an effective entry point into a sensibility that would become dominant by the film's release—an often drug-induced, often justified paranoiac sense of *meaning* that Tom Wolfe described as *"mysto."* Traveling with Ken Kesey's band of Merry Pranksters in 1964, watching former Beat turned acid-sage Neal Cassady toss a giant hammer into the air over his head while babies cried, music played, and someone discussed the relative merits of brushing one's teeth, Wolfe felt

> the general mysto steam... rising in my head. This steam, I can actually hear it inside my head, a great sssssssss... everything in everybody's life is... *significant*. And everybody is alert, watching for the meanings. And the vibrations. There is no end of vibrations.... Everyone is picking up on the most minute of incidents as if they are metaphors for life itself...[4]

He soon discovered it was contagious and spreading fast—it would influence the counterculture, feminism, and the witch film cycle that

---
4. Wolfe, 1968, 18-19, emphasis added.

attempted to understand both. The story of *Eye of the Devil*'s failure to capture the zeitgeist is a useful one on this score, wrapped in this mystical sense of deaths foretold and bad trips on the horizon: though Kim Novak shot about three quarters of Catherine's scenes in *Eye of the Devil*, she suffered a spinal fracture filming on horseback and did not ultimately play the role.[5] As her recovery lagged, she was replaced by Deborah Kerr.[6] The film was delayed again when MGM raised concerns that Catholics would take issue with its depiction of Père Dominic as a "heretic priest".[7] It was during these unfortunate delays that the film's marketing began to shift in ways that, like *The Age of Curiosity*, made the mysto steam begin to rise. The production began foregrounding the film's countercultural aspects, starting with the two up-and-comers playing Christian and Odile: David Hemmings, whose star would rise meteorically at the year's end with Antonioni's taboo-shattering *Blow-Up* (1966)—and Sharon Tate in her screen debut, only two years before she was ritualistically murdered by the "satanic" Manson Family.

The pop-cultural mood only truly began to catch up with Wolfe's "significant" vibrations almost halfway through the decade, just as *Eye of the Devil* first began pre-production. As Andy Warhol put it, "everything went young in '64", the year the oldest of the massive Baby Boom generation would turn eighteen.[8] Hundreds of Berkeley students occupied buildings on campus to protest the suppression of free speech by the administration, leading to a massive increase in national student organizing. Inside rapidly expanding groups like SNCC, CORE, SDS and others, who had already been protesting for civil rights and free speech for several years, tremendous numbers of women (mostly "college-educated women in their mid-to-late twenties who grew up in middle-class families") were beginning to gain the skills and connections to begin organizing themselves anew.[9] [10] The Civil Rights Act, which also included protections against sex discrimination, passed that fall. In a related win for the Free Speech Movement, the Supreme Court would radically loosen definitions of obscenity that spring in *Jacobellis v. Ohio* (the case most famous for Justice Stewart's remark on obscene material: "I know it when I see it")[11], a move with tremendous implications for the film industry.

Meanwhile, the same streak of hyper-individualism visible in the Port Huron Statement's concern for life as "personally authentic" was spreading still further. In July, writers in *Esquire* complained of an ironically named

---

5. Kleno, 1980, 230.
6. "Broken Vertebra Caused Kim Novak to Quit Movie", 1965.
7. Capua, 2010, 149.
8. Hoberman, 2005, 93.
9. Echols, 2019, 65.
10. Student Nonviolent Coordinating Committee, Congress of Racial Equality, Students for a Democratic Society.
11. Lattman, 2007.

"New Sentimentality", characterized by a loss of cultural cohesion and an interest in the self. In cutting terms, the writers mourned that while the Old Sentimentality had

> 'values' that everyone could see... Patriotism, Love, Religion... [the New Sentimentality] has to do with *you*, really just you... what goes on in your head, *really*, and in your heart, really... Personal interest is the abiding motivation... Self-indulgence used to be a bad idea. ... Now it is a virtue... because it tells us the truth about ourselves.[12]

This interest in the self, though cynically framed here, was part and parcel with the interest in creating alternative ways of being outside the context of the grey monotony of Cold War conformity. Kesey's Merry Pranksters embodied this ethos, exploring the *self* through acid, art, and experience, making meaning from within and reflecting it out again. This ideological stance, characterized by an odd blend of heightened pop-art irony and mystical earnestness, was heavily shaped by an awareness of the media theory of Marshall McLuhan (a friend of Kesey's). Leary conceptualized the mind as a computer in need of reprogramming, or a TV set flashing off impulses and signals.[13] Life, art, and politics began to blend into one massive media spectacle, a phenomenon that these groups celebrated, particularly through Acid Tests and multimedia psychedelic art shows. This belief, that the self could be molded to fit the desires of the individual like a movie of one's own making, was reflected in one art group, USCO painting the phrase "Just Us" above the doors to their home base.[14]

The New Left as well as the hippies (originally a shortened version of the term "hipster" popularized by the *San Francisco Examiner* 1965) were viewed by the mainstream with genuine panic, as harbingers of a hedonistic, nihilistic future. In a TV documentary on student radicals that year, Free Speech activist Michael Rossman described his generation as having "no ideology" except "society stinks."[15] In 1964, Susan Sontag claimed *Dr. Strangelove*, a favorite film of the college scene, typified what she called "nihilism for the masses...our contemporary form of moral uplift."[16] In 1965, Kesey interrupted an anti-Vietnam protest at which he had been asked to speak by saying "you know you're not gonna stop this war with this rally... that's what *they* do," before playing the harmonica so badly and for so long that he was forcibly removed from the stage.[17] At the same time, with drug law enforcement targeting political activists and countercultural

---

12. Benton and Newman, 1964.
13. Hoberman, 2005, 130.
14. *Ibid*, 54.
15. *Ibid*, 131.
16. *Ibid*, 92.
17. Turner, 2006, 64.

leaders, violent urban protests, and massive increases in the draft, so-called revolutionary nihilism didn't seem so unreasonable to many.[18] As R.G. Davis of the San Francisco Mime Troupe put it, for many at the intersection of the New Left and the counterculture, "operative paranoia is our appropriate state of being."[19]

The sentiment was familiar to the women of the New Left, whose presence in the movement was continually sidelined. In 1965, several women working within SDS raised issues of sexism at a convention, only to be catcalled off the stage by men screaming that they "just need[ed] a good screw."[20] At SNCC, feminist organizers Casey Hayden and Mary King published a memo titled "Sex and Caste", drawing parallels between racist and sexist oppression, arguing that misogyny within the organization kept women in subordinate positions, their attempts to advocate for gender equality met with derision and laughter by movement men.[21] Experiences of harassment, dismissal, and exploitation were commonplace for women in these spaces, especially women of color, a continual disregard that would add to the troubles of the Women's Liberation Movement by the decade's end.

By the time *Eye of the Devil* completed shooting in early 1966, these changes had burst into the mainstream. That year, the "Under Twenty-Five Generation" was declared *Time*'s Man of the Year.[22] LSD was criminalized in early 1966, and, according to *Time*, the drug was now a "disease striking in beachside beatnik pads and in the dormitories of expensive prep schools" causing psychotic breaks and infecting tens of thousands of college students.[23] A far cry from the miracle drug *Time* had celebrated in '63, now "LSD can kill you dead." One of the "Florid and Terrifying" drug's most concerning side effects according to this writer? Users "say it brings supernatural powers."[24]

LSD was on the mind, and even Roger Corman had tried it and found it eye opening. He was preparing a series of what he called "protest films", whose identifications lay with the outlaws over the Establishment, at a time when he said his "filmmaking instincts, like [his] stance in politics, were growing more radical."[25] After a series of successful biker pictures, Corman soon turned to a cycle of LSD films with many of the same actors, people he chose because they were "a hundred percent committed" to the cause of the countercultural and psychedelic revolution.[26] The films typically follow unhip "squares" as they have their minds blown by acid and free love. Though

---

18. Hoberman, 2005, 65.
19. *Ibid*, 130.
20. D'Emilio and Freedman, 2012, 311.
21. Hayden and King, 1965.
22. Hoberman, 2005, 160.
23. "An Epidemic of 'Acid Heads'", 1966.
24. *Ibid.*
25. Heffernan, 2015, 5.
26. *Ibid*, 8.

the trips are depicted as harrowing and frequently dangerous, more often than not, the characters realize their lives had been lacking some essential soul, now available in the druggy counterculture of the Haight-Ashbury,[27] already being described in highly cinematic terms: as one man said during the Trips Festival, a massive concert in the Haight that summer that seemed to inaugurate the movement, "When your feet hit the ground in the morning, you're in a grade B movie."[28]

Corman's acid films, though promoted as social problem pictures "based on the… tragic results from the use of LSD"[29] would be criticized as tacit endorsements of the drugs and hippie lifestyles they were associated with— but not rejected as the same old exploitation cheapies he had been producing only a few years before. *Variety* voiced this confusion clearly, wondering of the first of these LSD films, *The Trip* (1967), "Is Corman simply exploiting a new horror avenue or is this an honest attempt to reproduce . . . an actual hallucinatory experience?"[30] The film, which grossed over six million dollars on its $340,000 budget by the end of 1967, was heralded as a watershed by *Playboy*, which took the opportunity to interview Leary on the psychedelic experience under the banner "the real impact and import of *The Trip*." The guru, sensing opportunity, claimed that LSD was "basically a sexual experience", playing with mainstream anxieties and countercultural allure.[31] *The Los Angeles Free Press* called the film "an occasion for rejoicing . . . the purest cinematic exercise ever to come out of Hollywood."[32] Corman's films' successes, both critically and at the box office, marked the beginning of a new exploitation cycle that would trouble the boundaries of legitimate cinema. Culture, it seemed, was moving at an increasingly rapid pace, in increasingly high definition.

It's no wonder that *Eye of the Devil* couldn't keep up. Still, the production team certainly did try, releasing a promotional film about Sharon Tate. "She's today's kind of girl!" a male announcer enthuses over footage of Tate and Hemmings dancing at "one of the newest, *in*-est discotheques" in London. The short promo, *All Eyes on Sharon Tate* (1966), emphasizes Tate's beauty first and foremost, as well as her eagerness to please, rendering her non-threatening and docile (closer to Samantha than Odile) even while banking on the vicarious appeal of London's libertine mod scene, a psychedelicized subculture about which the term "moral panic" was originally popularized by sociologist Stanley Cohen.[33] Filled with vignettes of Tate posing for glamor

---

27. A neighborhood in San Francisco that quickly became the epicenter of the hippie movement.
28. Hoberman, 2005, 139.
29. Heffernan, 2015, 8.
30. *Ibid*, 10.
31. *Ibid*.
32. *Ibid*.
33. Cohen popularized the term in his book *Folk Devils and Moral Panics* in 1972, a study on mod and rocker subcultures in England.

shots and touring "swinging" London with Hemmings, the film positions her as the ideal balance of good looks and feminine humility. In a telling clip, an interviewer leadingly observes that "other rising stars will say, 'Please don't think of me as a beautiful woman, I'd like to play Shakespeare,' and that rings quite hollow" as the camera roves over magazine spreads of Tate. "Well I don't fool myself", she amicably replies, sitting on a couch, laughing, "I'd *love* to do light comedy." This strategic pivot is understandable since her second film (released in quick succession after *Eye of the Devil*'s setbacks), was her soon-to-be husband Roman Polanski's black comedy *The Fearless Vampire Killers* (1967). It does, however, strike a jarring note with the clip that follows it by less than a minute: the scene of Odile attempting to murder Catherine. Tate's threatening presence in this scene is reduced to a joke still further by David Niven's blithe commentary, "first of all, she's a *fabulous* looking bird," before throwing in "she's a very good actress" as an afterthought. Sharon Tate is, the promo insists, ultimately "a girl on the go-go", a comely *Playboy* pin-up of the sexual revolution.

Ironically, *All Eyes on Sharon Tate* had all the ingredients of one of the year's most important films: Antonioni's *Blow-Up*, released in December, would track David Hemmings through London's mod clubs, taking glamor shots of swinging beauties and attempting to solve a murder. This Italian import became one of the first films to be released in the US without a production seal to immense critical acclaim. Also condemned by the Legion of Decency, it was a runaway success with young people, struck a death blow to the production code, and opened the floodgates—in tandem with the *Jacobellis* decision and the success of exploitation-art films like *The Trip*—for more daring, sexually explicit filmmaking. In 1968, the Production Code would end altogether with the institution of the modern ratings system. Itself a subject of profound moral and media panic, *Blow-Up*'s blasé, nihilistic approach to international cool, struck a chord with the same college kids "gobbling" LSD and "losing their minds" over The Beatles. International films were beginning to compete with Hollywood's own product—and it was becoming clear that these typically wealthy, white, college-aged American young people (whom then-governor Ronald Reagan was faulting for what he called "the morality gap at Berkeley")[34] were becoming Hollywood's lifeline.[35] By 1972, people ages twelve to twenty nine accounted for 73% of ticket sales—and almost 80% of those with some college education claimed to "frequently go to the movies" while about half of non-college-educated respondents claimed only infrequent attendance.[36] In this period of Hollywood crisis, as Jack Valenti put it, "the future of the film business lies on the campus."[37]

---

34. Hoberman, 2005, 157.
35. Hoberman, 2005, 157.
36. Lewis, 2002, 189.
37. *Ibid*, 145.

Another trend was beginning to take shape on campus, with some of its roots drawn from the same British scenes that birthed both *Blow-Up* and *Eye of the Devil*: witchcraft. After the repeal of England's 1735 anti-witchcraft law in 1951, modern practitioners slowly began to gain public attention in the UK. Arguably the most famous of the 1960s was Alex Sanders, the founder of Alexandrian Wicca, a modern form of paganism that falsely claimed to have its roots in the kinds of Medieval occult traditions promoted by Margaret Murray's "witch cult" hypothesis. Sanders worked to promote his practice on television and in the British press, thereby becoming a go-to interview subject on modern occultism. In early 1966, he and his wife Maxine were hired as technical consultants on *Eye of the Devil*. "According to MGM", reads one article in *Kine Weekly*, "there are 30,000 witches in Britain—and two of them… are to 'perform ceremonial rites which are normally only performed in the presence of members of their Covens'" for the director and crew of the film.[38] [39] While films like *Night of the Eagle* insisted that "witchcraft lives today!" in their promotional work, these truth claims were restricted to the diegetic worlds of their films. In this advertisement, witchcraft had become truly real, grounded in the British occult revival.

Occult practices were already gaining attention in the American media by this time. Several years earlier, *Time* had reported that "1963, for no clear reason, has been a banner year for sorcerers" in a brief story that connected witches with grave robbery and Devil worship.[40] These unsavory associations in the press were often mixed up with a hearty dose of the erotic: a 1962 pulp paperback "history" of witchcraft called it the "disgusting" terrain of "bored, wealthy people who seek to recreate the orgies of the Sabbat in order to whet their jaded sexual appetites." Some conservative members of Parliament began advocating for new British anti-witchcraft laws in 1963 on similar grounds claiming that witchcraft "is a cover for sexual orgies."[41]

Witches were also entering the zeitgeist of sexual politics on the pages of *Playboy*, making the promotion of Sharon Tate's casting in *Eye of the Devil* appear even more savvy in retrospect. In 1963, Hugh Hefner wrote an editorial on the history of witchcraft as part of a series of op-eds called "The Playboy Philosophy", dedicated "to better understand[ing] this Sexual Revolution… [by] explor[ing] the origins of our present-day traditions and taboos regarding sex." In this piece, he argued, in an echo of Michelet, that historical witchcraft accusations were a product of "sexual hysteria" by the church that speak "to the extreme effect sexual repression can have upon a society… when church and state are one", the consequences of which were taken out on "poor women" as a means of regulating "private behavior…

---

38. Todd, 1966.
39. Buckland, 1974, 16-17.
40. "A Prevalence of Witches", 1963.
41. *Ibid.*

[through] psychological control, based upon terror."⁴² This editorial was a sort of philosophical companion to another, pulpier piece run the month before called "The Sabbats of Satan." Beginning with a lightly psychedelic illustration of a curvaceous naked woman cozying up with goats and demons, the piece supplied breathless descriptions of "comely" young women being burned at the stake and having sex with polymorphously perverse, gender-swapping devils and animals.

This piece, too, took its historical philosophy from the likes of Michelet and Margaret Murray, arguing that witchcraft "devil-cults" practiced in secret as a response to the oppressive feudal system held up by the church ("It was during the 14th Century that old pagan nocturnal rites became imbued with a fierce spirit of revolt, vengeance and despair").⁴³ These details also highlight the appeal of witches as hinging on the same paranoias already coursing through the culture of the '60s—hypersexual cults hiding in plain sight, threatening Christian religious consensus. While politics are obviously secondary in this piece (which spends more time on anecdotes of supernatural adultery, wife swapping, and "promiscuous lovemaking") this article importantly begins to associate witches with psychedelics as well as rebellion: "Witch ointment, which supposedly made witches capable of flying... produced in the witches a hallucinatory state in which they could actually imagine themselves and their fellow witches air-borne" using ingredients that are "well-known today."⁴⁴ The piece concludes, like AIP's advertisements for *Night of the Eagle* and *Eye of the Devil*'s belated promotional campaign, with the assertion that "Satanism... did not die with the Middle Ages. The arcane powers of blackness still hold their unnatural fascination." Taken together, these two pieces speak to the same tensions on display in Sharon Tate's Odile: the witch as sexy companion (a groovy Samantha) and the witch as a highly political figure representing a history of extreme chauvinism and women's attempts to fight back, often through taking control of their own sexuality.

In 1966, American witchcraft took off in practice as well as in theory. On Halloween night in San Francisco, former carnival organist, lion tamer, and police photographer Anton LaVey founded the Church of Satan, declaring it "the Year One" of "the Age of Satan." The church was founded as a secular, highly theatrical group dedicated to self-indulgence in all its forms, using Satan as a symbolic representative of the repressed. Though not literal in its endorsement of the Devil's existence, the group practiced ritual magic as a means of exerting control over their environment and their own mindset. For LaVey, as well as Michelet, "the Devil has been the guy that's kept the church in business for many, many years", providing "much needed

---

42. Hefner, 1963, 43.
43. Griffith, 1963, 146.
44. *Ibid.*

opposition" and stoking fear for which Christians should be thankful.[45] A natural-born showman, LaVey, who sported a pointed goatee and a shaved head, actively courted the American press in 1967, delivering a good-luck spell on The Tonight Show with Johnny Carson. In February '67, the new "satanic cult" was prominently featured in "The Feminine Eye" column in *Life* magazine, with rhetoric that aligned the group with the libertine, individualistic politics of the counterculture, albeit in a different aesthetic package: "The distinguishing feature of this new Satanic religion is that it has no concept of sin, hence it evokes no guilt", the article enthused.[46] On top of printing LaVey's Satanic call to individual freedom without shame, the article, like *Playboy* and the Alexandrians, emphasized the physical beauty of his more glamorous followers (one of whom requested the title "sorceress" because "Witch has sort of the connotation of cookie-lady now" almost certainly a denigrating reference to *Bewitched* [1964-1972]): actress Jayne Mansfield would be named a High Priestess in 1966. The church, it was repeatedly implied by its founder as well as the media, used sex in its rituals. As all of this would suggest, LaVey, used *Playboy*-style media savvy and theatrical stylings pulled from the horror film landscape—plastic horns, oversized coffins and beautiful women—to gain notoriety with more than a hint of the salacious, blending parody and sacrilege to re-inject these cinematic signifiers with the powers of darkness. Alex Sanders too would continue to encourage these heightened sexual associations while promoting his new sect of Wicca, allowing photographers and camera crews to film his young and attractive female followers—and vividly describing whippings as part of their practice.[47] By the time *Eye of the Devil* was released, Sanders even claimed that he had initiated Sharon Tate into Wicca and taken her to buy books on the occult during shooting.[48] Witchcraft, like LSD, was on the rise.

Neither the team's buzzy occult marketing ploys, nor Sharon Tate's beauty, nor even David Hemmings' sudden superstardom, could save *Eye of the Devil* at the box office when it was finally released in 1967. As with *Night of the Eagle*, some critics commended its roots in older horror cycles, with its "plot that resembles so many of those old black magic, mysterious cult pictures of the 30s and 40s."[49] Some, in an indication of the schism between the average critic and the average theatergoer, rated it favorably against the surrounding genre landscape, archly suggesting that at least, "as bad movies go… it's lots more fun than the current spate of motorcycle sagas" of the kind Roger Corman had popularized.[50] Like *Night*

---

45. "Anton LaVey on the Joe Pyne Show", 2012.
46. Alexander, 1967.
47. "The Coven of One's Choice." 1970.
48. Ellis, 2000, 157.
49. "FEATURE REVIEWS: Eye of the Devil", 1967.
50. Thomas, 1967.

of the Eagle, though, the film's biggest problem for critics still seemed to be one of credibility. The *Los Angeles Times* suggested that "In the days of H-bombs and Vietnam, gloomy castles with witches... hold little terror. The only way to play gothic terror today seems to be tongue-in-cheek and heavy on the grand guignol gore," likely a reference to Corman's cycle of Edgar Allen Poe films. The writer goes farther in this assessment, claiming the film would have been "helped... had the story been set in the past—the farther back the *better*", distancing modern reality from occultism completely.[51] In simple terms, the film was "unconvincing" in the same way *Night of the Eagle* was unconvincing—modern witchcraft was simply beyond belief for these mainstream outlets, even in the face of what would soon be called an "occult explosion"—and this film had none of the necrophiliac allure of AIP's *Black Sunday*. On that score, though, critics did find one element of the film praiseworthy: Sharon Tate's figure. "For male moviegoers who don't like this sort of medieval madness in a modern mold, there is stunning Sharon Tate, one of the most beautiful girls now in the movies, and she can act, too", *Box Office* crowed.[52] Even as the film's team worked to ground the occult in the very-real mysticism of the countercultural milieu of the present, a notable shift in marketing tactics that would only increase in the years to come, this prestige B-picture couldn't hold a candle to the occult allure of AIP's low-budget countercultural films.

Taken together, the cultural shifts surrounding *Eye of the Devil* make the film a useful relic of a movie business, a film culture, and a pop culture in crisis. The film's story of intergenerational conflict and anxiety—Catherine's sexual fear of Odile's youthful power, Phillipe's patriarchal impotence culminating in his murder by Hemmings' Christian, and the creeping sense that the younger generation will grow into something unrecognizable and evil under their parents' noses—reflects much of the panic on display in the headlines. Catherine's staunch dedication to her absent husband becomes tragic and inexplicable in the face of cosmic forces she doesn't understand. Parents and children, husbands and wives here become unfamiliar to one another in the face of cultural change presented as both modern and arcane. Catherine's grim decision to give up on her husband's birthright and simply "never come back" to the castle after his death is rendered moot by her child's secret commitment to his father's ancient Craft. The creeping mysto of the era could not be contained, here riding a wave of unacknowledged generational anxiety and overt erotic charge. In this light, the film and the shift in its marketing and reception across the three years of its development signal the rise of the most high-profile branch of countercultural witchcraft at this point in history: the groovy, sexy, evil witch of the mondo documentary, the softcore flick, and the exploitation film—here exemplified by Sharon Tate, the

---

51. Thomas, 1967.
52. "FEATURE REVIEWS: Eye of the Devil", 1967.

comely *Playboy* witch incarnate and the woman whose eventual murderesses would come to represent the darker side of this precise fantasy archetype.⁵³

On April 8th, 1966, *Time* released an instantly iconic, intensely controversial issue with the question "Is God Dead?" wailing from its cover in bold, red letters. In the article, the magazine's religious editor, John T. Elson, explores this question, arguing that America felt itself slipping into secular humanism: "'We are proceeding toward a time of no religion at all,'" one subject proclaims; "For many, that time has arrived", Elson answers. In the context of a pop culture increasingly dominated by films like *The Graduate* (1967) and a politics characterized by violence, "the anti-heroes of modern art endlessly suggest that waiting for God is futile, since life is without meaning... the Christian mood today... is that faith has become not a possession but a *hope*."⁵⁴ The anxiety in the article is oriented towards something broadly imagistic, predicated on the secularization of *pop culture* rather than a pure loss of faith itself (the article cites a poll claiming 97% of Americans still believe in God, though churchgoing had declined). By the article's close, the question has evolved, wrestling with the same issues of credibility on display in earlier reviews of films like *Night of the Eagle* and *Eye of the Devil*: "After Dachau's mass sadism and Hiroshima's instant death, there are all too many real possibilities of hell on earth" to compel belief in God, the article suggests; in this light, "how do men talk of God in the context of a culture that rejects the transcendent, the beyond?" At the same time, though, the writer's tacit focus is one of an *expansion* of spiritual possibilities and beliefs that stands in tension with any prior foreclosing of religiosity: "Why is [Jesus] a better focus of faith than Buddha, Socrates or even Albert Camus?" the article asks, not without alarm, when discussing debates around Jesus' literal relationship to God. These passages, taken together, point not merely to the simple decline in spirituality that so many readers wrote the magazine to protest in the weeks following the story, so much as a yearning for alternatives, for meaning, in a cultural and political landscape in which meaningless itself has become a focal point, and nihilism an "appropriate" response to mass death and mass injustice.

In an *Esquire* article in August 1966, David Newman and Robert Benton penned what could well have been a follow up to *Time*'s cover story, summing up the national mood with equal force:

[H]as it really been just six years, or are we all going crazy, it seems like it's been the Sixties forever...Luminaries come and go faster than a speeding

---

53. Mondo films are a subgenre of exploitation film that use the stylings of documentary to explore sensational or taboo subject matter, usually making outlandish or false claims in the process.
54. Elson, 1966, emphasis added.

bullet. Fads and fashions flame up and burn out in a week... this seems a good time to call for a halt. We have had enough! Enough! And so we benevolently announce that the Sixties are over. Let six years be a decade. Let the next four be a vacation.[55]

By August 1967, a vacation may have begun, though not the kind that the average *Esquire* reader would enjoy. The Summer of Love rang in the cultural primacy of the psychedelicized hippie counterculture and the campus radical—groups that had begun to adopt each other's aesthetics and sensibilities. The Doors (named for Aldous Huxley's classic psychedelic text *At the Doors of Perception* [1954]) released their first album while The Beatles' *Sgt. Pepper's Lonely Hearts Club Band* marked the group's own sojourn into the hallucinogenic and the mystical: Aleister Crowley and Huxley himself graced the cover alongside Marilyn Monroe and Carl Jung. Young people flocked to San Francisco by the thousands and began experimenting with communal living, sharing resources and attempting to organize themselves into something resembling a viable alternative to mainstream American life.[56] The counterculture had taken Leary's advice to "tune in, turn on, and drop out", first given at the San Francisco's event Human Be-In that spring, to heart.

The same year, the first truly countercultural witch film arrived, though in protean form and with zero fanfare: Herschel Gordon Lewis' genuinely bizarre exploitation film, *Something Weird* (1967), played on the drive-in circuit and around college campuses to young, stoned audiences. Like Sharon Tate's debut, this film was largely ignored; but it captures the period's frenzied pop cultural landscape, setting the stage for the cycle of witch films and occultism about to dominate the national conversation. Fittingly for this moment of radical change, *Something Weird* is a jumble of trends, combining kung fu, witchcraft, acid, and telepathy with a tepid police procedural plot: after being electrocuted by a falling power line, playboy Cronin Mitchell (Tony McCabe) develops extrasensory perception. Horribly disfigured and suddenly unemployed, he's forced to work as a psychic, wearing a disguise to hide his disturbing appearance after women begin to mock his advances. Soon, a witch (Elizabeth Lee) magically arrives in his living room. This witch is a textbook crone, complete with greenish skin, warty chin, and Wicked Witch cackle. She offers him a Faustian bargain—she will give him his looks back, provided he become her sex slave for the rest of his life. He agrees, his face is healed, and she disappears. Soon, he meets a beautiful blonde named Ellen at a bar (depicted as a well-off, single working girl in a short, tight dress) and she comes home with him, only to transform into the witch, delighted by her own trick. After this humiliation, she curses him

---

55. Hoberman, 2005, 153.
56. Turner, 2006, 32.

to see her true "ugly" form, seemingly for her own sexual amusement at his discomfort, while everyone else sees her as Ellen. The witch, then, is depicted as sexually voracious, sadistic, and emasculating.

The rest of the film follows the duo as they assist a karate-obsessed detective named Jordan (William Brooker) in his effort to stop a serial killer by using Mitchell's ESP—amplified by a dose of acid. The plot is loose and episodic, with interludes featuring sentient killer bedsheets, levitating chairs, and a ghost. After discovering his identity, Mitchell is eventually himself killed by the serial killer (a psychotic member of the homicide unit). The witch seduces Jordan as Ellen, then transforms into a crone while they kiss. Jordan flees in terror while she chases him, grinning from ear to ear, before he suffers a similar disfiguring accident to Mitchell's own. The film ends with the witch offering him her bargain, staring directly into the camera, and cackling her Wicked Witch cackle as fire fills the frame.

This ending marks another significant shift in the witch films of the era: in *Black Sunday* the evil Asa loses to true love. *Eye of the Devil*'s melancholic conclusion leaves the mere possibility of further havoc dangling as the credits roll. With *Something Weird*, for the first time the witch of this decade ends the film triumphant and unconstrained, ready to wreak havoc on any man she chooses, a parody of Helen Gurley's advice in *Sex and the Single Girl* that a woman's sexuality is a "powerful weapon." Where in previous films the erotic threat of the witch is obvious but still sublimated, here the '60s witch becomes a centrally sexual monster.

Something Weird, though thoroughly disregarded at the time, exists at a fascinating intersection between the overtly opportunistic, the psychedelic, the scientific, and the occult. When the film, the B-picture to Lewis' *The Gruesome Twosome*, finally arrived in Los Angeles in early 1968, one critic called it "amateurish" and "unrelieved trash."[57] Lewis, whose hyperbloody low-budget features quickly earned him the moniker "the Godfather of Gore", took advantage of the increasingly permissive atmosphere of the '60s to give audiences the red meat they craved—and had almost never seen on screen. Like Corman's psychedelic, rebellious countercultural films, Lewis' sparked genuine outrage and open censure, often getting confiscated by police for obscenity. This fleshier, goopier, even less reputable side of the American horror landscape over the course of the decade, as *Something Weird* begins to demonstrate, will converge on the art horror film—often through the overlapping avenues of the psychedelic and the occult.

In an interview discussing the film for its Arrow Video release in 2020, media historian Jeffrey Sconce called *Something Weird* a "dead end", framing it as having neither real precedent in the horror genre of the era nor real influence on other films following its release.[58] While this is true in some ways

---

57. Thomas, 1968.
58. "Weirdsville", 2020.

(it's unlikely that other filmmakers were actively drawing on this particular Lewis film), this statement obscures *Something Weird*'s debt both to the exploitation horror films about LSD so recently popularized with films like *The Trip* and to the broader psychedelic cultural milieu on campus. Many of these exploitation films dealing with LSD (part of a cycle of what I've called "psychedelic horror films" elsewhere[59]), responded to the moral and media panic around hallucinogens at the precise moment the government cracked down on their usage by playing up sordid stories of psychosis, murder, and suicide.[60] Here, though, as in Corman's countercultural films, *Something Weird* is doing something different—and, arguably, almost entirely unique: consciously and overtly bringing the occult and the psychedelic together, seemingly for the first time on screen. The film, according to interviews with Lewis, was written by a history professor named Jim Hurley, who was an "expert in ESP." Inspired to write the script by his concerns over Russian scientists' research into the field of "parapsychology"—research that had, in fact, been taking place in the Soviet Union throughout the decade—Hurley originally envisioned the film as a quasi-documentary about ESP's potential benefits to national security.[61] The script Lewis received was evidently dry and unmarketable, leading the director to change the story to make it, in his words, "more of a movie and less of a lecture on ESP."[62]

The film's origins in the Cold War laboratory and college classroom speak to a fundamental—and often overlooked—connection among different countercultural trends, namely the occult, the New Age, and the psychedelic. Like LSD itself, originally doled out for government research as a form of defense technology, psychic phenomena (like ESP) were studied by the CIA and the DoD as potential military tools.

The overlap between research into occult phenomena and psychedelics during this period begins at inception of both: Andrija Puharich, a Defense Department researcher, investigated both the use of hallucinogenic mushrooms *and* ESP phenomena during his time working for the US government.[63] Research into ESP necessarily included practices commonly associated with witchcraft, from astrological prediction and palmistry to hypnotism and telepathy. As one famous witch put it in 1971: "'modern research has found long names for the powers witches exercise: hypnotism, clairvoyance, mediumship, astral projection, extra-sensory perception, psychotherapy.' In olden times… all these things came under one heading: witchcraft."[64] Puharich was so associated with the supernatural and the occult in the '60s that he appeared as himself on an episode of *Perry Mason* entitled

---

59. McCarty-Simas, 2024.
60. For more on the psychedelic horror film, see McCarty-Simas, 2024.
61. "Introduction to Something Weird", 2020.
62. *Ibid.*
63. Dickey, 2017.
64. Martello, 1971.

"The Case of the Meddling Medium" as a member of a team assigned to debunk a potentially psychic murderer.

At the CIA, meanwhile, research into hypnosis and telepathy (mind control techniques investigated in tandem with the MKULTRA program on hallucinogens) involved direct consultation with England's most famous witch Sybil Leek, on issues related to witchcraft and the supernatural in the late 1960s, partially in response to Soviet-produced films purporting to depict telekinetic abilities from Russian witches and mediums.[65] Concerns around the "ESP gap" were so great for this particular group of researchers that Leek issued a warning to US government officials alerting them of the "great danger that within the next ten years the Soviets will be able to steal our top secrets by using out-of-the-body spies."[66] The battle for America's political place on the world stage was being fought on supernatural as well as psychedelic terms—the same terms that the counterculture would wage in its battle for America's spirit.

While the scientific association between psychedelic experiences and the supernatural may at first appear strange, their roles in the counterculture help explain their shared appeal (and their power to frighten). The same kind of fascination with the two phenomena as *related* on display in the US government can be glimpsed through the famous warlocks and psychedelic pioneers standing shoulder to shoulder on the cover of *Sgt. Pepper* as well as in *Playboy*, where witches' brews, made from "now familiar" drugs, were a means to reach "a hallucinatory state… [and] actually imagine… witches airborne."[67] Aldous Huxley's book on an incident of medieval witchcraft hysteria and demonic possession (*The Devils of Loudun*, published in 1953, the same year he began experimenting with psilocybin,) provides another glimpse into the connective tissue between these phenomena. Writing about why a group of nuns would accuse a priest of making a pact with Satan and come to believe it with such fervor that it destroyed an entire town and led to the much-liked priest's execution, Huxley argued that

> [The] urge to self-transcendence is almost as widespread and, at times, quite as powerful as the urge to self-assertion. Men desire to intensify their consciousness of being what they have come to regard as 'themselves', but they also desire… to get out of themselves… we find… a deep-seated horror of their own selfhood, a passionate yearning to get free of the repulsive little identity to which the very perfection of their "adjustment to life" has condemned them.[68]

---

65. Jacobsen, 2017, 80.
66. *Ibid*, 81.
67. Rickler, 1974.
68. Dempsey, 1972.

Witchcraft, he suggests, is one means of striving for this self-transcendence, allowing its adherents to connect to divinity through experience with its opposite. Both the belief in and/or the practice of witchcraft, as well as the use of psychedelics, can be understood as forms of self-transcendence on these terms (or, as the Beatles put it, as a "surrender to the void"). Nuns' religious visions, witches' spells, or hippies' acid trips *all* function as forms of personal revelation that, for many, help ameliorate the "horror" of one's own "repulsive little identity."[69]—a phrase that aligns perfectly with hippies who, as Theodore Roszak writes in his 1969 book *The Making of a Counter Culture*, pushed back against "the myth of objective consciousness" by advocating for a "return to transcendence" through drugs and alternative spirituality.[70] They can *all* be understood as means of turning on and dropping out. In the context of *Something Weird*, Mitchell's ESP abilities, the witch's spells, and the effects of government-prescribed LSD are visualized in roughly the same manner, echoing these shared cultural associations. The visual language of these scenes would have been familiar to anyone who had ever attended an acid test—or seen AIP's countercultural films. In this "scientific" exploitation of the horror film, the counterculture's aesthetic impulses came together in a new way, and echoes of this tendency can be found in even the most successful witch films of the period.

By the time Ira Levin published his bestselling tale of black magic in Manhattan in March 1967, the press was eager to mark *Rosemary's Baby* as a sign of the times: "As if we didn't have enough troubles with Vietnam, air pollution, and modern art, now we've got to wonder if our next door neighbors aren't witches," wrote one critic in the *New York Times*, in a marked shift from the *Los Angeles Times* response to *Eye of the Devil* only a few months before.[71] In fact, witches and Satanists now seemed to be an accepted element of 20th-century life according to the *Chicago Tribune*, whose book critic took *Rosemary's Baby* as an opportunity to write that

> [today] there is no city on earth without its secret coterie of Asmodeists and Satanists... the satanic dialect is supple and sophisticated as hell, and moves with the times... the blind adoration of Opposition, for its own sake, is a going religious concern.[72]

---

69. Huxley, quoted in Dempsey, 1972, 14.
70. Turner, 2006, 36.
71. Fremont-Smith, 1967.
72. Kersh, 1967.

Levin began researching his tale of demonic pregnancy in 1965, (rather casually deciding he was "stuck with Satan" because "ETs had already fathered children in *The Midwich Cuckoos*")[73] serving as an inadvertent chronicler of the not-yet-blooming occult revival. He published at the perfect moment to capture the zeitgeist. Passages from the book ran in women's magazines like *Cosmopolitan* as mysteries of the month, prompting credulous replies from readers in the following month's "Dear Cosmopolitan" section: "Ira levin certainly has a wild imagination", writes one, "and he makes me wonder— *could* it be?" Meanwhile, immediately below her, the self-described "chief warlock of the Central Chicago Coven" writes in to complain that witchcraft "is a religion just like any other but we have a tough public relations job ahead. To set the record straight… we don't worship Satan."[74] For that month's readers of *Cosmo* at least, unlike the film critics of the early '60s, witches certainly *could* be—there they were, writing to the editor.

In many ways, *Rosemary's Baby* serves as both the start and the pinnacle of the American occult revival on film, imprinting itself onto our collective unconscious. It became an inescapable shadow and point of comparison for every major witch film to come, while simultaneously using the witch films of the past as a central point of reference, making it an all-encompassing Ur-text for the genre. The story is likely a familiar one to most readers: it's 1965; a hip young couple, Rosemary and Guy Woodhouse, jump at the chance to move into a historic old apartment house in Manhattan (based on, and in the film, shot at the Dakota on West 72nd St) where some decidedly disreputable things happened at the turn of the century (devil worship, an exorcism-cum-lynching of a Satanist named Adrian Mercato). The couple has everything going for them, looks, money, upward mobility, seem to genuinely love each other, have a healthy sex life and talk about their future. After their elderly neighbors, Minnie and Roman Castevet, suffer the apparent suicide of the girl they'd taken in off the street, the couple agrees to visit and offer their condolences. But Rosemary, whose family instilled traditional values alongside a since-lapsed Catholicism, struggles with the irreverent jokes the pair make over dinner, and can't shake the feeling that Guy is hiding something when he starts going over to their apartment without her; however, when he asks her to have a baby soon thereafter, she puts her misgivings aside. On the day the Pope comes to Manhattan for a visit, their baby-making plans go awry when Minnie provides dessert and Rosemary falls unconscious. In her dreams, she sees Guy, Minnie, Roman, and a mass of naked strangers painting symbols onto her body in red and feels a male forcing himself on her. Even then, she begins to understand that her mind isn't playing tricks on her, taking in the horror of her circumstances: "This

---

73. Levin, 2012.
74. "Dear Cosmopolitan", 1968.

is no dream," she cries, "this is *really happening!*"⁷⁵ She awakens to find her body covered in long, angry scratches and leaves the city, distraught at what she still believes to be Guy's assault on her sleeping body and the nightmare it caused her, but eventually forgives him.

Soon, she discovers she is pregnant, and everything seems perfect. But as her stomach swells, her suspicions grow alongside it. Rosemary's dream apartment becomes a prison—she is isolated and afraid, ignored and actively misled by her doctor and her husband alike, alienated from the people in her life. She tries to escape to her original doctor, recommended by her friends, only to have him call Guy and Roman when she tells him they're witches. She tries to flee a final time, locking herself into her apartment, but she's dragged through a secret door between apartments to deliver her baby, exactly six months after Christmas day, 1966. When the elderly neighbors insist the baby has died, she doesn't believe them and stages an escape, grabbing a knife to protect herself and her child. Finally, she walks into a celebration for the newborn boy—who the witches insist is the son of Satan. Despite her panic she's drawn to the baby's side, cooing. The novel, according to most critics, leaves the question of witchcraft up for debate, dangling the possibility that Rosemary is suffering from a case of "prepartum hysteria" (furthering the association between feminine hysteria and witchcraft) brought on by her difficult pregnancy and the rape that precipitated it. The book's direct treatment of this subject was a bold one, with Rosemary's sense of violation made visceral, particularly when met with smug dismissal by a grinning Guy who calls the act "kind of fun in a necrophile way."⁷⁶

Rosemary's story also plays out some of the wrenching fears at the heart of another issue of the moment: abortion. The novel, released amidst raging debates over a woman's right to bodily autonomy, depicts the consequences of a woman's body outside of her control in cosmic terms, with sympathy rather than scorn, even as Rosemary herself rejects the possibility of an abortion outright due to her Catholic upbringing. As Levin wrote his novel in New York in 1966, NOW (the National Organization for Women) had just founded its first chapters, beginning its advocacy for birth control, sex education, and abortion reform. At that time, an estimated one million women received abortions illegally in the United States each year—5,000 to 10,000 of whom died from botched procedures.⁷⁷ By the book's release, other organizations within radical feminist groups had sprung up around the country helping women gain access to safe illegal abortions. Colorado decriminalized the procedure that year, unleashing a wave of protest from Catholics. Rosemary's physically and psychologically anguished pregnancy played out the reality that American women's bodies were, in fact, not their own in a period when

---

75. Levin, 1967, 81.
76. *Ibid*, 84.
77. Johnson, 2022.

spousal rapes like Rosemary's were legal in the US and abortions were not. Most of the story's horror is domestic, stemming from dinners and doctors and marital fights. The eerie control the men in her life have over her vulnerable body only compounds her feeling of helplessness when obvious signs of danger are waved away as normal. Her satanic doctor's paternalistic credo, "don't read books", echoed the plain reality that access to information around a range of options for dealing with complex pregnancies was being contested in court,[78] where rape cases had to be corroborated by eye-witness testimony,[79] in school, where sex education was under fire from the likes of the John Birch Society,[80] and in Church, where abortion and birth control were explicitly forbidden.[81] The battle for America's spirituality plays out in Rosemary's obstetrician's waiting room whether she likes it or not: *Time*'s "Is God Dead?" sits at her elbow. She skips to the entertainment section.

The film version of *Rosemary's Baby* (1968) began production almost as soon as the book was published and would come to represent several facets of the seismic cultural shift occurring in Hollywood as well. Shooting on a rapid schedule and set for release the following year, the film was originally set to be directed by B-horror icon William Castle, who had bought the rights after reading the book and seeing immediate potential for a big payoff ("even if they ban it, Catholics will go" he reportedly said).[82] But Robert Evans, the newly hired hotshot head of production at the floundering Paramount Pictures, had other ideas; he passed the script to Polish auteur Roman Polanski, who accepted, while Castle took on the role of producer. *Rosemary's Baby* became a financial lifeline for Paramount, which was suffering from the same crisis of confidence the industry had begun to face in the early '60s.

Around the time the team began adapting Levin's novel, the Production Code was in its final death throes; the script for *Rosemary's Baby*, much of which was taken verbatim from the book was eviscerated by the office who insisted that "no actual nudity" be used, and phrases like "shit", "whore", and "fun in a necrophile way" be cut.[83] Thankfully, before production began, Jack Valenti finally announced the end of the Code and the shift into a voluntary ratings system, citing "changing times":

> [I]nsurrection on campus, riots in the streets, rise in women's liberation, protest of the young, doubt about the institution of marriage, abandonment of old guiding slogans, and the crumbling of social traditions… it would have

---

78. Johnson, 2022.
79. "The Rape Corroboration Requirement" 1972.
80. As one author reporting on the subject put it, quoting from a John Birch pamphlet titled, "Is the School House the Proper Place to Teach Raw Sex?" "Sex education is un-American and it is anti-Christian. Those supporting it are 'dupes', 'degenerates', 'atheists', and 'filthy pervert'." Luther, 210, 1969.
81. Pope John Paul VI, 1968, 24.
82. Munn, 2018, 24.
83. *Ibid*, 28.

been foolish to believe... that movies, that most creative of art forms, could have remained unaffected by the change and torment in our society.⁸⁴

Rosemary's Baby would prove the right film to take on these ideas. The film's treatment of its feminist themes is visceral, pushing the questions of belief at the heart of older witch films into the present day with tremendous political force. By performing this political work from the perspective of a highly vulnerable pregnant woman, *Rosemary's Baby* takes the gothic, "women's picture" roots of witch films like *Night of the Eagle* a step further, insisting on audience identification with a woman's acute distress—if the gothic as applied to *Rosemary's Baby*

> transforms the lovely and the beautiful [the domestic bliss of an expectant mother] into the abhorrent [a body possessed, sapped by a demonic parasite]... [and] this transformation of the sentimental into the grotesque 'disrupts dominant culture's representations of family, heterosexuality, ethnicity and class politics⁸⁵

as feminist professor Karyn Valerius rightly suggests it does, it's no wonder the film has "invite[d] feminist speculation", since its premiere, when critics marveled at the horror of being in Rosemary's shoes.

In one scene, Rosemary is shown in what may well have otherwise been her normal life. Rosemary finally rebels against Guy, Minnie, and Roman's entreaties to her health, insisting her young friends come for a visit. Familiar vignettes from the era's exploitation films abound as the camera moves lightly through the crowd: women with bright eyeshadow and shimmering minidresses chat while a man in round sunglasses smokes a joint in the couple's bedroom. Rock music plays quietly, and people ask her if she's eating enough, if she's feeling okay. Finally, she breaks down in the kitchen. Her friends gather round her, hugging her and drying her tears, offering her the first unambiguously comforting physical contact she's received on screen and keeping Guy out with exhortations of "girls only." "Pain like this is a warning that something isn't right," they tell her, rubbing her shoulders, "you can't go on suffering like this!" In this moment, the possibility of feminist solidarity is briefly visible—an alternative timeline when "Rosie", as we poignantly learn her friends call her, can ask questions about her body and choose her own fate. When she tells Guy she wants a second opinion, he replies that it's "not fair" to her doctor. *"What are you talking about?"* she cries, eyes still red, pain still wracking her embattled body, "what about what's fair to *me*?" In its very structure and subjectivity, the film inhabits a question feminists had begun to ask already through consciousness-raising sessions, what activist Carol Hanish described as a burgeoning "understanding that our oppressive

---

84. Lewis, 2022, 136-7.
85. Valerius, 2005.

situations were not our own fault—were not, in the parlance of the time, '*all in our head*'."[86] Here, Rosemary's story can be read as a rejection of women's internalization of heteropatriarchal misogyny in the present, as well as the Christian "paradox of womanhood" that relies on similar self-deceptions. By viewing misogyny as a systemic problem, as, in Rosemary's case, a plot, she is able to free herself up and take control of her situation—to take on the same kind of understanding that would provide feminists "a lot more courage as well as a more solid, real foundation on which to fight for liberation."[87] When the baby is born, Rosemary's decision to claim it could be read as either a sexist surrender to her biology's maternal call or, more promisingly, a symbolic embrace of a future she actively shapes in keeping with the nihilistic spirit of the times—after all, the witches may have offered him the deal, but Guy's violence against her was of his own choosing; the witches' plot may have stolen her bodily autonomy, but the Catholicism she clings to had stolen it first. The structures of her life were never as sound as she believed. God is dead and life can be what she makes of her newfound Satanic power.

The film's frank visual treatment of its ideas also struck a chord. Even more than explosively successful New Hollywood breakouts like *Bonnie and Clyde* (1967), its elegantly varied cinematography (blending handheld and fish-eye lensing with chilly wides and classical dutch angles) brought the aesthetics of the arthouse mainstream. This sense of risk applied to what was in front of the camera as well: films with mature themes had already begun to dominate the box office alongside more sexually explicit material in 1966 (making up almost 60% of the films released by studios in 1967-8).[88] Polanski's presence, alongside the film's mature, topical themes and the novel's success with American readers made it the perfect opportunity for a studio comeback—as well as a changing of the guard in the horror landscape that had been slightly presaged by praise for serious B-horror films like *Night of the Eagle*. Even as William Castle and others promoted the film with his typical style of flashy gimmicks (a phone number advertised in newspapers that gave showtimes in ominous tones, encouragement in *Kine Weekly* for promoters to start "[h]arping on unexplained occurrences in the neighborhood… [to] encourage local newspaper editors to run a feature on witchcraft to help sell 'Rosemary's Baby'", a woman with a black pram and a devil doll inside it, lurking outside a theater in Austin, etc)—Paramount's marketing materials were minimalist, decidedly classy: a stark, acid-green modernist poster warning viewers to simply "Pray for Rosemary's Baby."[89] [90] [91]

---

86. Hanish, 2006.
87. *Ibid.*
88. Lewis, 2000, 146.
89. "Showmandiser", 1968.
90. Costigan, 1969.
91. "'Rosemary's Baby' Buggy", 1968.

Essays on the film recognized this shift in horror's fortunes immediately, with one critic, R.H. Gardner, explicitly noting that "[p]reviously [horror film] has been treated in the manner of a side-show attraction, but here it is being presented with all the accouterments... of the best cinematic art." With the appreciably prestige A-picture *Rosemary's Baby*, horror "[e]nters a new stage."[92] Tracing the evolution of the genre through the career of William Castle, Gardner points out that the once disreputable genre had become "a staple entertainment commodity, not only for the general public, but also for the intelligensia [sic] and the avant garde."[93] Indeed, the film's team included the editor of New Hollywood favorites like *The Graduate* (1967), the art director of code-breaking films like *Who's Afraid of Virginia Woolf* (1966), and independent auteur director John Cassavetes ironically cast as Guy Woodhouse, Rosemary's method-acting husband. Valenti and the majors had gotten their wish, finding a film that would appeal to the campus audience that suddenly constituted Hollywood's base—and it did so in defiance of the Catholic Legion of Decency (releasing the film without a rating) in another milestone moment for the industry. The film was given a C (for condemned) by the Legion for reasons beyond its explicit nudity. The Legion cited "the perverted use which the film makes of fundamental Christian beliefs, especially in the events surrounding the birth of Christ", insisting that "[t]he very technical excellence of the film serves to intensify its defamatory nature", in a sharp rebuttal to the shift in legal obscenity standards towards looking for "redeeming social value" or artistic merit.[94] Nevertheless, the film went on to become the eighth highest grossing film of 1968.

Perhaps most importantly for this analysis, *Rosemary's Baby* represents an inflection point between the witch film's older generic roots in women's pictures and the B-movies of the '30s and '40s and the modern countercultural witch, associated with the feminist movement, who had not yet come to the public's full attention on screen, consolidating a messy assemblage of themes into a recognizable—and replicable—model. The faded grandeur of the old apartment house and its elderly *nouveau riche* occupants contrasts with their young recruits (not to mention their chic home decor and *au courant* streetwear—Guy buys his shirts straight from ads in the *Times*) whose bodies they require to carry on their traditions. The film's running concern with the nature of reality, augmented by its surreal stylings and countercultural mystique, did belie the interestingly traditional depiction of witches at its core: as elderly crones eager to pervert the sanctity of traditional women's roles as mothers and wives. Called "a kind of creepy-crawling 'Bell Book and Candle'",[95] this transition is made visceral through the film's continual

---

92. Gardner, 1968.
93. *Ibid.*
94. "Condemned Rating by NCO To 'Rosemary's Baby'", 1968.
95. Clifford, 1968.

emphasis on generational divides and religious morality. The intensely modern style of the film itself carefully emphasizes this contrast between the old witches who haunt the halls of Rosemary's building and the next, more empowered generation Rosemary represents. The older actors "give the film a sort of instant mustiness… we feel instinctively that cinematic cobwebs are being spun before our eyes and that poor Mia is the unsuspecting victim", marveled *Newsday*.[96]

The *Newsday* writer's choice to name the actress rather than the character in his review speaks to a sensation the film seemed to elicit even from its detractors: credulity. Viewers seemed to believe in the film's diegetic reality and the mysto it speaks to so clearly, in stark contrast to the earlier witch films of the decade. The contrast between the classic B-stylings of the witches coven and the modern world, is bridged by Mia Farrow's performance—and the politics and persona she brings along with it. At its heart, *Rosemary's Baby* captured the anxious ambivalence of the *Time* piece whose cover (of both the novel and its adaptation) highlight so overtly. Rosemary is a representative of the slow secularization of American culture, a liminal character caught between the traditions she gravitates towards out of a sense of familiarity and the community she seeks out of need for recognition as an individual. While Rosemary herself is presented as a closet-traditionalist, as Polanski later put it, Mia Farrow, who by her own admission had originally wanted to be a nun, was by then a "flower child" "heavily into the whole range of crackpot folklore that flourished in the 1960s, from UFOs through astrology to extrasensory perception."[97] While Polanski may have been an atheist and avowed non-believer in the occult, his and Farrow's associations with the counterculture—and the film's use of psychedelic and countercultural occult aesthetics for its depiction of the Satanic impregnation—lent the film another layer of topicality. In an era when, as *Cineaste* cracked, "virgins [for sacrifice] are getting harder to find every day", critics predicted that "the younger generation will find it groovey [sic]."[98]

The film's promotional team chose to highlight this relationship to the counterculture in several ways. In a promotional film released in 1968, *Mia and Roman*, the actress is framed as a classic hippie chick. Polanski describes the "innocent" "playful" Farrow as having a "childlike attitude." As rock music plays quietly in the background, Farrow herself extols the virtues of peace and love while she dances and paints peace signs on her trailer.[99] Meanwhile, in the press, Anton LaVey began claiming that he had served as a consultant on the film, and even played the part of Satan himself during

---

96. Gelmis, 1968.
97. Munn, 2018, 78.
98. Adams, 1968.
99. Mia and Roman, 1968.

the rape (he did not[100] though *Variety* amplified his own tall tale in his 1997 obituary[101]), and reports of Sharon Tate serving "marijuana brownies" at "black magic rituals" at the Polanski home proliferated.[102] All these elements add a particular cultural cache to the proceedings—a countercultural aura of mysto. From the start, the team wanted to "[get] clear away from the usual method of treating dreams—the fog, etc—because dreams, in reality, can be real", opting instead for associative editing, dissolves, and jump cuts.[103] This vocabulary, already established in psychedelic horror films like *The Trip*, would be canonized by *Rosemary's Baby*. For the mass movie-going public, Satan was officially psychedelic.

The reaction was immediate: "Everybody wanted to see it. You couldn't go to a dinner party, you couldn't go out to the drugstore. Everyone was talking about, 'Did you see *Rosemary's Baby*?'" reported one producer.[104] The film's visions would prove strangely prescient: its dreams of ghostly Kennedys lost at sea would arrive exactly one week after the brutal and shocking assassination of Bobby Kennedy, whose presidential bid was viewed as the triumphant culmination of the youthful liberal promise of his brother's unfinished administration. His murder, along with Dr. Martin Luther King Jr.'s almost exactly three months previously, confirmed the worst fears of the era's seething paranoia. Rosemary's insistence that "now and then there *are* plots against people, aren't there?" after repeated allusions to the JFK assassination brought the political and the Satanic together with particular force that was quickly reflected out again. The trial of RFK's assassin, Sirhan Sirhan, was described in one outlet for example as "a real Hollywood voodoo thriller, Polanski style," replete with claims of possession and insanity—"Shades of 'Rosemary's Baby'."[105] The film would continue to haunt the upcoming election still more as graffiti was reported, declaring that George Wallace—the infamous anti-integration Alabama governor whose racist, populist campaign posited a violent rejection of civil rights and the New Left—"*is* Rosemary's Baby."[106]

As for the witchcraft itself, the film's emphasis on modernity, mundanity, and artifice brought its occult elements into reality. There is virtually no blood in the film, rather minor breaks in routine (a second blood test, a lost glove, an early arrival, a brief phone call) carry the weight of damnation under the surface, inspiring profound paranoia—the operative paranoia on display in American politics. One *Sight and Sound* writer grapples with this element of Polanski's filmmaking thus:

---

100. Park, 2012.
101. Variety, 1997.
102. Ellis, 2000, 169-70.
103. Munn, 2018, 43.
104. *Ibid*, 191.
105. Norma, 1968.
106. Women's Wear Daily, 1968.

> Shots from below insist on the mundane reality of feet, floors, thresholds... yet these are imbued with a *pointless significance* as they are distorted by the bizarre angle... Is the rain metaphoric of black magic, or is it simply rain, or is the whole thing a joke on metaphors?[107]

This semantic visual confusion, a flatness that suggests both black humor and black magic, evokes in this writer a description that speaks both to the radical nihilism of the era in terms uncannily similar to Wolfe's own description of the countercultural mysto ("everything is... *significant*... Everyone is picking up on the most minute of incidents as... metaphors for life itself").[108] In a moment when student revolutionaries began realizing that the government had actively infiltrated their organizations, and when the deaths of two icons of the liberal cause were murdered in such quick succession, the minor notes in individual lives (choosing to exit an event through a hotel kitchen or to step onto a motel balcony) *were* significant. Essays immediately connected this sense of nihilism to the film's seeming rejoinder to *Time*'s article, and to the bleak feeling that proliferated in this moment of crisis: "The film affirms that although God may be dead, Satan is not."[109] Yet Rosemary's belief in the latter:

> serves her in this new situation. Here is a child real enough to mother: she either accepts or ignores this mythic evil. This time she has evidence of the myth's reality of a completely different kind from any that is available for her Christianity. Belief in the mythic evil has given way to the pressure of another kind of belief based on a different mode of experience [the tangible *reality* of her occult experience, the tangible reality of evil]. The film has forced us to face two things. First of all we claim to assign belief to our myths; yet if we do so, it is a different kind of belief than that which we assign to 'reality'. *But our desire to hold belief is so powerful that under its pressure we can accept anything.*[110]

In this sense, the film plays out the subtext of the decade, depicting the desire for spiritual fulfillment in an era when traditional religion was viewed as one of myriad social institutions deserving of more-than-justified suspicion, culminating in a hippie-coded Satanic takeover of the American family. At its core, the film's continual refusal to ground the viewer in a comfortingly constructed, ontologically sound sense of reality—its successful insistence on Rosemary's subjective reality *as* reality itself, its meta casting choices and surrealist flare—radically aligned with the postmodern sensibility of the youth culture.

---

107. Houston and Kinder, 1968, emphasis added.
108. Wolfe, 18-19.
109. Lynn, 1968, 19.
110. Houston and Kinder, 1968.

Even the film's detractors noted its uncanny power: while Renata Adler was one of the few high-profile critics to dislike *Rosemary's Baby*, even she suggested that the film "[d]oesn't quite work... because it is almost too extremely plausible. The quality of the young people's lives seems the quality of lives that one knows... one gets very annoyed that they don't catch on sooner."[111] While Polanski claimed that his goal was to mirror the ambiguities of the novel, critics (and his star) were unswayed: "Author Levin left the reader to decide for himself, but at the end of the film director Polanski seems to be saying that Rosemary is indeed a victim of the old black magic", insists one, while Mia Farrow herself said she "thought it was clear" that the evil was real.[112] [113] "Is witchcraft practised in this day and age?" asks another critic, "I think we have... had ample evidence that it certainly is, in various forms, whether you believe it has any effect or not."[114] The new visibility of countercultural sorcerers like LaVey and Sanders spurred one review to sardonically suggest that the film, rather than offending Christians, might actually be

> disliked most by the witches themselves. Hollywood has been constantly attacked by pressure groups protesting against films that give their race, religion, or occupation a bad public image. Now the followers of the Old Religion will be invoking the studios, and sticking pins in directors, unless witchcraft is portrayed in a more favorable light.[115]

This line, snarky or not, would prove prescient, as witches *did* complain that the film misrepresented their practice, and depictions of the Old Religion evolved, even in the horror film. Witches had finally broken into the mainstream, and Rosemary was a hit. As William Castle's wife Terry put it, "Innocence was lost and the horror films were never the same... [*Rosemary's Baby*] ushered in an age... it was pivotal... it was the year the world changed."[116]

In his book, *The Bad Trip* (2019), James Riley takes *Rosemary's Baby* as the hinge upon which the so-called "death of the sixties" rests, using the Castevet's secret door into the Woodhouse apartment as his metaphor:

> All the terrible things that have happened to Rosemary in the film have happened because of that door, because her private space has not been private. Finding the door confirms all of Rosemary's worst fears: your house is not your own, your body is not your own, your child is not your own. The devil has dominion everywhere.[117]

---

111. Adler, 1968, 57, emphasis added.
112. Clifford, 1968.
113. *Roman Polanski on Rosemary's Baby*, 2012.
114. Costigan, 1969.
115. Lynn, 1968.
116. Munn, 2018, 188.
117. Lewis, 2022, 5.

Bringing this uncanny point home, a series of tragedies haunted the film's team, driving William Castle to declare (with his characteristic flare for publicity) that "the story of *Rosemary's Baby* was happening in life"[118]: composer Krzysztof Komeda would fall into a coma and die the year after the film's release; Castle fell sick with kidney stones from which he never fully recovered; and, on August 8th, 1969, the wannabe rockstar, racist New Age guru, and doomsday cultist Charles Manson would bring the film's "curse" full circle, ordering the murder of Polanski's wife Sharon Tate, the original *Playboy* witch, during an outing he called "creepy-crawling" in an eerie linguistic echo of how the film was initially described. Tate had reached genuine fame around the time Levin's novel was released, playing a tragic victim of Hollywood hedonism in the sordidly moralistic hit of the summer, *Valley of the Dolls*. Manson's brainwashed female followers, soon colloquially known as "Manson girls", stabbed her sixteen times, killing her: she was eight-and-a-half months pregnant. When Tex Watson, one of Manson's followers, found the door to the Polanski home open to him, he introduced himself to his victims thus: "I'm the devil, I'm here to do the devil's business." This moment, for Lewis, was the door, the entry into the dark side of the counterculture through *Rosemary's Baby*. Reflecting on the events of that night in her classic book of essays on the decade's end, *The White Album*, Joan Didion writes "'black masses were imagined, and bad trips blamed'... I remember this and also wish I did not: *no one was surprised.*"[119]

By the time Richard Nixon was inaugurated in January 1969, the counterculture had splintered, radicalized, and the "proto-feminism" of Rosemary was dismissed by some elements of the New Left as not going far enough, a sentiment that would prove equally fundamental to the countercultural witch cycle *Rosemary* gave birth to. The film was still top of the box office during the Democratic Convention in Chicago, when protestors were violently beaten by police, alongside *2001: A Space Odyssey* (1968), another vision of counterculturally-coded apocalypse. Reality had ruptured at last. "People across the political spectrum", reflects one historian, "believed that the country was moving inexorably toward revolution or fascism", including radical feminists.[120] The question for the witch subgenre to grow on in this new context, then, became: if America was experiencing a sexual revolution, and if the world was already so irreparably corrupt, to quote the title of a song Deep Purple wrote after the band saw the movie, if everybody else was taking the pill, "Why didn't Rosemary?"[121]

---

118. Munn, 2018, 195.
119. Didion, 2008, 42.
120. Echols, 2019, 85.
121. "Why didn't Rosemary?" in Deep Purple (album), by Deep Purple (1969).

Chapter Five

The Countercultural Witch as Feminist Symbol (1968-1973)

> "I have been invisible,/weird and supernatural./I want my black dress./I want my hair/curling wild around me./I want my broomstick/from the closet where I hid it./Tonight I meet my sisters/in the graveyard... watch for us against the moon./We are screaming,/we are flying./Laughing and won't stop."
> -Jean Tepperman, "Witch"[1]

Rosemary's Baby (1968) opened the cinematic floodgates for the witchsploitation cycle, and the films that followed would build on and respond to the feminist mold it introduced, taking on the youthful aesthetics and political sensibilities of which the occult revival was a thriving part. This chapter will explore first the witchsploitation cycle proper, unpacking different examples of the genre to understand the broader cinematic climate and the witch as a commoditized countercultural symbol, before turning to the most actively political, overtly feminist examples of the period.

Though *Rosemary's Baby* was responding to the political climate of its time, as Newman and Benton's *Esquire* piece calling for a halt to the sixties suggests, politics were simply moving faster than production schedules, and the movies to follow Polanski's would have even more novel forms of feminist activism to contend with. In 1967, anti-authoritarian groups like the Yippies (The Youth International Party) would pick up on the more performative elements of the hippie counterculture's political sensibility (the same kinds of theatrics adopted by Anton LaVey) and apply them to political activism through what became known as 'guerilla theater'. Unlike groups like SDS, this group, founded by Jerry Rubin, Abbie and Anita Hoffman, Paul Krassner and others, originated within the counterculture rather than the infrastructure of party politics. As Krassner described it:

> We needed a name to signify the radicalization of hippies, and I came up with Yippie as a label for a phenomenon that already existed, an organic coalition of psychedelic hippies and political activists. In the process of cross-fertilization at antiwar demonstrations, we had come to share an awareness

---
1. Tepperman, 1970, 16.

that there was a linear connection between putting kids in prison for smoking pot in this country and burning them to death with napalm on the other side of the planet.²

They focused on what they called "symbolic politics" rooted in McLuhanite theory, the art scene, and the drug scene. Characteristic actions were protesting the criminalization of psychedelics in 1966 by dressing as monks and sitting with store-bought mushrooms outside the California State House to "expand the consciousness of Mayor Shelly", or "form[ing] a magic ring around the pentagon", with the goal of levitating the building and "cast[ing] out evil spirits."³ ⁴ For groups like these, including the San Francisco Mime Troupe organized by Peter Berg, the media had become "more dominant than reality, and the way to retake the media was to create *alternative* realities"⁵ through political performance action and confrontational, experimental, and explicit art—a sentiment that *Rosemary's Baby* inadvertently adopted. It was also out of this theatrical milieu that radical feminism emerged. One of the Yippies' founding members, Robin Morgan, collaborated with feminist writer Shulamith Firestone in mid-1967 to form one of the most influential countercultural feminist groups of the era, NYRW (New York Radical Women).

While NOW (National Organization for Women) had begun organizing for women's rights in 1966, it was founded with the mandate to, in Betty Friedan's words, "reach out to the great silent majority of women who are shy, timid, afraid to speak out"—in other words, to the Rosemary's of the world.⁶ With an over 90% white majority membership throughout the decade, NOW was a traditionally political organization, focused on relatively cautious institutional change.⁷ Begun as a means of consolidating (and reinvigorating) a "robust but diffuse" network of aging women's advocacy groups, spread across obscure government departments and "women's clubs", NOW was careful to maintain a moderate image that would allow for maximal respectability to appeal to its affluent white base.⁸ The group thus avoided taking stances on controversial political topics, including the war in Vietnam. Friedan was also notoriously lesbophobic, calling lesbians a "lavender menace" that threatened women's empowerment.⁹ Friedan deployed oft-homophobic stereotypes against "radical" feminists as unfeminine and aggressive, accusing them of telling women to "make yourself ugly, to stop shaving under your arms, to stop wearing makeup or pretty dresses."¹⁰

---

2. Krassner, 2007.
3. Stephens, 1987, 291.
4. Hoberman, 2005, 179.
5. *Ibid*, 162.
6. Turk, 2023, 89.
7. *Ibid*, 117.
8. *Ibid*, 11-12
9. *Ibid*, 99.
10. *Ibid*, 100.

This denigrating stance was typical of the understanding of more radical feminists at the time. Loosely organized into "action", planning, and consciousness-raising groups, the women of NYRW embraced the "militant" stance that reformers like Friedan abhorred, openly including lesbians and focusing on what they called the issue of "male supremacy." The media seized on this schism between "moderate" NOW members and radicals like Morgan and Firestone, whose positions were indeed far more confrontational, arguing for example that marriage and the nuclear family, as well as the conventional beauty standards to which Friedan was referring, were central tools in the patriarchal oppression of women. Women, they believed, should be able to advocate for their own sexual autonomy and pleasure, and they facilitated this through sex education (in books like Firestone's *Dialectic of Sex* [1970] and Koedt's essay "The Myth of the Vaginal Orgasm" [1968]) and consciousness raising.[11]

These women harnessed *anger* as well as personal experience as a fundamental part of their political strategy. In 1969, NYRW staged an intervention at a New York hearing on legalizing abortion, having discovered that a panel of fourteen men and a nun would shape legislators' thinking on whether women would be able to control their own pregnancies.[12] At this action, women gave testimonials on their own experience with illegal abortions, complicated pregnancies, and sexual assault, telling the panel that "[t]he only real experts on abortion are women...who have known the pain, fear, and socially imposed guilt of an illegal abortion."[13] They were introducing one of the fundamental tenets of radical feminism in visceral terms, that "the personal is political", a phrase first coined by NYRW members that year. As Ellen Willis put it in her writing on the abortion event, "speak-out" actions like these, along with more theatrical forms of protest, helped to dispel her "deep feminine inhibitions against being nasty, and making myself conspicuous."[14] The mainstream was not pleased. Per the *Chicago Tribune*, "women's lib" groups "[had] intruded upon the American consciousness like a rude guest at an already uncomfortable party"; while NOW was "working quietly", "the women who burn bras in protest represent a novelty fringe."[15] As another article put it, radical feminism was "billed as a black comedy."[16]

In many ways, the women of NYRW embraced this sense of novelty and humor in their protests, gaining attention by adopting Yippie shock tactics, but without the drawbacks of working within a masculinist organization. The women's schism with the mainstays of the New Left came as a result of being ignored and undervalued: groups like SDS disregarded women's requests

---

11. D'Emilio and Freedman, 2012, 313.
12. Echols, 2019, 141.
13. Willis, 1969.
14. Press, 2022.
15. Turk, 2023, 87.
16. Lear, 1968.

to promote "women's issues" like childcare, birth control, and equal pay, while feminists were denigrated in publications like *Ramparts*, which ran a cover story on "women power" that dismissively called feminists within SDS "the miniskirt caucus."[17] The same sets of issues plagued feminists in the burgeoning Black Power movement—even as women like Angela Davis and Kathleen Cleaver became icons of Black radical politics, the structures of these organizations remained prohibitively and virulently misogynistic. In one infamous example, Stokeley Carmichael reportedly joked that "the position of women in SNCC is prone!"[18] Responding to this sort of attitude, Marge Piercy wrote: "A man can bring a woman into an organization by sleeping with her and remove her by ceasing to do so… for no other reason than that he has tired of her, knocked her up, or is after someone else."[19] Similarly, Ann Koedt described being "considered a sort of sex pool. The so-called 'emancipated male' wants women to be free because he thinks that means free love. It's the *Playboy* image… We want to get away from relating to men merely as sex objects."[20] [21] As this reference to "Playboy" free love would suggest, NYRW's actions were heavily informed by a perception of media as male-supremacist and objectifying. Their "purist approach to politics" was belied by a playful approach to action, crowning a sheep Miss America for example, or their "funeral procession" at the 1968 "counter-inaugural" protest in which the women performed the burial of "Traditional Womanhood" in Arlington cemetery.[22] Through stereotyped imagery and a sense of play, protest actions like these highlighted how women were dominated, even as the image of "militant, bra burning feminists" still carried associations of dour, drab "masculinization". As one woman put it, "suits have been replaced by the colorful dress of a turned-on generation of women who are asserting themselves as females as well as intellectual politicos."[23]

Given this vibrantly performative and strategically deployed rage, it is perhaps unsurprising that NYRW would be the group to take up that most anti-feminine archetype as a protest symbol. On Halloween 1968, Yippie Robin Morgan and NYRW "Media Women" member Florkia, founded W.I.T.C.H (a flexible acronym that often stood for "Women's International Conspiracy from Hell"), as part of a group of "approximately 13 other heretical women" who embraced "clownish proto-anarchism" and visual flare to gain attention for their causes.[24] In the group's "Witch Manifesto", left at the sites of its actions and reprinted in feminist magazines, witches

---

17. Echols, 2019, 109.
18. *Ibid*, 31.
19. D'Emilio and Freedman, 2012, 311.
20. Echols, 2019, 44.
21. Lear, 1968.
22. Echols, 2019, 57.
23. *Ibid*.
24. Morgan, 2014, 91.

were described as "theatre, revolution, magic, terror and joy", existing "in all women... Independent, sexually liberated, and revolutionary... the first friendly heads... the last living remnants of the oldest culture of all—one in which men and women were equal."[25] Clearly drawing on Margaret Murray's history of the witch (they reference her erroneous figure of nine million witch burnings), these anti-capitalist feminists brought together the psychedelic, the sexual, and the abject inherent in the witch archetype as a locus of countercultural feminist empowerment.

Groups like W.I.T.C.H. brilliantly blended the theatrical associations of witchcraft as a specifically pop cultural symbol and the intellectual and historical roots of witchcraft as a feminist tool and spiritual practice. Donning black pointed hats and cloaks, using broomsticks, and frequently invoking Satan, the women of these groups understood the paranoiac masculine fears around this archetype (as embodied by films like *Rosemary's Baby*) and would discuss her on those media-shaped terms: medieval Catholicism, as they put it, "characterized women as evil, 'the tool of the devil' (i.e. Eve and Mia Farrow)."[26] Where many radical feminist groups would trail NOW in organizing around women's financial security and empowerment, W.I.T.C.H. viewed women's oppression under capitalism and in the media as central parts of the same patriarchal system.[27] As Florika put it, each

> woman is directly oppressed and subjugated by the corporation wherever she functions as a consumer. Her mind is saturated with ads... she is not only projected by the mass media as an object and a commodity for consumption—she has in fact emulated and reinforced that image by becoming a self-conscious, self-acting commodity.[28]

Figures like Samantha in *Bewitched* (1964-1972), used to sell oatmeal during the commercial break, facilitated this subjugation, representing the woman as consumer. This understanding of the media, capitalism, and chauvinism was undergirded by the same references to Marshall McLuhan that appear in the writings of Abbie Hoffman and Timothy Leary. As Robin Morgan put it in an early W.I.T.C.H. pamphlet: "Witches [are] the original Mediums, and therefore the original Message", (a play on McLuhan's famous axiom "the medium is the message").[29]

For these women, witches played an important role in the broader history of women's economic oppression, as witch hunts formed part of "a class struggle. Women healers were people's doctors, and their medicine was part

---

25. W.I.T.C.H., 1970.
26. Taylor, 1973.
27. Echols, 2019, 80.
28. *Ibid*, 77.
29. Morgan, 2014, 97.

of a people's subculture."[30] At the same time, W.I.T.C.H. and groups like it were equally interested in mobilizing symbolic narratives around Wiccan *spirituality* as a form of activism, blending them with the potent historical narrative they were constructing: "Witches have always fought oppression (of women, and men as well) down through the ages," Robin Morgan explained of her choice of symbol, pointing to the history of the witchcraft accusations against midwives who assisted in both births and abortions.[31] Witches were the "original guerrilla fighters" against the Catholic church, against misogyny, and against capitalism. As one W.I.T.C.H. chapter described in the feminist press *Everywoman*, they were "leaders of the people, especially the peasantry, Persecuted and destroyed… by the Church and Feudal State because their leadership was dangerous to the ruling class."[32] With every action, article, and meeting, they suggested that underneath the broader archetypal anxiety was a history of the "'political suppression of an alternative culture and of a social and economic structure'" of men fearing "an organized society of women with its own structure and sacraments."[33] [34] The concept of organization in particular seemed to be at the heart of the archetype's appeal, particularly as framed by Murray's oft-cited thesis, which suggested women maintained secret societies. As Barbara Ehrenreich and Deirdre English put it in their 1973 manifesto *Witches, Midwives, & Nurses*: "First witches are accused of every conceivable crime against men. Quite simply, they are 'accused' of female sexuality. Second, they are accused of being organized."[35] With this in mind, the organization suggested that because the power to resist was inside every woman, "WITCHES ARE NOT DEAD. ALL WITCH POWER TO THE WITCHES."[36]

By reversing the negative stereotype around witches as evil and reassociating it with utopian metanarratives and folk histories of feminine solidarity and organization, the witch became a vibrant symbol of feminist activism that could be powerfully tapped by radical activists: "In the face of the repressive fatalism of Christianity, [witches] held out the hope of change in this world."[37] W.I.T.C.H. chapters spread around the country, particularly on college campuses, where young women took up the broom to hex (to list just a few) the deans of their colleges, men leaving burlesque clubs, and Pat Nixon. College witches in Indiana exhorted their administration with cries of "may your wives rise up and leave your houses. (hiss) May your daughters turn on you in anger for your weak minds. (hiss)… and may you meet a

---

30. Ehrenreich and English, 1973, 29.
31. Morgan, 2014, 90, 95.
32. "Women's Liberation" 1970.
33. Taylor, 1973.
34. Cowan, 1972.
35. Ehrenreich and English, 1973, 39.
36. Morgan, 2014, 90.
37. Ehrenreich and English, 1973, 49.

real castrating female."[38] Feminist presses ran articles on Wicca regularly, featuring interviews with Practitioners (who often explained that, as one woman put it, "Wicca is closely allied with all forms of the occult, including astrology, E.S.P, and astral projection," or that witches used herbs "for a sort of acid trip").[39] Taken together, the witch in this context becomes a symbol of feminist rebellion on multiple fronts, an insistence on women's independence from the patriarchy both politically and spiritually, through a rejection of internalized guilt and an embrace of new histories, historiographies, and states of consciousness—witches as a symbol became an embodied iteration of calls to create *alternative realities.*

In the wake of the Manson murders, though, the psychedelic aspect of witchcraft took on a darker valence as well, one associated more with brainwashing than individual freedom, bringing the broader public discourse around the overlapping interest in the occult and the psychedelic in line with that of the CIA and the newly inaugurated President Nixon. Where hippies had initially been described as largely peaceful and harmless (if misguided), the aftermath of the Manson murders warped this image.[40] Articles began calling them "severely emotionally disturbed people... totally devoid of human compassion... socially almost dead inside" who kill "to feel alive."[41] This description of hippies as zombie-like murderers was linked just as much to the occult as it was to LSD when word began to spread of Manson's predilection for sexual brainwashing through acid-fueled orgies and rapes (the exact kinds of sadistic occult sexual activity predicted by alarmist British M.P.s in 1963[42]). It is important to note that, while Manson did not truly practice any form of witchcraft, Wicca, or neopaganism, he appropriated elements from the amalgamated aesthetics of all three. In reality, he espoused a white supremacist mix of Scientology and New Age pop psychology to his followers—a combination that writers would quickly label "acid fascism" or the "Acid Right" to the peace and love of the "Acid Left." Yet press coverage continually emphasized the "Satanic" elements of his belief system, for example the fact that his followers called him both God and Satan interchangeably.

This kind of conflation between hippies, Satanists, and witches, already begun by coverage of theatrical groups like LaVey's church of Satan, is best exemplified by Vincent Bugliosi's best-selling account of the Manson trial, *Helter Skelter*. Released in 1974, the book serves as a succinct amalgamation of the kind of rhetoric that spread in the early 1970s about evil hippie cults. In it, Bugliosi suggests that Manson was "heavily into the occult." Most

---

38. "Witches' Curse." 1969.
39. Stern, and Strachan, 1970, 7.
40. "The Demon of Death Valley", 1969.
41. Wolfe, 1968, 30-1.
42. The year Parliament attempted to reinstate anti-witchcraft laws repealed in 1953.

saliently here, Bugliosi repeatedly highlights "witchy" elements of the Family's belief system, emphasizing that Linda Casabian claimed to have "believed herself to be a witch" while living at Spahn Movie Ranch with Manson, and that Susan Atkins spent time with Satanist Anton LaVey before joining the Family.[43] In this way, Manson's followers were quickly seized upon as a prime example of "satanic cult activity" that mixed acid, sex, and black magic. The sexual aspect of this archetype, (the "Manson girl" quickly became a subject of titillation as well as revulsion) was central to the way the Manson murders were received by the public: the women were constantly described as the products of broken homes and hippie adolescences, both "slaves" and "amazons", pantingly depicted as stoned, passive, and sexually available (i.e. "[Manson's] women lolled harem-like around the commune nude or bare-breasted, catering to his every whim").[44] Drug use was a central part of the sexual allure (Atkins was described as "a former acid-dropper and topless dancer").[45] These "witches", though young and sexual like their feminist counterparts, were by no means liberated; rather, they came to symbolize a rejection of the youthquake and a tacit need to return to traditional family values, proof that women needed to be protected and controlled lest they become monstrous, violent, and delinquent.

It is with both the feminist witch and the Mansonoid witch in mind that in 1971, sociologist Marcello Truzzi published an article in *The Sociological Quarterly* describing a phenomenon he had been tracking since 1967; he called it "the nouveau witch", and it is central to understanding the cinematic witch cycle of this moment. Taking a clinical, more economic approach to the broader countercultural ferment of the era, Truzzi pointed to the rise in occult belief and practice in America during this period "of great cultural significance... reflecting serious social conflicts and strains of macroscopic import."[46] Beginning in 1967, when Ouija Boards suddenly outsold Monopoly boards in the American market and the Church of Satan began to gain real cultural attention, "the mass media" began to "portray youth as adherents of occultism"—quoth the *Wall Street Journal* in 1969, "mysticism is becoming a big business."[47] In early 1970, *Newsweek* published "The Cult of the Occult", decrying the "mass phenomenon" of witchcraft that left "[millions... addicted to astrology, numerology, fortunetelling, and tarot cards."[48] Citing *Rosemary's Baby* and the Manson murders as points of departure, the article compares countercultural occultism to drug addiction and calls its followers sexual perverts and "nuts". Even as the article denigrates (nouveau) witches as "lonely", more "ludicrous than truly eerie",

---

43. Bugliosi, 2001, 437-8, 613-4.
44. "Demon of Death Valley", 1969.
45. *Ibid.*
46. Truzzi, 1971, 16.
47. *Ibid*, 16, 17, 18.
48. "Cult of the Occult", 1970.

it presents them as a microcosm for society's ills. That same year, *Cosmo* reported that "in the Age of Aquarius, astrologers are doing better business than psychoanalysts."[49] By 1972, *Time* ran a cover story on the "Occult Revival" that serves as a de facto follow up to its 1966 "Is God Dead?" cover: The "wave of fascination with the occult", the writer suggests, serves as a "substitute faith" for those who feel that the world is "out of joint" and that "the church [is] a mere authenticator of the Establishment." Speaking to the sexual element of the occult revival, the article also suggests that for these groups, Satan "is more often a type of magician playmate, the product of a *Playboy* culture rather than the malign personal being found in Scripture."[50]

Truzzi's article is an excellent portrait of myriad conflicting perceptions of these phenomena: describing the nouveau witch as a "youth phenomenon", Truzzi indicates that the "occult revival of the past five years... has become a marketing bonanza," complete with 1,750 regularly printed astrology columns in weekly papers by 1970 (up from only 100 twenty years before), the proliferation of merchandize like "astrology calendars, ashtrays, hairstyles, [and] sweatshirts," and an explosion of occult bookstores around college campuses (accompanied by a boom in occult paperbacks as well as reissues of older books on the subject—including Huxley's 1953 *The Devils of Loudun*).[51] Books on the history of witchcraft shared shelf space with occult self-help books like *The Modern Witch's Spellbook* (for "Improved Daily Living"),[52] *Teaching Yourself White Magic and How to Try it Out* ("a convincing rationale of why magic works"),[53] *The Complete Art of Witchcraft: Penetrating the Secrets of White Magic* ("You get the feeling you might like to take it up!"),[54] and *The Witches' Handbook* ("the 'supernatural' is...perfectly natural!").[55] Records with titles like *Seduction Through Witchcraft*, recorded by now-famous witches like Alex and Maxine Sanders or Louise Heubner—or those who played them in the movies like Vincent Price and Barbara Steele—proliferated.[56] Meanwhile, colleges across the country began offering classes on the history of witchcraft and sometimes whole degrees in the subject.[57] Others began offering "crash courses in palmistry", "reincarnation workshops, and classes in astral projections, numerology", and tarot from institutions as varied as countercultural centers like the Free University in San Francisco, to NYU and Berkeley, to the

---

49. Boeth, 1970.
50. "The Occult Revival: A Substitute Faith" 1972.
51. Truzzi, 1971, 19, 20, 23.
52. Riva, 1973.
53. Heriot, 1973.
54. Leak, 1973.
55. Grammary, 1973.
56. Price would star as a warlock in several films in Corman's Edgar Allan Poe cycle, as well as an inquisitor in the classic of the genre *Witchfinder General* (1968).
57. Boeth, 1970.

University of Alabama.[58] [59] Anton LaVey, too, began offering paid classes for witches, specifically focused on sex magic. "We are living in the only period in history", he proclaimed, "in which it is considered fashionable to be a witch."[60]

Truzzi's article attempts to categorize the swirl of participants in this occult revival (primarily young, "high-school or college age girls"), dividing representations of countercultural witches into three categories that align neatly with the cultural associations baked into the broader archetype: 1) College age witches who "belong to no organized group… have obtained their knowledge from their readings and conversations with others" and practice astrology and tarot (which they believe to be "scientific") largely for "entertainment", 2) Witches or "Satanic groups" (his shorthand amalgam "witchcraft-satanism" speaks to the broadness of the terminology in use at the time) drawn to the practice for sexual reasons ("one can read a great deal in the 'soft-core' pornographic literature… of sex clubs that incorporate Satanism and some of its alleged rituals"), and 3) Actual "satanic groups" like the Manson family that serve as an "outgrowth of the current narcotics or 'acid-culture' now found in various parts of the country", rather than as a product of genuine belief in the occult.[61]

For Truzzi, interest in the occult represents a form of mass "pop religion." He concludes by suggesting that "[l]ike astrology, witchcraft… represents a play-function for the major portion of its current popular audience… a fad of popular culture rather than a serious religious involvement."[62] And indeed, figures like Sibyl Leek were giving advice on how to be a "bewitching hostess" in *Ladies Home Journal* even as she was consulting for the CIA on the "ESP gap."[63] By the early 1970s, articles in the *Berkeley Barb* and *Playboy* poked fun at the "astral jet set", portraying them as spaced-out (if sexy) New Age nuts—one mentions a tarot teacher with a "very bewitching neckline", while another begins with an illustration of a woman's torso, cut off at the neck, holding a smoking martini in one beringed hand in front of her cleavage.[64]

This argument—that occultism during this period was an apolitical fad entirely devoid of sincere belief or political motivation—reflects the ambivalence of the phenomenon's reception: newly canonized, the nouveau witch was also quickly contested. A 1972 piece in *Cosmo* titled "Be a Witch!" highlights these contradictions between the witch as a symbol of defanged, commercialized sex appeal (Satanic woman as *Playboy* playmate) and the

---

58. "The Occult Revival: A Substitute Faith", 1972.
59. Fleming, 1972.
60. LaVey, 2003, 1.
61. Truzzi, 1971, 26.
62. *Ibid*, 26, 29.
63. "Bewitching Hostess", 1969.
64. Rickler, 1974.

witch as a symbol of genuine empowerment. After going into the "very serious and intellectual... scientific basis for understanding... magic," the article goes on to discuss the political implications of the rise in witchcraft: "Skeptic Owen Rachleff of NYU is convinced that witchcraft's growing popularity is connected with the powerful role played in the Craft by women," the article notes, "he wryly describes it as 'the first Women's Liberation movement.'"[65] This "wry", evidently displeased description, linking the renewed influence of feminist activism in the '60s with the rise in the practice of witchcraft speaks both to the visibility with which feminists appropriated the symbol and the anxiety this generated. But this description is dismissed by the writer: "other experts are not so *cynical* as Mr. Rachleff... the prime attraction of witchcraft is in its reputed power to work love spells," a breezily chauvinist reinstatement of the *Bewitched* ideal feminists rejected wrapped in the notion that to link feminism to pop culture was cynical.[66] The article concludes with a fluffy quiz, "find out if you have magical gifts", with questions like, "Am I fascinated by firelight? Do I like to gaze at the ocean, moon, and stars?... Do my wishes usually come true?" With articles like these actively dismissing the power of the witch as a political symbol as "cynical", or disrupting the "play function" Truzzi identified, the push-and-pull dynamics between Samantha and Odile are on clear display. By not allowing both facets of the archetype to exist in active tension, Truzzi also misunderstands the way in which performativity, irony, and politics coexisted with earnestness in the continually paradoxical blend of idealism, individualism, and collectivism that made up the countercultural political milieu of groups like NYRW and the Yippies—and particularly for the women of groups like W.I.T.C.H. From Ouija boards at slumber parties to broomsticks at abortion rallies, all of it existed in tension in the culture.

Taken together, the three poles of Truzzi's gamified pop religion help to parse the jumbled themes on display in *Something Weird* (1967) that later began the process of symbolic consolidation in *Rosemary's Baby*: the witch as a multifaceted representation of a malevolent sexual siren with psychedelically tinged, mind-altering powers hidden behind the facade of a hip young woman. While Truzzi leaves films out of his analysis, this archetype, incentivized by a "marketing bonanza", would appear *constantly* in the latter half of the decade, becoming a nearly unavoidable part of the pop cultural landscape, a representative of a particular kind of countercultural femininity characterized by her sexual voraciousness, her beauty, and her malevolence. Part of the reason why is simply a matter of timing: with her combination of sex appeal, violence, and druggy-visual flair, the nouveau witch came at exactly the right time for the seedier side of the New Hollywood to feel her magic.

---

65. Fleming, 1972.
66. *Ibid.*

By 1970, the same year "middle Americans" were declared *Time*'s "Man of the Year", a *Variety* piece announced a box office "dictatorship by youth"—the student demographic still claimed the majority of the ticket sales and Hollywood was forced not just to accommodate it, but to actively cater to it.[67] Even as Timothy Leary fled the country to avoid extended jail time on drug charges and Nixon formally declared his "war on drugs", one *Variety* item from November sang a different tune, addressing the subtext of this "youth dictatorship" head-on: "Don't get uptight about the potential audience" reads an internal memo from the marketing company advertising Disney's re-release of *Fantasia*. "These are nice, unwashed, potsmoking citizens. They like to buy tickets by the bundle... sell 'Fantasia' as you did 'Easy Rider'. Hip youngsters come to see it as a special kind of trip."[68] Similarly, even as conservatives on President Nixon's taskforce on pornography wrote that porn's presence in the culture "strongly paralleled the rise of certain extremist groups of nihilists," films with X ratings were making tremendous amounts of money and gaining a modicum of respectability.[69] The X-rated *Midnight Cowboy*'s Best Picture win in 1969 proved indicative: four of that year's top twenty grossing films were "adult", including Peter Fonda and Dennis Hopper's countercultural biker classic *Easy Rider* (whose extended acid trip sequence featured its own witchy hippie women).[70] As Disney's newfound acceptance of the "nice potsmoking citizens" market suggests, Hollywood's continuing decline in revenue (unemployment in the studio film business would hit a mind-blowing 42.85% in 1970) and the runaway success of these low-budget and foreign films, led regular theaters to begin screening pornography to stay afloat.[71] *Variety* soon reported over six hundred American theaters had started playing X (and "XXX") rated films. The pornographic comedy *Deep Throat* (1972) ushered in the era of what Ralph Blumenthal first called "porno chic". Advertised in outlets like *Variety* and the *New York Times*, the film, which those outlets would only demurely call "Throat" broke box office records (continuing to break the top ten after 48 weeks), and garnered fans like Truman Capote and Johnny Carson.[72] At the arthouse, Pauline Kael heralded Bertolucci's X-rated *Last Tango in Paris* (1972) as having "altered the face of the art form."[73] *Variety* began reviewing pornography alongside non-pornographic films and audiences

---

67. Hoberman, 2005, 268.
68. "Pot-Smoking Kids" (1970).
69. Hoberman, 2005, 336.
70. Lewis, 2002, 153.
71. *Ibid*, 151.
72. Blumenthal, 1973.
73. Haberski, 2014, 383.

of all kinds were trying out the trend.⁷⁴ The conclusion for critics seemed to be that raunch was finally out in the open: as Addison Verill wrote in *Variety*, whether or not it was the Age of Aquarius, the "Nixon-celebrated silent majority [may] be caught out at first base... a substantial segment of the general public is buying screen sex in all its variations."⁷⁵ On campus in particular, according to another gleeful report on the phenomenon, "A, B, C—they're strictly for schoolkids. R and X—that's where the money is. For the short term, anyway."⁷⁶

Already associated with the erotic, from drug-using Wiccans to Mansonoid sex slaves, the counterculture's interest in the occult was a perfect subject for the era of porno chic. *Rosemary's Baby*, with its increased "permissiveness" towards sex on screen, helped usher in a rash of more overtly sexual witch and occult-themed exploitation films. In 1971, *Playboy* even ran a spread in its "Sex in Cinema" roundup called "Bewitched, Bothered and Bedevilled" (with plenty of photos). Between 1972 and 1973 alone, *Box Office*'s "Looking Ahead" page announced more than ten low-budget films about witches, with titles like *The Sensuous Sorceress* (1972), *The Daughters of Satan* (1972), and *The Devil's Wedding Night* (1973). Many others were, like AIP's earlier witch films, foreign imports, from now-classic folk horror films like *The Blood on Satan's Claw* (1971) and *Witch-hammer* (1970), to video nasties like the West German *Mark of the Devil* (1970) and Italian mondo films (sensationalist pseudo-documentaries) like *Witchcraft '70* (1970).⁷⁷ Even more legitimate outlets like the BBC were eager to take advantage of the trend, offering the 1971 *The Power of the Witch: Real or Imaginary?*, a "documentary" that features the nude rituals of Alex Sanders' coven.⁷⁸ Each of these films took a conventionally conservative stance on its material, using moral panic as a cover for salacious subject matter. *The Power of the Witch* questions the reality of witchcraft ("Is it all just a delusion?... why do so many smart people believe in it?"), and presents the same arguments made in outlets like *Newsweek* about the occult revival (citing declining religious faith, delinquency, drug use), before turning to an cast of clergymen and "former cultists" who argue that young people practicing witchcraft "open themselves up to spirit possession." After showing photos of alleged grave robberies and openly claiming that Jayne Mansfield's death was a product of a Satanic curse, the film ends on a decidedly Corman-esque note: "Once

---

74. Lewis, 2002, 169.
75. *Ibid.*
76. Oldfield, 1971.
77. *The Blood on Satan's Claw* is a classic of the genre and shares many of the possible feminist readings I will employ in Chapter 5. It well deserves its own case study. Unfortunately, for the sake of brevity, this one didn't make it in—but an excellent analysis of this film appears in 2021 Kier-la Janisse's *Woodlands Dark and Days Bewitched*.
78. Pseudoscientific documentaries began to proliferate on British television in the early 1970s, exploring a range of conspiracy theories and myths, for example the theory that aliens built the pyramids.

you're in", a man intones as the camera rapidly zooms on a statue of Baphomet, "you've *sold your soul!*"

Meanwhile, *Witchcraft '70*, unfettered by television standards, takes an even more dramatic tone with its material, actively conflating any religion popular within the counterculture with Satanism (Hare Krishnas feature prominently). This film also focuses on the ceremonies of Alex Sanders' coven, simulating sexual rites even as it bemoans that in America "even the children of Satan have freedom of speech." These films, though theoretically engaging with all three of Truzzi's types of nouveau witches, emphasize the more fear-mongering, Mansonoid element of the archetype through their focus on villainous sexuality and drug use; any woman who practices witchcraft is, from this perspective, deluded and manipulated—or, as it's put in *The Power of the Witch*, "better off dead", and "certain to become a murderess at some point."

Witchsploitation films that engaged with the nouveau witch, focused on ambivalent narratives depicting women's sexual empowerment. An X-rated American documentary, *Satanis: The Devil's Mass* (1971) portrays the Church of Satan as a place for sexual exploration, interviewing LaVey's bemused neighbors as well as (mostly female) members of the coven who talk frankly about their increased practice and enjoyment of sexual freedom. The film, shot in a typically psychedelic style, features scenes of light flogging, simulated sex in a coffin, and naked women dancing with snakes. Clearly, in this context, the purpose of showcasing women's sexual liberation falls under the rubric of what Truzzi decried as "Playboy" sorceresses, but these women still served as a model for a form of sexual autonomy. The *San Francisco Examiner* dismissed Satanis as "flabby, talky, and tiresome", making the church seem "suspiciously like some sort of friendship club for bored, middle-aged people."[79] [80] *Variety* complained that some of the naked women were "fat... over 50 and a bit unjoined", ironically undercutting the suggestion that countercultural witches were simple playmates for men to ogle with flip sexism.[81] [82]

---

79. "March 5", 1970.
80. The *San Francisco Examiner* at the same time recommended instead Kenneth Anger's "fascinating" and "far more successful" short film, *Invocation of my Demon Brother* (1969), (a long-overdue film maudit featuring the Rolling Stones and originally intended to star Manson Family member Bobby Beausoliel as the devil). This film, notably, played sporadically on a double bill with *Witchcraft Through the Ages* (1968) on the college circuit, a re-edited, psychedelicized version of Benjamin Christensen's *Häxan* (1922) featuring narration by William S. Burroughs and an experimental jazz score by Jean-Luc Ponty. Like the film from which it is adapted, *Witchcraft Through the Ages* presents a sympathetic narrative towards witches that blames the Catholic church and hysteria for violence against women—though with an obvious relish for the wildly experimental, baroque torture on display. Both of these films speak to the fact that, at this point of rapid change for the film industry, young American filmgoers had an unprecedented range of choices as Hollywood studios came into competition with pornographers, avant garde artists, and exploitationeers; often, they were choosing psychedelic occult oddities like these, focused on witchcraft and with a decidedly countercultural appeal.
81. Har, 1970.
82. *Satanis* quickly became an easy visual shorthand for the era's occult boom, and sumptuously kitschy

Grindhouse films would begin to solidify these themes in a narrative context, bringing them closer to the feminist potentials implicit in the ending of *Rosemary's Baby*. *Mark of the Witch* (1970), a microbudget exploitation film set on a college campus and shot by a local production company in El Paso, taps into these same themes and anxieties. The film brings to life the tensions on display in *Cosmo*'s "Be a Witch!" article when Jill (Anitra Walsh), a "college co-ed" earning her degree in witchcraft, finds herself possessed by a witch burned at the stake 300 years before. At a book fair run by "the chicks", several women explain the popularity of witchcraft to an incredulous classmate ("You don't look like a witch? Are you on some kind of a Halloween trip in March?"). At a party, a group of unbelieving classmates performs a ritual from an old spellbook at their Professor Mac (Robert Elston)'s behest, a condescending experiment to prove that young people are "impressionable". The spell works, though, and the previously shy Jill becomes suddenly imperious, spurning her steady boyfriend, Alan (Darryl Wells) while courting Mac, revealed to be the reincarnation of a warlock who betrayed the witch's coven and sent her to the pyre. Much of the film's first half is dedicated to the vexation of these two men as the newly empowered Jill stays out late and refuses to do what they tell her to, sleeping with whichever of them she chooses.

During the rest of the film, she seduces several classmates, lures them to the woods for sex, and hypnotizes them for a ritual to reincarnate the rest of her coven. Here, too, the magic is depicted as psychedelic with rapid flash cuts between the past, the present, and associative imagery from both (flames, embraces, a cross), vividly tinted shots, and cycling rainbow lights. In the end, Mac manages to exorcise the witch from Jill's body, but is forced to join her in Hell. The last shot is Mac's own hanging, a clear recompense for the witch's murder. Amateurish or not, the film serves as an illustration of the way witches were beginning to full-throatedly represent sexual emancipation for women, particularly inflected by a knowledge of historical misogynist oppression as facilitated by newly dominant feminist discourse. This little-seen film, builds on the model offered by *Something Weird* and promised by the ending of *Rosemary's Baby*, presenting the witch as an unconstrained feminine force. In so doing, it speaks to the era's anxieties around the occult revival, feminism, and the Left's burgeoning awareness of systemic sexism.

The next year, another, more high-profile film, *The Mephisto Waltz* (1971) brought this subversive idea home, restaging the Faustian bargain of *Rosemary's Baby* but turning the tables on the men at the story's center. Directed by television veteran Paul Wendkos (with consultation from Anton LaVey), the film was dismissed as a "misshapen" knockoff of Polanski's film

---

shots of naked women, snakes, coffins, and skulls are frequently pulled from it to this day in documentaries on the period, often completely devoid of context. In the '80s, imagery from this film will appear again and again in the Satanic Panic specials that fomented the moral panic of the day.

(the similarities are glaring). This story's Guy and Rosemary are Myles (Alan Alda), a failed concert pianist turned music journalist, and Paula (Jacqueline Bisset), his wife. When Myles is sent to interview dying piano virtuoso Duncan Ely (Curd Jürgens), the couple are granted a place in the inner circle of what one critic called "chic, jet-set zombies" because Duncan admires Myles' large hands, well suited for difficult chords.[83] Soon, the happy pair finds themselves at odds, with Myles basking in the debauchery and attention, and Paula primly skeptical, leery of the LSD that infuses the reeling parties Duncan's sultry daughter, a self-described witch named Roxanne, (Barbara Perkins, the star of both *The Valley of the Dolls* [1967] with Sharon Tate and *Peyton Place* [1964-69] with Mia Farrow,) throws at all hours. Myles draws away from Paula, grows attracted to Roxanne, and by the time Duncan dies, has been willed the older man's entire estate—along with his soul, which Roxanne transfers to Myles' body with black magic. The film is structured as a psychedelic, sexual power struggle over matters of infidelity and incest, with Paula as its moral center: the magic itself always involves drugs that cause visions rendered like an AIP film, and Duncan and Roxanne are lovers whose union is made socially acceptable through Myles' body. Roxanne and Duncan-as-Myles plan to kill Paula, but not before he seduces her for his own amusement, introducing her to sex that's more passionate, violent, and fulfilling than she'd previously had with the real Myles. Though Paula initially tries to fight to get her husband's soul back through love, soon, like Rosemary, she discovers that in a world governed by forces more immediate and powerful than the Christian God, she can only fight back through black magic of her own.

In the film's frenzied climax, replete with wild canted angles and frantic crash zooms, she performs a pact with the Devil. Her lust for the new, more sexual Duncan-as-Myles is so great that she casts a spell to swap bodies with Roxanne, Duncan's incestuous lover, giving no further thought to the fate of her husband's soul. The film ends with Duncan-as-Myles becoming the unsuspecting victim of Paula-as-Roxanne's scheme and not the other way around. Paula's desire not for love but for sex has overcome the perverse parody of a romantic happy ending that the older Satanist and his daughter/lover believed they would finally achieve. As in *Mark of the Witch*, a marked shift has occurred—while each woman's descent into the world of the occult is clearly intended as tragic, even ruinous, it is also marked as a radical rejection of a normalcy that puts her at a disadvantage.

The Mephisto Waltz was dismissed in turns as pornographic "slick Hollywood trash", "mumbo jumbo" and "jiggery-pokery".[84] [85] One writer for the *Los Angeles Times* did recognize its merits as a sort of corrective to *Rosemary's Baby*:

---

83. Thompson, 1971.
84. "Feature Reviews: The Mephisto Waltz", 1971.
85. Rock, 1971.

> One of the questions about "Rosemary's Baby" is whether it would have been more exciting (and more honest) if Mia Farrow had known what the hell was going on and had fought back instead of being an inert carrier. "The Mephisto Waltz" begins promisingly because Jaqueline Bisset... is immediately suspicious, and skeptical and *furious*."[86]

While the rest of the review is derisive, this observation is fundamental to the broader shift in witch films as the '60s gave way to a new era. Further illustrating this shift, the critic noted that "the devil, who used to lose all the time, now *wins* all the time without ever having had to be in a fair fight."[87]

This trend was on display in another cinematic phenomenon within the early-1970s New Hollywood milieu: Blaxploitation.[88] In 1971, two low-budget exploitation films made by Black artists heralded the birth of this new subgenre: Gordon Parks' *Shaft* and Mario Van Peebles' *Sweet Sweetback's Baadasssss Song*. Blaxploitation introduced newly confident, self-assured paradigms for Black women on screen, exemplified by actresses like Pam Greer. Though centrally associated with crime films and thrillers, this subgenre included a number of horror films, some of which played with and subverted older witch tropes. The most notable example is AIP's *Sugar Hill* (1974), in which Diana "Sugar" Hill (Marki Bey), a nightclub hostess, enlists the help of a voodoo queen named Mama Maitresse (Zara Cully) to get revenge on mobsters who kill her fiancé. *Sugar Hill* is most often described as a zombie film, and for good reason—Mama Maitresse helps Sugar resurrect the bodies of slaves to kill the white mobsters. But the plot presents both women as witches, avenging angels who literally call upon the history of slavery to enact racial justice in the present. When they convene in Maitresse's old mansion, she tells the younger woman, "I can feel your anger and your pain, and I sympathize." In this way, this film's structure parallels many of the witch films examined here, tapping into female rage resulting from past injustice (here, slavery, there, femicide). *Sugar Hill* is distinct, however, in that the witches are allowed to be the unambiguous heroes of the narrative, precisely because blaxploitation films were geared towards an oppositional Black audience. While most of the white witch films posit a devil's bargain as a sort of unfortunate necessity, *Sugar Hill* stands alongside the most feminist films of this chapter, presenting its witchy protagonist as making a deal with the supernatural consciously and on her own terms. When Mama Maitresse helps Sugar summon the lord of the dead, Baron Samedi (Don Pedro Colley), she offers her soul. He asks her for sex instead, then agrees to help Sugar for nothing because of her bravery and self-assurance—"You're not afraid of me!" he remarks, looking

---

86. Champlin, 1971, emphasis added.
87. *Ibid.*
88. The term was originally coined by Junius Griffin, then-head of the NAACP.

petulant, before granting her his army and her request, revenge and "the power to destroy my enemies."

With these exploitation films as a point of reference for the timbre of the witchsploitation cycle at this point in time, I will now turn to several films that take an even more explicit approach to the subject of feminism across a range of contexts. Some were tremendously successful; some were dismissed as representatives of the broader exploitation cycle; others were simply underseen. Yet each of these films provides a nuanced window into the politics of the witch as a symbol for the Second Wave feminist movement.

In 1971, British provocateur Ken Russell followed up the disastrous failure of his musical adaptation of *The Boy Friend* with a series of X-rated films, the most controversial of which was his adaptation of Aldous Huxley's *The Devils of Loudun*. *The Devils* (1971) was the subject of countless competing articles, sometimes in the same publication, over whether the film was an empty, vulgar provocation or a particularly sordid piece of erotic art. In the US, showtimes were repeatedly canceled in the face of Catholic protest despite a strictly enforced X-rating.[89] The film follows a 17th-century French priest, Father Grandier (Oliver Reed), who mixes his devotion to the lord with his love of the erotic, regularly sleeping with the women who seek his spiritual counsel. The philosophy he espouses is essentially a rejection of Christian sexual repression: in his words, "The body can transcend its purpose. It can become a thing of such purity that it can be worshiped to the limits of imagination. Everything is allowed, all is right and such perfection lends for an understanding of this hideous state of existence." He also combines this heretical philosophy with a strong belief in independence for his walled city of Loudun, whose autonomy the French government seeks to dissolve by tearing down its ramparts.

Most of the film is dedicated to the hallucinatory postmodern journey of a hunchbacked nun, Sister Jeanne (Vanessa Redgrave), who becomes so erotically obsessed with Grandier, that she loses touch with reality and accuses him of witchcraft. As the characters wander through Boschian tableaus of sex, death, and destruction (pits of fecund corpses, glowing white churches, and mud on the hems of festival gowns), the entire convent is seized with this witch craze and devolves into excesses of the flesh. In a world in which "unmarriageable women" are abandoned to the convent, this guilty pleasure and the rampant destruction it causes is the only erotic outlet available. As Grandier describes it, after his arrest when he is finally able to see his accuser for the first time, "pain is sensuality… horror and lust… anything found in the desert of a frustrated life can bring hope, and with hope comes love, and

---

89. Curtiss, 1971.

with love comes hate, so I possess this woman, may God help her." Jeanne's claims to have a great need to be united with God, become hopelessly entangled with her sexual desire for the libertine priest. After Grandier's death, the walls fall and the city loses its quasi-democratic system of self-governance to the monarchy's despotic rule. Jeanne is eventually overcome with guilt and commits suicide. The film is a political feminist tragedy.

Though *The Devils* ultimately focuses on Grandier's noble quest for "purer" forms of transcendence, turning Jeanne into a monster controlled by her lust, this depiction is nevertheless run through with sympathy. Becoming a witch in this context, as Michelet described it, is the fault of the church and a fundamentally political act for otherwise disempowered women—it's an escape, a means of self-transcendence when religion becomes a dead end. In life, Jeanne is ugly, outcast, and rejected. But in her fantasies of demonic power, she can topple an entire political system and exact erotic agency over the otherwise unreachable target of her lust while still adhering to a perverse feminine role. The often violent orgy scenes are both abject and a form of exculpatory liberation, parties for those who choose to take pleasure in the pain the system causes them. Russell's Bacchanalian depiction of political and sexual heresy earned it outright denunciation from several conservative critics as well as the Church. It was called "a hymn to sado-masochism… vulgar, camp, and hysterical."[90] In an essay in *Film Quarterly*, though, Michael Dempsey described the film as a sort of exorcism, a rejection of repression itself and a search for purity that requires a journey through its opposite; "despite its X-rated torture, violence, and nudity, [*The Devils*] is a deeply Catholic film" not a rejection but a "fulfillment" of spirituality.[91]

All of this was linked, both in the film and in analyses of it, to the counterculture. Beyond the inherent connection between the film's source material and the head scene, the sensibility reflects Sontag's earlier "radical nihilism" as well as Huxley's search for "self-transcendence". As described in the *Film Quarterly* piece, "weariness with existence runs through Russell's work as a corollary to the quest for a better, more intense life," an escape from the world and the self.[92] The film also presents its courtiers as drag queens and punks, and its exorcist as an over-excited hippie gone rogue with Mick Jagger's shag and John Lennon's circular sunglasses, imagistically tying this narrative to the present. As one *New York Times* review put it, "Perhaps the devils of repression and fanaticism and hypocrisy that Ken Russell means to attack… are closer to the surface of contemporary life than most of us want to admit."[93] In this sense, *The Devils* becomes a fractured, frenzied encapsulation of the counterculture's understanding of witch lore.

---

90. Ford, 1973.
91. Dempsey, 1972.
92. *Ibid.*
93. Farber, 1971.

A similarly controversial film was Nicholas Roeg's *Don't Look Now* (1973), the lyrical story of John and Laura Baxter's doomed experience with ESP and witchcraft after the death of their daughter. Also given an X-rating in the US, specifically for a sex scene between its two stars that was so intense Warren Beatty, Julie Christie's then-partner, reportedly threatened to beat Donald Sutherland, believing that it was unsimulated. The film's marketing relied heavily on the cachet of this controversy, alluding to it constantly and putting this witch film (along with *The Devils* and others) at the heart of the conversation around sex and violence in film.

Don't Look Now plays with the conventions of witch lore and femininity throughout: after the distraught couple moves to Venice for John's work restoring an old church, the grieving Laura meets a pair of British sisters who tell her they can communicate with her dead daughter, Christine. These two women, one of whom is blind, evoke both the Greek Fates and the crones of pagan folklore. The three become close, holding seances that comfort Laura. Soon, she begins to process her grief. John meanwhile starts receiving warnings from the women that his life is in danger if he stays in Venice. A devout skeptic, he rejects their advice, even going to the police to report them on the suspicion that they plan to harm Laura.

This scene with the police is particularly illuminating in its depiction of masculine anxieties around the supernatural feminine, eventually making the contrast between the two main characters' points of view starker. John is repeatedly incapable of describing the two women as anything other than "old women". The police are sympathetic, telling him that "age makes women look more like each other... men, each becomes quite distinct. Women seem to converge." Here, shades of the fears evoked by *Night of the Eagle*'s (1962) descriptions of women again appear: Laura is becoming entangled in what John views as a form of abject collective femininity associated with the supernatural. John's death at the hand of another crone— this one perversely masquerading as his daughter—stems from his refusal to accept the supernatural. Speaking to the topicality of the subject matter, Donald Sutherland actually complained to Roeg that the film presented ESP in a negative light, telling the director that "ESP was a positive part of our lives and therefore we should make *Don't Look Now* a more educative sort of film," in a strange echo of *Something Weird*'s origins, "that the characters should in some way benefit from ESP," which he claims Roeg rejected.[94] Yet this critique of the film's portrayal only makes sense from the perspective of John's character. For Laura, the sisters' companionship and the aid of the ESP genuinely *is* a positive force, helping her assuage her grief, not just when Christine dies, but when John dies as well. The final scene shows the three women standing beside his coffin traveling through Venice, Laura dressed in

---

94. Sanderson, 1996, 18.

a dramatic black veil. She looks out over the water with an expression very similar to Rosemary's at the end of Polanski's film, no longer afraid, no longer in pain, but seemingly at some sort of newfound peace with the supernatural world around her. As she glides along the canal in closeup, a small smile plays around the corners of her mouth. Like *The Devils*, the supernatural here is a gateway out of the heteropatriarchal world and into another space, at once more hostile and more familiar, which takes on an emotional logic.

The film was not an immediate success, though some critics rightly predicted that it would become an enduring cult classic. It was described by the *New York Times* as "possibly the most subtle and sophisticated horror film ever made, and a profoundly unsettling warning of the precariousness of everything we take for granted."[95] This same review drew similar parallels between the counterculture and the film as were visible in commentary on *The Devils*, suggesting that

> over the last decade, a great many euphoric sages and plastic gurus have mindlessly celebrated the irrational or the supernatural, promising an easy salvation through Jesus or LSD. Roeg's mysticism is of a less comforting variety... contemplat[ing] all extremes—barbarism and madness, as well as ecstasy... Roeg is not advocating a return to religion or an immersion in the occult; his point is simply that reason is inadequate to deal with some essential questions—although the search for a transcendent, supra-rational understanding is treacherous and possibly futile, it is still one of the deepest human impulses. In his stubborn skepticism, John denies part of what it means to be alive.

Like *Rosemary's Baby*, this film's expressionistic, associative, even mystical editing style was a significant part of this thematic thrust, bringing it into conversation with the mysto of the era as it "obsessively assembles countless bits and pieces of object and incident" to create a tragic portrait of the devil's business.[96] Roeg's film, though tragic and largely hewn to John's rationalist perspective, takes on an arguably feminist timbre by suggesting that belief must expand with one's experiences, no matter how unbelievable, and positing that John's masculinity and Laura's femininity are fundamental to this process. Unlike in *The Devils*, Laura survives this tragedy.

While these two high-profile auteur art films made headlines for their controversial displays of sexuality, in December, 1972, George Romero, director of the watershed zombie classic *Night of the Living Dead*, released another supernatural art film that received virtually no attention, barely a passing mention in the trades. *Season of the Witch*[97]—another film

---

95. Farber, 1973.
96. *Ibid.*
97. This analysis of Season of the Witch is an updated and expanded version of an essay I originally published in *Film Inquiry*. See McCarty-Simas, 2022, "Season of the Witch."

brimming with social commentary, this time exploring the state of feminism at the beginning of the '70s and inspired by his research into real-world, contemporary witchcraft—has never received the same level of praise. Even after the success of *Night of the Living Dead*, Romero continually struggled to finance his films. To secure funding, then, he wrote several softcore sex scenes into what was then titled *Jack's Wife*, a choice that would lump the film in with the broader witchsploitation softcore cycle in the minds of distributors. Romero and his team were invested in the film, which White described as "his take on women's liberation." But despite his protestations, the distributor, Jack H. Harris Enterprises (who had most recently released *Beware! The Blob* [1972]), retitled the film *Hungry Wives* and marketed it as softcore porn. "It was an absolute bomb because people were thinking it was meant to be a porn film and it was not," White explained in an interview for the film's Arrow Video release, "it wasn't sold and promoted properly. *Nobody* saw this film."[98]

Season of the Witch masterfully synthesizes all the elements that characterized the witchsploitation cycle, combining them with an overt commentary on gender in suburban America, positing the occult revival as a gateway into feminist empowerment. The film is the story of a stymied housewife named Joan (Jan White) who finds herself drawn to witchcraft as a means to take control of her circumstances when her daughter goes off to college. Romero focuses on Joan's struggles contending with the social isolation—and desexualization—that middle-age represented for women at the time. Prominently featuring (and eventually named for) Donovan's classic '60s acid rock anthem "Season of the Witch", the film employs an abstract, almost cyclical narrative structure and avant-garde, psychedelic visual stylings to convey Joan's story in hyper-subjective terms. The film's queasy black-comedy, day-glo colors, fish-eye lenses, and jarring time jumps bear little resemblance to *Living Dead*'s crisp black-and-white cinematography and linear bottle-film structure, instead bringing *Season of the Witch* into closer conversation with countercultural films like *Head* (1968), *Rosemary's Baby*, and even John Cassavetes' classic of New Hollywood feminist hysteria, *A Woman Under the Influence* (1974), which followed a year later. It also reflects a powerful masculine ambivalence about "women's roles", Women's Liberation, and the power that femininity outside heteropatriarchal control holds over the popular imagination.

When *Season of the Witch* begins, middle-aged Joan finds herself trailing helplessly along a wooded path behind a man in a suit who ignores her as he reads the newspaper. He lets branches whip her across the face as he pushes ahead. She starts awake for a moment—only to find herself in another dream: this time, her husband slaps her with his paper and buckles a leash to the red,

---

98. McCarty-Simas, 2022, "Season of the Witch."

studded dog collar she suddenly wears around her neck. He leads her to a dog kennel, watches her get locked away, and departs for a business trip. In her next dream, the kennel becomes her house. When she catches her reflection in her bedroom mirror, she's become an elderly woman. The central tension of *Season of the Witch* isn't really witchcraft. It's the particularly ambivalent indignities of aging for women in the latter half of the 20th century—a fate that, effectively, turns women into crones. Joan increasingly finds herself alone in her suburban home once her daughter has gone to college; her husband, Jack (Bill Thunhurst), is no longer sexually interested in her and travels constantly for work; her friends talk about little more than bridge and the latest classes at the country club. Watching her daughter enjoy her sexually liberated youth while her older friends fall to pieces, popping pills to pass the time and speaking seldom, Joan is trapped in her home without a role to fulfill.

Not long into the movie, Joan, driven by curiosity, goes to meet the one local witch in town whose argument in favor of witchcraft reads like a passage from Betty Friedan. "I honestly think," the elegant older woman tells a nervous Joan, "that every woman underneath her prejudices knows that there is something out there that we haven't got the power to define." In other words, to quote *The Feminine Mystique*: "We can no longer ignore that voice within women that says: 'I want something more than my husband and my children and my home.'"[99] These feelings of middle-aged feminine alienation are taken as the film's urgent emotional center, treated seriously and compassionately at a time when they went largely unaddressed in the movies. As Molly Haskell wrote that same year in her investigation of women on screen, *From Reverence to Rape*, middle-aged women were treated as disposable commodities on screen and off, easily traded for younger girlfriends whose youth was seen by husbands as a mark of distinction.[100] Joan's story is a process of refusing to accept this death sentence, particularly in the realm of her sexuality. She seduces Gregg (Raymond Laine), a man her daughter, Nikki (Joedda McClain), has been seeing, but for whom she has no feelings. Her daughter's status as a hip college student, colors the film, allowing Joan access to the sexual revolution by proxy. The dynamic relationship between mother and daughter here is another element that makes the film significant—in an era when pairings between older women like Joan and younger men like Gregg were viewed, as Molly Haskell put it, as either "a joke or a perversion", Nikki insists her mother is beautiful and encourages her to see the younger man if she wants to.[101] Feminist writers like Haskell were criticizing the dynamics that made scenarios like these into objects of ridicule. In an echo of the metaphor at the heart of films like

---

99. Friedan, 1997, 78.
100. Haskell, 2016, 14.
101. *Ibid.*

Rosemary's Baby and implicit in the tenets of consciousness raising, Haskell writes that "[o]ne doesn't have to be inclined to the conspiracy theory to feel an unconscious drive working to keep women in their place, a taboo that has arisen out of a fear, or awe, of woman's greater survival and sexual powers."[102] In this context, the storyline feels particularly poignant.

The film plays with the same questions of belief that run throughout the films of the occult revival. Early in the film, Gregg humiliates Joan's older friend Shirley (Ann Muffly) by tricking her into thinking she's smoked marijuana and acting foolish. As in *Mark of the Witch*, he calls it an "experiment", a way to prove that people will experience what they believe to be happening whether it's true or not. This gambit reflects the film's investment with the dubious nature of reality that animates *Night of the Eagle* and *Eye of the Devil* (1966). "Being afraid is necessary to believing [in witchcraft]," the witch tells Joan after she's seduced Gregg with her newfound magic. "But don't use it lightly," the other woman cautions, "knowing you've abused it can destroy you. With fear at least." Soon after beginning her journey into witchcraft, Joan's nightmares of domestic purgatory become visions of sexually violent home invasion by the Devil. Joan's guilt at transgressing the norms of her social milieu and her family's Catholic faith (she performs her first spell on Ash Wednesday, in an echo of *Rosemary's Baby*) is transferred onto her newfound source of agency. Her guilt at her own need for sexual gratification warps into a violent destruction of her bodily autonomy. At the film's climax, Joan summons "one of the lords" of her Craft through a sexual ritual with Gregg, causing a skeletally patterned black and white cat to appear unbeknownst to her. Gregg dismisses her "way of showing faith" and mocks her for believing she's summoned the Devil.

After Gregg leaves, Joan—overcome with paranoia from her nightmares—shoots her husband through the door when he returns home unexpectedly. His death is crosscut with her initiation into her coven, which features her kneeling on all fours, neck tied with a red rope fashioned into a collar reminiscent of the one her husband held in her dreams. "Goddamn women," one of the cops at the scene of the murder exclaims, "they get everything in the end. They get it all from us." If, as Molly Haskell suggests, by "defying cultural norms... with men who want only to flatter and flirt with her," female characters "becom[e] 'unfeminine' and undesirable... in short, a monster", and Barbara Creed suggests, that "[t]he presence of the monstrous-feminine in the popular horror film speaks to us more about male fears than about female desire or feminine subjectivity,"[103] these men illustrate the central anxieties around feminism at the heart of the witch film—that a new conspiracy has emerged, orchestrated by women, to subvert

---

102. Haskell, 2016, 14.
103. Creed, 1993, 7.

masculinist cultural hegemony.[104] Soon after, Joan returns to her social circle looking markedly younger and more confident in herself. When her flustered friends comment on it, she replies "I'm a witch," with a faint glimmer in her eye. Nevertheless, she's still introduced to newcomers as "Jack's wife", continually underestimated.

Ultimately, the film's stance on witchcraft is open to several interpretations. Romero's emphasis on autosuggestion and fear, paired with the stylistic parallels he draws between sexist American paternalism, Catholic guilt, and witchcraft (i.e. the witches' red rope replacing the husband's red dog collar) could suggest that the film's tragedy lies in Joan's inability to take responsibility over her own circumstances and her reliance on external systems of control. Romero actually said something to that effect, arguing that

> [T]he fact is that every forward motion in the film is caused by [Joan]... yet she needs to be able to say, "The Devil made me do it!" Which at once is the plight of womanhood, or any minority, and the genocide—it's very hard to perceive yourself as the cause of something that might make it better.[105]

This suggestion, that witchcraft as a source of personal fulfillment and agency can function as a kind of guilt trap, is not the most fulfilling feminist message, though Romero may take a sympathetic stance on the matter. It suggests that any search for feminist agency on Joan's part is hampered by her awareness of her own victimization. In short, that she remains trapped within the "paradox of womanhood". Yet the fact that Joan's final ritual *does* seem to summon the skeletal cat leaves open the possibility that her magic was real, and opens up more affirmative readings. While Romero argues that the moral of the story is that Joan's self-doubt and reliance on witchcraft ultimately prevents her liberation, it's also easy to read her link to witchcraft as her way to break free: Witchcraft as self-advocacy and control.

Either interpretation airs the same anxiety on the part of the dominant culture: women's bids for autonomy will, in the words of the cops at the film's climax, "take everything" from men. As such, they are to be feared. The men's dismissals of witchcraft throughout the film allow male viewers to view feminists as histrionic and flaky in the same manner *Playboy* and *Cosmo* readers could. However this demonization of witchcraft affirms the notion that even occult-oriented feminism like witchcraft is destabilizing to masculine authority. At the same time, the fact that the filmic text resists an easy dismissal of Joan's powers, and the ease with which she learns to use them with a little help from other women, undergirds the same message— women's solidarity is a genuine threat to the heteropatriarchy. In both

---
104. Creed, 1993, 4.
105. Williams, 2015, 53.

contexts, calling Joan "Jack's wife", even after her husband's death at her hands, rings hollow not just because she killed him, but because that moniker never accurately encapsulated who Joan was as a woman.

Given its softcore-style marketing, it is unsurprising that this relatively challenging, genre-bending, explicitly feminist film would be overlooked at the time of its release. But *Season of the Witch* was not alone that year in being lost in the wash of witchsploitation and arthouse porn. Another explicitly feminist witch film, a Japanese import called *Belladonna of Sadness* (1973), was similarly overlooked. Where Romero only used explicit sexuality as a tool to get funding, however, in *Belladonna*, sexuality was central, both in its marketing and its message from the outset.[106] "This is porn [...] but make it a pure love story," the director, Eiichi Yamamoto told his team of his vision for his pioneering work of psychedelic, avant-garde erotic animation.[107] This film is an ecstatic freakout about a Medieval peasant woman who becomes a witch; it's composed of a series of largely still watercolor paintings interspersed with bursts of rapid, lyrical animation. Inspired by the aesthetics of thirteenth-century tarot decks, its eclectic visual palette includes iridescent acrylics and delicate pencil work (the film was marketed to compete with another psychedelic classic, 1968's *Yellow Submarine*, which only arrived in Japan in the early 1970s). It features a score that combines experimental jazz and noise music, partly inspired by Pink Floyd and created by one of the earliest Japanese artists to use a Moog synthesizer.[108] *Belladonna* is also based directly on Michelet's *Satanism and Witchcraft*.

The film's "pure love story", ostensibly between two French peasants, Jeanne (Aiko Nagayama) and Jean (Katsuyuki Itô), is much more about women fighting against the violent ravages of sexism, alienation, and burgeoning capitalism than it is about genitalia, though there are plenty of those (everything is sex, except sex, etc.). When it comes to sex, Jeanne's journey is defined by her vulnerability as a woman: she is raped by her feudal overlord and his entire court as punishment when her betrothed can't afford her dowry, then by the Devil himself (an impishly seductive Tatsuya Nakadai). And when it comes to animation, sex itself seems to have been beside the point: Kuni Fukai, the film's art director, said, "I wasn't thinking about the erotic when I was painting," he laughed, "I painted even the erotic scenes as abstractions ... I found the forms interesting."[109] This sentiment would seem at odds with a film that features near-constant graphic nudity, but the film's meditations on gender and power somehow take center stage even in, and perhaps even because of, its most creatively Bacchic sequences.

---

106. This analysis of *Belladonna of Sadness* is an updated and expanded version of an essay I originally published in *The Brooklyn Rail*. See, McCarty-Simas, 2023.
107. "Eiichi Yamamoto Interview", 2016.
108. *Ibid.*
109. "Kuni Fukai", 2016.

Belladonna of Sadness, much to the director's surprise, proved most popular with the same college-aged women bringing radical feminism to the foreground of politics in the late '60s and early '70s. Yamamoto briefly contemplated cutting the pornographic scenes in deference to what he assumed would be this more sensitive audience, but to do so would have been to miss the point. Around the same time, reporters noticed that in Paris, screenings of the Italian softcore film *Emmanuelle* (1974) "comprised of 75 to 80% women."[110] The same trend was visible in the US when Columbia Pictures released *Emmanuelle* as its first X, marketing it to women with the tagline "X was never like this". Women were seeking out sexuality on screen, particularly in films that emphasized a woman's agency and pleasure—or that treated the sexualized power dynamics women experience with nuance and empathy. Yamamoto's film, with its blend of erotica, violence, and anti-establishment feminist politics, lays out a nuanced case for the relationship between misogyny, capitalism, and religion that doubtless struck a chord with the young feminists coming of age during the occult boom. Much of *Belladonna*'s politics are pulled directly from Michelet's philosophical frame—here visualized as a heavily pop cultural, 20th-century acid trip. As described in Chapter 1 of this book, the central, radical thesis of *Satanism and Witchcraft* is that the oppression of women under Christianity and Feudalism in the Middle Ages is at fault both for the existence of witches *and* for men and women's suffering alike, trapping them with guilt, shame, and division: drawing on historical understandings of femininity as inherently linked to nature, healing, and to the erotic body, Michelet argues that "nothing is impure but moral evil. Everything physical is pure; nothing physical can properly be ... prohibited in deference to an empty idealism, or worse still a silly feeling of repulsion."[111] Thus, the Christian feudal system's demonization of sex, midwifery, and natural healing created the witch by forcing women into league with the Devil, whose realm (earth, nature, the erotic) was now necessarily their own. Under this system, women become outlaws, and "is not Satan the outlaw of outlaws? ... He gives his followers the joy and wild liberty of all free things of Nature, the rude delight of being a world apart."[112]

In *Belladonna*, Jeanne's downfall is largely a sexual one, yet, significantly, tied to the use of rape as a tool of political and social control, forced on her by a Christian understanding of sex as sin. It's only after this ordeal that she summons the Devil, praying, "I want power! Someone help me!" The Devil appears as a delightfully literal phallus, rising from the tip of her spinning wheel. Jeanne's deal with the Devil disrupts traditional notions of morality and horror, flipping the script on heteropatriarchy through violent abnegation. His possession of her body is depicted as its own form of

---

110. Lewis, 2002, 228.
111. Michelet, 1998, 86. This quote also evokes Grandier in *The Devils*.
112. *Ibid*, 70.

parasitism. At this stage, her powers are economic as well as sexual, and soon she earns enough money selling cloth to the slavering townsmen that her husband, Jean, becomes the town tax collector. But participating in the noxious economic system only brings more strife, leading to his ruination when his subjects are unable to pay. Finding his own power stripped, he too (as the Devil initially did) rapes and beats Jeanne, drinking himself into a daily stupor. Yet, that same sexual relationship is also her path to salvation. Fleeing into the woods after her husband's betrayals, Jeanne willingly gives her soul as well as her body to Satan. "My wife," he rumbles, "what do you want to do?" "Anything," she murmurs, floating naked, looking up through her eyelashes at his now-enormous figure, "so long as it's bad."

Like *Season of the Witch*, *Belladonna* rejects the madonna-whore dichotomy[113] that feminists were criticizing while turning pornography into a site of overt political commentary about women's experience. Where Jeanne believed being the Devil's wife would turn her into a monster, having bought into the Christian understanding of her sexuality as sinful, she wakes to find herself even more beautiful than before: "Who says anger and hatred are ugly? You have become ... radiant. More beautiful than God," Satan tells her, her body engulfed in stunning runs of psychedelic flowers. Temporality ruptures and the screen explodes with a cavalcade of atemporal imagery from the Statue of Liberty to disco dancers to Apollo 11, thrusting her into the progressive flow of history. She heals the plague-riddled with belladonna flowers, both poisonous and beautiful; she invites them to orgies and eases their own sexual shame. "I want to become a horrifying woman," she sighs to the Devil. The anger and hatred he invokes are purifying emotions: anger at her violation, hatred at her oppressors and the system that protects them. To be horrifying, as the women of W.I.T.C.H knew, is to be subversive, to shock and overthrow those in power. Yamamoto makes this rage manifest, masterfully rendering it with kaleidoscopic wrath and hallucinatory avant-garde exuberance. Jeanne is eventually burned at the stake for her crimes against the state, an image that pervades witchcraft media as the ultimate form of defeat and abuse, femicide and oppression. Yet, watching her demise, the crowd of women begin to transform: their faces change, each one becoming Jeanne's. Every woman has the power to make the same pact, the feminist conspiracy from Hell hides under the passive faces of old women and young girls. "Time passed", a title tells us, before Jeanne's figure, fabulously, transfigures into Eugène Delacroix's *Liberty Leading the People*, breasts bared. The erotic becomes a tool of power and liberation, a harbinger of revolution specifically geared towards women rather than as a generic symbol of patriotism. Jeanne becomes a martyr, yes, but her murder is remade into a symbol of enduring hope for feminist resistance.

---

113. Bareket, O. et al, 2018.

These two sadly underseen films signal the genuinely subversive potential of the witch as a cinematic signifier: with their ample use of experimental visuals and avant-garde, non-linear storytelling, *Season of the Witch* and *Belladonna of Sadness* took full advantage of the era's increased openness to sexuality on-screen, using it to tell nuanced stories of women's alienation, objectification, suffering, and, eventually, empowerment. Films like these are essential to the witch's status as a feminist archetype in film, setting the stage for the witch films of the 2010s with their brute-force polemic even as classics like *Rosemary's Baby* concretize the ambiguities at the heart of the subgenre.

But 1973 proved to be the final real year of the witchsploitation era, even as many of its best entries were released—though as their commercial deadfalls also indicate, to diminishing returns. Part of this decline arguably comes from the death of porno chic, sped along by a series of unfavorable Supreme Court decisions placing limits on the exhibition of sexually explicit films in theaters and the transportation of such "obscene materials" across state lines in 1973. By 1974 X-rated films had lost much of their legitimacy as well as their distribution network, making it even harder for films as provocative and explicit as *Belladonna* and *Season of the Witch* to gain traction.[114] Jack Valenti's choice to keep sex in the movies at arms-length had proved prescient, pointing to a conservative turn in the culture and political landscape on the horizon. The next chapter will explore the death of the witchsploitation cycle—and the death of the sixties.

---

114. Lewis, 2002, 212.

Chapter Six

The End of the Countercultural Witch Horror Cycle

"Nobody was really surprised when it happened, not really, not at the subconscious level where savage things grow."
-Stephen King, *Carrie*[1]

"Lately, I've had a new worry. The success of *Rosemary's Baby* inspired *Exorcists* and *Omens* and lots of et ceteras. Two generations of youngsters have grown to adulthood watching depictions of Satan as a living reality. Here's what I worry about now: if I hadn't pursued an idea for a suspense novel almost forty years ago, would there be quite as many religious fundamentalists around today?"
-Ira Levin, "Stuck with Satan"[2]

The same dynamics that sparked the decline of the porno chic era could be seen in the waning power of the Second Wave Women's Movement. The passage of *Roe v. Wade* in January 1973 fundamentally altered the landscape for American women's health, affirming their bodily autonomy and saving countless lives in the process.[3] But, as Katherine Turk describes in her book on the history of NOW, even in the face of victories like this and the passage of the Equal Credit Opportunity Act the following fall, "by 1973 the radical feminist movement was actually in decline."[4] Many radical groups like NYRW had already disbanded by 1969, splintering into smaller organizations or joining the more moderate NOW; by the mid-1970s, those that had taken their place were losing political relevance in the face of the strange confluence of feminist victories *and* increasing social conservatism. Even NOW found itself facing a funding cliff and splintering priorities that would precipitate its declining influence into the '80s. Radical feminist groups were also shifting their emphasis towards what was becoming known as "cultural feminism". In Turk's estimation, this form of hyper-individualistic feminism served as a natural outgrowth of the rejection of "male culture" so fundamental to the already-separatist women's movement. As the economy finally slowed after

---
1. King, 2011, 3.
2. Levin, 2012.
3. The 1973 Supreme Court decision that enshrined abortion protections in American law.
4. Turk, 2023, 198.

decades of post-war prosperity and even the Left became weary of years of political turmoil and violence, cultural feminism

> held that women possessed distinct values and should honor them by fostering their own 'women's culture'. Rather than participating in institutions built by men—especially the economy... their sex should carve out their own spaces and institutions where they could build community.[5]

This impulse, ironically, fostered a kind of *political escapism* similar to that which Leary and the hippies had advocated at the height of the Vietnam War, in this case what one radical group called a "female '*counter-reality*' and counterculture."[6] This departure from concerted political action has been critiqued as a form of "trickle-down feminism"—in the same manner that the counterculture's ostensible rejection of the dominant culture via rural communalism was often funded by wealthy parents at the expense of working-class people of color in the west and southwest who were priced out of their homes by these "utopianists".[7]

In both cases, utopian ideals and mystical inclinations came together to foster a neoprimitivist binarism on questions of gender. Rural hippies embraced an understanding of femininity predicated on domesticity and childbearing (per the *Whole Earth Catalog*: "a girl just becomes so... so *womanly* when she's doing something like baking her own bread in a wood stove... It turns me on."[8] According to Lois Brand, visiting a New Mexico commune "wasn't that far removed from what I'd grown up with at home," where men made the decisions and women made the beds).[9] Meanwhile, radical feminists like W.I.T.C.H. founder Robin Morgan were shifting their positions into markedly spiritual and bioessentialist territory, suggesting that "female biology is the basis of women's powers. Biology is hence the source and not the enemy of feminist revolution."[10]

While the Second Wave was never especially inclusive of queer people—particularly trans women—this shift into "female culture" calcified in the early 1970s, partly through neo-pagan rhetoric about matriarchal lineages, Wiccan femininity, and the power of the womb. By the turn of the next decade, Wiccan spirituality became commonly associated with radical feminist values as a result of now-classic texts like Starhawk's 1999 *The Spiral Dance* (a self-described feminist and environmentalist Wiccan Ur-text that positively discusses the author's history of feminist protests, while also unfortunately engaging in bioessentialist notions of Goddess worship,

---

5. Turk, 2023, 191.
6. Echols, 2019, 182, emphasis added.
7. For more on this see Turner, 2006, 78.
8. Turner, 2006, 76, 77.
9. *Ibid.*
10. Echols, 2019, 250.

describing womanhood through strict conceptions of the author's "body, in all its *femaleness*, its breasts, vulva, womb, and menstrual flow, [as] sacred.")[11] Ironically the counterculturalists, whom feminists had previously scorned as encouraging a "*Playboy* mentality", and many feminists *themselves* were now singing a similar tune about raising children over protesting wage inequality, deemed less consequential in a "broken system". This bioessentialist turn to mysticism, made feminists "[l]ess concerned with reforming society than with developing forms that would prefigure the utopian community of the future," a reorganization of priorities that co-opted "the personal is political" into what Alice Echols called a "solipsistic preoccupation with self-transformation."[12][13]

This change towards self-transformation was in many ways an embrace of the capitalist paradigm that, just a few years before, was viewed as one of the central pillars of the heteropatriarchy (for radical feminists) and for the military-state (for the New Left). Explaining this shift across the counterculture, Echols draws on Richard Flacks' history of the period's liberal movements, which describes this departure from traditional political organization and action in similarly bleak terms. Linking feminists to the Yippie milieu from which they emerged, he writes:

> This kind of politics could lead to 'a search for personally satisfying modes of life while abandoning the possibility of helping others to change theirs.' Thus the idea that 'politics is how you live your life, not who you vote for,' as Jerry Rubin put it, could lead to a subordination of politics to lifestyle.[14]

Many feminists who had once used the symbol of the witch as a more fluid signifier—at once historical, imagistic, symbolic, and folkloric—thusly refocused on the quality of feminine divinity and the potentials of "women's culture" to create an independent economic bubble for "women-aligned" women at the expense of solidarity with women as a whole.

By 1973, articles on the politics behind the history of the witch, though still prevalent in feminist presses, frequently competed for space with articles on Truzzi's more consumerist, lifestyle witch: coverage of the 1973 Witchcraft and Sorcery Convention for example focused more on the cost of talismans, amulets, and potions than on politics. This tendency towards consumerism had been heralded several years before in a *Time* article warning that hippies were capable of destroying the economy with their ideology ("What will happen if millions of youths turn against the material rewards... that have motivated so much American progress?"[15])—before

---
11. Starhawk, 1999, 14, emphasis added.
12. Echols, 2019, 16-17.
13. *Ibid*, 137.
14. *Ibid*, 17.
15. "Graduates and Jobs: A Grave New World", 1971.

suggesting that, in light of an economic downturn, hippies were joining the economy instead

> "Business? Like wow! Most of my friends are in business", explains one barefoot boy in bell-bottoms and beads, referring to the lucrative new counterculture enterprises that constitute what is sometimes known as *Hip Capitalism*. Hundreds of erstwhile flower children have become proprietors of record stores, organic-food shops, restaurants and boutiques.[16]

By this point, prominent figures in the counterculture like Stewart Brand of the *Whole Earth Catalog* had fully embraced this point of view, branding themselves "far out entrepreneurs" in the publication and even saying, "I've yet to figure out what capitalism is, but if it's what we're doing, I dig it… responsibility is individual stuff" rather than the purview of communities, a fascinating if paradoxically unsurprising assertion from one of the staunchest supporters of the creation of America's rural communes.[17]

Meanwhile, witchy cultural feminists were becoming more mystical. An op-ed by a self-described therapist and occultist in the feminist newspaper *Her-Self* encouraged those in the medical profession to give more "credence to the reality of psychic phenomenon… dismissed clinically as… as being either psychotic or borderline psychotic." She concluded that her interest in the occult had led her "views of what is 'true' knowledge [to change] drastically."[18] [19] Only a few pages away, research into "astrological birth control" was heralded, alongside credulously framed claims that this "rhythm plus" method was 98% effective.[20] By 1975, feminists were publishing articles with titles like "Will the Women's Movement Survive?" that, responding to "cultural feminism" and "women's culture", portended, "without a movement to support it, consciousness veers off, turns inward toward self-hatred or destructive mysticism, and finally dies."[21]

The primary culprits for the decline in feminist power, though, were the conservatives gaining political ground and the broader mood in the country. The combination of consumerism and mysticism dominating feminist and hippie circles had by this time gone mainstream—giving birth to what Tom Wolfe would bleakly label the "Me Decade" in 1976. This famous if curmudgeonly diagnosis of the countercultural ethos as an experiment in self-absorption nevertheless drew cutting parallels between the spiritual experimentation and the devolution of politics into religion and the craze for self-improvement, eventually birthing the socially conservative coalitions of the '80s, from

---

16. "Graduates and Jobs: A Grave New World", 1971, emphasis added.
17. Turner, 2006, 99.
18. Golden, 1972, 7.
19. Taylor, 1973, 4.
20. Stern, 1972, 7.
21. Echols, 2019, 283.

fitness-obsessed yuppies to reactionary evangelicals. "It is entirely possible," Wolfe argued, "that in the long run historians will regard the entire New Left experience as not so much a political as a *religious* episode wrapped in semi military gear and guerrilla talk." He provocatively suggested that rather than kill God, the hippies inadvertently resurrected Him:

> What finally started attracting young people to Christianity was something the churches had absolutely nothing to do with: namely, the psychedelic or hippie movement. The hippies had suddenly made religion look hip. Very few people went into the hippie life with religious intentions, but many came out of it absolutely *righteous*.[22]

This, combined with the permission granted by the inward-seeking nature of the counterculture and the previously-named New Sentimentality deadened political activism in exchange for vanity—a new car or a new wife or a new cause. In perhaps his most flagrantly condescending turn in an already-dismissive essay, Wolfe applied this lens to the feminist movement to suggest that feminism, rather than a product of genuine political ardor, had been a similarly narcissistic project all along, a means to "to elevate an ordinary status—woman, housewife—to the level of drama." Ironically, this chauvinistic perspective leads Wolfe to miss the insight of his broader point: that the notion of the personal as political could be coopted by women who, rather than work towards structural feminist change, having already tuned in and turned on, wanted, finally, to drop out.

It is unsurprising that in the early 1970s the creeping decline in the occult revival was accompanied by what was becoming known as the Jesus Revolution. A new wave of religious revivalism had, as Wolfe observed, swept many former hippies and made its way into the mainstream alongside a political conservatism exemplified by Nixon's reelection in 1972. That election, in contrast to the ferment of '68, was characterized by lethargy: a 55% turnout, lower than the previous several cycles, despite the recent decrease in the voting age.[23] A prescient 1971 Time article, "The Alternative Jesus: Psychedelic Christ" put a fine point on the disillusionment Wolfe would eventually periodize. "Jesus is alive and well and living in the radical spiritual fervor of a growing number of young Americans... The Jesus revolution... heaps scorn on the message that God was ever dead."[24] The article points to the tumult and disappointment of the counterculture (contrasting John Lennon's quip about the Beatles being more famous than Jesus in '66 with George Harrison's "My Sweet Lord" in '70) with drastic terms meant to mark the end of the occult revival as surely as the "Is God Dead" cover had marked its beginning in 1968.[25]

---

22. Wolfe, 1976.
23. Hoberman, 2005, 258.
24. "Alternative Jesus", 1971.
25. *Ibid.*

Acid trips in the seventh grade, sex in the eighth, the Viet Nam War a daily serial on TV since you were nine, parents and school worse than 'irrelevant'—meaningless. No wonder Jesus is making a great comeback. The death of authority brought the curse of uncertainty. As Thomas Farber writes in *Tales for the Son of My Unborn Child*: "The freedom from work, from restraint, from accountability, wondrous in its inception, became banal and counterfeit. Without rules there was no way to say no, and worse, no way to say yes." The search for a "yes" led thousands to… the occult and even Satanism before they drew once again on familiar roots.[26]

By 1973, this same upswing of religious conservatism was being sold as its own form of empowerment in Marabel Morgan's bestselling Christian "marriage guide", *The Total Woman*, which warned women that their husbands' "masculinity might be threatened by [their] paycheck" and suggested they keep themselves "feminine, soft, and touchable" to compensate: "If you're stingy in bed, he'll be stingy with you."[27] This religious return, so heavily inflected with anti-feminism and a re-investment in "traditional women's roles", is visualized with almost uncanny precision in another occult horror film from 1973, this one decidedly more popular than *Season of the Witch* or *Belladonna of Sadness*: *The Exorcist*. This film, though not explicitly about witches, is based on a book that *is* and draws on the mythos—the *mysto*—around witches in the post-Manson end-of-the-'60s to dramatize a story of religious faith (and traditional gender roles) tested, and ultimately regained for a mosaic of non-normative characters. It also embodied the subgenre's more conservative subtext: without religion and a man in the house, women's bodies, minds, and sexualities could run dangerously out of control. Critics who asked why God never got a fair fight in the movies needed look no further.

Like *Rosemary's Baby* (1968), William Friedkin's classic horror film has been discussed *ad nauseum* since its release, and for good reason. Not simply the story of the exorcism of young Regan MacNeil (Linda Blair) by Father Damian Karras (Jason Miller), the film was viewed as an exorcism of the culture itself, with all the excretions, emanations, and profanity that come with that rite. *The Exorcist* in many ways synthesizes the era's tortured push-pull relationship with the horror film as legitimate *objet d'art* and as obscene commercial refuse degrading an already-fallen culture. The film's reception itself became a sensation, with breathless accounts of hours-long lines and even ticket scalping upon its Christmas release, despite reactions that were reportedly fearful and physical. "The men flee and the women vomit", one usher gleefully told the *Los Angeles Times*, while the *New York Times* credulously shared accounts of heart attacks, miscarriages, and even

---

26. "Alternative Jesus", 1971.
27. Morgan in Du Mez, 2020, 60-2.

commitments to psychiatric hospitals during screenings in the city.²⁸ The *Boston Globe* wrote about one Catholic schoolgirl making friends "sleep over for the past three weeks because she's afraid", and though framed as moral outrage, stories like these served as their own Corman-esque exploitation-style marketing campaign, naturally adding to the film's popularity.²⁹

The moral panic around the film was magnified by its accessibility. Seemingly given the high cost of *The Exorcist* to Warner Bros. (dramatically inflated during the famously difficult shoot), the MPAA had granted the finished product a lenient R-rating as opposed to an X, which, by December 1973, would have doomed Friedkin's film to almost certain box office failure. Many of the more outraged reviews of the film focused on this—that the film's generous helping of blasphemies and violence could be accessed by children whose unscrupulous parents might reason that "'Rosemary's Baby' wasn't that bad", only to find themselves watching "an obscene abomination… the most obvious X-rated movie ever made."³⁰ This was a hot topic upon the film's release, spawning panicked articles detailing the film's scenes of masturbation, highly detailed surgical operations (interestingly, the sequences when Regan undergoes an angiography or spinal tap come up in almost as many reviews as the former did)³¹ and decapitation. The film's grip on the populace was viewed as its own form of "possession"—one that, according to reviews, could harm real-life children. Yet in the context of the occult revival, the film seems perfectly designed to reassure viewers of the power of religion, harnessing the cynicism of its era not to suggest just that the Devil is everywhere, but that God is too.³²

Where films like *Rosemary's Baby* deconstruct the nuclear family from within in the mid-60s, *The Exorcist* presents the MacNeil household as already broken by the early '70s: successful actress Chris (New Hollywood star Ellen Burstyn), split up from her husband, is left to parent Regan alone while on location for her next film, *Crash Course*, (what one review called a "dreary film about student protest") set in Georgetown. In the only scene where Chris is shown filming *Crash Course*, (she later quips it's "kind of like the Walt Disney version of the Hồ Chí Minh story"), she complains that the script "makes no sense"—to her, the protesting students' political demands, the administration's position, and her own character's relationship to both, are confusing; but the writer is abroad, unreachable. She pushes her way to the front of the rowdy crowd of parodically bearded, turtlenecked extras and cries into a borrowed megaphone that the students are morally

---

28. Goodman, 1974.
29. Kelly, 1974.
30. Howard, 1973, 3.
31. Gehnis, 1974.
32. As Friedkin described his worldview in his 2017 documentary about real-life exorcism, *The Devil and Father Amorth*, "My own belief is that there's a far deeper dimension to the universe. We know there is evil. There is also good. And if there are demons, there must be angels."

contradicting themselves: "If you want to effect change, you have to do it within the system!" Chris soon finds it impossible to take her character's advice in her own life, trying to connect pieces of a puzzle the rationalist systems of modern life are incapable of putting together.

Chris' twelve-year-old daughter, Regan, begins the story as an almost parodic portrait of innocence, drawing childlike pictures in marker and begging her mother for a pony. When she begins playing with a Ouija board in the basement, though, she soon loses her rosy-cheeked charm. Symbols of hope have gone sour: sweet Regan urinates in the middle of a cocktail party, tells an astronaut he's going to die on his next mission, begins shouting profanities in a deep throaty growl (this Devil's voice was performed, notably, by a woman), and shows signs of physical deterioration that no one can explain (though the doctors try, first diagnosing her with "nerves" in a now-familiar nod to the relationship between "hysteria" and witchcraft, then concluding that she suffers from a kind of "disorder rarely seen these days outside of primitive cultures", the *belief* that she is possessed, in an echo of the genre's primitivist roots brought to the fore in the film's opening passages in Iraq). The film, which follows Chris' fruitless attempts to get her daughter the help she needs, ultimately resorting to exorcism, is, in essence, a story of lost innocence for everyone involved—a refutation of the "dreary", feel-good portrait of an earnest college professor with a cause (bringing the students and the administration together) she plays in the retrograde '60s-style *Crash Course*.

The film goes out of its way to conflate Regan's troubles with the Devil and the troubles of modern life: as audiences' disgust with the angiography scene attests, even as Satan—and eventually her exorcist—put Regan's body through unholy torture, the establishment's approach to the girl's problem prove no better, turning out to be physically and psychologically anguishing, and ultimately useless. Like Rosemary before them, Chris and Regan are stranded in a maze of masculinized, impersonal bureaucracy made even more impenetrable when Chris' alcoholic director, Burke Dennings (Jack MacGowran), dies mysteriously, thrown from Regan's bedroom window in an otherwise empty house. Regan, Chris fears, will end up in prison or an asylum for life. Father Karras' life, too, is shaped by crushing and impersonal forces: the poverty of his priesthood leaves his elderly ailing mother alone in a deteriorating tenement of a neighborhood gone bad, eventually forced into an institution where she dies alone, unable to afford better care. In cruel circumstances like these, the film suggests, it's easy to see Satan's work everywhere. Karras' crisis of faith (the film's genuine emotional core—Karras eventually becomes the film's protagonist) and implied repressed queerness (more explicit in William Peter Blatty's 1971 novel but referenced in the film) speak to the same broader cultural fear that Levin's novel does—that God *is* dead, leaving humanity, as embodied by two vulnerable women, alienated and susceptible to evil forces. All of these things, from the urban panic to the exploding astronauts to the voices in her Ouija board, are posited as signs of the times; the overwhelming sense, for every character, is that the future no longer holds promise.

The Exorcist, though not about witchcraft *per se*, does take the trappings of the occult revival as a central element of its backdrop, putting this story in direct conversation with the kinds of Mansonoid black magic that dominated discourses around the "death of the sixties" by 1973. As Regan's condition deteriorates and both psychiatry and physical medicine prove useless, the Georgetown church where Karras works, is vandalized: a statue of the Virgin Mary is defaced and desecrated. Soon after, Dennings is killed, and a homicide detective, Lt. Kinderman (Lee J. Cobb), is brought in to investigate. His first step is to reach out to Father Karras in his position as the psychiatrist for the Georgetown University Jesuits out of concern that the desecration and Dennings' death are connected, a theory he broaches to Karras by asking: "What do you know on the subject of witchcraft? From the witching end not the hunting end?" Karras explains that he wrote a paper about Black Masses and witchcraft in college "from the psychiatric end". The detective finally explains that "on the one hand you've got a witchcraft kind of murder [and] on the other, you've got a black mass type desecration of the church," and suggests the two might be connected through witchcraft or Satanism. Karras demurs, the subject is dropped, and the scene ends. While this brief scene is the only one in the film to address the subject head-on, it shapes the cultural architecture of the story—a detail that didn't go unnoticed by conservative viewers like David Sterritt, the long-time critic for the *Christian Science Monitor*, who argued that there was a

> hidden reason for the instant 'Exorcist' success: the past few years have seen a burgeoning popular interest in occult matters ranging from astrology to witchcraft. The Exorcist panders to this fascination, seeking to legitimize the occult by rooting it in establishment settings and institutions. Thus the heroine is no wild-eyed hippie, but a sweet suburban youngster... In short, 'The Exorcist' promises a trendy guided tour through the darkest depths of demonology, with famous filmmakers as our guides.[33]

In William Peter Blatty's novel, written in 1971, discussions of witchcraft abound—during the party when Regan urinates, for example, a conversation about the church desecration (explicitly described as including sex with the statues) leads to a familiar series of exchanges about "witch cults being around" in the modern day ("'I heard a statistic once about something like possibly fifty thousand Black Masses being said each year in the city of Paris.' 'You mean *now*?' marveled Chris").[34] Later, Father Karras describes

---

33. Sterritt, 1974.
34. Blatty, 1994, 64.

Satanism passively as a "pathology" characterized by "people who can't have any sexual pleasure unless it's connected to a blasphemous action" and who perform Black Masses and witchcraft "as the justification".[35] The novel had spent 57 weeks on the *New York Times* bestseller list (17 in the number one position) and had sold over seven million copies upon the film's release, suggesting that a significant portion of the audience would have, like David Sterritt, had this additional context in mind while watching Friedkin's adaptation. The fact that these kinds of exchanges are largely removed from Friedkin's final version speaks to the relative oversaturation of these narratives by 1973—the cycle was reaching its conclusion—but also demonstrates that the subject was familiar enough that one brief scene evokes an entire cultural context and accompanying set of anxieties, here imposed on the young Regan in a new way: where before girls and women getting entangled with the Devil were presented as fundamentally autonomous—desiring, and activiely sinful (making pacts with Satan), from Manson girls hungry for sex to co-ed witches hungry for revenge—here Regan's possession is *not* her fault or her choice. Rather, it is an indirect product of parental discord and a lack of paternal supervision. Thus, it becomes easy to read the film's focus on her possession in a more reassuring way, pushing concerns about women's *desire* for sexuality into the shadows, turning Regan's overtly infantilized adolescent body into an abject spectacle of sexual violence and torture, making her into a pure victim rather than an agent.

But through Karras' exchange with Kinderman, we *can* also understand Regan as a witch, performing Black Masses in empty churches by night off-screen, with her own body. While in the film the discussion of Satanism ends when Kinderman suggests that the church desecrator is a "psychotic priest", in both versions, the audience knows that *Regan* is the true culprit. Viewed from this perspective, recontextualized as a form of unholy manipulation, *The Exorcist* becomes a repudiation of films like *The Devils* (1971) or *The Mephisto Waltz* (1971), making Black Masses objects of perverse horror rather than sexual fascination. In an era when young women playing with Ouija boards were already causally assumed to be witches, these implied scenes of Black Mass are loaded with political and sexual subtext, history, and folklore. But where those subtexts typically hold erotic fascination, here they are made truly horrifying—in need of an exorcism.

Both Chris and Regan's transformations over the course of the film could be viewed as a repudiation of the 1960s ethos around gender and sexuality. Regan's possession shocked audiences for its depiction of a twelve-year-old girl as an abject sexual being. The innocent girl on the cusp of puberty becomes a writhing, swearing, sweating, self-mutilating monster strapped to a bed. This grotesque depiction of pubescent sexuality becomes especially

---

35. Blatty, 1994, 156.

potent in the context of a cultural panic around young women "revolting" against their parents, rejecting religion, "dropping acid in the seventh grade and having sex in the eighth", right around Regan's age. As Stephen King put it, "religious trappings aside, every adult in America understood what the film's powerful subtext was saying... the demon in Regan MacNeil would have responded enthusiastically to the Fish Cheer in Woodstock."[36] [37]

Chris for her part is transformed from a wealthy working actress to a stay-at-home mother. Where before she boldly denigrates her husband for his absenteeism from Regan's life, not calling her on her birthday (an exchange a tearful Regan overhears in an early scene, enforcing the sense that her lack of a father figure leads, in part, to her possession), she eventually finds herself housebound and desperately reliant on men to protect her, laundering Karras' shirts clean of vomit and waiting downstairs while he and Father Merin (Max Von Sydow) conduct the exorcism. While the film does suggest that "effecting change" for Regan is impossible for Chris within the modern medical system, she is instead forced to seek refuge within an even older masculine bureaucratic system—the Catholic church. At the film's end, the mother and daughter leave the house together for Europe, Chris having decided to take time off to spend more time with her child. Regan, offered a return to innocence, has no memory of her possession or exorcism. At a moment when discourse around the Jesus People movement proffered stories of young women and girls, burned out on drugs until they accepted Christ and embraced celibacy, this story takes on broader cultural implications; if Regan's run-in with the Devil represents a debauched, witchy adolescence in the shadow of the kinds of counterculture her mother's film so dismissively depicts, Karras' Jesus-like sacrifice and the girl's born again innocence offers an alternative—as one Christian rocker put it in *Time*, "Forget your hexagram/ You'll soon feel fine/ Stop looking at the stars/ You don't live under the signs."[38] That *Time* article goes on to suggest that, through Jesus, teenagers suffering from "recurring unscheduled [acid] trips" were shaking those unpleasant memories and regaining their normalcy, their innocence: "My flashbacks are gone!"[39] The same could be said for Regan.

For all the outrage around *The Exorcist* as a corruptor of innocence, many critics understood its potential as a form of moral edification. Even as parents and theater owners condemned the film as obscene, "not suitable for a mass audience", and even an "immediate assault upon the emotions" of young audience members "as real as that of any child-beater's fists", Catholics

---

36. King, 2010, 179.
37. The "Fish" Cheer, a call and response between Country Joe and the Fish and its audience ("Gimme an F!" etc.) done before their anti-Vietnam track "I-Feel-Like-I'm-Fixin'-to -Die", actually became the even more appropriate "Fuck" variation of the cheer at Woodstock, a change Regan no doubt would have approved of.
38. "The Alternative Jesus: Psychedelic Christ", 1971.
39. *Ibid*.

called the film "a great religious experience" and the Catholic Legion itself deemed it fully suitable for adult audiences.[40] Friedkin hired a priest as a consultant—another stark point of contrast to previous films whose publicity boasted technical assistance from Alex Sanders and Anton LaVey. This priest, Father O'Malley (who plays Karras' friend Father Dyer), served a political purpose during the film's tumultuous release arguing its spiritually uplifting power: "in a time... [of] 'live fast, die young, and have a pretty corpse'... [*The Exorcist*] raises the possibility that God exists... that in the darkness we can discover the light."[41]

Father O'malley wasn't the only one suggesting that *The Exorcist* was a blessing in disguise for American audiences. The same outlets that held up *The Mephisto Waltz* as an example of Satan's cinematic dominion were changing their tune en masse. The *Chicago Tribune* published several pieces defending the film: Gene Siskel argued in his column that it was "a warm, almost tender experience that reminds one of the necessity of believing in something... neither antireligious nor anticlerical", pointing out that the clergy are the most powerful characters in the film.[42] Slightly later into the film's run, the *Tribune* doubled down on its defense, publishing a piece by a University of Chicago graduate student who argued that "a 14th-century audience would have loved 'The Exorcist'" because it demonstrates "the darker side" of humanity while concluding, like any medieval story of diabolism worth its holy water, that "God, thru His earthly instruments, is triumphant."[43] Arguments like these were echoed more casually by audience members quoted in *Newsday*: "A girl at a Commack high school recently voiced a typical reaction to 'The Exorcist' when she asked: 'Was the film made to scare people back to church? Because that's what it's doing to most of the people I know who've seen it."[44] And the film critic for the *Afro-American* hammered home this point more viscerally when she wrote that after "two aspirin and a stiff drink" she "couldn't sleep... the only relief I could find was in Jesus.... The best comment I could make about 'The Exorcist' is: It will cause many a person to... renew his faith in his God."[45]

By 1974, when William Peter Blatty was accepting his Oscar for *The Exorcist*'s screenplay, the peak of the occult boom seemed to be ending. But one more story would shape the trajectory of American cinematic witches that year: Stephen King's runaway bestselling first novel, *Carrie*. King has

---

40. Meacham. 1974.
41. Champlin, 1972.
42. Siskel, 1973.
43. Dewell, 1974.
44. Gehnis 1974.
45. Brown, 1974.

explicitly acknowledged that writing *Carrie*, the story of a girl who develops supernatural, "witchlike" telekinetic powers with the onset of her first menstrual period, was a product of his anxiety surrounding the gains made by Women's Lib by the early '70s.[46] "*Carrie*" he says, "is largely about how women find their own channels of power, and what men fear about women and women's sexuality... the book is... an uneasy masculine shrinking from a future of female equality." King has also written that Carrie White serves as a foil for "any student who's ever had *his* gym shorts pulled down in Phys Ed or *his* glasses thumb-rubbed in a study hall," assuming a masculine perspective on her character, a downtrodden girl whose explosive violence is triggered by her mistreatment at the hands of other more socially powerful girls at her high school.[47] King's novel, though, tells a different story from the earlier entries into the era's canon of witchy women, in a sense building on the recuperative conservatism of *The Exorcist*. Carrie, failing to fit in as the prom queen, is turned into a monster and burned at the stake. As feminist academic Shelley Stamp writes of Brian De Palma's 1976 adaptation of *Carrie*, arguably the last film of this cycle, "Carrie is not about liberation from sexual repression," as films like *Belladonna of Sadness*, *Season of the Witch*, or *The Mephisto Waltz* explicitly are, "but about the failure of repression to contain the monstrous feminine."[48]

Carrie is often identified as a turning point for the horror genre.[49] Critics couched assessments of the film in telling qualifiers like "Now that devilry and exorcism have pretty much *run their course* (at least until the release of an *Exorcist* or *Omen* sequel) things like telekinesis and reincarnation are getting equal time."[50] This last statement, with its implication that Carrie White's telekinetic powers are a sort of bottom-of-the-barrel supernatural gimmick, is oft-repeated by puzzled critics. In her fiftieth anniversary retrospective on *Carrie* in 2024, novelist Margaret Atwood suggests that "all the quasi-scientific hocus-pocus about the genetic inheritability of telekinesis is just cover-up... you can't just say 'miracle' or 'witch' anymore and get instant

---

46. King, 2010, 180.
47. *Ibid*, 185, emphasis added.
48. Stamp, 2015, 340.
49. In his book on 1980s horror, *Sickos! Psychos! Sequels! Horror Films of the 1980s*, film historian John Stell describes *Carrie* as the beginning of the 1980s slasher cycle due to its status as a "teen" horror film, and for its "surprise ending" in which Carrie returns from the grave in a dream, a trope that carries through in many '80s slashers (12). By contrast, in her seminal article "Bringing It All Back Home: Family Economy and Generic Exchange" film theorist Vivian Sobchack calls *Carrie* the end of a cycle of horror films about "demonic children", begun with *Rosemary's Baby*, which represent the child as a monstrous Other, an evil imposed onto the family by external, uncontrollable forces, eventually suggesting that the films of the 1980s identify the father as the site of familial horror from within the family (179). I disagree with this characterization (Rosemary's baby is a product of her husband's betrayal as much as it is the spawn of the Devil), but Sobchack's periodization nevertheless mirrors my own; I would posit *Carrie* as the last major entry in the 1960s feminist witch cycle.
50. Taggart, 1976.

credibility."[51] In the context of this analysis, though, (as well as tacitly in its association with astrology in the 1976 review), it becomes clear that Carrie's telekinesis is one of the more overt concessions to the broader scientifically-coded New Age milieu from which the witch cycle emerges, beginning with *Something Weird* (1967): ESP of all types and witchcraft were viewed by most at the time as *one and the same*.

The failed repression in *Carrie* is, unlike in *The Exorcist*, ambivalent—making the film an important point of transition for witches in film. The story is likely familiar. After her classmates violently bully Carrie White (Sissy Spacek), for not understanding that she's gotten her period at 16, Sue (Amy Irving), a popular peer with a guilty conscience, conspires to give Carrie the ultimate high school experience: a dream date to the prom with her jock boyfriend. Carrie's fanatically religious and abusive mother (Piper Laurie) forbids Carrie to go, locking her in a closet full of religious paraphernalia, berating her for getting her period, viewing it as an expression of sin. The girls who mocked Carrie are banned from the prom, and, blaming Carrie, seek revenge. When Carrie finally arrives at the dance, her night is made perfect when she's named prom queen in a secretly rigged election orchestrated by the jealous Chris (Nancy Allan) as a cruel prank. When she rises to be crowned, Chris and her friends drench her in pigs' blood, a reminder of her original humiliation. Carrie, practically possessed by rage and betrayal, transforms into a wraithlike angel of death, slaughtering her classmates with her telepathic powers in the decade's most triumphant (if ultimately doomed) vision of feminine rage, revenge, and vindication at injustice. When Carrie returns home, her mother stabs her. Carrie responds in kind, telepathically stringing her mother up with every knife she can find in a mocking recreation of Jesus' death on the cross. The pair then burn to death in the house, which has been set ablaze by Mrs. White's votive candles.

In many ways, the film is as fundamentally conservative as King's comments on his story would suggest. Carrie's willful exploration of her sexuality spurs the development of her powers *and* her period in the story's opening passage of the young woman enjoying the feeling of her body in the school shower (which De Palma openly shoots like a softcore *Playboy* fantasy). In so doing, the film embraces the conservative roots of witch-lore, or "makes its ancient and deadly sex-and-sin equation with breathtaking boldness," as the *Los Angeles Times* put it.[52] Carrie's mother, who could easily be read as a representative of a resurgent religious right, is ultimately unable to prevent Carrie from attending the prom (her goal for most of the film) or from expressing this burgeoning sexuality, thus Carrie finds herself mocked and abused by her classmates, and ultimately she becomes a monster. However, in the film's climax, Carrie's guilt at her

---

51. Atwood, 2024.
52. Thomas, 1976.

powers overwhelms her (a feminized "hyperemotionality"), leading to her death. As her burning house comes crashing down, Carrie's powers, and her mother's, are destroyed, eliminating both poles of the monstrous feminine in the film—the young, sexual "witch" and her overbearing, overzealous witch-mother. Some critics recognized this at the time. Critics recognized this at the time: some denigratingly noted that the film displays "offhand misogyny",[53] while others replicated that misogyny—Roger Greenspun suggested in *Film Comment*, "I can't imagine feminists will care for this, but it seems logical that an action beginning with Carrie's first menstrual flow… should climax in an inferno of blood-become-fire"—as though this folkloric turn were a biologically-imposed inevitability rather than a narrative choice.[54] This review also echoes religious assessments of *The Exorcist*, pointing out that "the dreadful pronouncements of Carrie's sex-obsessed God-crazed mother are *never wrong*. She knows the devil when she sees him. And she knows a young girl's adolescence contains the potential for the destruction of the world."[55]

Yet *Carrie* defies simple characterization. The climax is undeniably cathartic for an audience whose sympathies have been aligned with the bullied girl. In this way, even more than *The Devils*, the film could be read as a feminist tragedy. Imagistically, too, it builds on the potential for unleashed powers promised in the closing passages of *Rosemary* and *Don't Look Now* (1973)—even if that hope for witchy liberation is dashed in the end. Though Carrie is killed at the film's close, her presence haunts its final moments. Sue Snell, her innocent "pure" classmate, is wracked by guilt and plagued by nightmares. In the film's last, most surreal scene (it was shot in reverse to add a sense of uncanniness), Sue walks up to the ruins of Carrie's house where a gravestone is planted with graffiti that reads "Carrie White burns in Hell". She kneels in front of it, and Carrie's badly burned arm suddenly thrusts itself out of the ground, reaching out for her. In Stamp's words, "Carrie is… relegated to Sue's dream life, a figure of the feminine unconscious returning to terrorize" the "correctly" feminine character, suggesting that the monstrous feminine embedded in the female psyche is perpetually threatening to break loose, irrespective of the short-term repression represented by Carrie's death.[56]

"Although the centuries of witch hunting were a terrible time for women," Nel Noddings observes, "they were the last age in which the ancient power of women—real or imagined—received explicit recognition."[57] The same could be argued of even the most repressive films of the 1960s horror cycle,

---

53. J.M., 1976.
54. Greenspun, 1977, 14.
55. *Ibid*, emphasis added.
56. Stamp, 2015, 342.
57. Noddings, 1989, 47.

when witches were occasionally able to survive to the end of the film. Some of them were even almost able to smile. As I will demonstrate in the rest of this book, feminism could never be fully rolled back—no matter how hard conservatives would (and still do) try. In the years following the death of the sixties, numerous feminist films would be released to great critical success, from *Alice Doesn't Live Here Anymore* (1974), to *The Stepford Wives* (1975) to *3 Women* (1977), to *9 to 5* (1980). But already by 1976, films like *Carrie* and *The Exorcist* proved, as one writer put it, that the American "spiritual climate ha[d] changed" and after the never-ending sixties, America once more definitively "*want[ed]* to believe"—in God as well as the Devil. Isaac Asimov said of *The Exorcist*'s success that "all that it prov[ed]... is that the number of sane rational people in the world is very few." In Part 2, as I explore the Satanic Panic through the witch films of the next era, this seemingly cynical statement will prove prescient as the long afterlives of the countercultural occult boom take on tremendous political significance for the feminist movement and beyond.[58]

---

58. Briggs, 1974.

PART TWO

Unpleasant Dreams:
Feminism, Satanic Panic
and the Witch Films of the 1980s

Chapter Seven

Look What's Happened to Rosemary's Baby

"The most volatile element in our culture is the pressure inside the family unit."
—Jack Nicholson, 1980[1]

"Curse the day you didn't pray for Rosemary's Baby."
-Tagline, *Look What's Happened to Rosemary's Baby* (1976)

While enough witches had haunted American screens in 1972 and '73 to form a respectably sized coven, by 1974, the cinematic season of the witch seemed to be ending with the Age of Aquarius. In 1976, when *Carrie* was released, horror was losing respectability once more. In the 1980s, the way witches were depicted on screen changed significantly, more commonly found on VHS or cable than the big screen, with many more male practitioners of the Craft taking center stage. Hidden in these shifts are significant political implications. Part 2 will work to answer several questions about the witch films of the next decade: How does this body of work respond to the films of the previous decade's witch cycle? How does Satanic Panic inflect the witch films of the 1980s? Considering these questions, what does the evolution of the witch as a figure in the films of this era say about the media ecosystem of the 1980s? And, finally, what can be extrapolated from this body of work about the state of feminism, the anxieties around women's and queer people's empowerment, and the backlash to both in the 1980s?

In 1976 while *Carrie* was burning up the big screen, another, far lesser-known witch film was released—this one with politics much more prescient of the coming moment. It aired on ABC as a Halloween special. *Look What's Happened to Rosemary's Baby* was a sequel no one asked for, not based on a novel (Ira Levin wrote the unrelated *Son of Rosemary* in 1997) and only loosely informed by the original film. Considered one of the best horror films of all time, *Rosemary's Baby* (1968) has also been accepted as a feminist classic; its depiction of a woman whose guilt-ridden relationship to her own lapsed Catholicism puts her at the center of a spiritual conflict of epoch-defining proportions, resonated profoundly in a rapidly changing culture: Guy's scathing reaction to Rosemary's new, "fashionable" short haircut is an

---
1. In Baxter, 1997, 310.

encapsulation of the rising anti-feminist sentiments of the time which posited that the Women's Movement was robbing women of their femininity. In the 1960s, God was indeed dead, and *Rosemary* had spawned a new unholy messiah. Just as the original Rosemary brought these cultural concerns to the fore, its made-for-TV sequel (released shortly after the Hyde Amendment instituted the first significant cuts to abortion access after *Roe v. Wade*) in many ways predicts that cycle's decline—and the hardline conservatism that was soon to follow in the age of Reagan's "morning in America".[2]

In this new film, released post Nixon's resignation, after the Vietnam War finally came to a lurching close, and during the presidential election cycle that would put the last Democrat in the White House for over a decade, Rosemary is transformed.[3] In *Look What's Happened to Rosemary's Baby*, gone is Mia Farrow's iconic pixie cut, replaced by a carefully coiffed chin-length bob. Rosemary (now played by Patty Duke) is also, in a shocking departure from the original film, now a devout Christian.[4] She sports a large gold crucifix and a renewed faith in the sanctity of her maternal bond with her demonic offspring that inspires her to steal him back from the coven and flee. She takes her son Andrew/Adrian (his given and Satanic names) to a synagogue, hoping to weaken his connection to the coven. When this tactic fails, she entreats the befuddled congregation to "Pray! Please pray!" and cries out to God when her crucifix burns an impression into Andrew/Adrian's chest. Nevertheless, she bundles up her son and takes him across the country to California. Before she can arrive, however, the boy is stolen from her by, in Minnie Castevet's words, a "two-bit hooker" named Marjean whom the coven has conscripted.[5] As soon as the child is out of her arms, Rosemary disappears from the film, last seen on an empty bus, her fate out of her hands as she bangs on the glass and calls her son's name. This image haunts Andrew/Adrian's nightmares: a pure

---

2. Another film, released only three months later on New Year's Day in 1977, even more obviously exemplifies the '70s cycle's decline—John Boorman's *Exorcist II: The Heretic* is still one of the most infamous cinematic disasters of all time, receiving vitriolic pans (Vincent Canby [1977] called it "spectacular[ly] fatuous") and to this day considered among the worst films). It was pulled from theaters and recut the first week of its run, to still more derision. *Exorcist II* as a parallel narrative to *Look What's Happened to Rosemary's Baby* is an even more potent illustration of the string of letdowns emerging in horror in the late 1970s as the returned to its more commercially-oriented, non-arthouse mean, relying on the sequels and knockoffs that would become standard fare in the 1980s.

3. Adding to the melancholic resonance of this ill-fated project, *Look What's Happened to Rosemary's Baby* was directed by New Hollywood editor Sam O'steen, whose work includes *The Graduate*, *Chinatown*—and the original *Rosemary*.

4. At the same time Mia Farrow was playing Rosemary for Polanski, Patty Duke, who began her film career starring as the young Hellen Keller in *The Miracle Worker* (1962), was playing Neely, the tragic protagonist of *Valley of the Dolls* alongside Sharon Tate. Where Rosemary's interactions with occultism and Women's Lib in Polanski's film leaves her arguably more liberated than before, Neely's involvement in rock n roll counterculture in *Dolls* leaves her twice divorced, addicted to drugs, and out of work by the time she's thirty, a cautionary victim of the counterculture.

5. In another sign of the times, Marjean is played by actress Tina Louise, who also had a starring role in another film adaptation of an Ira Levin feminist classic, *The Stepford Wives*, less than a year before, in 1975.

mother he doesn't really remember. As an adult, raised under the auspices of his replacement mother (Marjean), he's drawn to the rock 'n' roll lifestyle, of which his best friend, Peter (whom he calls a "hippie Jesus freak") thoroughly disapproves.[6] Peter espouses a Christian perspective, more evangelical than Catholic, while the coven encourages Andrew/Adrian to smoke grass, drink hallucinogenic wine, and dance to rock 'n' roll because its sexuality "corrupts the innocent," a conservative characterization of the type the original film never deploys—recall, Rosemary's "hip" friends in that film are her potential way *out* of the coven.

Look What's Happened to Rosemary's Baby is an exploration of the struggle between good and evil for the soul of Rosemary's son, a boy who, the film continually points out, never had a father (or a nuclear family) to teach him right from wrong, subjected to the influence of a group of witches who share the hedonistic fruits of the counterculture with him. This theme, witches as *malevolently* disrupting the nuclear family and undermining paternal influence (as opposed to deconstructing it, often to the woman's liberatory benefit), would become all the more common in the 1980s, when fears around the rising divorce rate, single and working mothers, and "latchkey kids" arriving home to empty homes and omnipresent television sets would frequently play out in a new era of witch films, suggesting what children needed were stable homes and "traditional values." When Jack Nicholson discussed his interest in playing Jack Torrance in *The Shining* (1980), he cited as motivation his belief that the "pressure inside the family unit" would be a central, driving tension of the coming decade. While in that film Jack is blamed for his family's unhappiness, more often in the 1980s, the demonized culprit is the working or absentee mother, from *Friday the 13th* (1980) to *A Nightmare on Elm Street* (1984). By the conclusion of *Look What's Happened to Rosemary's Baby*, the morally upright Andrew (no longer Adrian) meets an attractive young doctor who offers to help him escape the mental institution where the coven has placed him. The doctor seduces him, revealing herself to be a member of the coven, raised specifically to be impregnated by Andrew with the Devil's *grand*child—for Andrew, no woman can be trusted. Where previous witch films often explicitly addressed nuanced questions of feminism, here these questions are sublimated back into archetypes, either madonnas or whores, seductresses, and she-devils, and the narratives put forward regularly center the stories of men over women.

Look What's Happened to Rosemary's Baby, for all the ways it reflects the ascendant New Right, is still a product of an era in flux, still in the shadow

---

6. "Jesus freak" is a pejorative term native to the 1960s that refers to members of the Jesus Revolution, the upswell of evangelical activism and organization that reoriented the ethos of other countercultural movements (from music to political activism) and appropriated them into a Christian mold focused on pacifism and the Bible. The word "freak", here, as in "acid freak" connotes a particular countercultural association and involvement, as is implicit in Andrew/Adrian's association of the term with the word "hippie."

of the New Age counterculture that, though waning, maintained a degree of cultural cachet. *Rocky* (1976) may have been number one at the box office that year, but *The Omen* (1976), another tale of Satanic apocalypse shot through with spiritual and political paranoia, was number six. "Feel-bad movies" like *The Omen*, which concludes with the President of the United States adopting the Antichrist, certainly reflected the attitudes and paranoias of the moment, but in the upcoming age of blockbuster filmmaking, they would no longer dominate the culture, replaced by more optimistic forms of myth-making. If the counterculture was flirting with "hip capitalism" in the early '70s, by now the transformation from "Yippie to yuppie" was complete. Jerry Rubin, who had come to countercultural prominence condemning Wall Street, could now regularly be found there, staging what he called "business Be-Ins."[7] Jane Fonda was hawking her home workout tapes and starring alongside folk icon Kris Kristofferson in *Rollover* (1981), a financial drama marketed with the tagline "The most erotic thing in their world…was money."[8]

The remnants of New Age thinking on display in the ill-conceived follow-up to Polanski's classic, would in many ways remain central to the decade to come, but, in the 1980s, these cultural forces would be downplayed and redirected into a more reactionary Christian mold. The astrologer Nancy Reagan employed to help prepare her husband's schedule from 1981 until 1988 was deliberately kept a secret, while the president's personal friendships with fundamentalist evangelical leaders like Rev. Billy Graham were highly publicized. By this time, concerns that former DJ Bob Larson had expressed in his 1971 book *Rock & Roll: The Devil's Diversion*—that occultism in "hippie communities" constituted "blasphemy"—had gone mainstream, with high-profile events like the Parents Music Resource Center's infamous Congressional hearings investigating sexually explicit and "occult" music in 1985. Taken together, these trends point to a significant piece of the puzzle in the evolution of the witch film in the 1980s, the reactionary pushback to the culmination of all these elements (sexual liberation, feminism, drugs, alternative forms of spirituality), namely: "Satanic Panic."

Throughout the '80s, parents would claim that covens of Satanists covertly ran daycare centers as a means of, among other things, practicing witchcraft, assaulting minors, using them in rituals, producing child pornography, performing thousands of forced abortions a year to "sacrifice babies," and murdering an astronomical 50,000 children each year.[9] [10] The lack of *any*

---

7. Goldstein, 2024.
8. Kristofferson, best known for his classic folk rock oeuvre, anti-war activism and presence in films like *A Star is Born* (1976), *Heaven's Gate* (1980), and *Cisco Pike* (1971), also headlined a festival billed as "Christian Woodstock" in 1972, attended by 100,000-200,000 Christian students at the beginning of the Jesus Revolution (Du Mez, 47).
9. Lanning, 1992, 3.
10. The total number of murders in the United States at this point in history according to the FBI report on Satanic Ritual Abuse is "'only' about 23,000 murders a year. Those who accept these stories of mass

evidence only fueled the belief in a massive Satanic conspiracy, termed "Satanic Ritual Abuse". These allegations, fomented by tabloid journalism and constant media coverage, from pop-psychology literature for those who claimed to have escaped from these covens to testimony from born-again "former Satanists" on TV and in paperback, became a source of global anxiety, particularly in the US, Canada, and the UK throughout the 1980s.

Satanic Panic pervaded pop culture and broadened its scope to include campaigns against "Satanic" goth and punk subcultures, cartoons with supposed hidden sexual and demonic subtext, and fantasy role-playing games like Dungeons & Dragons, which, as early as 1979, some religious groups and parents' organizations had linked to teenage suicides, murders, and the literal practice of witchcraft.[11] Primetime specials, morning news segments, paperback exposés, and reams of articles abounded. Satanic Panic was a multifaceted phenomenon, broadly synthesizing many of the overarching conservative fears of the moment in a religiously-inflected appeal to "Save Our Children", by rigidly upholding the heterosexual nuclear family against gains made by the Women's Movement and Gay Liberation. In a decade in which televangelist and Moral Majority leader Jerry Falwell called NOW "the National Order for Witches", the historical link between witches and the fear of women's empowerment (deployed as a tool of liberation by feminists during the '60s occult revival) became explicit, and used as a conservative weapon.[12]

The phenomenon of Satanic Panic was quickly understood to be a modern "witch hunt", a media-driven manifestation of the culture's social conservatism taken to its most extreme.[13] While the Panic is most famous today for its pulpy, salacious media coverage, at the time it played an instrumental role in the anti-feminist backlash; it was used as a cudgel against the working mothers whom feminism had worked so hard to empower. Following the Panic's hysterical logic, these working women had neglected their children by exposing them to childcare services. The panic also had a homophobic inflection: many of the most high-profile daycare workers accused of being "Satanists" and "warlocks" were men whom the media implied were gay pedophiles.[14] On top of all that, the panic was shot through with the period's anti-drug "Just Say No" rhetoric, with one FBI investigator claiming that Satanists regularly "seduced" teenagers into "practicing animal sacrifice" by offering them "free vodka", "free sex", and cocaine).[15]

---

human sacrifice would have us believe that the satanists and other occult practitioners are murdering more than twice as many people every year in this country as all the other murders combined." Similarly, the number of child kidnappings a year at this time was somewhere between 250 and 550 (mostly teens, not infants) (Lanning, 1992, 19, 6).
11. Allison, 2014.
12. Casta, 2004.
13. Cockburn, 1990.
14. Beck, 2015, 267.
15. Devil Worship: The Rise of Satanism, 1989.

Yet, for all of the media ubiquity of Satanic Panic, Hollywood remained remarkably quiet on the subject. In his 2011 book *Conspiracy Films: A Tour of Dark Places in the American Conscious*, Barna Williams argues that this silence from the film world had a simple explanation: who would want to see a film about child sexual abuse? "Although Satan-themed films like *The Exorcist* (1973) were major trend-setters in the '70s," he writes, "by the time a real Satanic fear was making the news, Hollywood appeared to have lost interest… [this theme] is just too gruesome a topic for 'popcorn' entertainment."[16] The drop-off in horror films about witchcraft could be put down to the combination of oversaturation, i.e. the waning of the late '60s to early-mid '70s occult revival, and a new interest in this facet of the occult whose focus on deeply gruesome supposed-crimes against children and animals made for, simply put, a bad time at the movies. As some film critics and historians have pointed out, other facets of the Panic were quickly absorbed into the horror landscape, for example a small cycle of "80s heavy metal horror" or several films in which demonic possession and new technologies are combined to explore concerns over latchkey kids' access to the world outside their parents' control via the internet, television, and dial-up services.[17] At the same time, more grounded forms of antifeminist horror filmmaking were coming to the fore in the form of erotic thrillers like *Fatal Attraction* (1987) and *Body Heat* (1981) that posited wealthy or career women as murderous destroyers of the nuclear family. Yet Satanic Panic, which explicitly depicted people as "witches", held such powerful sway over the culture that to suggest the films of the period could avoid its influence entirely would be naive.

While few of the witch films released during this period address Satanic Panic head-on, the presence of the phenomenon, frequently called an "epidemic" in the press, hangs over these texts. In his study of 1980s neo-noir, Foster Hirsch describes the looming, yet shockingly unaddressed threat of another, tragically literal epidemic in the 1980s, AIDS, as

> "background 'noise' to the conflation of sex and death in the decade's neo-noir cycle. In these films," he writes, "the traditional link in noir narratives between sex and catastrophe is no longer merely symbolic or moralistic, although no noir film has addressed AIDS directly or enlisted it as a narrative cause."[18]

For the witch films of this period of Satanic Panic, the threat presented by this classic horror monster and anti-feminist scapegoat, defined by her anti-maternal, "anti-feminine" wrath, becomes equally literal, and

---

16. Donovan, 2011, 130.
17. For more on this, see Deighan, 2016 and Ferguson, 2016.
18. Hirsch, 1999, 9.

equally unaddressed, yet nevertheless hangs over the film landscape from *Ghostbusters* (1984) to *Fatal Attraction*. While in the previous cycle, witch films demonstrated relatively consistent narrative structures, themes and motifs, here, the films form a far less coherent corpus, taking several different approaches to their subject matter that reflect both the witch film's lack of popularity *and* the shifting meanings of the witch as a symbol during this period. Much as multivalent, fraught popular cultural understandings around AIDS presented what Paula A. Treichler called "an epidemic of signification", or a "chaotic assemblage of understandings [that]... [set] forth fantasies and speculations as though they were logical deductions", using scientific and medical discourses as a legitimizer for preconceived, homophobic understandings of the disease, Satanic Panic's meanings were also "a story, or multiple stories... read to a surprising extent from a text that does not exist"—in this case a hysteria whose thorough documentation belied a fundamental lack of evidence for accusations of child abuse and Satanic ritual murder.[19] The texts that *do* exist, the witch films of the 1980s, reflect these same confusions and, in so doing, encapsulate the fraught social and psychic conflicts of the decade.

By the end of the eighties, seeds of doubt had already begun to discredit many elements of the Satanic Panic. Yet, for the witch, as well as for feminism, the damage had already been done. In tabloid TV journalist Geraldo Rivera's infamous special on the issue, *Devil Worship: Exposing Satan's Underground*, released a few days before Halloween 1988, witch films themselves are used as evidence of the scope of the Satanic "epidemic" of child abuse, further linking Hollywood filmmaking to the Panic the industry largely chose to ignore. "Remember the movie *The Exorcist*?" Geraldo asks to open one segment on real-life exorcisms. Clips from *Rosemary's Baby* in particular are highlighted again and again, played stripped of context and reframed not as a woman's struggle with her faith and her autonomy, but as further proof of the need for a federal crackdown on the specter of many of the boogeymen of the Reagan era now past, namely secularism, teenage sexuality, queer liberation, and equal rights for women thinly disguised as murderous teenage warlocks in love with heavy metal, massive covens of Satanic pedophiles, and occult abortionists infiltrating "good neighborhoods". In a section on "babies being bred for human sacrifice", Geraldo turns to a small screen: "This is no dream", Rosemary cries, expression barely legible through the snow of a VHS transfer, "this is *really happening!*"

---

19. Treichler, 1987, 11, 16, 19.

Chapter Eight

The Roots of Satanic Panic (1977-1983)

In order to understand representations of the witch in the films of the 1980s, more context on the origins of the Satanic Panic, both in film and in the broader sociocultural history of the era, is essential. While the Panic is typically understood to have taken place between 1983 and 1989, as I have already suggested, much of the cultural iconography employed during this period was a product of the previous decade. The continued presence of these older films and the politics that motivated them in the culture (in reruns, at video stores, and in Satanic Panic media), looms over the cultural production of the 1980s, recontextualizing the witch films of this era not as their own cycle but as an aesthetic and thematic *grappling* with—and, mostly, a rejection of—the previous one.

Just as in her classic book on 1980s Hollywood cinema, *Hard Bodies: Hollywood Masculinity in the Reagan Era* (1994), Susan Jeffords suggests that Ronald Reagan didn't so much cause the Reagan Revolution as "the circumstances made it possible for him to stand at the head of a changing social and political situation,"[1] the iconography of the witch films of the long sixties took on a second life in the 1980s. New meanings both informed *and* shaped the rapidly changing political and technological landscape— centrally defined here by a sweeping cultural backlash to feminism and a reinstatement of masculinist values, the rise of evangelical Christianity in politics and media, and the proliferation of cable television and VHS, technologies that brought the perceived dangers of the outside world into the home.[2] Through a brief investigation of these elements, I will argue that American culture in the late 1970s and early 1980s was the perfect place for a uniquely media-driven, politically and religiously potent hysteria like the Satanic Panic to take shape: these oft-conflicting yet strangely aligned cultural forces came together to sell Satan and his disciples at a premium, and to a public more than eager to buy.

The pervasive antifeminist sentiment of the 1980s, beyond an obviously negative reaction to women's gains, was also a reaction against the perceived feminization of *men* as a result of the more forgiving gender norms emerging from the previous decade. Anxieties around America's perceived lack of machismo bled out into what so-called "men's movement" leaders termed

---

1. Jeffords, 1994, 5.
2. *Ibid.*

a broader "crisis of masculinity" in the 1980s: "something [was] wrong" with men in the 1970s, Robert Bly explained in his 1990 book *Iron John: A Book About Men*. Though "loved by their mothers" and wives for it, "1970s males" had become dangerously soft, excessively "gentle" in a way that, per Bly, went against their nature.[3] [4] This refrain, so common to the men's movement, would be answered by Ronald Reagan, who won men's votes by three times the margin he carried women by in 1980 and in 1984, and was the choice of 71% of white males under the age of thirty, a demographic that had historically favored Democrats.[5] This shift was seismic—in 1976, by contrast, there had been no significant difference in men and women's support for either candidate.[6] [7] When asked about this gendered dynamic, one voter told the *New York Times* in 1984 that "... at work the guys stick to Reagan primarily because they see the race as women versus men."[8]

Similar calls to reinstate men's "traditional" heteropatriarchal role in society were underway in the evangelical community. By the mid-1980s, over 40% of Protestants and almost a third of all Americans described themselves as "born again".[9] This demographic quickly aligned itself with the Republican party and became a vocal and influential force in the politics of the decade through leaders like Revs. Jerry Falwell, Pat Robertson, and Jim Bakker, who organized politically with groups like The Moral Majority (founded in 1979) and Focus on the Family (founded in 1977). Reagan, their overwhelmingly preferred candidate, championed policies that facilitated the erosion of the most threatening feminist gains, becoming, for example, the first president to endorse the idea of a constitutional ban on abortion.[10] Abortion was one of many issues used by conservative politicians and evangelicals alike to adopt deliberately positive "pro-family" rhetoric. This strategy, projecting benevolence to cast opponents (in this case pro-choice feminists) as villainous, is exemplary of how Republicans commanded dominant discourse. The approach was well outlined in a *Playboy* article on televangelism from 1982 that argued that

> "[a] good part of the far right's success lies in its remarkable skill with words: 'pro-family' and 'pro-life' are an image maker's dream. Not only do they

---

3. Faludi, 2020, 77.
4. Jeffords, 1994, 7.
5. Thompson, 1989, 253.
6. "How Groups Voted in 1976", 2023.
7. Chaturvedi, 2016.
8. Dowd, 1984.
9. "The 2004 Political Landscape", 2003.
10. Interestingly, abortion was not viewed as a central issue for evangelicals until the early-mid 1970s (coinciding with *Roe v. Wade*), when it became a "unifying" force for pan-Christian activism. Prior to this period, abortion was largely viewed by this demographic as a "Catholic issue." For more on this, see D'Emilio and Freedman (2012).

raise the Jesse Helmses and Phyllis Schlaflys to a kind of sainthood but they make the rest of us seem to be anti-family and, believe it or not, anti-*life*."[11]

Film critic Andrew Britton accurately describes this same rhetorical push as "mobili[zing] the utopian imagination," a ploy that proved profoundly effective in soothing anxieties around shifting social demography (in 1980 the divorce rate in America had increased 200% since 1960 and only 3/5ths of households had a "traditional" two parent configuration), even as proposed Republican policies (banning sex education in school, eliminating no-fault divorce, etc.)[12] [13] would worsen living conditions for those most vulnerable to these shifts. At the same time, paranoid, apocalyptic mentality so often associated with fundamentalism was essential to the evangelical worldview. Falwell for example, redirected and rejected the New Age sentiments of the '60s and '70s, claiming that the 1980s would be characterized by a battle against the forces of Satan (citing the cultural liberalism that defined the Age of Aquarius); for his followers, politics during this time became a "Holy War"—one whose battlefields were often pop-cultural.[14]

The Evangelical "Holy War" on the media of the 1980s far predated the Reagan Revolution and the Satanic Panic, originating in the prior decade alongside the feminist witch films of the previous cycle.[15] Yet it wasn't until 1980, with Lawrence and Michelle Pazder's bestselling "memoir", *Michelle Remembers*, that these texts went mainstream. Described by many as the de facto Ur-text of the Satanic Panic, the discredited book recounts a year in Michelle's childhood when she claims to have been kidnapped by a satanic cult (of which her mother was purportedly a member) and routinely tortured, raped, and used in rituals to summon Satan, only to be saved by the Virgin Mary.[16] The book was written in collaboration with her therapist (and soon-to-be husband), Lawrence, who claimed that he had helped her "recover" these traumatic, previously "repressed memories" from her subconscious. Depending on its audience, *Michelle Remembers* could be a cautionary tale on daytime television or a manual for spotting signs of cult activity at law enforcement and psychology conferences. The mainstreaming of reactionary

---

11. Roeder, 1981, 102.
12. Britton, 2009, 108.
13. D'Emilio and Freedman, 2012, 331, 349.
14. *Ibid*, 349.
15. In the early 1970s, for example, members of the evangelical community began releasing "personal accounts" of induction into "satanic cults" as the Jesus Revolution began, most notably Mike Warnke's quickly discredited potboiler *The Satan-Seller* (1972), that were heavily peppered with sordid descriptions of drug addiction, animal mutilation, child rape, and human sacrifice in service of black magic. The book was a tremendous success in evangelical circles but made less of an impact on mainstream pop culture.
16. Within several years Michelle Pazder's family came out to prove that she wasn't kidnapped—her yearbook photo from the year she was supposedly missing was easily available at her elementary school. That no reporter thought to fact check Michelle Remembers speaks to the credulous political climate and superstitious mentality of the time. For more, see *Satan Wants You* (2023).

occult paranoia is of fundamental importance to both the politics and the filmmaking of this period. Ultimately, critics' suggestions that the popularity of *The Exorcist* (1973) represented "a revolt against reason and science and an inclination to search for extra-rational transcendent claims of truth" proved prescient. By the mid-80s, Isaac Asimov's quip that Friedkin's film's grip on the country "is proving... that the number of sane rational people in the world is very few" would take on startling and genuinely frightening ramifications.[17]

Hollywood in the 1980s was responding to the same (re)masculinizing and traditionalist impulses as American politics, neatly summarized by President George H.W. Bush when he claimed that "the Reagan administration changed the nation's movie preference from *Easy Rider* to *Dirty Harry*."[18] Studios had, in fact, reasserted control, with muscle men such as Arnold Schwarzenegger and Sylvester Stallone ruling the box office with entries like *Predator* (1987), *Commando* (1985), *Rambo* (1985) and *Rocky* (1976).[19] The decade's slasher cycle, which had begun taking shape in the late 1970s with the release of now-iconic entries like *Halloween* (1978) was, at least on the surface, similarly conservative.[20] These films, with their mostly male villains (who film historian Tony Williams broadly termed "[p]atriarchal avengers"), were understood by many at the time to represent the darker side of this shift towards the hard-body film, or what Andrew Britton called Hollywood's "blatant apology for the patriarchy."[21] The slasher formula popularized during this period ritualistically eliminates characters who have sex and drink or do drugs, typically leaving the virgin to survive, exemplifying a "Just Say No" attitude that lingers long after Freddy (or Jason, or Michael) has been, temporarily, vanquished.[22] Similarly, a cinematographic glorification of the aesthetics and values of the so-called "Nifty Fifties" was more firmly entrenched in the 1980s in loving paeans to suburban life like *E.T.* (1982) and *Back to the Future* (1985). These texts nostalgically valorize the American family imperiled by the slasher cycle. To quote Andrew Britton, "Nothing is

---

17. Briggs, 1974.
18. Hoberman, 2019, 324.
19. Jeffords, 1994, 24-5.
20. The exact history of the slasher cycle that became associated with the pervasive, ritualistic copycatting of its 1980s entries is often contested. For example, some cite Italian giallo films as early as the 1960s as slashers in the classic sense. Others point to *Black Christmas* (1974) as the first of this cycle. Regardless, it is clear that films with a shared "sex = death", masked killer formula came to real prominence in American horror and pop culture in the late 1970s, growing in popularity in the 1980s. Carol Clover's classic text on the slasher *Men, Women, and Chainsaws* (1992), which I employ liberally in other parts of this book, compellingly argues that the slasher can be read more progressively through the Final Girl, but here a more surface level, obvious reading is prudent—taken as a broad corpus, these texts were contemporaneously understood more by the *Scream* (1996) rules for surviving a horror movie (sex = death) rather than by their subsequent psychoanalytic reclamation.
21. Williams, 2015, 192-3.
22. Britton, 2009, 128.

easier, in the conventions of the horror-thriller, than to take the transcendent value of home and family completely for granted."[23]

In the 1980s, Hollywood also found itself facing unprecedented levels of competition from other forms of film entertainment, themselves driven by conflicting impulses and ideological uses. Home video technology (i.e. VHS) was exploding in popularity, reaching genuine ubiquity in 1985, just as the Satanic Panic was in full swing and when 50% of television households reported owning a VCR.[24] [25] As one National Institute of Health study described it, by 1982 "more Americans have television than have refrigerators or indoor plumbing."[26] This new technology, along with an expanding cable market, altered the film landscape in powerful ways, rapidly variegating sources of "news" and information with tabloid-style programming (infotainment) that would become central to the proliferation of the Satanic Panic, and allowing consumers to rewatch films—including, notably, films from previous eras—at home. In the '60s, access to witch films from earlier period was limited to the sporadic campus screening of *Häxan* (1922) or *The Wizard of Oz* (1939) on TV; now, the video store provided viewers with their first taste of cinematic instant gratification.

In his article, "Horror Movies at Home: Supernatural Horror, Delivery Systems and 1980s Satanic Panic", Drew Beard argues that this nascent phenomenon allowed the supernatural films of the 1970s to have unexpected, powerful "*afterlives* [...] haunting the public imagination far beyond the limited secondary markets faced by older films prior to the advent of cable and the VCR," thus contributing to the imagistic "feedback loop" of Satanic Panic;[27] films like *Rosemary's Baby* and *The Exorcist*, he points out, were among the first to be released on VHS and played often on cable at the height of the Panic, becoming part of the phenomenon's rhetorical framework (see Geraldo Rivera's *Devil Worship* special, described in chapter 7).[28] The cinematic "afterlives" of the supernatural films of the 1970s, particularly the witch films, became crucial as the decade progressed: the themes, iconography, and even the *plots* of these films became part of the fabric of both the Satanic Panic and of the movies, ingrained and deeply familiar, used both as a sort of "proof" of Satanic influence, and imagistically rejected and deflated in the '80s witch film, as the vestiges of a once influential (counter) culture now rendered comic and impotent.[29]

---

23. Britton, 2009, 146.
24. Hilderbrand, 2009, 36.
25. de Atley, 1985.
26. Graham, 2016, 90.
27. Beard, 2015, 212, 213.
28. *Ibid.*
29. The confluence of new technologies, politics, and paranoia in this era, and its impact on the pop-cultural and political landscape, recall Henry Jenkins' notion of "convergence culture" in the 2000s. While he bounds this form of "performative", "collective", "participatory culture" to the 2000s and beyond, his definition strongly evokes the Satanic Panic as a phenomenon: "[A] cultural shift as

Cable and VHS also gave the public much freer access to explicit sexual material than was possible before the rise of the "straight to video film" and the loosening of broadcast TV standards. While concerns around cable and VHS pornography proliferated—reaching their height in this decade with the 1986 Meese Commission study on the effects of pornographic materials on children, evangelical groups and church organizations were producing their own video content, from sermons to music videos, protesting "blasphemous" forms of secular entertainment. Citing videos like *Youth Suicide Fantasy: Does Their Music Make Them Do It?* (1985) and *Exposing the Satanic Web, Not Just Fun and Games* (1989), W. M. Conley's article, "The Tracking of Evil: Home Video and the Proliferation of the Satanic Panic", traces these forms of evangelical media production to argue that "[b]y creating a network of communication and distribution, evangelical home media was able to garner ideological legitimacy through isolating itself to other like-minded Christians," creating an echo chamber in which otherwise unbelievable claims seemed credible.[30]

The same dynamics were playing out on television: In 1984, a *Time* article cited a study estimating more than "thirteen million television viewers watched religious programming the previous year, most of it from evangelicals."[31] At the height of his viewership at the beginning of the decade, Rev. Fallwell's program *The Old-Time Gospel Hour* reached 18 million viewers; Pat Robertson's *The 700 Club* reached 16 million TV households in 1985.[32][33] "Televangelists" became a tremendous social force, both fomenting Republican social policy and the Satanic Panic. The first legal cases over "subliminal" pro-Satan messaging in 1981 stemmed from a woman who claimed to have heard about the phenomenon on *Praise the Lord*, a religious talk show hosted by televangelist Paul Crouch.[34] In 1981 Falwell's Coalition for Better Television threatened to boycott the networks for their sexual content and "immoral" depictions of violent behavior and drug use because, as John Brackett puts it in his article on Satanic Panic and rock music, "repeated exposure to morally objectionable behavior and images on network television had a *direct*, negative influence on America's

---

consumers are encouraged to seek out new information and make connections among dispersed media content", ultimately leading to strange outcomes when "the power of the media producer and power of the media consumer interact in unpredictable ways" (2012, 2-3). He points to the 1980s as the beginning of the media consolidation that eventually makes convergence possible, but again, his suggestion that, in a convergence culture, "new media and old media... interact in even more complex ways" rather than linearly superseding one another, brings to mind the cinematic "afterlives" at the heart of the Satanic Panic's television and tabloid media ecosystem (11, 6). This idea will become progressively more salient to the witch in my book, when I draw connections between the Satanic Panic as a media system in the '80s and QAnon in the late 2010s and early 2020s.
30. Conley, 2016, 234.
31. Hughes, 2017, 711.
32. D'Emilio and Freedman, 2012, 350.
33. Buursma, 1985.
34. Brackett, 2018, 277.

youth."[35] Meanwhile, as the decade progressed, shows on Christian networks openly discussed graphic allegations of sexual violence against children and pregnant women and promoted religious videotapes that included images of real naked bodies, dead animals, and mutilated murder victims.[36] [37]

Like evangelical texts concerning satanic cults, concern over television's corrupting pull on the young was also not new: a 1972 Surgeon General's Report titled "Television and Growing Up: The Impact of Televised Violence" cited a "suspicion that there was a direct line from too much childhood television watching to delinquency and a rising crime rate."[38] However in the 1980s, this anxiety was less about violent behavior and more about thinly veiled fears for the very souls of America's children. Early examples of panic over rock music and its supposed link to Satanism and suicide were made in arguments over proposed bills banning "backmasking", or the inclusion of messages audible only when a record is played backwards, California Assemblyman Paul Weyman cited the "risk" that such messages "can manipulate our behavior without our knowledge or consent and turn us into disciples of the Antichrist."[39]

If, as *Michelle Remembers* co-author Lawrence Pazder put it, Satanists' sexual abuse of children was at base about "destroying faith in God," the fears on display in religiously motivated attempts to regulate these new media phenomena were about *maintaining* that same faith, come Hell or high water.[40] And these moral crusades had a tremendous impact across the creative spectrum even *before* the Parents Music Resource Center began its 1985 clampdown on "filthy" music.[41] Michael Jackson's iconic 1982 video for his spooky single, "Thriller", sold 9 million copies, but after Jehovah's Witnesses threatened Jackson with excommunication, he added a disclaimer: "Due to my strong personal convictions, I wish to stress that this film in no way endorses a belief in the occult."[42] [43] This sort of caution pervaded the decade.[44]

---

35. Brackett, 2018, 275-6.
36. "The Devil Worshippers" (1985). *20/20*. ABC News Productions.
37. "Devil Worship: Exposing Satan's Underground." The Geraldo Rivera Show. (1988).
38. Graham, 2016, 88.
39. "Rock Demons", 1982, 53-54.
40. "The Devil Worshippers", 1985.
41. The committee was responsible for, among other things, championing the "Parental Advisory" sticker on music.
42. Rusnack, 2016, 194.
43. Griffin, 2010.
44. Controversies around perceived "blasphemies" in music videos also encompassed non-occult displays of sexuality and uses of religious iconography: Madonna's music video for "Like a Prayer", originally intended to be sponsored by Pepsi and shown during primetime at the 1989 Super Bowl, was pulled from its slot and chopped up to avoid showing (among other things) images of Madonna kissing a Black saint in a church and singing in front of burning crosses. The Vatican even attempted to facilitate a Catholic boycott of Madonna's tour that year. The video nevertheless received MTV Video Music Awards' Video of the Year (Lambe, 2019).

Through a combination of new media technologies and religious revivalism, the stage had been set for a broader witch hunt that spanned from America's living rooms to its classrooms, and eventually, to its courts. But as concerns around "backmasking" in metal albums and "repressed" memories of cannibalistic covens would suggest, these battles were being waged both on a highly public stage and, its proponents insisted, on the subliminal level of ambiguous signifiers and tacit influence. Witch films of this period should be understood as having been contemporaneously received in this context and, within it, on the terms of the occult revival gone to seed. To quote the 1972 federal report on TV and violence, "It would be desirable to look upon television drama and cartoon programs—crude as they may be—as *folk literature*...[and] to investigate the latent symbolic 'messages' that even violent television plays and cartoons may convey."[45]

The films of the turn of the decade (loosely between 1977 and 1983) reflect the transition taking place across the culture and cannot be accurately described as a "cycle". As a corpus they are contradictory and form a bricolage of a culture in turmoil as the film and television industries adapted to new political circumstances. To reflect the scattershot nature of this period for the witch film, I've selected three films whose histories are themselves scattershot, and that *failed* to attract the public interest. I do so in order to set the stage both for later films (providing a roadmap to the base elements that become denser and more confusing as the Panic breaks into the mainstream in 1984,) and to ask, given this charged environment, why did these movies fail?

The Devonsville Terror (1983) has all the experimental flourishes and sharp feminist bonafides of some of the past decade's strongest entries, but its eventual focus on its male characters' perspectives signals the genre had definitively changed direction by the early 1980s. Directed by Rainer Werner Fassbinder and Andy Warhol collaborator Ulli Lommel, this dreamy, heavily Freudian low-budget film, shot in Wisconsin in 1982, fell almost immediately into the video store discount bin.[46] Inspired by the Salem Witch Trials, the director set out to make an explicitly "feminist film"—a stark contrast to almost all the '80s films to come in this subgenre.[47] [48] The narrative blends historical persecution with modern antifeminism through the stories of three young, college-educated working women whose move to a small town foments a violent conservative reaction. The film opens in 1693 with several

---
45. Graham, 2016, 89, emphasis added.
46. Beauparlant, 1982.
47. "Interview with Ulli Lommel", 2016.
48. The film was co-written with Lommel's partner Suzanna Love in a rare instance of women's involvement behind the camera in witch films during this period (though Love plays down the degree of her involvement with the script in interviews ("God Is A Woman", 2016).

slasher-style scenes of witch burning and torture, here framed as acts of sexually sadistic gendered violence (one woman is killed after being caught having sex with her lover and refusing her tormentors' advances). Replete with uncomfortably wide-lensed closeups from the scantily-clad victims' perspectives, the film emphasizes the lascivious expressions of the women's tormentors who eagerly demand they recount their erotic encounters with the Devil, making an otherwise conventional sequence of titillation into an indictment of violence against women.

In the present, the male descendants of these hypocritical, erstwhile Puritans—themselves characterized as morally bereft, clannish and unpleasant—sit around their kitchen table after one of them delivers the Sunday sermon and discuss the anniversary of these past atrocities. They insist that they're "very, *very* different" from their ancestors, even as they complain about their unfortunate legacy rather than acknowledging the actual harm their families inflicted. Their own chauvinism becomes murderous when Walter (Paul Wilson), the head of the clan and the town's pharmacist, smothers his bedridden wife to death, annoyed with her chronic illness. Soon, Jenny (Suzanna Love) arrives in town to teach at the small school and meets Walter at his pharmacy. The man immediately feels entitled to Jenny's sexual attention, imagining her naked and as his fawning, doting housewife in a series of hallucinatory vignettes, soon stalking her in the evenings.

For the rest of the film, Jenny and her two friends, Chris (Mary Walden) and Monica (Deanna Haas), become a lightning rod for the town as they are systematically harassed, their homes encroached upon, and their livelihoods—eventually their lives—threatened. Jenny's central transgression touches on a classic conservative issue, religion in school, when she answers a little girl's question "Is God a man or a woman?" with a nuanced response citing multiple cultures' deities and systems that evoke radical feminist thinking, concluding that "It's only in fairly recent history since Judaism that God the Father has taken over." In a town whose witches were burned for "not having the fear of God in their heart," this response is met with accusations of blasphemy and lesbianism. Jenny's two friends also represent different '70s-coded liberal values (one is an EPA scientist testing the water for pollution and the other is a radio DJ who uses her advice talk show to introduce housewives to feminism, in one case instructing a caller to tell her husband to "take a hike!"). Though other women faintly try to support these three, the men, led by the descendants of the Puritan inquisitors, begin to reject them, calling them "witches" in a direct invocation of the persecution their families enacted.[49] Walter quickly decides to kill them. As tensions rise, everyone is plagued by dreams of the town's past crimes (presented

---

49. In a 2016 interview, Suzanna Love describes the shoot as echoing these dynamics, with the cast and crew being refused service at coffee shops in Tomahawk, Wisconsin where they filmed "because we looked like hippies." ("God Is A Woman")

in a characteristically '70s manner as psychedelic visions complete with kaleidoscopic colors, flash cuts, slow dissolves, and inserts of mushrooms), while Walter is inflamed by dreams of sexual teasing and humiliation by these attractive, liberated "witches."[50]

Thus far, the film effectively blends the conventions of the '80s slasher with '70s feminist messaging about the relationship between sexual liberation, feminism, and witchcraft accusations. The most powerfully feminist element of *Devonsville* is that the accused women have no guilt or shame for their independence. Unlike Rosemary Woodhouse or Joan Mitchell (George Romero's frustrated housewife in *Season of the Witch* [1973]), who struggle with Nel Noddings' "paradox of womanhood", and eventually *become* agents in their own stories, the women of *Devonsville* are *already* feminists, knowledgeable about this history of women's persecution and willing to enact change not only for themselves but for other women.[51]

Yet, the film weakens its stance by centering the story of the town's patrician doctor, Dr. Warley (Donald Pleasance, Père Dominic in *Eye of the Devil* [1966] and Michael Myers' doctor in *Halloween*), above those of the women. Dr. Warley narrates large stretches of the film, lamenting his own family's involvement in the 17th-century murders. His guilt, he tells us, manifests in a "curse": worms that systematically eat away at his flesh when new instances of persecution arise and that will eventually kill him if he can't help these new victims. It is *his* investigation into the new crop of femicides, as well as Walter's committing them, that drive the plot forward, leaving the women largely passive for long stretches of the film. The literal gnawing guilt at his family's historical, murderous misogyny is elegantly illustrated at various opportunities as representative of men's tangle of desire and rage. One well-drawn scene shows a hypnotized man describing the motivations behind his family's violence by responding to the question, "Why does she deserve to die? Why do you feel so good she's dying?" with a frank description of the connection he feels between masculinist rage, resentment, and sexual desire: "She wouldn't let me... it's her own fault... she teased me... she turned me on..."

---

50. *Devonsville*'s use of psychedelic imagery is also connected to the subgenre's countercultural past through Jenny's lessons to the children—her discussion of God's gender takes place during a lesson on mushrooms and mycelia networks. She concludes, before telling the children that God is a woman, that "mother nature always builds out of decay" in a manner that already suggests a broader rejection of Christian frameworks, a rejection solidified at the film's conclusion when the witch's ghost, possessing Jenny, takes retribution on the Christian townsmen.

51. The choice to cast the third woman as an environmental activist is another characteristically '70s touch in the film, which links the men of the town's reticence to accept these women with their investment in the capitalistic destruction of their lived environment through deforestation. This connection also serves, for the townspeople, to link the women to stereotypes around femininity's closeness to nature, an element used in witch lore to render witches as uncontrollable, dangerous, and abject for their lack of "civilized" domestication *and* tie them to the past era's counterculture—one man venomously calls this character a "nature freak".

The film's commentary on violence and misogyny, so clear in its depictions of men's anxieties and women's persecution, gets watered down by the conventional slasher plot that eventually takes center stage, and by the eventual imbalance in perspectives. By the film's conclusion, the previously strong female characters are either dead or in states of supernatural passivity: Jenny is routinely hypnotized by Dr. Warley, who discovers through "past life regression" late in the film that she is the psychic descendant of one of the murdered witches, a contrivance that undercuts the film's larger feminist allegory in which men paint *any* "rowdy" woman as a witch in a sexist world.[52] The men, for their part, lose some of their nuanced characterizations, becoming generic murderers or saviors rather than people with complex psychology. While the commentary in the film is clear, it gets lost in its final passages.

It is possible to see this shift towards men's stories as a bellwether for the future of the subgenre, though even then, the film's depiction of men's guilt at their own power, their contradictory fear at the encroaching loss of it, and their sexual frustration at the prospect of empowered women is far more direct than the decade's later entries. Nevertheless, *Devonsville*'s capitulation to generic convention ultimately kneecaps its effectiveness as a feminist allegory: a possession plot takes over as Jenny's body is inhabited by the angry ghost of the dead witch who smites her captors with lasers from her eyes.[53] Jenny, the only woman to survive, leaves town without a final word, while Dr. Warley egotistically (and ham-fistedly) narrates over pages from his diary, "I am redeemed. The Warley curse of the worms is cured. All who were guilty are gone or soon to be brought to Justice. The Devonsville Terror is over." This flaccid elision of the women's presence (particularly given that two out of the three are dead) and emphasis on a man's redemption exemplifies the tensions on display in the film. A story that began as a metaphor for gendered guilt and culpability is reduced to a man literally saving his own skin. Nevertheless, it's unlikely that any of Lommel's intended feminist arguments were appreciated by audiences at the time: *The Devonsville Terror* was never theatrically released due to a series of lawsuits over rights between production companies and eventually appeared on VHS in 1983, sandwiched between fare like *Deadly Eyes* (a Canadian cheapie about giant rats) and *Friday the 13th Part II* (1981) in promotional material. This sort of haphazard marketing and unceremonious

---

52. It's ironic that, as with many of the films in this period, though many of its characters' politics center around tacit forms of hippie-bashing, these same conservative figures also engage in New Age practices like "past life regression", a discredited therapeutic practice that was, along with ESP and telepathy, treated with some credulity in the 1970s.

53. The possession narrative here is at least inflected with the same feminist rage that tinges the rest of the film, unlike other more high-profile iterations that had already come to characterize much of the decade's highest-grossing horror films: the year of *The Devonsville Terror*'s production, *Amityville II: The Possession* (1982) made a strong showing while *Poltergeist* (1982) dominated the box office for weeks, ending the year with a spot in the box office top ten.

release all but guaranteed that the film would not reach a broad audience interested in more than its status as one of countless slashers to watch with friends on a Friday night.[54]

Not only directors with arthouse bonafides were taking a stab at the witch film in the early 1980s; B-movie directors and '60s and '70s exploitationeers with a nose for a quick profit likewise turned to the genre, finding their hopes similarly dashed in the face of changing cultural headwinds even as they took diametrically opposed approaches to the subject matter. Bert I. Gordon, the low-budget genre draftsman best known for his giant monster movies (*The Amazing Colossal Man* [1955], *Empire of the Ants* [1977]), had first turned to witch horror in the early 1970s with *Necromancy*, the story of a man (a depressingly befuddled Orson Welles) who, consumed by the death of his son, turns to black magic to resurrect him via human sacrifice. This film has many of the tenets of that cycle, with a strong female lead, psychedelic sequences, and elliptical editing. In 1981, Gordon returned to the witch genre with *The Coming* (titled *Burned at the Stake* on VHS). The film's plot is somewhat like *The Devonsville Terror*, with a frame narrative in the 1690s and a possession narrative in the present. Also like *Devonsville*, the film draws parallels between capitalism, conservatism, and the misogyny of witch crazes, though in this case greed is foregrounded as the film presents another religious hypocrite as the true villain: in a re-imagining of the Salem Witch Trials, Reverend Parris (John Peters) manipulates Ann Putnam (Susan Swift), into condemning her peers in order to consolidate power and claim their land. This choice shapes the historical record to elevate economic and misogynistic context through this narrative of greed—"witches" did lose their land when accused, though there is no evidence of the overt, outlined plot the film depicts. In the present, a young girl, Loreen (also Susan Swift) becomes possessed by a spirit whom her mother comes to realize is the ghost of Ann Putnam. Her possession, clearly a miniature rehash of *The Exorcist*, deteriorates in a predictable manner and leads to violent behavior that (unfortunately) takes up much of the film's runtime.

As in *The Devonsville Terror*, the film decenters the women's narratives in favor of a man's, attempting to explore questions of guilt and responsibility for past harms but never truly succeeding. In the film's alternative history, Dorcas Goode, the youngest person accused during the real witch trials, is executed. The spirit of her father, William Goode (David Rounds), appears in the present to exonerate his daughter, revealing Ann's false accusations to Loreen and her mother and thus becoming the film's heroic protagonist. This dense, muddled narrative seems aimed to attract viewers of possession films, supernatural and psychological thrillers, science fiction and slashers alike in one 85-minute jumble. As if to illustrate this, a haphazard slasher

---

54. "Halloween Horror Film Weekend", 1983.

plot is introduced midway through the film—again recentering the story of a male policeman searching for the killer—which ultimately reveals that the ghost of Rev. Parris, the original instigator, is the murderer and that Ann's ghost is trying to help correct the same historical injustice as William Goode, astral projecting back to the 17th century to save Dorcas. Here a modern witch is introduced as a comic sidekick to William and the police investigator—helping save Loreen from her possession and helping Ann's ghost save Dorcas as well—depicted as a mildly ridiculous, overly serious, wildly eccentric goth who nevertheless aims to save the day. This is an extreme departure from the powerful and threatening witches of '60s and '70s films like *Season of the Witch*. At the film's climax, the Rev. is exposed, and William Goode and Ann Putnam are sent back to the past, spirits at rest.

Though initially scheduled for theatrical release, like Lommel's film, *The Coming* was instead pushed to television in 1981, playing sporadically during off hours, again eliminating much of its potential audience.[55] Even more than in *Devonsville*, the men's are the more propulsive stories. The witches themselves are depicted as cartoonish oddballs with names like "Merlina". In the end, the family is restored in both timelines, elevating the centrality of traditional values over the ostensibly progressive narrative of political and religious corruption that, the film argues, incited the Salem Witch Trials. The descent into generic convention, begun with the conclusion of *Devonsville*, comes into full flower in *The Coming*, an overstuffed, quasi-feminist picture that seems to epitomize a horror landscape in transition.

While both *The Devonsville Terror* and *The Coming* were still languishing in post-production, another, more conservative, film finally had its television release after years of delays. *Witches' Brew* (1983), like *The Coming*, was at base a product of an earlier era. Though its director, Richard Shorr, would win an Academy Award in 1988 for his sound editing on *Die Hard*, when production began on *Witches' Brew* (set to be an NBC Movie of the Week in 1978) his highest-level credit to date was sound-editing a 1973 grindhouse-style rock 'n' roll horror musical called *Son of Dracula*, starring Ringo Starr. The task of directing the film proved too much for Shorr, who was eventually barred from set after numerous "yelling" conflicts with Lana Turner, who co-starred. After NBC halted production for a year, prolific TV and B-science-fiction director Herbert L. Strock (whose credits read similarly to Bert I. Gordon's—*I Was a Teenage Frankenstein* [1957], *The Crawling Hand* [1963]), was brought on to finish the film, reshooting long stretches and overseeing its editing.[56] The completed film was never theatrically released, nor was it the NBC Movie of the Week. Instead, it played sporadically on cable at odd hours before appearing on video store shelves in 1985.[57]

---

55. unkle lancifer, 2013.
56. Weaver, 1999, 329-30.
57. Lor, 1985.

Where *The Coming* is most notable for its muddled feminism and adoption of slasher and time travel elements, *Witches' Brew* is most notable for its steadfast retrogradeness and trite misogyny—and its source material.[58] The film is an adaptation of *The Conjure Wives*, the same book from which *Night of the Eagle* was adapted in 1962; the differences between the two adaptations are stark, and deeply telling of the direction the country's politics had moved in the intervening decade. It follows a housewife, Margaret (Teri Garr, between her role in *Close Encounters of the Third Kind* and her Oscar nomination for *Tootsie*) locked in a battle of the sexes with her college professor husband Joshua (Richard Benjamin), who refuses to acknowledge the influence her hobbyist magical practice has on the success of his career. Haphazardly blending screwball comedy and surreal possession horror, the film depicts the couple's lives coming dangerously unraveled when Margaret undoes all of her prosperity spells on the eve of a big promotion. Halfhearted hijinks ensue, with Joshua facing misfortunes ranging in size from a shaving cut to an attempted assassination, as he refuses to acknowledge his wife's influence. While in theory a crash course in appreciating the lengths to which a stay-at-home wife goes in order for a working man's life to work could serve as a critique of condescending paternalism, the film instead opts to present witchcraft as both a trivial hobby and a dangerous, often disgusting practice to be avoided, throwing into direct tension two representations of the witch that will become fundamental as the decade wears on. Joshua demeans his wife and her magic at every turn, laughing at her and demanding she spend "less time on [her] hobby and more time being a wife" when she gives him cereal for breakfast (he throws it at a wall) and growing frustrated when she insists she's capable of more than accompanying him to faculty dinners. Nowhere to be found are the philosophical concerns at the heart of Sidney Hayers' AIP adaptation, which probed questions of belief through a gendered lens, presenting the couple as (more or less) intellectual equals, doing field research together; here, the story's marital conflict hinges on the retrograde notion that a woman's place is in the kitchen. The film's sympathies clearly lie with Joshua over Margaret, reveling in his misfortunes for his lack of belief, but presenting the witchcraft that evidently protects him from catastrophic harm as ridiculous and childish—Margaret chants her nonsense-syllable spells with the broadly comedic gravity of Vincent Price, covers her husband in bat guano, and leaves him to sit out under the moon rolling his eyes. The film practically begs for a sitcom laugh-track.

The paternalism of Margaret's treatment is matched by the film's denigration of its other female characters. One of these, a student named Joanna (Ellen Farran), is presented as a 1960s-style "radical" student activist

---

58. Lor, 1985. Though one of the few reviews I was able to find of the film, which the author begins by stating was only written "for the record", insists that the film's "key point of historical interest" is its shared plot points with the Steve Martin/Lily Tomlin vehicle *All of Me* (1984).

sporting a mullet and a black turtleneck. When Joshua fails her for the semester, she retaliates by attempting to assassinate him with a sniper rifle. Similarly, all the other faculty wives (headed by "Vivian", Lana Turner in her final film role) are presented as conniving, untrustworthy power-seekers with no moral compass, summoning the Devil to win their husbands' or sons' promotion and spend the raise themselves. These women's spells are presented in more surreal, threatening fashion than Margaret's, introducing a stylistic schism between magic more aligned with the aesthetics of the '70s witch cycle (these may not be housewives with a chip on their shoulders practicing sexual, psychedelic magic, but they're certainly a sitcom-appropriate, G-rated echo) and magic safely confined to the strictures of helpful witch housemates, like those in *Bewitched* (1964-1972) and the 1950s classic of domestic house-witchery, *Bell, Book and Candle* (1958), ultimately rejecting the more modern witch depiction so soundly as to destroy her entirely.

These elements present Margaret's helpful spellcasting as a sort of barrier that not only upholds the nuclear family (the film ends with a magical ceremony to ensure their next child is a boy) but protects Joshua from the machinations of various liberal boogeymen, from feminist radicals to gay men—in what is structurally presented as the ultimate humiliation, a male student accuses Joshua of sexual harassment. In this sense, Margaret's magic is a patriarchal tool and cover to confirm Joshua's heterosexuality, as well as make him breakfast and help him get that promotion. But Joshua's rejection of her magic is also a form of cosmic realignment and re-masculinization, a contrast to the other passive husbands reminiscent of Robert Bly's invective against the "soft" men of the '70s. As the film progresses, Margaret loses control over her magic, and by extension the narrative, when Vivian performs a body swapping ritual to take possession of her body in a quest for youth. Joshua eventually learns of the possession and the mounting danger and reads up on his witchcraft in order to save the day and his wife, now a damsel in distress. He eventually performs a spell Margaret herself couldn't and burns Vivian to death, excising the evil from their home and restoring their family to order. By violently punishing other witches for wielding power out of their own self-interest as opposed to their male family members, and by depicting Joshua as ultimately *more* magically competent than Margaret when called upon, the seeming return of "balance" and "respect" Margaret earns from Joshua is profoundly undercut, painting women as fundamentally subordinate to their husbands in an almost literal return the "Nifty Fifties". *Witches' Brew*'s final line breezily summarizes the film's ultimate message, a far cry from the source material's tortured ambiguity that rejects the notion that the couple was anything other than perfectly happy before their brush with devilish feminism: "I'm so glad things are back to normal."

With these three examples—early 80s films whose low-budget exploitation-style productions emphasize elements deemed (correctly or not) to be profitable and engaging to audiences of the period—I aim to highlight several key elements of the witch films at this moment of cultural realignment. These key elements are: 1) overt examinations of women's roles often shot through with conservatism, a dynamic I will come to describe as a "veneer of feminism", 2) an emphasis on the male characters that often undercuts any genuine female subjectivity, 3) cross-genre bricolage (science fiction elements, liberal use of variegated, often disconnected horror tropes, overt and broad use of comedy, etc.), and 4) temporal or narrative distancing (i.e. frame narratives, time travel plots, epistolary forms) that hold the threat of witchcraft at somewhat of a distance. As the Satanic Panic shoots into the public consciousness and Hollywood produces some of its biggest successes in "popcorn" filmmaking, these elements will both remain and take new forms as other new tropes—ones which I will argue also define the state of feminism and the mentality behind the Satanic Panic—begin to dominate the subgenre. All three of these films were commercial disasters. The concerns they attempted to embody were very much on the public's mind—concerns about women's roles, concerns over children's education and religion's role in public life as the evangelical movement gained political purchase. Yet they failed to catch on. Satan was selling, but not this way. America needed a new nightmare—a new scapegoat—and, soon, they'd find one.

In March 1984, after several months of frenzied police activity, almost the entire faculty of the McMartin Preschool in Manhattan Beach, California, was charged with a collective 115 counts of child abuse against over forty young children in their care. These arrests were initiated in mid-1983 by a set of bizarre allegations against a male teacher named Ray Buckey by Judy Johnson, the mother of a two-year-old at the school. She soon claimed that Buckey and the other teachers at the preschool were "witches" who drank blood, wore black robes, could fly, and who used her son and his classmates in violent, sexual, Satanic rituals intended to summon the Devil. Johnson, it was eventually revealed, was a diagnosed schizophrenic, self-medicating with alcohol; she would be found dead from liver failure just two years into the trial.[59] [60] But the shocking persecution of the McMartin family that resulted from her feverish accusations spanned the remainder of the 1980s and captivated America's imagination, serving as a bellwether for the nation's fascination with Satanic cults in general. The next chapter will explore how this fascination seeped into the witch films of this decade, occluded by a veneer of feminism.

---

59. Beck, 2015, 109.
60. Hughes, 2017, 692.

Chapter Nine

Backlash, Comedy, and the Witch Film

> "Women are discovering they *can't* have it all."
> -Paul Weyrich, 1988[1]

Witches were everywhere and nowhere in the films of the 1980s, and this chapter will investigate their most prominent iterations. In the straight horror films of the 1980s, witches in the traditional sense were rarely the central villains. As antifeminist backlash realigned discourses around women's "empowerment", an ethos of so-called "postfeminism" began to pervade, suggesting that women had already achieved equality, *and* that any more freedom would only harm them. The Satanic Panic employed these same discourses as a cudgel against working women (female teachers and the "negligent" mothers who remitted their children into their care were cast as witches). The culture more broadly was also leveling a similar set of complaints against horror films, often by presenting them as "pornographic". This chapter will investigate the witch films of this era on these terms, situating them in the conflictingly inflammatory and placatory discourses of the backlash and Satanic Panic, particularly in the arenas of the supernatural comedy and the erotic thriller.

Susan Faludi's 1991 book on the state of feminism in the 1980s, *Backlash: The Undeclared War Against American Women*, begins with a paradox: according to the media, feminism had achieved its goals by 1980, yet "behind the news, cheerfully and endlessly repeated, that the struggle for women's rights is won, another message flashes. You may be free and equal now, it says, but you have never been more miserable."[2] Her explanation of this rhetoric, backed up through careful case studies, is that mass media in the '80s insisted that "women are unhappy precisely *because* they're free. Women are enslaved by their own liberation," a contention made as a response to the progress women were *still* making in the 1980s.[3] The decade saw a tremendous surge in women's employment (including to higher office), the passage of no-fault divorce laws in all but two states (New York and South Dakota), more women receiving higher education, the expansion

---

1. In Faludi, 2020, 242, emphasis added.
2. Faludi, 2020, 1.
3. *Ibid*, 2.

of Title IX,[4] and an increased awareness of marital rape and spousal abuse.[5] Women in the workforce represented a particular strain on heteropatriarchal gender roles and masculinist cultural hegemony—a primary source of this fear that, Faludi argues, spurred backlash.

Within this paradox—feminism's continued gains in the face of adversity and the media apparatus that suggested the feminist movement had already "ended"—lies the birth backlash (and what some would soon call postfeminism), a rollback not only of women's legal rights, but, almost more centrally, a breezy dismissal of even the *need* for those rights and dignities in the court of public opinion. Faludi calls the backlash an "insidious" "preemptive strike" "triggered by the perception—accurate or not—that women are making great strides" before larger social change can truly be made, "designed to make women think that the hard work is over."[6] This backlash in popular culture leads to a "feedback loop" that parallels the discourses of Satanic Panic, using the media infrastructure to shore up the legitimacy of antifeminism, thus swaying public opinion in a manner that specifically delegitimates women's employment, and thus, their material and emotional independence. She analyzes, for example, rafts of articles in outlets like *Time* and *Newsweek* amplifying a study (even after it had been discredited) that warned women of a "marriage crunch", under which single women above thirty-five had only a 5% chance of marriage that by forty dropped to a miniscule 1.3%.[7] Meanwhile, newscasters warned of "a full-scale female invasion" of the workforce, and doctors began calling endometriosis a "career woman's disease", in essence suggesting, along with the marriage study, that working could ruin a woman's chance at ever having a family life.[8] The narrative around these studies was presented as a sort of pro-woman warning: women don't *want* to be lonely, thus, these stories are *helping* women's lives and protecting their futures by getting them out of the workforce *before it's too late*.

Faludi cites women reporting they hadn't been thinking about getting married or having children at all until coverage of these fictitious "trends", reiterated in countless outlets and in wildly successful films like *When Harry Met Sally* (1989), that told them to fear their "biological clock."[9][10] Meanwhile, a study *Newsweek* left unpublished until years later found that "71 percent of mothers at home wanted to work, and 75 percent of the working mothers

---

4. A landmark 1972 law prohibiting sex-based discrimination from schools and businesses receiving federal funding.
5. A spate of laws passed in the '80s addressed violence against women in a variety of forms, from the 1985 Family Violence Prevention and Response Act and the designation of October as Domestic Violence Awareness Month in 1989.
6. Faludi, 2020, 10-11.
7. *Ibid*, 25, 43.
8. *Ibid*, 53.
9. *Ibid*, 33.
10. Sally: "I just said to myself, you deserve more than this, you're 31 years old and the clock is ticking."

said they would work even if they didn't need the paycheck." The outlet, after shelving this survey, instead continued publishing stories asserting that "the myth of the Supermom is fading fast—doomed by anger, *guilt*," that is, guilt at leaving their children in the care of someone else like a daycare provider, "and exhaustion".[11] These campaigns to delegitimize feminist gains, along with the evangelical right's more explicit "pro-family" anti-feminism, paint feminism as the source of women's suffering rather than of self-fulfillment, particularly in the realm of employment. This turn, like the witch hunts of the Middle Ages, highlights the link between the figure of the witch and the threat women's empowerment poses to heteropatriarchal capitalism: when women make financial gains, they become witches whose femininity, maternal instincts, and sexuality become suspect. The backlash could be seen as working to reinstate exactly the form of internalized guilt and moralized self-regulation that plagued characters like Rosemary: Nel Noddings' Christian "paradox of womanhood" in a new form. Unfortunately, the rhetorical turn on the label "feminist" can also be linked to the "sex wars" between sex-positive (or "pro-sex") feminism and anti-porn feminism at the time. The former, led by figures like Gayle Rubin and Ellen Willis, continued to champion women's sexual liberation while the latter, headed by the likes of Catherine McKinnon and Andrea Dworkin, argued that most forms of sexual expression (but particularly pornography and sexualized advertising and film) were violence against women. This latter, more conservative contingent aided and fomented the backlash, eventually becoming synonymous in the public consciousness with the label "feminist" and thus giving the impression that feminism itself was "no fun".[12]

Nevertheless, backlash was, and remains to this day, primarily perpetuated by men. A 1988 American Male Opinion Index poll found that "no more than 5 to 10 percent of the men surveyed 'genuinely support women's demands for independence and equality'", "less than one fourth of men supported the women's movement", and that "the most substantial share of the growth in men's support for feminism may have occurred in the first half of the '70s, in that brief period when women's 'lib' was fashionable".[13] The question of feminism's status as "fashionable" is essential to understanding the mechanism of backlash—a succinct way of demonstrating that feminism had already "won" was to posit it as out of touch, out of style, boring, and

---

11. Faludi, 2020, 103, emphasis added.
12. Sex-positive feminists were largely ignored by the mainstream media and culture (for being "sluts") or delegitimized, as in the case of sexologist Shere Hite, precisely for their sexuality. Hite's explosively popular 1978 book on female sexuality, *The Hite Report*, suggested that the majority of women don't achieve orgasm through penetration alone—a fact that proved threatening to heterosexual men who smeared her for this finding. Her 1981 book on male sexuality similarly suggested men feel pressure to perform, lack intimacy, and find patriarchal heteromasculinity damaging and isolating. Hite was eventually driven out of the country entirely after it was revealed that she had posed for *Playboy*, a fact used to discredit her as a serious thinker. For more on this, see *The Disappearance of Shere Hite* (2023).
13. Faludi, 2020, 74, emphasis added.

even a little silly. This rhetorical move ties into the use of comedy in the witch film and will become central to how the witch (an already feminist-associated symbol as the films of the 1960s cycle and early '80s films like *The Devonsville Terror* [1983] demonstrate) is depicted, as I will describe in the pages to come.

By the mid-'80s, damage to feminism's image was done, and the paradox of womanhood was returning to the public consciousness, even if women didn't leave the workforce or the single life *en masse* as was so hopefully predicted. A December 1984 *Time* cover story entitled "Sex in the '80s: The Revolution Is Over", suggested that, largely thanks to women realizing they'd been "*tricked*" by the sexual revolution "into playing the *male*'s game of easy sex, in the 1980s, [a] sexual revolutionary at a party, chattering on earnestly about sex as a natural function, a panacea and the cutting edge of social change, would quickly end up standing alone." Even as the article self-congratulatingly points out that "[t]he sexual revolution has not been rebuffed, merely absorbed into the culture," it continues to emphasize women's investment in traditionalism by insisting that even among "females exposed to the heaviest *antifamily* criticisms" of the '70s, in Reagan's America, "marriage became something hip, ambitious women could do." This argument presents the counterculture (and by extension feminists "tricked" into enjoying sex) as boring (and masculine) and monogamy (and conservative values) as "hip" (and feminine); it reasserts traditionally gendered expectations of behavior with the language of a fashion trend, and folding in conservative presentations of feminist sexual liberation as anti-family at the same time—the uncouth "revolutionary" at the party, male or female, is replaced with a new "trendsetter", the monogamous woman.

Here we see that the paradox of womanhood, reiterated through the '80s culture of backlash, had evolved: because the gains women were making proved impossible to ignore, as the insistence on feminism's "absorption" into the culture attests, these excerpts demonstrate the way antifeminist backlash necessarily includes empowering language for women—a veneer of feminism. This move was in part supported by a real wing of conservative feminists (anti-porn advocates), who, by aligning themselves with evangelical activists and conservatives on these issues, inadvertently imply that traditionalism was inherently feminist, in women's best interest. The *Time* article cheerfully concludes that, by 1984, "[t]here is much talk of pendulum swings, matters coming full circle and a psychic return to prerevolutionary days," declaring, "We are in a '50s period again." As Faludi put it, articles like these popularized the sense that "[f]eminist anger, or any form of social outrage" in the 1980s "is dismissed breezily—not because it lacks substance, but because it lacks '*style*'... feminism is 'so '70s', pop culture's ironists say, stifling a yawn."[14] Like the "soft" politics of Jimmy Carter, sex for women was very much "out of fashion"—but this was, the media argued, because that's what women wanted.[15] In the most insightful line in the *Time* article, one interview subject summarizes the attitudes that define the backlash and the paradox of womanhood: "Beneath the veneer of liberation," provided by the ethos of the sexual revolution, "we have a residual guilt;" a guilt the backlash eagerly fomented.[16] [17]

The backlash's two biggest targets during this period, as Faludi's case studies and this *Time* article suggest, were working women and sexually liberated women—the same kinds of women who have been accused of witchcraft since the Middle Ages. It is unsurprising that, according to many of its proponents, the conspiracy alleged by the Satanic Panic was at its heart the fault of working mothers degrading the traditional family. From the daycare scare to concerns around Satanic rock music, coverage of the Panic consistently blamed apathetic mothering for children's demonic woes. High-profile TV specials on Satanism and devil worship often foregrounded mothers lamenting their "neglect" of their children: "I feel *very guilty* that I didn't pay attention," the mother of a teen who committed suicide says in Geraldo Rivera's *Exposing Satan's Underground*. "Parents, pay attention!" she urges, in response to questions about her son's love of metal bands, and the "hideous" "Satanic" artwork on their covers, "Satanism isn't a harmless fad or a passing phase." Articles covering alleged Satanic sex rings emphasized that many of the women who had been implicated were divorced, suggesting that the "deterioration of the family" (though never the absent father) was at fault. As Debbie Nathan wrote in *The Village Voice* "it seems the weaker the family gets, the holier its image… if the private family is sacred, the public child-care center is profane. If stay-at-home mothers are holy, then the people they pay to take care of their kids when they escape from the house are *witches*."[18] Not only were the mothers too busy working to keep their children out of Satan's clutches at fault, but according to the FBI's report on the daycare panic, women made up "as many as 40-50 percent" of all accused individuals, a notably higher rate than in any other kind of child

---

14. Faludi, 2020, 86, emphasis added.
15. The article does accurately predict periodizations like my own by suggesting that "[f]uture historians of the movement, in fact, may set the years of sexual revolt at roughly 1965 to 1975."
16. Leo, 1984.
17. This quote is in reference to the rise of herpes in the 1980s, a sexually transmitted disease outbreak that received much more mainstream coverage than did AIDS for the first several years of the decade. This article for example never once mentions AIDS, but the complete quote here, which comes from a doctor studying herpes, reads: "Beneath the veneer of liberation, we have a residual guilt, and the idea that promiscuity breeds disease falls on prepared ears", a line of argumentation that parallels both questions of feminist *and* sexual liberation and violently homophobic discourses around AIDS.
18. Beck, 2015, 160, emphasis added.

abuse allegations.[19][20] Looking at these claims together, it is easy to read Jerry Falwell's accusation that "feminists had launched a 'satanic attack on the home'" between the lines.[21] Satanic Panic was, in this sense, an extension of the backlash against women.

Horror films, as I suggested in the previous chapter, were blamed for the explosion of "satanic" violence, by anti-porn feminists and evangelicals alike, marked as pornography with dangerous real-world effects—but in the context of backlash, this claim takes on a new valence. The Meese Commission Hearings on pornography in 1985 and '86 were held only blocks from the McMartin pre-trial in Los Angeles (mentioned in chapter 8), often with the same set of witnesses, particularly FBI investigator Kenneth Lanning whose work on child abuse extended to child pornography. Its members, including prominent anti-porn feminist Andrea Dworkin, endorsed the notion that slasher films were themselves literally "pornographic".[22] This argument dovetailed with broader anti-horror film arguments being made at the time by conservatives that, in addition to their degraded status as pornography, the proliferation of horror films was actually *the fault of feminists*: "By making the 'violence' of abortion more acceptable," one writer argued, "women's rights activists made it all right to show graphic murders on screen."[23] These arguments, taken together, are another fundamental element of the regulatory, backlash-fueled impulses on display in the moral framework of the Panic. As the Meese Commission strove (unsuccessfully) to link the distribution and consumption of pornography to child abuse, claiming that child porn was the most lucrative part of that industry (more profitable than Hollywood by one exaggerated accounting the commission heard), Satanic Panic media used horror films as a bridge between the two.[24] The narrator of "The Devil Worshippers" (1985) then questions the ethics of allowing films like *Damien: Omen II* (1978), or *Exorcist II: The Heretic* (1977) on shelves at all by repeatedly stressing, with a disgusted expression and a wave around the horror section of a video store, that this supposedly dangerous material is—like working mothers, abortion, and no-fault divorce—"all perfectly legal."[25]

---

19. Lanning, 1992, 15.
20. Interestingly, even though Faludi never references Satanic Panic or witchcraft accusations directly, she does describe the antifeminist attacks on daycare at the time as critics "[p]ainting devil's horns on mothers who use daycare and daycare centers themselves", a clear, if tacit, reference to the controversy (57). This feels like a deliberate choice in the book, perhaps made in order to avoid an unsavory, "illegitimate" subject in order to preserve her professional tone and credibility on the book's release in 1991 when the Panic was already a sore subject for most Americans.
21. Faludi, 2020, 244.
22. Beck, 2015, 136.
23. Faludi, 2020, 3.
24. Hefner, 1990, 45.
25. "The Devil Worshippers", 1985.

✻

1984 proved to be an inflection point for the 1980s. The same year *Time* declared the sexual revolution officially over and Ronald Reagan won his second term in a historic landslide, several American towns banned trick-or-treating for fear of poisoned Halloween candy. As one writer put it, in truly witchy fashion, that "plump red apple" from the "kindly old lady down the block…may have a razor blade hidden inside."[26] [27] By spring 1984, news outlets were reporting upwards of 350 young victims in the McMartin Preschool case; the coverage became inescapable on television, in tabloids, and, briefly, in mainstream media as well; the Satanic Panic had begun in earnest.[28] That same spring, another, even more powerful supernatural phenomenon took America by storm: *Ghostbusters*.

It might seem strange to find a case study of one of the most famous *ghost* comedies of all time in a book on witch films, but, examined more closely, *Ghostbusters* employs many of the tropes of the witch film—from possession narratives to Pagan gods to shadowy (oc)cultists—and in so doing neatly exemplifies how these tropes will be used in the subgenre for the rest of the decade. Ivan Reitman's runaway blockbuster supernatural comedy could be viewed as the film that finally found the right narrative and tonal strategy to profit from the broad-ranging fascination with the occult in American culture. J. Hoberman links the film's success to the blending of reality with media in the culture at this point in the decade, citing Baudrillard's assertion that "cinema and TV are America's reality!" and suggesting that its conservative politics resonated with "[t]he Reaganist vision of 'America'… founded on religious certainty, which is to say supernaturalism… (*I ain't afraid of no ghost*)."[29]

In this sense, the film represents what the decade of Satanic Panic logically could have continued to produce as successful transmedia pop-objects in the years to follow; but the success of *Ghostbusters* was never replicated. What did *Ghostbusters* get right that the others got wrong? Here, rather than view *Ghostbusters* as a direct expression of the supernatural fears of its increasingly Satanic cultural moment (when viewed in relation to its

---

26. Poole, 2019.
27. The mid-80s Halloween candy scare is another perfectly illustrative example of the obstinate illogic of the Panic: even after a comprehensive 1985 study had found no evidence of *any* examples of strangers harming other people's children with Halloween candy in the past 30 years, a breathless report still described how "over the past several years, several children have died and hundreds have narrowly escaped injury from razor blades, sewing needles and shards of glass put into their goodies by adults." In 1984, however, a man named Ronald Clark O'Bryan was executed for poisoning his *own* son with a cyanide-laced pixie stick, paralleling the way Satanic Panic covered concerns around incest and child abuse *within* the home with the specter of shadowy Satanists hiding in plain sight outside of it. (Best and Horiuchu, 1985), (Poole, 2019).
28. Beck, 2015, 702.
29. Hoberman, 2019, 269, 226.

less-than-successful witchy progenitors in the few years prior—which failed to capture the public's imagination in part for their stodgy, out-of-fashion directness with their subject matter) *Ghostbusters* can be viewed as both *dismissing* (using a veneer of feminism) and *eliding* (downplaying backlash antifeminism through comedy) the supernatural anxieties of the period rather than expressing them directly, a pivot in the subgenre during this decade that replicates backlash strategies.

Often, analyses of the turn to supernatural comedy and horror parody in the 1980s dismiss it an expression of audiences' weariness with the material, a claim that's worth examining. The horror comedy reigned supreme in the 1980s across subgenres, from *An American Werewolf in London* to *Killer Klowns from Outer Space*. Supernatural horror films according to Drew Beard, "became objects of parody and camp... increasingly associated with low-budget schlock."[30] Hoberman concludes his analysis of *Ghostbusters* similarly, stating that while *The Exorcist* (1973) had been treated as politically significant under Nixon, "a decade later, as yippies gave way to yuppies, *Ghostbusters* replayed *The Exorcist* for laughs," a framing that suggests laughing at Dana's possession in *Ghostbusters* is less political under Reagan than screaming at Regan's possession was under Nixon.[31] This argument (both with regards to witch films and to horror in general), is, in my opinion, too broadly dismissive. As I discuss in Chapter 8, the "afterlives" of films like *Rosemary's Baby* (1968) (as outlined by Beard) certainly had a fundamental role in shaping the witch films of this decade, but to suggest they simply reduce the previous era's themes into comic simulacra is an insufficient explanation. The trend towards comedy in horror across the board, I argue, speaks to much of the politics of the time, predicated on the dual strategies of dismissal and elision.

Considering the context of the period—namely the heightened concern over Satanic involvement in children's minds and women's bodies—there is room for a more political interpretation of this shift towards comedy in the witch film—here, unexpectedly epitomized by *Ghostbusters*. The film follows a group of broke paranormal researchers, Peter Venkman (Bill Murray), Ray Stantz (Dan Aykroyd), and Egon Spengler (Harold Ramis), looking for a new income stream after being fired from Columbia University. They set up their titular, tacky ghost extermination service as a rash of hauntings strikes New York City. Dana Barrett (Sigourney Weaver), a cellist and one of their first customers, is soon possessed by a Sumerian demigod named Zuul, who aims to use her body and that of her comically irritating yuppie neighbor, Louis (Rick Moranis), to open an interdimensional portal, summon its ruler (named Gozer) physically, and bring about the Apocalypse. The gang, joined by Winston Zedd (Ernie Hudson), must save the world from these demons

---
30. Beard, 2015, 221.
31. Hoberman, 2019, 225.

and get the girl, while fighting off interference from a pesky EPA agent (William Atherton) concerned that their illegal ghostbusting nuclear reactors just might pose a threat to the populace (his concern is of course presented as outrageous). The film is recognizably conservative in its depiction of this fight between free enterprise and an overreaching government, which, like *The Devonsville Terror*, is characterized by the oft-hippie-coded, never-macho EPA through its representative whiney pencil pusher.

The film never fully leans into its horror elements, nimbly parodying the fears underneath the tropes through irony, distance, and laughs. Dana's possession in particular highlights masculinist concerns over an unregulated sexually desiring (and desirable) female body, but renders them amusing and safe. Before her possession, Dana is a beautiful, self-assured working woman, in control of her life and sexuality, but once possessed, the implicit threat inherent in her combination of sex appeal and upward mobility transforms her into a super-strong sexpot (a transformation we see recur constantly in possession films)—yet, here, rather than cower at her demonic shrieks of rage and levitating sexual advances, Peter rebuffs her condescendingly ("Take me, subcreature"..."Oh, Zuulie, you nut!"). Gozer further highlights this gendered anxiety: played by Yugoslavian model Slavitza Jovan, Gozer is marked as a figure of gender trouble. Realizing that the godly embodiment of interdimensional destruction is female, Ray is confused: "I thought Gozer was a man?" Egon grimly replies, "It's whatever it wants to be", linguistically dehumanizing the character before settling on feminine pronouns. Gozer's low, gravelly voice (performed, like Regan's growl in *The Exorcist*, by a woman), David Bowie-esque haircut, and lanky, muscular physique also mark her as a threateningly androgynous figure, even an overtly queer, if deeply ironized, threat (Peter laments at one point during Dana's possession that "it seems that *the Goze* has been putting some moves on *my* would-be girlfriend!"). Order is restored in the end however, in a climax Andrew Britton describes as a sort of "gang rape" of Gozer via exploding proton beams ("let's show this prehistoric bitch how we do things downtown!"), used to reassert an obviously gendered sense of normalcy.[32] After he proves his facility with a positron collider, the newly unpossessed Dana falls limply into the previously-lame Peter's arms. That being said, their relationship had been blossoming to begin with: Peter openly admires Dana's tenacity and career-mindedness (and figure) and Dana finds Peter's eccentric slobbishness charming. Ultimately, though, *Ghostbusters*, like *Devonsville*, falls back on more sexist conventions of gendered passivity for Dana, transforming Signourney Weaver, icon of late '70s feminist horror classic *Alien*, from a working woman to a laughable monster to a damsel in distress to a loving girlfriend. Yet, we know, this transformation is—as it would be for any

---

32. Britton, 2009, 121.

woman over thirty-five in the '80s according to *Newsweek*—*what Dana wants*, providing these antifeminist tropes a veneer of feminism.

Andrew Britton's contention (like Hoberman's), that *Ghostbusters* is "the definitive Reaganite text" in his article "Blissing Out: The Politics of Reaganite Entertainment" serves as an excellent point of entry into questions of comedy and deflection in '80s witch horror. Britton contends, as I do, that the film's parodic use of 1970s possession narratives, as films in the witch subgenre then echo, functions as a cover for its conservative ethos, a means of "promoting indifference":

> [T]he genre's new solipsism serves to mystify the monster's function as [a Freudian monstrous Other] by focusing our attention on narrative procedure in the abstract [i.e. generic convention] and by systematically trivializing character so as to preempt any complex emotional involvement in the action—indeed, to promote indifference to it.[33]

In other words, by laughing at Gozer or Dana rather than fearing them, and by relying on such overt references to the horror genre to elicit those laughs, these feminine monsters (and the horror genre itself) become toothless. Gozer is, in essence, the Devil in this story, but distanced from questions of literal Satanism by a substitution for ambiguous neo-paganism ("Gozer was real big in Sumeria")—in other words, witchcraft by another name.

The actual reason for Dana's possession notably draws directly from '60s witch films, but its framing speaks to the elisions and dismissals of backlash politics: an eccentric European architect named Ivo Shandor built Dana's Upper West Side apartment building in the early 20th century so his "secret society" of "Gozer-worshippers" could perform "bizarre rituals" to bring about the Apocalypse, using a woman's body as a sexual conduit.[34] The fact that the plot of *Ghostbusters* is predicated on what essentially amounts to a sped-up version of *Rosemary's Baby* without the words "witchcraft" or "Satan" (or "Dakota") is easy to miss—this dense piece of exposition is delivered in less than 90 seconds of screentime. Interestingly, even as these revelations are met with glibness from the Ghostbusters (Peter breaks out into a rendition of "Santa Claus Is Coming to Town"), the narrative requires credulity in this particular bit of occult backstory above all else to function: Ivo Shandor and his followers are depicted as ridiculous for their "bizarre" belief in Armageddon, but, as Egon tells the group, "now it looks like it's *actually happening!*" Mirroring a narrative technique employed in many of the witch films to come, this underhanded assertion of the realities of Satan worship

---

33. Britton, 2009, 112.
34. The apocalyptic rhetoric used in the film also speaks to the evangelical, supernaturalist mentality of the period so often referenced by President Reagan. The otherwise secular Ghostbusters quote from Revelation while discussing the impending arrival of Gozer, here presented as a sort of Antichrist precipitating the End of Days.

strongly resonates with the kinds of occult ritual practice being described in courthouses and on TV sets across the nation (Geraldo's use of Rosemary's dismayed cries to contend that human sacrifice is also *"really happening!"*).[35] Nevertheless, its comedic tone and self-referential, generically-rigid-yet-ironized set of occult symbols and plots, like all Reaganite entertainment in Britton's terms, "refers to itself in order to persuade us that it doesn't refer outwards at all. It is, purely and simply, 'entertainment'… as a commodity to be consumed rather than as a text to be read" which in so doing "tell[s] us that we are 'off duty' and that nothing is required of us but to sit back, relax, and enjoy"—in other words, it's only a movie.[36]

Its supernaturalism makes *Ghostbusters* an opportune entry point into the parodization of the witch films of the 1980s, many of which transcend both the horror *and* comedy genres, entering the realm of the cult film (a category the ironic, solipsistic *Ghostbusters* itself could have easily fallen into had it failed). The films I will analyze for the rest of this chapter, for their similarities, demonstrate a range of political and aesthetic sensibilities. But the strategies these films deploy—dismissal and elision, a veneer of feminism and comedy—as necessitated by the conservative framing of the culture, nevertheless come through in each, to varying degrees and with varying effects.

Wicked Stepmother (1989), directed by beloved genre impresario Larry Cohen was never intended to be a blockbuster. This low budget ($5 million) film was, like *The Coming* (1981) in the previous chapter, simply meant to turn a profit, and, with a cast of reliable comedic performers like Colleen Camp and the almost unbelievable presence of Bette Davis in a starring role, it seemed likely to. Yet, after a series of unmitigated disasters on set, most importantly, Davis' choice to withdraw from the film after only half of her scenes were shot (this strange performance, in an odd echo of Lana Turner's role in *Witches' Brew* (1980), would be her last screen appearance), the film floundered, was subject to bizarre rewrites, and ultimately, bombed.[37] It tells the story of a young yuppie couple, Jenny and Steve (Camp and David Rasche), who return home from a vacation to find that Jenny's elderly father, Sam (Lionel Stander), has married Miranda (Davis), a woman who they

---

35. Indeed, star and co-screenwriter Dan Aykroyd is a self-described spiritualist who firmly believes in the occult. His first draft of the screenplay was 180 pages long and stuffed to the gills with folklore, myth, and New Age beliefs, liberally sprinkled with multidimensional travel, past life regression, and demonology. The credulity of the underlying subject matter, more than simply being interesting, also speaks to the genuine pervasiveness of these forms of belief at the time. In other words, it's not a stretch to read real-life gravity in the Apocalyptic visions of *Ghostbusters* (Goldberg, 2023).
36. Britton, 2009, 100-1.
37. Spain, 1989.

find entirely unacceptable. Miranda is, of course, a witch. One who, as it turns out, is wanted in five states for marrying lonely older men for their money and killing them off. Interestingly, her marriage con (she's beaten the marriage study's astronomical odds for her age group five times over!) is characterized as her *work*. The detective on her case calls her "clever, ruthless, and very professional", negatively conjuring up images of sex work as well as financial entrapment, a detail which puts her in conflict with Sam's family over questions of authentic, feminine love and a masculinized, "professional" simulacrum of it, throwing her gendered role as a wife into disarray. This geriatric gold digger is also, much to the couple's dismay, a smoker, a meat eater, and a TV watcher—she gets dear old dad hooked on daytime game shows while she makes herself at home filling the house with acrid clouds of smoke and using their shared funds as she pleases. After Davis' departure, the plot was changed such that Miranda has a daughter, Priscilla (March 1982 *Playboy* Playmate of the Month, Barbara Carrera), with whom the older woman shares a conveniently shapeshifting human body and a cat's body (or, rather, a cat puppet), allowing the young, alluring Priscilla to take Miranda's place in the house, adding insult to injury by sleeping with Jenny's husband as well as her father. The film is largely a battle of wills between the frumpy, uptight Jenny and the sexy, conniving Priscilla/Miranda (Carrera is forced to talk to the cat as though Davis were still in the film), to see which of them will run the household. It concludes when Sam, using the magical gift of knowing the answer to any question, helps Jenny casts a spell to trap both witches inside the cat and bring the house back to order. The film, which *Fangoria* called "mind-bogglingly awful" and an "unmitigated disaster", quickly left theaters for an unceremonious home video release.[38]

Wicked Stepmother embraces the worst tendencies of retrograde films like *Witches' Brew* while attempting to update them for the 1980s. Miranda and Priscilla provide ample opportunity for a variety of witch jokes, from dismissive gross-out gags about older men having sex with younger women, to dismissive gross-out gags about older couples having sex at all. Priscilla is presented as promiscuous, with most of her screen time devoted to jokes about her cleavage. The elderly Miranda's open discussion of her enjoyment of sex is conversely held up as the worst of all of her offenses to American dignity and decorum. The two characters largely represent a disruption to the nuclear family, emasculating Sam and ousting Jenny's role in the kitchen. Most interestingly, the film doesn't seem to believe that a witch as an archetype could be frightening on her own terms. When Jenny and her husband arrive home and meet Miranda for the first time, as dramatic *Psycho* strings play, Miranda is presented in fractal close-ups, each of which embodies a different slasher monster: she has Freddy Krueger's knife-hands and Jason Voorhese's

---

38. Dr. Cyclops, 1990, 30.

hockey mask, cigarette stuck through one of the holes ("Call me mamma," Davis' voice drawls). In this throwaway scene, this 96-pound witch is both erased, supplanted by more familiar (notably large, phallic, and male) boogeymen of the period, and at the same time paradoxically imbued with the power of each of them to bring terror to the suburbs—if largely through the forces of high cholesterol and tobacco. The witch here is not a frightening figure, but a cypher which connotes one, what Britton would call a solipsism and what Baudrillard would call a simulacrum. Finally, the fact that Sam, Jenny's father, literally "knows best" and is the one to ultimately save the family from these intruders—Jenny tries and fails to take "witch classes" to get rid of them but finds herself to be "a lousy sorceress"—not only harkens back to the politics of *Witches' Brew* but adds insult to injury.

Teen Witch (1989), takes the conservatism of witch comedies like *Wicked Stepmother* a step further. Couching itself in the postfeminist rhetoric of independence and choice, *Teen Witch* could theoretically be construed as employing a veneer of feminism, but its chipper devotion to stereotypical femininity, rigid heteropatriarchal gender roles, and self-abnegation for women, reveals that threadbare occluding tactic as farce. This musical coming-of-age film has become a modest cult success, though not to the degree of *Elvira*, and not for the same reasons: along with its more conventional songs, it features a series of bizarre, stilted "rap" scenes performed by its white characters that have become an object of perplexed millennial nostalgia since it aired on ABC and Disney Channel in the 1990s. The film follows Louise Miller (Robyn Lively), an unpopular teenage girl who, on her sixteenth birthday, finds that she is the reincarnation of a 16th-century witch. With the help of Madame Serena (Zelda Rubinstein), she quickly uses these powers to make herself popular, beautiful, and desired, but has second thoughts, wondering whether relationships made by magic are meaningful. In the end, she renounces her powers, deciding to get the boy the hard way. This tepid, feel-good message ("The real magic is believing in yourself! If you can do that you can make anything happen!"), though, means little as her place atop the high school pecking order remains even after her magic is gone.

Replete with songs like "I Like Boys!" that implore young women to stop playing "in the dirt" and start "putting on some lipstick to attract some boys," the film's portrayal of conformism is parodically uncritical, predicated on finding self-worth in heterosexual romance over friendship or genuine, independent self-actualization. While Louise insists that overall, "I want to be me!", what that means is never made clear, sidestepped in favor of a new glamorous outfit and a ride in her boyfriend's car. The most significant element of this flagrantly conventionally conservative film for the purposes of this analysis, is its eerie inversion of *Carrie* (1976). Louise's popularity is only "authentic" when she accepts her role as a cool girl in a purely passive way, allowing the film to deride the agency provided by her witchcraft as manipulative and immoral. Here *Carrie*'s blend of witchcraft and danger remains but means the power to control men. Like Carrie White, Louise seems to fear her own power—her popularity spell brings alarmingly enthusiastic throngs of admirers swarming to her windows, fans that she, at heart, doesn't feel worthy of, even though her powers are naturally occurring and therefore an extension of the natural "authentic" self she's ostensibly seeking. Where Carrie dies powerful, Louise remains popular at the cost of this inner strength. In this sense, the film's barely-feminist gestures towards authenticity bring to mind arguments made by New Right figures who suggested feminism was "antidemocratic", providing women undue power, while as one Christian self-help book claimed, true feminine "power" comes from "submitting to your man."[39] Ironically, Louise's arc *unironically* depicts backlash rhetoric accomplishing its goals, positing this turn positively: her dismay over her feelings of guilt, the sense that none of her good fortune is truly her own, reflects the internalized guilt at the heart of the backlash. At the film's conclusion, the witches are symbolically defeated and a final song plays over the credits, undercutting once more any gesture towards an embrace of authenticity and individuality: "I'm gonna be the most popular girl... gonna change my hair and makeup soon you're gonna see... gonna be so different that you won't recognize me..."[40]

Horror comedies in general reflect an ideological balance that tends to disarm the political power of their subject matter. As Cynthia J. Miller and A. Bowdoin Van Riper write in their introduction to *The Laughing Dead*, the injection of overt comedy alters the ideological and affective impact of horror profoundly:

> Traditional dramas show us characters who—because they inhabit the same reality we do—have problems that can resonate uncomfortably with our own... Horror and comedy, carefully reined in, can do the same.... Allowed to run unchecked, however, both genres dissolve their characters' everyday realities so throughout and so extravagantly... they announce themselves as *fantasy*. Recognizing them as such, we are reassured... that nothing similar could happen to *us*. Freed of such worries, we are free to laugh, and we do.[41]

The two films of this section uncritically embody the reactionary heart of backlash politics, and do so *openly*, with none of the insidious complexity of effective backlash rhetoric. The persistent presence of films like these throughout the decade speaks to the reflexive conservatism of the period,

---

39. Faludi, 2020, 307, 438.
40. Though it's purely a teen comedy film, *Teen Witch* shares some strange DNA with the horror film: In addition to the inclusion of *Poltergeist*'s (1982) Zelda Rubinstein, Joshua John Miller, who plays Louise's younger brother, is the son of playwright and actor Jason Miller, Father Karras in *The Exorcist*. Joshua also plays a pre-teen vampire in Kathryn Bigelow's *Near Dark* (1987) (Stratford, 2013).
41. Miller and Van Riper, 2016, xvi.

however their critical and commercial failure, I argue, represents a deeper failure to capture the evolving nature of antifemism in America. Figures like Miranda, Priscilla, and Louise are clear, unsubtle blueprints for classic "bad" (i.e. sexual, nonreproductive, rowdy, indecorous) and "good" (cooperative, conformist, feminine, passive) witches, and audiences were disinterested in both, finding them narratively and tonally boring, old fashioned, and out of touch in much the same way "feminism" was, if for converse reasons. As films like *Witches' Brew* illustrate, by the mid-1980s, open, trite chauvinism, explicitly and directly tied to the creaky plot devices (devoid of broader political context) used here to depict them (i.e. the *Bewitched* [1964-1972] formula which one critic astutely calls "anti-magic" in *Teen Witch* for its conformist, disempowering message to women)[42] were no longer palatable to audiences or critics. Out-and-out spoofing, elevated, theatrical sexism, and solipsistic generic referentiality to formulas past without the gestures towards a postfeminist perspective that mediate sexism and, by extension, drive the political tightrope acts of films like *Ghostbusters*—or the two films to which I will now turn—transform these films into precisely the kinds of laughable failures Drew Beard suggests the genre itself to be composed of: "Low-budget schlock" with political implications.[43]

In the spring of 1987, three of the most famous women in Hollywood, Cher, Susan Sarandon, and Michelle Pfeiffer, starred alongside Jack Nicholson in a film to which *Playboy* dedicated a full two-page spread in Bruce Williamson's annual "Sex in Cinema" roundup. The header read "Witching may make it so: from occult rites to devilry, strange things are happening" in the films of 1987. *The Witches of Eastwick*, George Miller's R-rated supernatural sex comedy based on John Updike's novel by the same name, was a box office hit, and its sexy setup and superstar cast garnered this strange film a tremendous amount of media attention and popular hype. The film's main point of interest at the time of its release was its kitschy, raunchy premise: in a small New England town, three lonely single women, Alexandra (Cher), Jane (Sarandon) and Sukie (Pfeiffer), wish for a man one lonely night, and get more than they bargained for when a wealthy eccentric, Daryl Van Horne (Nicholson) arrives, buys a mansion, and introduces the women to a life of hedonistic sex—and witchcraft. Their wild self-indulgence offends the town's sense of decency as parodically embodied by local scold Felicia Alden (Veronica Cartwright). While the three friends learn to let their hair down (literally, their perennially postcoital manes were much discussed in reviews), Felicia transforms from devout wife to rabid proselytizing harpy (with the Phylis Schlafly updo to

---

42. Westbrook, 1989.
43. Beard, 2015, 221.

match) after a strange, seemingly supernatural accident leads her to a broken leg and an ambiguous case of hysteria the doctors (like Regan's in *The Exorcist*) wave away with medical jargon and a shrug. The film is structured as a sex comedy, with Van Horne comically seducing each woman separately by playing to her interests, before revealing to all three that they've been sharing a man and then forming a *ménage à quatre* in his new mansion. The town resents and ostracizes them for their newfound licentiousness and both Jane and Sukie lose their jobs. Eventually, the women decide they've taken things too far when they accidentally kill Felicia, promptly break up with Daryl and discover they're all pregnant. In a frenzied climax, Daryl reacts violently to his rejection and causes Sukie's pregnancy to complicate, bringing her to the verge of death. The three women cast a spell that first humiliates Daryl and then banishes him. Each woman carries her baby to term and they share the mansion to raise their combined brood.

The sexual liberation of these three famous, beautiful women on screen is obviously much of the film's draw, and one of the central sources of *Eastwick*'s profound political ambivalence. The film is far less explicitly socially conservative than the Updike novel upon which it is based, a liberalizing turn that *The Christian Science Monitor* bemoaned in its film review: in the book, written in 1984 but set in the early '70s, "the witches' casual mischief is of a piece with the casual relationships of the sexual revolution" wrote David Steritt—who had criticized *The Exorcist* and the broader "burgeoning popular interest in occult matters"—and their "giggly" violence is by extension, "a symptom of larger ills in society" (i.e. what he dismissively terms "the 'peace' movement").[44] In the film, he concludes, "the witches are sociologically on their own. So much for *Eastwick* as a microcosm, and the story as a cautionary fable." The film in many ways does strive to present as a feminist narrative, putting itself in conversation with the counterculture its '70s-era stars so obviously represent, though adapting the story to suit the particularities of '80s backlash politics. The three women start the story single and independent, like the witches of *Devonsville*, share drinks and laughs, talk frankly about divorce, child-rearing, and money, smoke a little weed, kick a powerful man to the curb, and end their adventure single once more and rich to boot. Ultimately, these three wildly charismatic stars opt for the power of sisterhood (literalized through Alexandra's army of ceramic Gaia statues, common to the matriarchal lore of the '60s) over a man, and stand up to the moral consensus in the process. The film even includes a monologue about the history of witchcraft as a form of capitalistic misogynist oppression almost identical to *Witches, Midwives, and Nurses* (1972). In Daryl's words:

---

44. Sterritt, 1987.

The entire witchcraft scare was started by the medical profession trying to get midwives out of the birthing business... just another example of male dominated professional society exploiting females for their own selfish purposes.... when they're confronted by a woman with obvious power [...] what do they do? Call them witches! Burn 'em, torture 'em, til every woman is afraid: Afraid of herself, afraid of men, and for what? Fear of losing their hard-ons.[45]

One reviewer, Jay Scott, calls *Eastwick* "a revolutionary, revisionist feminist theory of 'herstory'."[46]

Yet, this surface narrative, this veneer of feminism that shows three women magically resurrecting free love for the '80s, belies the ways in which the film *does* adhere to Updike's model of conservative politics and sexual caution. The witches' power seems to stem from Daryl's impending presence in their lives, and they never truly learn to control their newfound magic, liberally coded though it may be. They cast their first spell (a thunderstorm) to stop a school principal's interminable speech about "disintegrating values, [and] children exposed daily to the hazards of divorce," obvious references to the conservative, evangelical turn in American culture at the time and which almost every character is bored by—the scene cuts between the speech and sleeping audience members. Yet, they do so accidentally and without an understanding of how. Daryl must teach them to cast real spells, and there is no evidence they can exert any power at all after he is banished. This narrative defanging, parallels the argument Karen Hollinger makes about *Cat People* (1982) and the cinematic antifeminist backlash in this era: the witches of *Eastwick* may cast spells, but like Irena's new brother in the '82 adaptation, Daryl holds the true power in this backlash-era film.

In another example of the film's underlying conservatism, Felicia, though comedic in her depiction as an overzealous bully who literally drives her browbeaten husband to drink, is in a certain sense still the moral heart of the film. She continually warns her husband and the three witches that Daryl is dangerous and is proven right when he tries to murder all three women. Before this, even as she lambasts the women for a familiar raft of parodic Satanic Panic-style charges at them, her tone soon softens: "I have nothing against a good fuck, but there is danger here and somebody has to do something about it!" rendering her ultimately reasonable, under her exterior "pro-family" conservatism. Her death, a product of the women's annoyance at her constant interference in their lives, is the film's turning point, the traumatic event that snaps them out of their erotic ennui and into action.

Yes, their sexual liberation is depicted as largely harmless, but its cost nevertheless proves too high. Their unfulfilled desires result in their cosmic

---

45. For more on this, see Ehrenreich and English, 1973.
46. Scott, 1987.

punishment, ostracization, and a death. The monologue about the political history of witchcraft accusations is delivered by the film's trickster Devil, proven to be hollow, a way to sleep with Alexandra, an old school "feminist". Here, the three women are literally "tricked", as *Time* suggested feminists were, "into playing the male's game of easy sex" by Daryl, the proverbial, "sexual revolutionary at [the] party." Plus, like any cautionary fable worth its salt, all three sexually autonomous women get pregnant (a notable change from the book that further marks the film as a product of its postfeminist, New Traditionalist era). And they couldn't be happier to become mothers and swear off men, settling down in suitably modest attire to enjoy their newly minted lives as homemakers.

Critics picked up the ambivalence of *The Witches of Eastwick*, voicing many of the tensions at the heart of the backlash using the film as a lightning rod. It was frequently discussed in "battle of the sexes" terms, with reviewers offering their own metacommentary on the debate and its minutiae. Most critics settled somewhere in the middle, expressing confusion at the film's refusal to take a side; even as one critic calls the film "a brilliantly conceived metaphor for the battle between the sexes", they conclude it nevertheless "never really solves the riddle" of men and women's relationships.[47] As Bruce Williamson put it in his *Playboy* review where he calls the witches "sex slaves", the film "leave[s] the viewer with but one burning question: '*Huh?*'"[48]

This response to the film's backlash attitudes and its "empowering" bonafides, occasionally evoked prose so tortured as to be genuinely amusing. The same critic who called the film a "revisionist 'herstory'" and a "supernatural feminist farce", Scott, also calls the three leads "the bitches of Eastwick" for complaining about their single status and then immediately engages in bizarre, rhapsodic objectification: "The three witches of Eastwick make up a creamy Neapolitan dish–strawberry, vanilla and chocolate"— he means their hair color. He follows up on this metaphor with the even more degrading suggestion that while the "lusty and warlike" Daryl "loves licking his Neapolitan dish… he doesn't respect it."[49] Interestingly, this critic's interpretation of Daryl's witchcraft monologue is that it amounts to "crackpot feminism of the Andrea Dworkin variety (he maintains the women historically persecuted as witches were chosen because they were intimidating women capable of causing men to lose their erections)", demonizing feminist political history along with the chauvinist Devil who so conveniently misuses it. This critic is, engaging in backlash by deflecting *men*'s fear of women's empowerment ("fear of losing their hard-ons") onto

---
47. Jagr, 1987.
48. Williamson, September 1987.
49. Scott, 1987.

sex-negative "crackpot feminism" and thus *women* not wanting sex.[50][51] Not that the kind of feminism Daryl parrots matters much to him in the end; when the witches leave him, he reveals his true chauvinism, screaming: "I want somebody to wash these shirts! I want somebody to pay a little attention to me! I want a little respect! I want somebody to take care of me for a change!"

Ultimately, *Eastwick*'s gendered power dynamics demonstrate that, under its veneer of feminism, for these witches, feminism is indeed "the Great Experiment That Failed." In review after review, Nicholson is declared the winner of this battle of the sexes: "Miller and his collaborators may have given their bias away by casting Nicholson" writes one on the question of gendered power, "it makes eminent sense that it would take three of them to control one of him."[52][53] As Roger Ebert succinctly put it, "it's Nicholson's show."[54]

At the same time, women wanted to support this film precisely for its veneer of sex-positive feminism. In a 1987 article on what then-*Guardian* critic Nancy Mills hoped would be a rise in films about female friendship, *The Witches of Eastwick* is held up as a sign of progress—and the obstacles yet to be overcome—for films with multiple prominent female characters. "[Studios] seem to think that if you don't have a strong male lead you don't have anything you can advertise," she writes, quoting screenwriter Carol Sobieski. "Look at *The Witches of Eastwick*," she continues, "that's Jack's picture. In John Updike's book, the women were much more interesting. But the choice was to go away from the book."[55] Even though Updike's treatment of his characters was commonly understood to be deeply sexist, the sketchy characterizations of the film's female characters put Sobieski in the position of defending the novel for featuring complex female leads, villainized or not.

Filming *Eastwick* proved to replicate these dynamics—Cher has repeatedly stated in interviews that director George Miller initially told her she was "too old" and "not sexy enough" for a role in the film, and that

---

50. Scott, 1987.
51. This conflation evokes the story of Shere Hite's discreditation in the media as described in footnote 100 and was a common line of argumentation against pro-sex (pro-empowerment in the bedroom) feminism.
52. Scott, 1987.
53. Casting Nicholson, an iconic countercultural sex symbol, also ties witchcraft and the demonic to the counterculture. Bruce Williamson's "Sex in Cinema" piece features another man much less prominently than Nicholson, in a small box in the corner of the page: in a spread otherwise dedicated to witches and warlocks, giant of countercultural exploitation and arthouse films, Dennis Hopper (*The Trip* (1967), *Easy Rider* (1969), etc.), is mentioned for his role in David Lynch's *Blue Velvet* (1986). "Jack Nicholson has a hell of a time playing Satan," Williamson writes, "but Dennis Hopper is a far scarier personification of evil as torch singer Isabella Rossellini's nemesis in *Blue Velvet*, already a hit on the video-cassette charts" ("Year in Movies"). This inclusion of Hopper's non-supernatural, drug fiend and queer-coded sex pervert—recall the late scene when he smears makeup on his lips, kisses Kyle MacLachlan's Jeffrey, and tells him he'll "send [him] a love letter… you know what a love letter is? It's a bullet from a fuckin' gun… I'll send you straight to Hell, fucker!"—is extremely telling for the expansive way the witch and the Devil are associated with the counterculture at this time. Nicholson may be the Devil, but he's not as dangerous as this faded hippie demon (Williamson, November 1987).
54. Ebert, 1987.
55. Mills, 1987.

she had to fight with him to win her part, undercutting the clear power of casting women over 40 in sexual roles.⁵⁶ Once on set, according to a 1987 interview with the cast, Pfeiffer and Cher attested that "neither... had any control over their parts in 'The Witches of Eastwick'... 'Less than zero. The witches had no influence on anything,'" forcing these powerful stars to lean on Nicholson's influence on set, "because there really was, like, no one else to go to. It was Jack and The Girls. And The Girls kind of were, like, at a very low level."⁵⁷ In 1988, Cher was even more explicit in her critique of the film in a *Playboy* interview:

> On the set of *Witches*, I thought the women were treated really, really badly.... One day, I had a fight with [producer] Jon Peters, and he said, 'You're angry with me. I'm upset. Can I buy you a dress? Or a bracelet?' I just looked at him and said, 'What do I look like, a showgirl and you're Flo Zigfield?'... It was all kind of hysterical.⁵⁸

The objectification, minimization, and misogyny implicit in the sex-negative message at the heart of *Eastwick* is effectively occluded by a veneer of feminism and empowerment within the text, which remains a classic of the subgenre to this day, and which is of course an ambivalent postfeminist text open to, and often inviting of, liberal readings.

The reason this elision is so effective, as my analysis of *Ghostbusters* would suggest, is the film's status as a heightened sex farce, which leaves us, in the words of Miller and Riper, "free to laugh" at the "fantasy" of these three women's brush with sexual autonomy as they settle into their real lives as mothers, having beaten the highly publicized "odds" of birth as single, older women. Much as Andrew Britton suggests Reaganite entertainment announces itself as inconsequential, many reviewers dismissed the film's politics: *The Witches of Eastwick* is "a great time at the movies."⁵⁹ However as its critical reception, and the reactions of its female leads attests, the film's attitude serves as the perfect encapsulation of ambivalent backlash politics—and it succeeded on this basis like no other witch film of the decade.

While Cher, Susan Sarandon, and Michelle Pfeiffer may be the most famous, it was arguably Elvira, the late night TV horror hostess played by former Vegas showgirl and improv comedian Cassandra Peterson, who was the most visually iconic and ubiquitous witch of the '80s. Instructed to create a

---

56. Real, 2020.
57. Geringer, 1987.
58. "Cher's Raciest Interview Yet", 1988.
59. Kehr, 1987.

character with a "sexy Morticia Addams" look, Peterson combined a "Valley Girl" persona with a costume that evoked a punk version of '50s horror hostess Vampira.[60] Peterson's syndicated show, *Elvira's Movie Macabre*, ran on KHJ-TV in Los Angeles from 1981 to 1985, beginning when she was thirty, putting her in conversion with the "older" women of *Eastwick*.[61] [62] During its run, *Elvira* became a national presence (and an omnipresent underground goth sex symbol, or what Peterson called an "underground-pop-culture thingy"),[63] hosting Halloween specials on national networks throughout the decade, appearing on late night comedy shows (guesting with Vincent Price on the *Tonight Show* for example), and negotiating a number of successful deals for herself, (Elvira costumes and comic books, shoots for men's magazines, ads for beer, etc.) that raised her profile enormously.[64]

Elvira's first Hollywood film, *Elvira, Mistress of the Dark* (1988), is unique among 1980s witch films, navigating the backlash to present a genuinely feminist witch. It also provides an excellent entry point into using the sensibility of the cult film to understand the tensions inherent in this task. The winking PG-13 film, directed by *SNL* producer James Signorelli and co-written with Peterson and *Pee-Wee's Playhouse* writer John Paragon, was considered a flop on its release, even on its microbudget, and received derisive pans from critics who dismissed Elvira as a bimbo and the film as a vehicle for rote sex jokes. The film found tremendous success on home video, however, reaching number twelve on Billboard's US Top Video charts, becoming one of the 60 best-selling videos of all time (at least according to Peterson), and attaining NBC's highest rating in its time slot during the 1990 season.[65] Its idiosyncrasies and secondary market success take this film, a loving spoof of the kinds of cult horror films Elvira introduced on her show, itself into the realm of the cult film.

Inspired, per Peterson, in part by *The Wizard of Oz* (1939), *Elvira, Mistress of the Dark* blends punk rock nonconformity and sex-positivity

---

60. Peterson, 2023, xii.
61. Cotter, 2017, 32.
62. Vampira actress Maila Nurmi sued Peterson for copying her iconic look as Vampira—a suit she lost. The association with Vampira, the horror hostess and proto-goth pinup, is an interesting one. In many ways, Vampira is a precursor to the '60s countercultural witch—Maila Nurmi, the actress who played Vampira, first as a horror hostess on *The Vampira Show* (1955-6) and then in Ed Wood's cult classic *Plan 9 From Outer Space* (1957) also plays a "poetess" in Corman's 1959 *The Beat Generation*, a beatnik spin on the juvenile delinquent films AIP was already producing in vast quantities, bridging the divide between the blonde 'hip' witch of witch romances like *Bell Book and Candle* and the horror witches of the 60s with her witchy supernatural screen presence. Nurmi, whose costume was itself inspired by the as-yet-unnamed mother of the Addams family comics (who would formally become Moriticia the witch in the 1964 television adaptation) was also rumored to have cursed her ex-boyfriend James Dean soon before his death (Nancy, 2023). The urban legend tells that when she was asked why she kept an altar with a picture of Dean, she replied "I'm a witch!" (Janey, 2018). Vampira also served as a visual inspiration for Maleficent, the evil witch-queen in Disney's *Sleeping Beauty* (1956) (Greene, 2014).
63. Peterson, 2023, xvi.
64. Cotter, 2017, xvi.
65. *Ibid*, 213.

with a fairytale-style conventional narrative structure and a pervasive air of PG-13 inoffensiveness to create the most openly feminist witch film of the decade. Triumphantly placing her subversive punk witch in the role of Dorothy, *Elvira* exists in a cult film tradition from the outset, beginning with a clip from a Roger Corman film and a characteristic run of corny jokes from the skimpily clad hostess, playing herself ("It's me, Elvira, the gal with the enormous... ratings") When she finishes up recording this segment, after threatening to castrate the new station owner who sexually harasses her ("You said she was a nympho!" he wails to her producer in confusion), Elvira quits her show in the hopes of starring in a burlesque solo act in Las Vegas, but doesn't have the cash to reserve the venue. As soon as she realizes her problem, she receives a letter telling her that her Aunt Morgana has died and left her something in her will, to be collected in Falwell, Massachusetts.[66] "Is that timing or what?" she asks, looking directly to camera with a grin. The opening scene establishes the film's forthrightly sex-positive brand of feminism that flies in the face of the backlash attitudes of the day—Elvira consistently sexualizes herself (she is "the girl who puts the boob back into boob tube" after all) but refuses to allow others to degrade her for it (she sneeringly dismisses a woman who asks her if there's "anything that could possibly shame [her]") and establishes in the first five minutes of screentime that her self-awarely slutty punk look does not make her automatically sexually available or open to strangers' advances. She's frank and deliberately transgressive, warning the unending barrage of harassing men and prudish women she's faced with, to watch themselves, or else, throughout ("If I want your opinion, I'll beat it outta ya"), while also making unabashedly sexual—if cheekily corny—advances to men constantly ("My name's Elvira but you can call me... tonight"). This last also puts her in conversation with burlesque icons like Mae West, whose play with stereotypical versions of "excessive" erotic femininity led Pamela Robertson to coin the phrase "feminist camp" to describe their liberatory subject position throughout her 1996 book on the subject, *Guilty Pleasures: Feminist Camp from Mae West to Madonna.*

The film continues apace, incorporating conventional fish-out-of-water comedy beats into its zero to hero plot—while also overtly referencing elements of the Satanic Panic. Upon arriving in Falwell, Elvira becomes the subject of a town-wide witch craze (that is, adulation from the kids, panic from Falwell's very own "Morality Club") virtually identical to the harassment Eastwick's witches face at Felicia's hands. She soon finds that her aunt has left her only a tumbledown mansion, closer to the set of *The Munsters* than a home, an adorable dog (whom she gives a punk makeover and names Algonquin), and a cookbook, leaving her Vegas dreams dashed.

---

66. Possibly a reference to Rev. Jerry Falwell.

As she tries to sell her new fixer-upper to raise the cash for her burlesque show, she defies the cartoonish Christian crusaders and introduces the youth to extremely well-mannered nonconformity. While teaching the kids it's okay to wear makeup and listen to rock, she strikes up a chaste romance with the benignly hunky, largely empty-headed manager of the local movie theater, Bob (Daniel Greene). The Morality Club, headed by a woman named Chastity Pariah (Edie Mclurg), finds Elvira's largely wholesome (if buxom) antics dangerously inappropriate, working to bar her from legitimate employment and to keep her away from the children "for their own safety" ("One of *those people* comes into town, next you know you'll have sex ed in the schools and they'll be passing out condoms to kindergarteners!" she hisses during a meeting).

These plotlines work to illustrate the hypocrisy of puritanical crusades, render consensual sex and open, playful displays of eroticism, harmless, and present these dowdy society women as harmful for evoking sexualized Satanic threats to the children, adding another layer to the film's progressivism. While Felicia's rage in *Eastwick* may be presented as ridiculous, she is correct that the women present a danger to the town. Here, the boys under Elvira's tutelage may get an eyeful, and the once-frumpy young girls may wear a little eyeshadow, but over the course of the film, the kids largely learn to become better citizens—they paint houses, wash cars, and take care of each other. Meanwhile Chastity Pariah and her ilk brand Elvira a witch and attempt literal murder by witch burning, complete with Girl Scouts roasting marshmallows over the coals in a true lesson in poor moral education. Their hypocrisy is further illustrated when Elvira slips them a love potion at a Morality Club picnic, leading to the amusingly transgressive image of these church ladies and gentlemen engaging in the PG-13 equivalent of an orgy. Everyone has sexuality, but Elvira stays true to herself. Peterson's Elvira persona is self-consciously punk in its stylings, rebellious and anti-conformist in its sensibility, and liberal in its ideological bent.[67] In her memoir, Peterson describes the impact the feminism of the film had on fans at the time:

> Fans have told me, sometimes between sobs, that *Elvira, Mistress of the Dark* made a huge impact on their lives. The movie is the story of a misfit who, even though she's mischaracterized by almost everyone she meets, overcomes conflict, accomplishes her dreams, and in the end, even gets the guy... she unapologetically flaunts her sexiness, but is also fiercely independent, strong, and self-empowered... Throughout the film, Elvira is subjected to sexual harassment, false accusations, and being judged on her appearance alone,

---

[67]. On this note, the film is self-consciously political in myriad ways—Peterson, who came out as bisexual in 2023, would align herself with queer activism throughout her career, for example doing strip teases to raise money for AIDS research and serving as Grand Marshall for the West Hollywood Pride Parade in the early 1990s—and the film is dedicated to her friend and *Elvira* collaborator Robert Redding, who died of AIDS in 1986. (Peterson, 240, 213-14).

but she demands respect without ever having to compromise her (however warped) integrity... She's tough and flawed, but also exudes a vulnerability that connects with people, making her an odd, yet positive role model.[68]

This reception is a far cry from the ambivalence of *Eastwick*'s release. Indeed, the hypersexual Elvira is not only the unmitigated hero of the film, the moralists apologize to her, and she gets her Vegas show and a wholesome boyfriend, too—giving this film the most overtly feminist narrative in this chapter. In this sense, where *Eastwick* epitomizes the backlash's combination of dismissal through comedy and elision through a veneer of feminism, *Elvira* reorients these two approaches, using comedy and familiar generic conventions that *evoke* a familiar veneer of feminism to present a genuinely empowering sensibility.

In navigating the fraught terrain of the backlash and Satanic Panic era, though, *Elvira* interestingly shies away from the witch as a frightening figure, engaging in another form of distancing—a hewing of the witch as an archetype into two pieces, only one of which represents literal danger. In other words, for Elvira to be a feminist "good witch", the film gives its audience a "bad" witch. Elvira herself highlights the political valence of the witch, i.e. the historical figure of the falsely accused woman, rather than the monster of a fairytale. She's not a witch at all at the beginning of the film, only her Aunt Morgana's cookbook (actually a grimoire) gives her the ability to do magic at all. And when it comes to black magic, Elvira (like Jenny in *Wicked Stepmother*) turns out to be a poor practitioner: the strongest spells she casts are accidental, like thinking she's making a casserole until a monster jumps out of the dish. She is only a true witch in the eyes of the Morality Club, a threat to normalcy.

This is shored up by her direct opposition to a dark, malevolent figure, the folkloric archetype of the witch—a villain to be burned: uncle Vincent (W. Morgan Sheppard), an evil warlock trying to bring about the apocalypse by becoming Master of the Dark. Imposingly British, Vincent could be the villain of a Hammer horror film. Elvira's ostensibly disruptive presence proves the town's only salvation, solidifying her true role, not as a "witch", but as normative zero-to-hero. She finally manages to defeat the warlock, but largely passively—she sports a ring given to her by her aunt that primarily deflects spells rather than casts them and she never successfully *fights* Vincent, magically or otherwise.

Thus, the film suggests, the evangelical-coded Morality Club shouldn't have been worried about her in the first place—Elvira is a witch in the symbolic, political sense, a woman persecuted for her (functionally normative, if flamboyant and overt) sexuality. As in *The Witches of Eastwick*,

---

68. Peterson, 2023, 213-14.

false accusations of witchcraft distract from a *real* Satanic evil threatening real Armageddon on this town. As for Elvira, she does become the Mistress of the Dark, but only briefly. At the film's climax, she leaves the spellbook in the burning building, and once it burns, she no longer holds any power. Elvira returns to (relative) normalcy, as a (relatively) nonthreatening mortal. These elements—so central yet so peripheral to the film's message of empowerment and gleeful takedown of its moralizing antagonists—replicate the placatory gestures of *Eastwick*, themselves a far more nuanced echo of the restrictive logics of films like *Teen Witch* and even *Wicked Stepmother*. In the '80s, even the gutsy, truly feminist witches are denied the supernatural powers of their '70s feminist predecessors. Indeed, in the political climate of the 1980s, Elvira's provocations might not necessarily even bring the word "feminist" to mind—feminists were, after all, generally considered to be dowdy man-haters and lesbians, not sexy vamps.

The film's cult sensibility and broad comedy are at the heart of this distancing technique. As Barry Keith Grant writes in his essay "Science Fiction Double Feature: Ideology in the Cult Film", what "makes cult movies *cultish* is their ability to be at once transgressive and recuperative, in other words, to reclaim that which they seem to violate."[69] In this case, Elvira's showy sexual transgressions are titillating, but cover for the modest, recuperative quality of her wholesome impact on the town.[70] Grant suggests that cult films at base "presen[t] a conflict between the normal and the Other," that becomes pleasurable by "making a clownish spectacle—of caricaturing—the normal while minimizing the threat of the Other" through a similar form of caricature.[71] This is certainly true of Elvira, whose punk trappings are themselves countered by her ditsy valley girl persona, and her nemesis Chastity Pariah, whose prim smile and demure manner of speaking covers a steely ambition, an ability to swear a blue streak, and an apparently boundless sexual appetite. "As in classic genre film," Grant concludes, "the viewer ultimately gains the double satisfaction of both rejecting dominant cultural values and remaining safely inscribed within them," in this case, by rooting for the goth with a heart of gold.[72]

As progressive as Elvira's feminism is, it is much easier to accept presented in this safe, distanced form (through the ironized generic self-referentiality highlighted by Britton), softened by the ample visual spectacle of a conventionally attractive, skimpily-clad female body (sex-positive empowerment, the film smartly assures us, means more sex, and who doesn't want that?) whose inquisitors only the most puritanical could identify with.[73]

---

69. Examples include *The Rocky Horror Picture Show* (1975), *La Cage aux Folles* (1978), and *Beyond the Valley of the Dolls* (1970).
70. Grant, 2008, 78.
71. *Ibid*, 86, 78.
72. *Ibid*, 78.
73. In this sense, Elvira may have been the perfect character to navigate the Satanic Panic so successfully—

"This tendency toward caricature" of normativity, Grant posits, "may be essential to the cult film, making an otherwise bitter pill somewhat easier to swallow. While cult movies gain some appeal through this textual strategy, they lose much potential power." Grant also suggests that the often liberal political content of the cult film is largely beside the point for its audiences—he uses the anecdote of genre convention-goers booing George Romero off stage as he discussed the politics of *Night of the Living Dead* (eager to get to the gore) to indicate "the fact that the film can be read as a biting critique of the American middle class accounts for little of its cult appeal."[74] For all of its feminist bonafides, reviewers focused largely on *Elvira*'s "stupidity", insisting on its inanity in parodic terms that rivaled only the film's own: "This film is aggressively, tirelessly, fearlessly stupid. If being stupid were a cause, *Elvira, Mistress of The Dark* would be its Mother Teresa",[75] one critic chuckles, while another spends almost as much time as the film does on jokes about Peterson's "milky white bosom."[76]

The broad quality of *Elvira*'s humor, as well as its parodic style of critique make it much safer, sillier, sexier, and most importantly, more reassuring than the witch films of the previous decade which insisted time and time again that the beautiful witches next door, evil or not, had the supernatural power to defend themselves and make things happen. Even as *Elvira* exuberantly satirizes the social climate of the time, skewering many elements of the Satanic Panic, the choice to make the film's true villain a warlock speaks to a conservative, latently homophobic trend that pervaded the subgenre and runs counter to the film's progressivism. This detail is most important as a means of demonstrating the conservatism inherent in the dismissive, fantasy-coded and cross-genre popular stylings spoofed by cult and cult-adjacent films like *Elvira* and *Ghostbusters*. Ultimately, *Elvira*'s pro-sex message works to show that weird or not, this witch isn't scary at all.

Having delved into the witch films of this period, it becomes clear that these seemingly innocuous supernatural and horror comedies are a locus of complex cultural re-articulation, absorbing backlash and Satanic Panic discourses and projecting them outward through the classic figure of the witch. With this in mind, I have argued that some of the failure of the lower-profile examples of the subgenre comes from their approach to this re-articulation, using comedy to soften the witch as a dangerous presence, but

---

as fellow cable horror hostess Penny Dreadful puts it, horror hosts "take such delight in showing you that which is forbidden and appalling.... But in a nice way. You see, the horror host has always been a pal to children. We're the friendly creepies who help you through that scary movie" (Prasch, 2).

74. Grant, 2008, 81.
75. Pevere, 1988.
76. Brit, 1988.

also opting to cleave the witch from the context of the Panic and presenting their antifeminist, backlash conservatism openly (doing away with what I have called a veneer of feminism or a postfeminist stance), typically through the deployment of older, creakier generic tropes (*Wicked Stepmother*'s "boring" gold digger narrative and *Teen Witch*'s "anti-magic" approach to the teen comedy). The more successful films use comedy, like *Ghostbusters*, to de-legitimize and render the witch safe, while also placing her in spoofed, satirical conversation with the moral panics of the day around women's roles, and actively employing a veneer of feminism. As Thomas Prasch writes in his analysis of *The Fearless Vampire Killers* (1967), "Precisely because of the distancing effects of laughter," horror comedies (like *Elvira*) are free to use horror tropes to address more serious subjects.[77] In *The Witches of Eastwick*, this postfeminist stance, in tension with the film's underlying conservatism, perfectly encapsulates the fraught place feminism (or women's empowerment, for those who rejected the label) held in mainstream culture at this point in American history. *Eastwick*'s reception by critics and audiences plays out these tensions, while its production history and narrative power dynamics demonstrate the unfortunate reality that women's gains were being attacked, that feminism, contrary to much public discourse, had not "already won." I've used *Elvira, Mistress of the Dark*, an enormous underground cult success, to highlight the ways in which these discourses are malleable: this film flips these tropes and narrative approaches on their head, using its cult sensibility to present its feminism with the same comedic tone and a similar plot to *Eastwick* to a more unambiguously feminist end, but defanging the witch as an archetype in the process, ultimately suggesting that Elvira may be a witch, but she's not a threat.

This raises a final question for this chapter: if witches *per se* are no longer threatening in this decade—largely disappearing from traditional horror films and appearing again and again in the horror comedy—but the archetype clearly holds powerful sway over the culture in the context of the Satanic Panic (as is so obviously spoofed in both *Eastwick* and *Elvira*), where are the truly frightening cinematic women (the true witches) of this era, and what do they look like? The answer begins to appear in a marked *absence* in the witch film narratives. In a period wherein, as Susan Faludi puts it, society was "[p]ainting devil's horns on mothers who use daycare and daycare centers themselves," none of the witches I have described maintain traditional, 9 to 5 employment. None end their films as the kinds of working women the backlash was so violently rejecting. The archetypal process of disaggregation performed in *Elvira*—between the witch as a demonic, violent force and the witch as a persecuted woman—focuses solely on the witch as a sexual figure, allowing Elvira herself to be a liberatory champion for women and

---

77. Prasch, 2016, 5.

nevertheless relatively non-threatening in the context of a Panic predicated on the demonization of working women. According to purveyors of Satanic Panic, the real-life witches of Reagan's America may cast hexes, but they don't wear pointy hats in small town grocery stores or schools. Enter one of the most singularly successful genres of the decade: the erotic thriller.

Much has been written about the demonization of the working woman in the erotic thriller, particularly in the context of the period's antifeminist backlash, but it becomes particularly salient in the context of the witch film and takes on an even stronger resonance when contextualized by the Satanic Panic. Rather than provide an overview of the genre and its historical context/reception, I will instead turn to the most famous and successful film within it, *Fatal Attraction* (1987) to unpack its significance to the archetype of the witch, how it was understood contemporaneously in this context, and how it served as a cultural release valve for the brutal misogyny and fear lurking beneath the humor in the witch horror comedy. *Fatal Attraction* was the second highest grossing film of 1987 (the year Bruce Williamson highlighted as replete with cinematic witches[78]) and garnered six Oscar nominations. Its cultural impact can't be understated, taking on a quasi-midnight movie relationship to its male viewership wherein crowds of men hurled misogynist epithets at its working woman antagonist, cheering on her death, and encapsulating for many the potency of misogynist backlash in the country.[79]

In *Fatal Attraction*, married, upper middle class everyman Dan (Michael Douglas), has a brief affair with Alex (Glenn Close), a high-powered colleague he meets at a company party. They carry on their relationship at her apartment downtown, on a weekend when Dan's wife, Beth (Anne Archer), is looking for a home upstate that symbolically connotes the end of his virile life and the beginning of his "settling down". When he eventually breaks it off, citing his happy marriage, Alex tries everything to get him back, from flattery and manipulation (she tells him she's pregnant—he isn't sure whether to believe her) to blackmail to open stalking, and ultimately, violence. The film's tone shifts wildly from the first half to the second, going from the careful character studies of a romantic drama to the hectic foreboding of a horror movie. Her rage at his scorn becomes psychotic, taking on the almost supernatural quality of a slasher villain's pursuit of their victims: she throws acid on his car, appears seemingly out of thin air at his office and then his country house at strange hours, kidnaps his daughter, Ellen (Ellen Latzen), and attempts to murder Beth. In the end, even after Dan drowns her in a bathtub, Alex comes back from the dead, rising from the water with a butcher knife for one final (literal) stab at the nuclear family before Beth shoots her to death. The film ends in a closeup on a photograph of the happy nuclear family she attempted to destroy.

---

78. Williamson, September 1987.
79. McCarty-Simas, Payton, 2022. "'single White Female' at Thirty."

The obvious channeling of backlash rhetoric in the film is intimately tied to the witch as an archetype, in this case overtly tinged with the narrative conventions of the Satanic Panic. Overall, Alex is consistently masculinized, an anti-maternal threat to the nuclear family. Her interest in having Dan's child is presented as pathetic at best even as she faithfully espouses the rhetoric of the backlash that so scorns her: "I'm thirty-six, Dan," she says, incredulous when he asks for an abortion, "this may be my last chance to have a child." Her perverse baby fever drives her to kidnap Dan's child, an act that evokes both the baby-eating witches of folklore and the lurking elementary school Satanist pedophiles of the '80s. Crucially, this scene of child endangerment is the turning point that unites the family for the climax. Immediately after Beth has kicked Dan out of the house for his cheating, she sends Ellen to daycare, which she has just begun at the midpoint of the film. That day, Alex poses as Ellen's mother and picks her up, associatively presenting daycare as dangerously negligent for remitting Ellen into this stranger's care. When Beth arrives at the school, the kidnapping is treated almost supernaturally—another young child, first shot in ominous silhouette, tells her simply, "She's gone," before the editing takes on a highly associative, elliptical quality unlike any other sequence in the film: as Beth frantically searches her wooded neighborhood (shot in a series of frantic whip pans in a film otherwise devoid of them), Alex takes Ellen out for ice cream, then to a boardwalk, holding her hand and towering over her in a long, boxy black leather coat that, along with her hair, evokes the queer villain of De Palma's *Dressed to Kill*.[80]

The pedophilic overtones of the scene are overwhelming. The pair are shot on voyeuristic long lenses and at dramatic, destabilizing dutch angles that mark this otherwise wholesome scene as illicit, unpredictable, and unsafe. This threat of violence is heightened by the associative cuts back to Beth in her car, who grows progressively more frantic.[81] Eventually, as Alex and Ellen get on a rollercoaster together and careen down a steep slope, expressions eerily blank then suddenly animate as they scream for the drop, Beth is suddenly, shockingly, hit by another car seemingly out of nowhere. It is as though the monstrous Alex, in replacing Beth, has cast a spell over both mother and child. When Alex drops Ellen off at home, seemingly unharmed, the jumps in narrative continuity leave a sense of foreboding and uncertainty as to what happened to the child. Alex finally asks for a kiss, which is shot at an obscuring angle, leaving the impression that the woman and young girl have kissed on the lips. Divorce, or even the man's (justified) expulsion from

---

80. This evocation of gender trouble, specifically the "transvestitism" of (spoilers) Michael Caine's character in *Dressed to Kill*.
81. The elliptical, surreal quality of this scene in *Fatal Attraction* even recreates the aesthetics of the witch films of the previous decade—the editing of this scene is far more reminiscent of *Don't Look Now* (1973) or even *The Devonsville Terror* than comparable erotic thrillers from the time or other Adrian Lyne films. Thus, the film form here also affirms Alex's status as a witch *generically* rather than just tonally or associatively.

the household, as the Panic's rhetoric suggests, inevitably allows pedophilic witches access to American children. The supernaturalism of this scene is brought into the home when Alex boils the family's rabbit (an unsubtle sign of innocence) in an enormous pot, like a witch's cauldron. Even Alex's last name, Forrest, like her uncontrollable mane of hair, links this refined working woman with the dark, uncontrollable world of the witch.

The connections between backlash and *Fatal Attraction* weren't missed by critics, and it became a source of innumerable commentaries on the film. In his 1986 review for the *Washington Post*, Richard Cohen calls it the "ultimate nightmare... for the women's movement" for its reversal of the celebratory rhetoric of older films about career women, calling it the beginning of "a new stereotype", namely "the crazy career woman". Here, it "is the non-working wife-*cum*-mother who is the paragon of mature womanhood... [s]he is complete unto herself."[82] In other words, it is she who "has it all". The review is extremely direct in its detailed assessment of the problem of feminist backlash:

> Just a short time ago, women were told to follow the career path. A job... would add up to fulfillment. When that turned out to be not always the case, a counter-prescription was offered: stay home, stay pregnant and, in the process, stay happy. This is the chirpy advice of anti-feminists.[83]

Nevertheless, Cohen concludes with a concession to Britton's thesis in "Blissing Out" by suggesting that while the trend may be concerning, "[a] movie is just a movie, and too much should not be made of it. It's doubtful that the makers of 'Fatal Attraction' were attempting to make a statement about feminism."[84] Originally, the film's female producer had indeed intended to make a statement on feminism—a positive one.[85] *Fatal Attraction* originally sympathized with Alex, meant to depict the complexity of relationships between married men and single women. It was Douglas, then a megastar, who forced changes because he refused to play a "weak, unheroic character". He also (infamously) stated doing press for the film that he was "really tired of feminists, sick of them," because "[t]hey've really dug themselves into their own grave. It's time they looked at themselves and stopped attacking men."[86] This film, as in each case in this chapter, is not just a film, but a reflection of the politics of its time.

Ultimately, *Fatal Attraction*'s perfect replication of backlash discourse, and its deployment of horror film tropes and witchy iconography, demonstrate

---

82. Cohen, 1987.
83. *Ibid.*
84. *Ibid.*
85. Leading 20th Century Fox as the first female studio head in Hollywood history in 1980, Sherry Lansing would go on to become the CEO of Paramount Pictures in 1992 (Galloway, 2017).
86. J. Hoberman, 1995.

what the tangled landscape of the witch film in the 1980s had otherwise either struggled to or flat-out refused to, articulate directly.[87] For Faludi, the marital films of the 1980s in general often depict antagonistic wives as "virtual witches, controlling and conquering their husbands with a supernatural and deadly precision," while in this film, outside Alex's apartment, the anti-familial home she has created for her married quarry, the oil drums "burn like witch's cauldrons."[88] Pauline Kael, meanwhile, literalizes *Fatal Attraction*'s subtext and in so doing brings the cinematic witch and the feminist together more directly than any other film in this chapter:

> The horror subtext is the lawyer's developing dread of the crazy feminist who attacks his masculine role as protector of his property and his family. It's about men seeing feminists as witches, and, the way the facts are presented here, the woman *is a witch*.... This shrewd film also touches on something deeper than men's fear of feminism: their fear of women, their fear of women's emotions, of women's hanging on to them. "Fatal Attraction" doesn't treat the dreaded passionate woman as a theme; she's merely a monster in a monster flick. It's directed so that by the time she's wielding a knife... you're ready to shriek at the sight of her.[89]

Without ever invoking any element of the Satanic Panic directly, the film draws upon the culture's fascination with evil women and the occult, in a manner similar to Foster Hirsch's description of "background noise", the term he uses to explain the simultaneous unspeakability and omnipresence of the AIDS epidemic in American neo-noir cinema at the time. In these films, he says, "the traditional link in noir narratives between sex and catastrophe is no longer merely symbolic or moralistic, although no noir film has addressed AIDS directly or enlisted it as a narrative cause."[90] For the witch films of this period of Satanic Panic, the threat presented by this "monster in a monster flick", already an obvious anti-feminist scapegoat, becomes equally tinged by the decade's very own unsavory, unmentionable witch craze.[91]

In a climate where backlash rhetoric predicates itself on a veneer of feminism (the illusion that women are the decision makers at the center of their own conservative regression back into the home) it becomes essential for feminist archetypes to lose their danger. In this environment, working mothers are blamed for the dissolution of the nuclear family: in my case

---

87. True to form, the film employs a veneer of feminism by presenting Beth, the domestic angel, as her very own "patriarchal avenger". After warning Alex, "if you ever come near my family again, I'll kill you," she does. As one Paramount executive put it, Beth "terminate[s] the bitch with extreme prejudice." (Galloway, 2017).
88. Faludi, 2020, 150.
89. Kael, 1987, emphasis added.
90. Hirsch, 1999, 9.
91. On this score, the film was also received as an AIDS metaphor by many critics. This continued direct relationship between the Satanic Panic and AIDS will become more overt in the next chapter.

studies literalized through the Satanic Panic, the father or husband (or lover, in the case of *Fatal Attraction*) is never to blame. In an environment wherein witches and feminists are simultaneously rendered non-threatening *and* vilified, blamed (via the divorce rate, women's entrance into the workforce, legal abortions) for the suffering of the nuclear family's decline, the archetype, like the feminist movement, becomes split. Men need not fear the woman in the pointy hat and the broomstick, rather their fears are far closer to home, even *in* their homes, as well as in their boardrooms, their children's classrooms, and everywhere they turn. Witches *were* everywhere in the 1980s, and thus they faded into non-seriousness and obscurity on our screens, supplanted by "bitches" like Alex Forrest whose death men cheered like she was Jason Voorhees, Michael Myers, and Freddy Krueger all rolled into one. In 1984, during the presidential campaign, then-Vice President George H.W. Bush debated Democratic Vice-Presidential nominee Geraldine Ferraro, the first woman to ever run for the role, who was subject to constant misogynistic attacks; when it was over, Bush smugly told the press he had "kicked a little ass."[92] When asked for her opinion on Ferraro, Barbara Bush laughed. "I can't say it," she said, "but it rhymes with rich." Later, when pushed to elaborate on the comment she insisted that the word she had in mind wasn't in fact "bitch", but simply "witch."[93] While only the latter would be acceptable for the wholesome, devoutly religious wife of the Vice President of the United States to say about another woman, the subtext was obviously the same.[94]

---

92. Groer, 1988.
93. "Bush's Wife Assails Ferraro, But Apologizes", 1984.
94. Fascinatingly, in pieces that mention the incident as early as 1992, this infamous gaff is transformed, recalled by journalists in at least three articles as Barbara Bush saying "rhymes with witch", a misremembering that both brings out the subtext of the insult and underestimates the meanings of her actual choice of phrase in the mid-1980s when the archetype of the witch was highly visible, and highly threatening, in the culture (Walker, 1992) (Black, 2004), (Swann, 2004).

Chapter Ten

Witch Films, Satanic Panic Specials, and "Morale-Boosting Entertainment"

"This is no dream, this is really happening!"
-Rosemary Woodhouse, *Rosemary's Baby* (1968)
-Rosemary Woodhouse, *Devil Worship: Exposing Satan's Underground*[1]

By 1992, American culture had performed a new exorcism—excising the Satanic Panic itself from the mainstream. At the turn of the decade, Satanic Ritual Abuse had become a thoroughly disreputable subject. As Francis Fukuyama posited "the end of history" and a new "culture war" was officially named and declared, several of the few accused who were ever actually convicted of pedophilia in the swaths of daycare abuse cases in the United States, had already had their convictions overturned or had been released, though many would remain on federal sex offender registries for years to come. Soon-to-be presidential candidate Pat Robertson founded The Christian Coalition in 1989, pushing provisions against "witchcraft", "channeling", and even yoga in Washington State's 1992 party platform; however, that year the state's Republican candidates were trounced, losing control of the state Senate entirely and finding their numbers in the House shrink from three to just one.[2] This change came in tandem with an increasing disreputability of the evangelical agenda at the heart of the Satanic Panic. In the late 1980s and early 1990s, scores of once-untouchable televangelists like Rev. Jim Bakker, host of the successful television ministry *The PTL Club*, were exposed for embezzlement and sexual abuse in their congregations.[3] More broadly, opinions of the McMartin case were changing in the wake of overturned convictions and the exposure of unprofessional interview techniques of underage witnesses.[4] Pop culture, too, reflected these changes: while in October, 1989, a serious procedural drama (somewhat inexplicably) called *Do You Know the Muffin Man?* (1989) depicted the defendants of the (still-ongoing) McMartin trial as literal blood-drinking witches on screen, guilty beyond a shadow of a doubt, in 1995 an HBO film called *Indictment:*

---

1. Woodhouse clip in *The Geraldo Rivera Show*, 1988.
2. Edsall, 1993.
3. Schmidt, 1987.
4. Cockburn, 1990.

The McMartin Trial, depicted the accused as the victims of a witch hunt by power-hungry politicians and moralists. The first film, a piece of fiction—disguised, like any other Satanic Panic special, as a morally inflected warning (a number for a child abuse hotline flashed before every commercial break)—was one of the top ten films watched on television that week, while the second film was nominated for nine Emmys in 1992, winning four including Outstanding Made for Television Movie, demonstrating the radical rejection of the Panic by the culture.

Throughout the last several chapters, I have worked to demonstrate that the witch films of the 1980s exist in a tense, often paradoxical relationship with the Satanic Panic, a phenomenon which insisted on the reality of real-world Satanic conspiracies, occult ritual murder, supernatural pedophilia, and demonic cannibalism, while often citing fictional horror films as evidence for all the above. This last phenomenon, itself a deliberate conflation of reality and fiction, speaks to a broader political climate in which films, music, and other forms of pop-media were being treated by politicians, religious leaders, and conservative feminists alike as powerful "pornographic" objects capable of real-world harm, often at the level of the subconscious in the form of subliminal messages. This is also reflective of the broader hyper-saturation of media in public life, a phenomenon that would bloom into what became known as "the 24-hour news cycle" during the trial of OJ Simpson in 1994.

With regards to the Panic itself, as I discuss in Chapters 7 and 8, the rise of evangelical conservatism, VHS culture, and the proliferation of Hollywood films on cable television allowed older occult and witch films, most powerfully *The Exorcist* (1973) and *Rosemary's Baby* (1968), to "haunt" American audiences in the '80s, taking on new morally-coded cultural valences in these "afterlives" which would not have been possible in decades past. The witch films released in the 1980s, I have suggested, operate not as their own cycle, but as a response to those older films, received well past their initial release by a culture radically different from the one filmmakers were originally responding to. As such, the preponderance of supernatural comedies about witches during this period should be understood as more than a simple exhaustion with the subject, a cycle gone to seed, but as an uneasy re-articulation of themes which continued to hold powerful sway over this new, hybrid cultural landscape in the form of background noise alongside the continued, though embattled, gains made by the women's movement in a time of backlash. In Chapter 9, the witch horror comedies of the 1980s reflected the complexities of backlash's rhetorical strategies, namely elision (a veneer of feminism) and dismissal (comedic stylings meant to suggest that "the witch", a classic specter of feminism, was no longer a threat), largely sanitizing this archetype to present her as safe, silly, and sexy rather that a threat to the dominant order. I have worked to present these films, which responded to the previous cycle of witch horror, themselves unpacking the rise of feminism, the counterculture, and civil rights movements of the '60s and '70s, as a significant, if confused, vector for a culture undergoing a mass pushback to these same phenomena—in short, the messy process of the burgeoning acceptance of marginalized groups in America.

In this concluding chapter, I will put the witch films of the 1980s in direct conversation with the most (in)famous form of Satanic Panic cultural production, the so-called "Satanic Panic special" on television and video, as a means of understanding these films more coherently as a placatory, recuperative response to a rapidly changing social and political landscape. I suggest that these horror comedies serve as a conservative form of morale-boosting entertainment amidst a hysterical phenomenon which spurred a crisis of signification within the genre and the culture writ at large. As I discussed briefly in each chapter of this section, many "news" programs on television, often forms of "infotainment", alongside straight-to-VHS media, covered elements of the Satanic Panic in more detail and with more credulity than in any other venue in the decade. Programs like (among others) Geraldo's *Devil Worship: Exposing Satan's Underground* (1988), *20/20*'s segment, "The Devil Worshippers" (1985), and multiple episodes of *The Oprah Winfrey* Show dealing with "Satanic Worship" in 1988 and '89, promulgated the Panic even after less credulous outlets began calling it a "witch hunt". These shows strategically deployed clips from horror films like *Rosemary's Baby*, in one instance calling it "the movie that's been described as the best advertisement that devil worship has ever had," and in another using it as "evidence" of human sacrifice.[5] [6]

Even as the hosts and guests of these programs strove to ban horror films, the genre's visual and narrative vernacular bled into their rhetorical strategies, which used dramatic horror fiction to push the boundaries of credulity into the realm of supernaturalism, panic, and hysteria. As Sarah Hughes explains in her article, "Tabloid Media and the Satanic Panic", the "alleged legitimacy of these claims" about Satanic Ritual Abuse on numerous shows (including, in addition to Geraldo and Oprah, *Sally Jesse Raphael*, *The Morton Downey Jr.* Show and others) "was bolstered by the use of anecdotal evidence… and dramatic reenactments that often revolved around extremely intimate situations", shot like outtakes from a slasher.[7] As early as 1984, the year the McMartin trial began and *A Nightmare on Elm Street* was released, "a TV Guide cover asked, 'Is Local News Going Too Far?'"[8] That isn't to say that people lost faith in this programming—shows like these contributed to an almost universal assumption of guilt for the McMartin trial's defendants as late as '89 when the vast majority of charges had been dropped or thrown out of court.

---

5. "The Devil Worshippers", 1985.
6. *Devil Worship: Exposing Satan's Underground*, 1988.
7. Hughes, 2017, 701.
8. *Ibid*, 701, 700.

Taken together, these specials display the same formulaicness that slashers (and erotic thrillers) do, citing the same criminal cases and instances of violence over the years, interviewing the same bench of guests, and even using the same film clips and turns of phrase. Just as the scattershot witch films of the era become more discernible as backlash entertainment, when viewed in conversation with the erotic thriller cycle of the period, I would argue, these specials constitute their own form of witch horror cycle, far more gripping than their multiplex counterparts, played out with deadly gravity on primetime, and under the guise of the public's edification in the same way older era's exploitation films paraded as moralistic "hygiene films". David Canfield argues similarly, suggesting that Christian videotapes about satanic and occult conspiracies served as a "covert horror culture" for evangelicals in the '80s.[9] In this sense, witches' paradoxical omnipresence and marked absence from successful mainstream horror films becomes more comprehensible—the niche had been filled not only by the erotic thriller, but also by the nightly news, both of which stressed that the Devil was a woman (or a gay man) and Hell was a place on earth. This exploitation framework also aids to resolve the strange, tense relationships shows like these maintained between reality and fiction, providing clearer readings of marketing for Oprah's 1988 special, visibly designed to piggyback off of the success of Geraldo's show: "*Satanic Worship!*" it reads, "It could be the plot of a horror movie, but it's not."[10] In the '80s, it never was. But then again, it never truly needed to be. Shows like Oprah satisfied the desire to explore the subject, leaving the horror genre itself scrambling to its own legal defense, as fact and fiction lost their ontological stability. Ironically, here, these entertaining products of "covert horror culture" themselves served as "evidence" against innocent teachers and parents, swaying public opinion and leading to the wrongful imprisonment of dozens on thinly disguised charges of witchcraft. As one reporter wrote of Geraldo's special, these kinds of anti-Satanic crusades, rooted in discourses around the "pornographic" could themselves be seen as "pornography masquerading as journalism."[11]

The reappropriation of horror and exploitation film's generic codes to render otherwise unbelievable, quasi-mythic tales of Satanic Ritual Abuse legible, also highlights the "multiple, fragmentary, and often contradictory" nature of Satanic Panic's fundamental claims. As Paula Treichler says of discourses around AIDS circulating at the same time,

> [T]he AIDS epidemic is simultaneously an epidemic of a transmissible lethal disease and *an epidemic of meanings or signification*...This epidemic of

---

9. Canfield, 2016, 269.
10. "The Oprah Winfrey Show - Satanic Worship!", 1989.
11. "NBC's Obscene Masquerade", 1988.

meanings is readily apparent in the chaotic assemblage of understandings of AIDS that by now exists… But scientific and medical discourses have traditions through which semantic epidemics as well as biological ones are controlled, and these may disguise contradiction and irrationality… In writing about AIDS, these traditions typically include characterizing ambiguity and contradiction as nonscientific (a no-nonsense let's-get-the-facts-on-the-table-and-clear-up-this-muddle approach), invoking faith in scientific inquiry, taking for granted the reality of quantitative and/or biomedical data, deducing social and behavioral reality from quantitative and/or biomedical data, [and] *setting forth fantasies and speculations as though they were logical deductions.*[12]

In the case of AIDS, the logic of biomedical discourse as a rubric belies the fundamental homophobic "fantasy" of much of what was being said about the disease at this point in history. In the case of Satanic Panic, this "fantasy" of mass abuse and witchcraft similarly bypasses contradictions and leaps in logic through a matter-of-fact style and a reliance on faith in the police and the judicial system to act rationally, while also invoking the codes of the horror film to make seemingly fantastical claims feel both reasonable, logical, and *real*, thereby "disguise[ing] contradiction and irrationality."

The witch films of the 1980s perform a similar operation, using comedy and postfeminist rhetoric as mediating tactics to render homophobic and misogynistic moral codes tacitly legible while remaining emotionally palatable. If AIDS is to Treicher "a story, or multiple stories, and read to a surprising extent from a text that does not exist: the body of the male homosexual" which "people so want-need-to read… that they have gone so far as to write it themselves" in a manner wherein "multiple meanings, stories, and discourses intersect and overlap, reinforce and subvert each other," the Satanic Panic takes this a step further, replacing the gay man specifically with a broader indictment of multiple groups who fall under Susan Jeffords' rubric of the "soft body."[13] Thus, as a result of Faludi's "feedback loops" of "media pop culture and advertising" which "perpetuate and exaggerate [their] own false images of womanhood" in films like *The Witches of Eastwick* (1987) and even *Ghostbusters*, the stories of witches take on countless meanings, fracturing under the burden of this epidemic of signification, which renders the sign of the witch contradictory—illegible to the point of laughability.

In his 1992 FBI memo unpacking the Satanic Ritual Abuse panic, investigator Kenneth Lanning discusses these feedback loops as self-fulfilling prophecies:

---

12. Treichler, 1999, 11, 16, emphasis added.
13. *Ibid*, 19.

> The amount of sexually explicit, occult, anti-occult or violence-oriented material available to adults and even children in the modern world is overwhelming. This includes movies, videotapes, television, music, toys, and books. There are also documentaries on satanism, witchcraft, and the occult that are available on videotape. Most of the televangelists have videotapes on the topic & that they are selling on their programs. The National Coalition on Television Violence News (1988) estimates that 12 percent of the movies produced in the United States can be classified as satanic horror films. Cable television and the home VCR make all this material readily available even to young children. Religious broadcasters and almost all the television tabloid and magazine programs have done shows on satanism and the occult... Some well-intentioned awareness programs designed to prevent child sex abuse, alert professionals, or fight satanism may, in fact, be *unrealistically increasing the fears* of professionals, children, and parents and *creating self-fulfilling prophecies*.[14]

Even within this accurate assessment of the impact of this "covert horror culture" on politics, pop culture, and law enforcement practices however, Lanning himself puts forward a shockingly inflated statistic for the number of "satanic horror films" produced in the United States a year—similar to the inflated numbers of "unreported satanic kidnappings" as seen in Chapter 7—reflecting the perceived pervasiveness of the phenomenon and its outsized impact on culture as well as highlighting just how diffuse and illegible a category the "satanic horror film" had become. While books like *Saturday Morning Mind Control* insisted that "when children imagine and role-play that they have occult power, they actually open themselves up to accepting an occult mind-set", and that "there is actually a demonic realm that your child could summon up by accident", the passage above cited from Lanning's report literalizes this strange form of satanic conjuring, an extension of what J. Hoberman calls "supernaturalism" stemming from all corners of the culture during this period up to and including President Reagan himself.[15] Lanning's "self-fulfilling prophecy", then represents an entire nation summoning a belief in demons through its pop-culture (television, films, music, etc.) and sparking a witch hunt as a result.[16]

In *20/20*'s special on "devil worship", after the host points to the "perfectly legal" yet implicitly immoral "seemingly harmless types of entertainment" on offer in the horror section of a video store, he turns to the camera to tell the audience to "take a look at the numerous films that involve Satanism: most were popular films in their day, but *even today*, if one is inclined to believe in Satanism, it's a way to actually *see* the devil and perhaps be inspired."[17]

---

14. Lanning, 1992, 26.
15. Graham, 2016, 91.
16. *Ibid.*
17. "The Devil Worshippers." (1985). *20/20*. ABC News Productions.

After describing the occult content of films like *Damien: Omen II* (1978), he turns to a climactic clip from *The Exorcist*. As the ghoulish Regan laughs, the towering Father Merin cries, "*I CAST YOU OUT!*" recontextualized (like Rosemary in Geraldo's show) as if to exorcize these "pornographic" horror films themselves from video stores. In his introduction to his own special, Geraldo insists that "this is not a Halloween fable," like the era's witch horror comedies. "This is a real-life horror story." If the Panic is truly a "feedback loop" related to and reflective of antifeminist and anti-gay backlash, these witch horror comedies must be read in this context as well as a response to this atmosphere, as what the Surgeon General's Report on violence in fictional media calls *"folk literature."*[18] In a context in which horror movies were both held up as vital "proof" of abuse of which there was no other evidence (i.e. clips from *Rosemary's Baby* in segments on "breeding babies for human sacrifice") *and* decried as sinful filth, capable of indoctrinating children into satanic cults, the '80s witch film's comedic overtones, veneer of feminism and underlying moral conservatism work to bypass these overwhelming paradoxes, both archetypally for the witch and generically for the horror film. In so doing, these films also assuage popular anxieties about a changing society—concerns that, to quote Pat Robertson, the "feminist agenda . . . encourages women to leave their husbands, kill their children, practice witchcraft, destroy capitalism, and become lesbians."[19]

In her analysis of 1940s horror comedies, Christina Knopf suggests that their elision of direct references to Nazism *occluded* rather than denied a preoccupation with the war. Though these films "rarely made explicit reference" to the conflict "lest the fantastic bloodletting... come too close for comfort to their counterparts in reality... nonetheless... films inspired by the grim realities... reflected the public's war-related angst, paranoia, and *guilt*" through a lens of comedy.[20] "The addition of comic elements to these [horror] films," rather than continue to perpetuate the collective angst at hand, she argues, "[gave] form to audiences fears and faith... providing contrast to crisis" and "emotional catharsis."[21] This catharsis, she argues, springs from horror narrative's ability to "give substance to fears" *and* "[allow] audiences to face them" through the "distancing" effect of laughter—a combination she terms "morale-boosting entertainment."[22] Almost every witch comedy from the 1980s fits this definition, making the specters of women's liberation safe and amusing for conservative audience members while also spoofing those same religious, moralistic frameworks and rendering *them* safe for more liberal audiences, attempting to thread the needle of public opinion

---

18. Quoted in Graham, 2016, 89.
19. "Robertson Letter Attacks Feminists", 1992.
20. Knopf, 2016, 25.
21. *Ibid.*
22. *Ibid*, 27, 26.

to parody the Satanic Panic in its totality and serve as "morale-boosting entertainment" no matter which side of the divide a viewer happens to be on. Concerns around child molestation are held at a distance through the more familiar fairytale image of baby-eating witches and rendered safe when the witch is caricatured as laughable (*Witches' Brew* [1980]), shown to mean well (*Elvira*), disempowered and "properly" gendered (*Eastwick*) or simply burned at the stake. Nevertheless, the films also clearly reflect another prevailing sentiment of the time, what the 1984 *Time* story calls "a residual guilt" around sexual liberation; in this case, the films speak to a broader guilt about women progress in society, a backlash mentality that works to reinstitute Noddings' paradox of womanhood (see Chapter 1) that would be too painful to address without the "morale-boost" of a good laugh.

As Lanning concludes his assessment of the Satanic Panic's appeal, "it is a simple explanation for a complex problem. Nothing is more simple than 'the devil made them do it.' If we do not understand something, we make it the work of some supernatural force."[23] The Panic was a sort of mass "denial" of complex changes in the culture, from working mothers to the burgeoning acceptance of queer people that would only grow as the century wore on. Articles on the McMartin trial at the turn of the decade echoed this sentiment, suggesting that "[s]ociety seems to have a periodic need for witch trials. At the onset of the Reagan era… the hunt went back to the traditional exorcism of Satan, whose horns and cloven feet assumed the form of the local daycare teacher."[24] As it became clear towards the decade's close that the progress women and queer people had made in the 1960s and '70s—and continued to make in the '80s—was not going to be unilaterally reversed, even in the face of a mass witch hunt, the Satanic Panic, the very phenomena that conjured up witches to frighten the citizens of America into metaphorically burning their neighbors at the stake, were themselves rejected, dismissed, as Elvira closes each episode of her *Movie Macabre*, as "*unpleasant dreams.*"

---

23. Lanning, 1992, 19.
24. Cockburn, 1990.

INTERLUDE

Notes on the Postfeminist Witch Film (1990-2013)

Chapter Eleven

Riot Grrrls, Girl Power, and the Bitchification of the Witch

"So, what I want to say is... This world is bullshit. And you shouldn't model your life—wait a second—you shouldn't model your life about what you think that *we* think is cool, and what we're wearing, and what we're saying and everything. Go with yourself. Go with yourself."
-Fiona Apple, 1997[1]

The witches of the late 1990s and early 2000s are undoubtedly some of the most iconic characters in the entire history of this archetype on screen, leaving an indelible mark on the witch's pop cultural trajectory and shaping our current framework for understanding her as a specifically feminist symbol in the process. Because this era is likely the most familiar to most readers, and because there is a tremendous amount of writing on the films of this period, I have taken a different approach to this interlude than I have in Parts 1 and 2.[2]

The following several chapters are looser, shorter and more episodic, highlighting the way a bricolage of competing feminist discourses were actively applied to the Y2K witch film, by their audiences as well as their critics. I will come to argue that the witch films of the '90s in particular, though viewed as a cinematic high watermark for the witch film, are still often challenging and tangled texts that reflect the ambivalent politics of their moment. Shaped by neoliberal postfeminism in a political climate hijacked by a still-ascendant, religiously-inflected conservatism, these films were admirably responding to a virulent, bloviating culture of chauvinism with actively and explicitly feminist intent—speaking to a generation of girls who grew up alongside Second Wave feminism, made more accessible by virtue of this highly visible history, itself ironically *amplified* by the likes of Rush Limbaugh calling women "feminazis."[3] Where the backlash '80s met feminist activism with a yawn, the backlash '90s helped bring it front and center—with vein-popping rage and condescending disdain—on talk

---
1. Apple, 1997. "This World Is Bullshit", Jan 1, Video Music Awards, Los Angeles.
2. For more on the witch of the '90s, see, among others, *Lights, Camera, Witchcraft* by Heather Greene and *The Science of Witchcraft* by Meg Hafdahl and Kelly Florence.
3. Williams, 2015.

radio and the 24-hour news cycle. The differing approaches the filmmakers I discuss take to the subject of empowerment for women, however, speak to the still-fractal nature of feminism during the period of regrouping that followed the brutal defeats and disappointments of the '80s. These case studies will serve as a brief tour of feminism's big pop cultural comeback, from the Third Wave and the Riot Grrrl movement to the postfeminism these groups were rejecting, and the "Girl Power" that eventually supplanted them both in the cultural spotlight. I will work to answer several questions: How did this new generation of feminists take up the witch as a symbol and to what end? How is the '90s feminist witch shaped by the countercultural witches of the '60s occult boom? How can these characters be understood in an era of pop-cultural primacy for the "bitch" and why do they continue to hold such powerful iconic sway?

On June 29, 1998, *Time* pulled a familiar black and red design from its back catalogs, replacing the burning question that so haunted *Rosemary's Baby* (1968) ("Is God Dead?") with a new one: "Is Feminism Dead?" the cover asks, showing a line-up of women staring directly at the camera, their names listed above, in a neat row. Presented as a feminist chronology to the present, the cover bore the black and white faces of Susan B. Anthony, Betty Friedan, Gloria Steinam, and, to represent the '90s, Ally McBeal in full color. "What a comedown for the movement," Ginia Bellafante writes, "much of feminism has devolved into the silly. And it has powerful support for this: a popular culture insistent on offering images of grown single women as frazzled, self-absorbed girls."[4] The piece works to suggest that whereas the older pioneers on the magazine's cover were engaging in activism, the women of the '90s put their stock in, among other things, "mindless sex talk" and "airy—sometimes even ludicrous—mini-memoirs meant to expand our understanding of female experience," citing *Cunt* and *The Vagina Monologues*.[5]

This cover is an instructive entry into the complex, often agonizing world of '90s feminist discourse for several reasons. In some ways, the author's criticisms of what she insistently calls postfeminism are more than justified—she charges corporate interests with promulgating tepid portraits of women as beautiful, man-crazy babies and feeding off their insecurities to sell beauty products. In fact, these denunciations spoke to the kinds of dissatisfaction feminists had begun making at the top of their lungs in 1991, when Susan Faludi published *Backlash* and Clarence Thomas' senate confirmation became a national spectacle that sparked urgent debates over

---

4. Bellafante, 1998.
5. *Ibid.*

sexual harassment and institutional misogyny.[6] It does, however, *perpetuate* all these problems in the same breath, replicating these backlash-style discourses in its very premise: Ally McBeal, unlike Gloria Steinem or Susan B. Anthony, was not an activist. She wasn't even a real person. She was the title character on a TV show, created by the very masculinist institutions the author aims to critique—"and what did David Kelley have to say about Ally as a feminist?" Bellafante asks, scathingly quoting the showrunner, "'She's not a hard, strident feminist out of the '60s and '70s. She's all for women's rights, but she doesn't want to lead the charge at her own emotional expense.' Ally, though, is in charge of nothing, least of all her emotional life"—an accurate assessment of any fictional character's worldview, if not of the real-life feminists who, like Bellafante, had been debating Ally's merits in journals like *Feminist Media Studies* since her debut.

This fundamental category error, the conflation of media representations of feminists and feminists themselves, provides an insight into the rapidly shifting media landscape of the '90s—and the terms of the debates that dominated the culture. The already-saturated landscape Baudrillard described in the '80s only picked up in this decade, with the increased presence of cable television, talk radio, and the nascent internet alongside the booming indie film scene (think *Clerks*, [1994]) and a strong period for Hollywood—all of which came with a particular postmodern meta-referentiality (think *Scream*, [1996]). Concerns over the real-world impact of media on culture in the '80s had bled into every element of American life by the '90s. Feminists' focus on now-familiar issues of "representation" and what became known as "cultural studies" became so dominant—recall the media primacy of Naomi Wolf's *The Beauty Myth* and the success of Camille Paglia's *Sexual Personae* in 1990—that, as this *Time* story indicates, some believed feminism had lost sight of "real-world" issues, becoming image-obsessed and solipsistic. Indeed, postfeminism's prominence at this point was itself a product of the landscape of media studies—the result of what Angela McRobbie describes as the new "feminist reflexivity" within cultural studies in the '90s.[7] Feminist media scholars like Rebecca Feasey highlighted the fact that Second Wave feminism (particularly in the aftermath of the "sex wars"), was often "underpinned by a hostility toward the popular", framing this renewed interest in pop-cultural analysis and representation as a response to the fact that "our initial ideas of what feminism was about were *formed through the popular* in the 1970s and 1980s."[8] As such, feminists were indeed discussing *Ally McBeal* as a microcosm for heteropatriarchal hegemony in an era when

---

6. During the confirmation process for still-sitting Supreme Court Justice Clarence Thomas, a former law clerk accused Thomas of sexual harassment. She was vilified in the press, by Senators, and by Thomas himself. For more on this, see *Race-ing Justice, En-gendering Power: Essays on Anita Hill, Clarence Thomas, and the Construction of Social Reality* (1992).
7. McRobbie, 2007, 256.
8. Feasey, 2006, 4.

the successes of women-led films like *The Witches of Eastwick* (1987) and rom-coms like *When Harry Met Sally* (1989) in the late '80s had led to the proliferation of films "for women". The Bechdel Test was going mainstream and rightly so.[9] These debates, though, in McRobbie's view among others, were a product of the same neoliberalism that birthed postfeminism and meant, in part, that "'emancipatory politics' ha[d] given way instead to life politics", an argument that echoes the critiques of "cultural feminism" in the '70s.[10]

All the same, academics duking it out over television or the merits of Nora Ephron films weren't the heart of feminist *activism* during this period—and real feminists responded to *Time*'s postfeminist cover story with open frustration. "We got smart and *Time* declared us dead," Erica Jong wrote,[11] while Judy Mann argued that

> [t]he media has paid scant attention to a wealth of world-class feminist scholarship that has emerged over the past 20 years, while it made a star of Camille Paglia, an intellectual buzzsaw-cum-publicity hound. Time magazine's article is yet another unfortunate example of this—fixing its sights on people who have no relevance to the women's movement and have done nothing to advance the welfare of women, and then hauling out the death knell of the movement, which, in typical *Time* fashion, it never quite sounds.[12]

The article was diagnosed for what it was: more backlash. "When feminists are scholarly and serious, we see such articles as 'Why don't feminists smile?' and 'Where is the humor?'... [Here] the writer condemns women for supporting Clinton, ignoring the fact that the only available alternative was a fundamentalist-controlled-Dole," another complains.[13] One writer even pointed out, echoing Faludi's thesis, that *Time* "ha[d] run scores of stories like this long before [this particular author] was born."[14] The broad conclusion scores of female journalists made in concert—a unified front in legacy outlets, newly prolific feminist presses, and women-run women's magazines alike that spoke to the undeniable progress feminism had, in fact, been making—was that

> [w]e are in the midst of an unfinished revolution. The older troops are exhausted and their replacements (our daughters) are just getting the hang of

---

9. A metric for measuring a film's representation of its women characters created by lesbian cartoonist Allision Bechdel: to pass, two women have to speak to each other in the film about something other than a man.
10. McRobbie, 2007, 260.
11. Jong, 1998.
12. Mann, 1998.
13. De Hon, 2016.
14. Jong, 1998.

it. They are about to reframe the debate and shape it to their own uses. They are about to turn the revolution around and make it new. This is good. It also takes time. Of course, there are miles to go before we sleep, but it's not as if nothing happened... *Time*'s idiotic cover story on feminism is, in short, a symptom of what's wrong, not an analysis.[15]

"Is Feminism Dead?" and its reception speak to the way backlash rhetoric had insidiously evolved in the intervening decade, coming full circle by the end of the millennium. Even as many young women continued to espouse the backlash line, actively disidentifying with "feminist" as a dusty, superfluous label, Second Wave feminism had also become canonized, embedding itself into the education system since the 1960s, with the entrenchment and growth of "Women's Studies" departments after the field's founding as an official academic study in 1979. Similarly, as Lisa Levenstein notes in her book *They Didn't See Us Coming*, feminists took advantage of new modes of communication in their activism, giving rise to a powerful feminist "blogosphere" (i.e. sites like *Jezebel*) to disseminate feminist ideas: "by the end of the 1990s, anyone looking for feminism no longer needed to attend a march or a conference... All they needed was a modem, a computer, and a phone line."[16] But these newly-educated and, importantly, self-educated feminists were now being treated as bimbos rather than harpies—becoming what some denigratingly called "lipstick feminists".

Meanwhile, in 1991, the torturous experience of Clarence Thomas' confirmation hearing atomized the next generation of already-primed young feminist activists. During the hearings, Anita Hill, a young, Black conservative lawyer, accused then-nominee for Supreme Court Justice Clarence Thomas of sexual harassment and was excoriated by senators and in the press—in a particularly insulting incident, Senator Orrin Hatch accused her of plagiarizing her allegation (that Thomas had put a pubic hair on a soda can) from *The Exorcist* (1973).[17] Phyllis Schlafly called the well-documented sexual harassment accusations a smear orchestrated by the "feminist mob", while Thomas called it a "lynching."[18] As these loaded statements indicate, the hearings were highly racialized as well as gendered, and Thomas successfully used his marginalized status as a Black man (he was consciously appointed by George H.W. Bush to replace Thurgood Marshall, the first Black Supreme Court Justice) as a wedge against accusations of misogyny made by conspiratorially-framed feminists, presented by defenders as white. Despite the evidence against him, he was confirmed in October 1992. The tactics used by the Justice to deflect the accusations weren't missed by Black feminists.

---

15. Jong, 1998.
16. Doherty, 2020.
17. C-Span, 2018.
18. Du Mez, 2020, 146.

Indeed, one of Hill's lawyers was Kimberlé Crenshaw, who had coined the term "intersectionality" in her 1989 essay "Demarginalizing the intersection of race and sex". The public humiliation and victim-blaming of the hearings, alongside another major blow to *Roe v. Wade*—*1992's Planned Parenthood v. Casey* decision which replaced strict protections against restrictive abortion legislation with the far more surmountable "undue burden" standard—sparked a massive revitalization of the feminist movement.

These defeats for women tapped into the simmering rage of a feminist movement on the ropes with misogyny fresh on its mind. More women ran for (and won) elected positions in the aftermath of the Thomas hearings than at any previous point in history, prompting reporters to label that year, "The Year of the Woman". NOW regained much of its strength after *Casey*, organizing a 750,000-person March for Women's Lives that April. Rebecca Walker's "Becoming the Third Wave" was directly spurred by her *anger* at the Thomas fracas. Calling the hearings "an assault on the human spirit" in specifically intersectional terms, Walker framed her argument as a wrathful manifesto:

> The backlash against U.S. women is real... I intend to fight back. I have uncovered and unleashed more repressed anger than I thought possible... Let Thomas' confirmation serve to remind you, as it did me, that the fight is far from over.[19]

She insisted that to overcome institutional misogyny, it would be essential for women to "join in sisterhood with women when often we are divided, to understand power structures with the intention of challenging them." Meanwhile, in Olympia Washington, Kathleen Hanna, then twenty-three, was starting a pop cultural rebellion in the punk scene with her band Bikini Kill. The "Riot Grrrl Manifesto", spread using the DIY ethos of punk through self-published zines, channeled a similar fury, calling on young women to identify as riot grrrls and participate in the subculture

> BECAUSE doing/reading/seeing/hearing cool things that validate and challenge us can help us gain the strength and sense of community that we need in order to figure out how bullshit like racism, able-bodieism, ageism, speciesism, classism, thinism, sexism, anti-semitism and heterosexism figures in our own lives./...BECAUSE we hate capitalism in all its forms /... BECAUSE we are angry at a society that tells us Girl = Dumb, Girl = Bad, Girl = Weak./BECAUSE we are unwilling to let our real and valid anger be diffused and/or turned against us via the internalization of sexism.../ BECAUSE I believe with my wholeheartmindbody that girls constitute a revolutionary soul force that can, and will change the world for real.[20]

---

19. Walker, 2002, 86.
20. Hanna, 1991.

The manifesto, and the raucously queer movement it represented, took "girls" seriously, mixing real-world intersectional politics with art and music and community. The riot grrrls actively worked against an atmosphere of sexism in the punk scene, calling out rape culture, sexual harassment, and slut-shaming.

> "Everyone was saying 'feminism is dead' and I had just found it", Hanna said later, "And I was like, if feminism doesn't need to exist anymore and we live in a 'post-feminist' society... why is the rape crisis phone ringing off the hook all night long?"[21]

Like W.I.T.C.H., the largely middle class, white and suburban riot grrrls weaponized sexist stereotypes used against them, labeling their bodies with words like "bitch", "slut", and "whore" to espouse actively sex-positive feminism. The stereotype they chose, however, rather than the witch was simply the girl—as Part 2 concludes, "witches" and "bitches" were practically the same thing.

This particular reclamatory gesture, embracing the "bitch", is in some ways the connective tissue of the feminist movements of the '90s. United in their rage if not in their activism, as Allison Yarrow points out in her book *90s Bitch: Media, Culture, and the Failed Promise of Gender Equality*, the women of this moment embraced the "bitchification" of feminism, weaponizing the hostility used against them to produce reams of incisive, intersectional academic work on the one hand (other authors have credited the '90s with the "professionalization—one might even call it the bureaucratization—of feminism"), alongside, as Kat Stratford put it in *10 Things I Hate About You* (1999), "angry girl music of the indie rock persuasion."[22] While a wave of women entered politics to fight the uphill battle against backlash conservatism and feminist academics made drudging, thankless rounds on the nightly news to spar with Christian culture warriors, riot grrrls and bitches alike did what in the '80s would have seemed impossible. As Beth Ditto, lead singer for punk band The Gossip put it in her introduction to *Riot Grrrl: Revolution Girl Style Now*, "for the first time in history, valley girls were feared... Riot Grrrl... turn[ed] academia into an accessible, down-to-earth language, making feminism a trend for the first time in history."[23] These skater punks, queer goths, and rebellious girls in combat boots and sparkly eyeshadow, who spent the time they weren't rocking out publishing reams of DIY zines full of poems and essays about sex, drugs, rock n roll, and making the world a better place, made feminism *fun* again.

---

21. West, 2018, 16.
22. Doherty, 2020.
23. West, 2018, 36.

But turning this renewed energy and determination into real-world gains would prove a constant and largely re-infuriating struggle. As Karina Longworth explains in the "Erotic 90s" season of her cinema history series, *You Must Remember This*, "though there seemed to be an enormous amount of sex in the culture in the 1990s"—on the news, with scandals like teenage Amy Fischer murdering her lover's wife and OJ Simpson (allegedly) murdering his wife and her lover; on television, with popular shows like the *Red Shoe Diaries* (1992-1999); and in film, with hits as varied as *Basic Instinct* (1992) and *Pretty Woman* (1990)—the effects of backlash "were not subversive undercurrents by the time Bill Clinton was elected in 1992. They were the meat of the culture."[24] Between 1987 and 1995, the budget of Focus on the Family, James Dobson's evangelical anti-gay, anti-choice organization, had ballooned from $34 million to over $100 million.[25] While Clinton's embrace of the neoliberal center aided Democrats recovering political ground after a decade of Republican control, opening the door for long-term feminist gains, conservatives continued to push a repressive social agenda, continually embattling any kind of progressive legislation. As such, the entire era's politics were defined by retrenchment and forced moderation of an already moderate Democratic mainstream. Even as Bill Clinton passed the Family and Medical Leave Act in 1993 and the Violence Against Women Act in 1994 after vehement lobbying from women's groups like NOW, while he had originally proposed a bill that allowed gay people to openly serve in the military, the result of bitter conflict with republicans like Newt Gingrich led to "Don't Ask, Don't Tell" instead. Gingrich and others popularized a brasher, more vitriolic form of conservatism than had previously dominated the party in the '80s, taking advantage of the newly minted 24-hour news cycle to keep Democrats off-balance—"one of the great problems we have in the Republican Party is that we don't encourage you to be nasty," he famously lamented, arguing that "the number one fact about the news media is they love fights... When you give them confrontations, you get attention."[26] At the 1992 Republican convention, Pat Buchanan used the term that fundamentally underpinned the terms of this form of rhetorical combat: "There is a religious war going on in this country. It is a *cultural war*... this war is for the soul of America."[27]

The newly declared culture war's disastrous impact on women's empowerment is clearly on view in the systematic disempowerment of First Lady Hillary Rodham Clinton over the course of the decade. Clinton went from a successful lawyer actively participating in the Second Wave in the '70s, to *repeatedly* apologizing to housewives for responding to an attack

---

24. Longworth, March 2023.
25. Du Mez, 2020, 85.
26. Coppins, 2018.
27. Buchanan, 1992.

against her status as a working woman during a '92 primary debate with the quip, "I suppose I could have stayed home, baked cookies, and had teas, but I decided to fulfill my profession." In that same remark, her argument that, as a lawyer, she had worked "to assure that women can make the choices, whether it's full-time career, full-time motherhood, or some combination,"[28] fell on deaf ears: "If I ever entertained the idea of voting for Bill Clinton" one woman wrote to *Time*, "the smug bitchiness of his wife's comments has nipped that notion in the bud."[29] Hillary faced similar scandals that year during the Gennifer Flowers incident when she said on 60 Minutes "I'm not sittin' here some little woman standing by my man." These "gaffs" were presented as evidence for the "moral decay" of social liberalism—and, just as importantly, of Hillary's failures as a *woman*.[30] Hillary Clinton, who only took her husband's name a decade into their marriage, was a "feminazi".

But as repeated references to "postfeminism", from Faludi to Ally McBeal attest, questions of what feminism even was in the bleak, confusing wake of the Reagan-Bush years tied feminists into internecine academic knots over the meaning of the term even as the girls of Generation X were staking out new territory as members of the movement's Third Wave. With these battles unfolding, as the "Is Feminism Dead?" cover attests, what I called backlash's "veneer of feminism" (what Faludi calls postfeminist rhetoric), had by the end of the millennium *absorbed anti-backlash discourse itself as a new tool of backlash*, blaming feminists for the "death" of feminism *again*—this time by labeling them trivial or shallow or slutty on top of the usual charges of man-hating and dowdiness.

By 1993, Bikini Kill and riot grrrl had been mischaracterized so many times in the mainstream press that Kathleen Hanna called for a media blackout, inadvertently ceding the narrative of the movement in the process. Around the same time, corporations, and Hollywood, began taking note of teenage girls as a lucrative market, giving rise to what was quickly labeled "girl power" as a discourse and a marketing tool in the vacuum of activist voices. Commonly associated with The Spice Girls, girl power discourse was a highly individuated, specifically neoliberal form of feminist signaling, that encouraged women to empower themselves as unique agents rather than members of any feminist coalition, specifically through capitalistic consumption, i.e. buying "girls rule!" t-shirts and watching *Bridget Jones' Diary* rather than attending a Take Back the Night protest or crossing evangelical picket-lines outside abortion clinics. Girl power was an offshoot

---

28. Jamieson and Gabbatt, 2016.
29. Du Mez, 2020, 140, emphasis added.
30. The Lewinsky scandal was also used by Pat Robertson as evidence of the counterculture's continued pernicious influence. He contended, that alongside the socialist, feminist, anti-family Hillary, the sexually rapacious, pot-smoking ("I did not inhale"), first Boomer president had "'debauched, debased, and defamed' the Presidency, turning the White House into a 'playpen for the sexual freedom of the poster child of the 1960s'" (Du Mez, 2020, 143).

of a broader postfeminist ethos that pervaded like a haze of trendy perfume, obscuring broader feminist goals even as it undeniably popularized some forms of empowerment to women and girls. Girl power's ethos of consumerism *did* encourage a broader range of positive media representations for women and girls in the middle of the decade with affectionate portraits of womanhood like *Clueless* (1995; whose Valley Girl star mixes references to Monet with her diet of Beevis and Butthead), *10 Things I Hate About You* (whose iconic "bitchy" feminist hero reads *The Bell Jar* and listens to Bikini Kill—her paramour pretends to love The Raincoats to get her attention), and *Reality Bites* (1994; whose star-crossed superwoman debates feminist politics and the economy with her parodically cynical slacker lover, while her yuppie suitor insists he, too, "know[s] why the caged bird sings").

Witches fall into the dead center of the girl power milieu of the mid-late '90s, encapsulating both the ways Third Wave feminist ideals were being foregrounded in pop culture and, at the same time, undercut by neoliberalism, individualism, and the hobbling forces of the now-mainstreamed conservatism of the Moral Majority. Beginning in 1995, interest in Wicca spiked among teenage girls because of shows like *Sabrina the Teenage Witch* (1996-2003) and, more importantly, Andrew Fleming's *The Craft* (1996). Such revival, immediately remarked in the media (called the "Teen Witch Phenomenon" by religious scholar Denise Cush), was received with alarm in a culture that had only fully put the Satanic Panic to rest about a year before.[31] This fascination, so similar to the nouveau witch of the '60s occult revival, was immediately linked to both countercultural New Ageism *and* the Satanic Panic, and discussed on feminist terms: one 1998 article by an evangelical author lamented that "radical feminists" (divorced from its original meaning, now a culture war-era insult) like Silver Ravenwolf were indoctrinating young girls into a dangerous religious practice while encouraging safe sex and polyamory on websites like witchvox.com.[32] Citing a smattering of born-again former hippies (who had made their living off of the Panic in the '80s with alarmist books like *Like Lambs to the Slaughter: Your Child and the Occult* [1989]) and the head of Focus on the Family, she argues that "witchcraft is 'narcissistic, amoral and pleasure seeking—the perfect postmodern religion for the nineties.'"[33]

Interestingly, Ravenwolf's classic Wicca primer, *Teen Witch: Witchcraft for a New Generation* (1998), begins with an introduction meant to combat the rhetoric of the Panic: "Okay—you've picked up this book and you're going through minor coronary arrest," she begins, but

---

31. Cush, 2007, 45.
32. Edwards, 1999, 23.
33. *Ibid.*

[b]efore you rush into their room and put them on a plane to the nearest church camp... you can stop worrying that [your] child... will attack you in the dark with a butcher knife and try to sacrifice Fluffy when your back is turned. It ain't gonna happen.[34]

The book espouses the precise kind of feminist Wicca I explore in Part 1, using the author's personal experience as a thirteen-year-old picking up a pack of tarot cards and a copy of Sibyl Leek's *Diary of a Witch* in 1969 as a segue into explaining the now-familiar histories (two million dead witches, Goddess worship, feminine solidarity with nature, etc).[35] She lists books by authors from the occult revival in her recommended reading list. The book couches its particular feminist neo-paganism in references to hiding in your room with your CD player and going to the mall with your friends, but the concepts remain entirely unchanged. Books like these pervaded in the mid-late '90s as in the late '60s—titles like *Where to Park Your Broomstick: A Teen's Guide to Witchcraft*, *To Ride A Silver Broomstick: New Generation Witchcraft*, and *Living Wicca* became familiar sights at Barnes & Noble.[36] "The problem is that this younger generation has grown up with magic and occult" lamented the head of an "anti-New Age" action group, echoing the precise kind of language constantly applied to Third Wave feminism, "they have the internet websites and primetime TV is *Buffy the Vampire Slayer* (1997-2003) and *Sabrina*. All this stuff makes Wicca seem natural to them."[37] By the year 2000, witches dominated on television: *Charmed* (1998-2006) would become the longest running series with all-female leads, adding to the supernatural landscape established by, yes, *Buffy* and *Sabrina*, shows that re-popularized the kinds of storylines begun with *Carrie* and cleaned up in the white-rapping musical bomb *Teen Witch* in 1989—by then a cult classic on Disney Channel.

The Craft, though, is by far the most influential touchstone for this micro-occult revival, credited by many girls as their entry into Wiccan practice and solidifying the association between witchcraft and '90s goth subcultures.[38] Conceived by *Flatliners* screenwriter Peter Filardi, who would go on direct a film about one of the most infamous cases of the Satanic Panic,[39] the film was both explicitly feminist in its intent and a tremendous financial success,

---

34. RavenWolf, 1998, xiii.
35. *Ibid*, xx.
36. Manoy and Apostolides, 2002.
37. Edwards, 1999, 25.
38. Not even two years later this connection would be obvious enough to appear in *Scooby Doo*: As Thorn, the lead singer for the vampiric Wicca girl band the Hex Girls in *Scooby Doo and the Witch's Ghost* (1999) drawls, "we're eco goths."
39. The film, *Ricky 6* (2000), is about teen heavy metal fan and frequent psychedelic drug user Ricky Kasso, a.k.a. "The Acid King", who commanded his friend to "say you love Satan" before stabbing him to death in the woods near his home. The story was featured prominently in both Geraldo's *Devil Worship: Exposing Satan's Underground* (1988) and *20/20's The Devil Worshippers* (1985).

particularly with teenage girls. Building on the punk feminism of *Elvira, Mistress of the Dark* (1988), *The Craft* brought the New Age sensibility of Ravenwolf's radical feminist neo-paganism together with the heretofore negatively associated occultism of metal subcultures, imbuing the latter with the former's specific brand of feminism.[40] This connection nicely crystalizes the witch archetype's status as a sort of oppositional sponge, a vector for whatever flavor of rebellion suits the anxieties of the moment—a sensibility that *The Craft* captures perfectly.

Andrew Fleming has repeatedly emphasized that the concept he pitched Columbia Pictures for *The Craft* wasn't about devil worship. Raised with what he called "a little bit of a hippie upbringing", he wanted to make his witches "recognizable to Wiccans", playing on the question, "What if those four girls people stare at at lunch… were witches and… looked like they were in The Cure?"[41] A gay man, he also explicitly wanted the film to champion "outsiders" and "people on the margins". Drawing on recollections from his "torturous" time in high school for rewrites, the film's producer, Doug Wick, said he injected these archetypal outcast teens with "specific pain", imbuing his witches with distinctly intersectional identities. This pain was thematically linked to the political history of the Second Wave countercultural witch from the start: "I was very aware that [witchcraft is an] age-old metaphor for talking about female empowerment, and the sort of mysteries of women and their connection to nature in terms of reproductivity," Wick said, and "I've always been very interested in female empowerment."[42] Filardi, for his part, recalled later that, "Doug and I spoke for hours about magic, mushrooms and ecstasy" as well as "the world of teen Satanism and that volatile cocktail of hallucinogens, metal and magic… I remember telling him that magic is historically a weapon of the underclass," explicitly threading the imagistic and thematic needle of the psychedelicized occult boom of the '60s and the heavy metal bust of the '80s.[43] In a film that begins with an alt-rock cover of The Beatles' psychedelic classic "Tomorrow Never Knows" these influences are manifested most directly through visualizing magic as MTV-style psychedelic flash-cuts—Medieval witch illustrations, eyes, the ocean, pentagrams, tarot cards, etc. The production also, like the films of the occult revival, publicized their employment of a Wiccan "witch consultant" on set. She herself claimed to have only "become a witch at sixteen because

---

40. Interestingly, in the evolution of the witch as a non-normative threat, the association between witches and punks can be tied to the witch's broader history as a countercultural signifier. As exemplified by a June 1984 *Playboy* article, "Skank or Die" (Young, 1984), about '80s punk, there seemed to be a sense that, regardless of their antithetical aesthetics, punks were actually the spiritual successors to hippies: "This armadillo of sociomusical evolution ['80s punk] is emerging rabid and snarling from under a rock in suburbia, much as the hippies slithered out in 1966 or so", "[punks] are all naive teenage twats trying to offend their parents… they're just like hippies", "[punks] are no better than stoned-out hippies," etc.
41. "Directing *The Craft*", 2019.
42. "Producing *The Craft*", 2019.
43. Jacobs and Brucculieri, 2016.

Donovan wrote a song called 'Season of the Witch'. I do not underestimate the impact of the media on teenagers and this movie was brewed up for the teenage audience."[44]

Produced on the early side of the commodification of teen girl culture, the studio was leery of what they viewed as an "edgy" product, particularly in an atmosphere that was still, as Wick put it, a "very male time at the studios."[45] Indeed, the top grossing film of 1995 was a literal holdover from the '80s hard body era: *Die Hard with a Vengeance*. "The whole idea of a girl-centric teenage movie that was dark, there weren't really a lot of antecedents for that. It was pre-*Buffy* and it was before *Scream*," recalled Fleming in a 2016 interview. *The Craft* was indeed part of a rising tide of girl-centric horror, part of what Alexandra West called "the 1990s teen horror cycle", exemplified by films like *I Know What You Did Last Summer* (1998). These films would eventually come to be understood as, in part, an offshoot of "branding" of grunge, punk, and alt post-Nirvana, as well as a revision of the '80s slasher cycle and an appeal to the newly powerful suburban teen market (almost half of Americans lived in the 'burbs by the start of the decade).[46] But before *Scream*, and with regards to this film in particular, concern over the film's "edginess", was also a product of the Panic—the film's surprising R-rating, per Fleming, came as a result of industry nerves at the sight of "devil worship and teenagers in the same movie"; in retrospect, this ostensibly limiting move for a film designed to appeal to teens actually *aided* it, giving its already-outsider appeal an added sheen of the forbidden for teens sneaking into an R-rated movie at the multiplex.[47]

The Craft tells the story of formerly suicidal new girl Sarah (Robin Tunney), who befriends a group of outcasts, Nancy (Fairuza Balk, a real-life Wiccan), Bonnie (Neve Campbell), and Rochelle (Rachel True) on her first day of Catholic school. Sarah is initially nervous around the three goth girls, and Chris (Skeet Ulrich, who would star in *Scream* alongside Campbell only a few months later), a popular jock, warns her that they're "the bitches of Eastwick"—an insult off-handedly tossed at the leads of the actual *Eastwick* in reviews, now brought full circle. Nancy, who Chris calls a "huge slut", is a working-class girl with an abusive step-father; Bonnie is ashamed of the disfiguring scars that mar her body after a fire; Rochelle, who's Black, is tormented by a racist white girl named Laura (Christine Taylor, familiar as Marcy in *The Brady Bunch Movie,* [1995]), who uses racial slurs and compares her ginger-tinted curls to pubic hair. Once Sarah joins their coven, they take strength in their shared social ostracization, comforting and defending each other. In a poignant embodiment of the

---

44. Yohalem, 1998.
45. "Producing *The Craft*", 2019.
46. West, 2018, 132.
47. "Directing *The Craft*", 2019.

power of their solidarity, they raise up Rochelle, levitating her feet above the ground, holding her up with their minds. In this image, as in the party scene in *Rosemary's Baby*, a vision of genuine feminist solidarity is hopefully and clearly visible, even allowed to play out for long stretches of the film. In Nancy's iconic, grinning declaration that "we're the weirdos mister", an embrace of the witch's rebellious, empowered, outsider status is visible.

After Chris slut-shames Sarah, the women get magical revenge on their tormentors. Their spells work: Chris falls madly in love with Sarah (much to the bemusement of his sexist jock friends—"what are you the Stepford boy?"). Meanwhile, Bonnie's scars heal, and Rochelle's racist bully loses her long blonde hair. Nancy's circumstances are the harshest: she faces rampant slut-shaming at school and the threat of sexual abuse by her stepfather in her ramshackle home with only her alcoholic mother for company. Eventually, she gives her stepfather a heart attack and she and her mother receive a large life insurance policy, bringing them out of poverty. The overwhelming consensus from the girls: they deserve it.

This kind of wrathful, gleefully outsider feminism was very much in keeping with the pop cultural mood by 1996, even beyond the riot grrrl scene that Nancy and the gang would almost certainly be a part of (when she learns that Sarah tried to kill herself, slitting her wrists "the right way", as Bonnie knowingly points out, Nancy raises an eyebrow: "punk rock", she concedes). In *Bitch: In Praise of Difficult Women*, Elizabeth Wurtzl's follow-up to that Gen X classic *Prozac Nation*, she articulates the rage of the decade's feminism from the perspective of that particularly gendered epithet, already so associated with witches. Pointing to the rise of feminist zines like *Bitch*, she argues that

> [b]ad girls understand that there is no point in being good and suffering in silence. What good has *good* ever done? We women still only make seventy-one cents, on average, for every man's dollar. We still have to listen to studies telling us that a single woman over the age of thirty-five best avoid airplanes because she is more likely to die in a terrorist attack than get married (and even after Susan Faludi refuted the numbers, we still had to hear Rosie O'Donnell point out in *Sleepless in Seattle* that the study, "feels true, even if it isn't")... we're stuck with Clarence Thomas on the Supreme court. So why be good? Anita Hill, a good girl if there ever was one... still had to listen to Orrin Hatch read to her from *The Exorcist*.[48]

As Katt Shea, the director of *The Rage: Carrie 2* (1999), described her (equally tragically flawed) take on the goth '90s witch, "I hoped to bring the pain and triumph of being a social pariah to life. To be blunt and honest. It's a movie about revenge and bullies getting what they deserve. We can't do that in

---

48. Wurtzel, 1999, 8.

life, we get to do that in our fantasies and movies."[49] [50] From this perspective, the catharsis offered to the goth kids who made *The Craft* a classic is obvious and satisfying, harsh or not, part of the enduring appeal of this film—and the appeal of the "teenage witch phenomenon", whose practitioners, per one study on the commercialized Wicca of the '90s "admitted to copying some of their rituals" from films like *The Craft*.[51] The depictions of these women's misery is poignant and visceral, detailed and realistic. With these frank portrayals of the complex and interwoven challenges facing young women, from poverty and racism to sexual harassment and abuse—the exact battles being centered by feminists like Rebecca Walker and Kathleen Hanna—this coven literalizes the rage undergirding feminist manifestos like Wurtzl's or Bikini Kill's ("I used to say that I hated men... I guess I actually did").[52] And their wrath *must be collective* to function: they are a unit, a harmonious quartet, calling on the powers of nature to re-order the universe.

Tragically, the film takes a turn for the conservative and traditionally moralistic. Sarah, the only witch presented as "natural" (having inherited her gift from her mother where the other women learned it themselves), becomes the hero and Nancy the villain, with Bonnie and Rochelle as her evil henchwomen. The girls' spells are suddenly depicted as "going too far" (the ironically Biblical golden rule is invoked),[53] but the moral valences behind this presentation are complex. Bonnie's circumstances don't change, but Sarah finds her new self-confidence and sexual assertiveness "narcissistic", complaining "You used to be nice!" Rochelle's racist tormentor's hair continues to fall out, a detail presented as a pitiable escalation, but which seems entirely logical in context; the only truly dramatic change is in Chris, whose obsession with Sarah takes a grim turn when he tries to rape her. Nancy reacts with full, traumatized force. She goes to his house and seduces him, disguising herself as Sarah. This scene recreates many of the most elemental anxieties of witch portrayals, women seducing and tormenting men as a means of exerting sexual control. Sarah stops her, obviously disgusted with this "bad" witch, and Chris disingenuously apologizes. "He's *sorry?*" Nancy spits, laughing with outrage, "The only way you know how to treat women is by treating them like *whores*! *You're* the whore!" Nancy shakes with rage, shaking her head violently and repeating, "He's sorry, he's sorry, he's sorry!" like an evil incantation. The window flies open behind the boy. "*Sorry my ass!*" She roars. Chris, cowering in terror, flies backwards, falling to his death.

---

49. Shea, quoted in West, 2018, 90.
50. In that film, as the title attests, Carrie's (punk rock) rage is fleshed out as more than justified, with much of the film's runtime spent knife-twisting the bullying in even more detail. Still, Carrie dies in the same tragic way.
51. Cush, 2007, 49.
52. Bellafante, 1998.
53. "Do to others as you would like them to do to you" Luke 6:31.

The dynamics on display in this important scene, clearly meant to connote Nancy's turn into villainy, recall the panicked reactions male audience-members and critics had to *Thelma & Louise* (1991) several years before. That film, which portrayed what Pat Morrison in the *New York Times* astutely called the kind of "violent revenge fantasy for women that Hollywood had been making for men for decades", made some male critics so nervous as to declare it, quite confidently, "fascist."[54] Using the logic of *Thelma & Louise*, Nancy's actions are a form of cathartic anti-misogynist vigilante justice. In *The Craft*, however, the viewer is hewn to Sarah's perspective throughout Nancy's moving and fiery monologue. Sarah, who gives Nancy looks of outright horror as she lambasts her would-be rapist and their mutual sexual harasser, is the film's most normative witch, hewing far closer to the *Sabrina* mold than the others in terms of wealth and status. In portraying this "natural" witch as "good" and the other three as, eventually, literally evil, stereotypes around a particular kind of upper-middle-class white femininity as "pure" are reasserted, shattering the solidarity that previously guided the film's narrative. By the film's final passages, the three "evil" witches are framing Sarah for a murder she didn't commit. ("You know," Nancy falsely claims in one of the more overt fabrications in the film's witch-lore, "in the old days, if a witch betrayed her coven, they'd kill her.") Nancy attempts to stab Sarah to death, only for Sarah to invoke the powers of Manon on her own and defeat her with her superior, "natural" craft, torturing Bonnie and Rochelle with images of their skin marred and their hair falling out before restoring order to the world. "Now who's pathetic?" she asks Nancy, who lies prone on the floor.

Adding insult to injury, the last two scenes show Bonnie, Rochelle, and Nancy humiliated by the now-haughty Sarah, losing their powers as punishment for their transgressive anger. Nancy for her part is locked in an institution, her face covered in scratches and her arms and legs tied down with enormous straps, moaning and screaming about her powers, made disturbing and disturbed, powerless and insane. "I'm flying!" she wails, a tragic parody of her previous cries of rage, before a nurse forcibly injects her with a sedative. The frame dissolves into dissociative close ups. She smiles, mania in her eyes, looking directly into the camera. This concluding image, a cruel tonal shift from the rest of the film, flies in the face of the upbeat alt-rock that covers the credits, any message of "female empowerment" crushed by the uncritical use of the same imagery of "hysterical" witches that feminists critiqued as far back as *Häxan* (1922).

Critics universally excoriated this strange moralism, even while they celebrated *The Craft*'s overall tone and depiction of powerful young women. "As vampires and werewolves are to teenage boys, witches are to teenage

---

54. Morrison, quoted in Longworth, April 2023.

girls—scarily sexy, omnipotent alter egos born of raging hormones and the lust for power that comes from being disrespected all around," Amy Taubin writes, and *The Craft* is "more on the mark in its detailing of mid '90s girl life than one expects than from a Hollywood product." But "when, at the very end, the 'law' enters the picture to put the grrrl world in order. I was really pissed."[55] [56] "OK, we get it: Kinky sex and the occult are bad, right?" moans another writer, "because 'The Craft's' target audience - trendy adolescents - is usually turned off by such prim finger-wagging, Fleming masks this '700 Club' message with a raucous MTV veneer."[57] Critics across the board also highlighted the unnecessary and surprising trivialization of the three "bad" witch's serious problems: "Rochelle becomes racked with guilt after seeing her bald schoolmate crying in the shower. (Why? Who cares if a bigoted cheerleader loses her hair?). Bonnie becomes unduly narcissistic after the scars come off. (Wouldn't anyone in that situation?)"[58] asks one, while another muses that *The Craft*'s conclusion "[a]ll but adopts the snob's viewpoint... Are we supposed to think Nancy has a greater propensity for evil because she lives in a trailer park... and is Sarah good because she lives in a multimillion-dollar hacienda?"[59]

Even as oppositional viewers have still turned the film into a cult classic, relishing these punk rock witches and their riot grrrl revenge, the ultimate failure of *The Craft* is one of intersectionality. In this sense, Fleming's film could be viewed as a microcosm for the ways postfeminist "girl power", with its emphasis on capitalist consumption and tacit conformity to a neo-conservative moral framework, overtook genuinely intersectional Third Wave feminism in the public eye. Doug Wick, the film's producer, rather defensively mused in 2016 that "in retrospect one solution [to the film's hated ending] would have been where the girls unite to stop some form of the patriarchy... but that really wasn't in the DNA of that story."[60] This non-excuse, which is the closest any member on the team has come to acknowledging the perniciousness of the film's denouement, feels less like a clear answer and more like a lack of imagination—a response to the suffocating social conservatism that soaked into the cultural product of the moment, seemingly despite the artists' best intentions. The teen girls watching the movie seemed to agree: in Cush's study of the "teen witch phenomenon", in response to her questions about *The Craft*'s anti-magic message, a group of 16-year-old girls snarked, "we do Media Studies,

---

55. Taubin, 1996.
56. Taubin ends her review with a bit of advice that accurately sums up how jarring the ending feels in context: "My advice: after the big scene with the 500 snakes, giant water bugs and assorted creepy crawlies, get the jump on everyone else and head for the exit"
57. Hamilton, 1996.
58. *Ibid.*
59. Wilmington, 1996.
60. "Producing The Craft", 2019.

we know how these things work."⁶¹ And scholars were making the same conclusions: as one frustrated academic intervening in the thorny debate over the meaning of "postfeminism" as applied to films like *Pretty Woman* put it, "However problematic, *some* form of feminist discourse is occurring within these women's films for the 1990s."⁶² This exhausted concession—the same kind of compromise that forced Hillary Clinton to remind the public that her chocolate cookie recipe had won a contest even as she demanded the United Nations recognize that "women's rights are human rights once and for all"—seemed to be the best the embattled, embittered feminists of the '90s could squeeze out of mainstream culture.

There were, however, two smaller witch films at the end of the decade that offered an outlet for feminist anger without the pejorative stance of *The Craft*. *Eve's Bayou* (1996) and *Practical Magic* (1998), the former an indie success story, the latter a mainstream commercial bomb that has since been reclaimed, both effectively build on the promise of solidarity offered by the opening passages of Fleming's film. Here, women create support systems for each other to overcome the forces of misogynist oppression, actively and deftly subverting the stereotypes of the subgenre, maintaining women's power, and presenting magic as a foundation for future feminist solidarity rather than a disruptive force that undercuts it.

Eve's Bayou, the directorial debut of then-actress Kasi Lemmons (perhaps best known at the time for her supporting role as Clarice's friend Ardelia in *The Silence of the Lambs*, [1991]), was a breakout indie success upon its release in 1997. While the booming indie film scene of the 1990s was overwhelmingly white and male (the Weinstein/Miramax era introduced the world to the "film buff" as we know him—*Pulp Fiction* [1994] dorm poster and all), it was, alongside the New Queer Cinema, accompanied by a so-called "Golden Age" of Black cinema. "This is the best time in history to be a black filmmaker", said director Reginald Hudlin in a piece titled, "In Hollywood, Black Is In."⁶³ This shift was, in part, market driven. As Barry Reardon, Warner Bros. distribution head, cynically reported to the *New York Times* in 1990, "with the success of such films as 'The Color Purple,'" a film notably led by a cast of Black women "There are no minuses [in making Black films]. Any time a genre... makes money, it becomes accepted."⁶⁴ With these shifts in the filmmaking landscape, Lemmons was able to escape the string of "Black best friend" roles she had been stuck with as an actress and

---

61. Cush, 2007, 49.
62. Brundson, 1997, 85, emphasis added.
63. Greenberg, 1990.
64. *Ibid.*

produce her Southern gothic, magic realist drama. It was received by the press as a "small miracle", making almost $15 million off of its $4 million budget.

Inspired by the styles of Toni Morrison and Gabriel García Márquez, the film follows a multigenerational Black family on an island called Eve's Bayou. The film is explicitly folkloric and matrilineal: the town's Biblical name is drawn from the story of a formerly enslaved woman with a knowledge of herbal medicine, Eve Batiste, who was freed after helping nurse a French aristocrat back to health. "Perhaps out of gratitude," the narrator tells us, "she bore him sixteen children." This narrator (Tamara Tunie) is a rare presence, only bookending the film and framing the story, set in the '60s, as a hazy object of retrospect. She is another Eve Batiste, a descendant of this ambiguous sexual legacy of slavery, assault, and pain. This ambivalent, opaque opening detail shapes the rest of the story, which follows the Baptiste clan through the summer this ten-year-old Eve (Jurnee Smollett) kills her father with voodoo. Eve and her older sister, Cisely (Meagan Good) vie for the affection of their father, Louis (Samuel L. Jackson). One night after a party, Eve accidentally sees him having sex with Matty Mereaux (Lisa Nicole Carson), his friend Lenny (Roger Guenveur Smith)'s wife. She tries to tell Cisely, who angrily tells her she misunderstood, narrating an alternative version of the scene where nothing is wrong, showing Louis and Matty laughing innocently together.

These interwoven frames of memory and perception are central to the story's multiple generations of women—particularly Eve and her aunt Mozelle (Debbi Morgan), both of whom have the second sight. Though Mozelle's powers are decidedly witchlike, she insists on the term "spiritual counselor" for her work as a psychic. This distinction is dramatized through contrast with another character, Elzora (Diahann Carroll), who throws the bones for cash at the town market, dresses in long flowing robes, and whom Mozelle hissingly calls a "sideshow witch!" Eventually, after Cisely's fights with her mother (Lynn Whitfield) have piqued, something violent occurs in the house: Cecily tells Eve (in a narrated scene) that Louis kissed and groped her. Eve's rage at her father grows apocalyptic. She runs into Lenny at the market, and, telling him she's looking for apples in a particularly Biblical allusion, mentions that his wife and her father spend time together when he's out of town. After Mozelle refuses to help, she approaches Elzora, the film's true witch, to perform a spell to kill Louis as revenge, and eventually, Lenny shoots him. Afterwards, however, Eve finds a letter recounting Cesily's molestation from her father's perspective (over another version of the scene), accusing Cecily of initiating the encounter and assuring his wife that he pushed her away. Devastated, Eve takes Cecily's hands and uses the second sight to access her memories. The scene repeats one final time—but ends before the truth is revealed. "I don't know!" Cecily cries. The two girls hold hands and look out over the water, the truth ambiguous. Eve drops Louis' letter into the pond.

Eve's Bayou takes many of the themes addressed only briefly in *The Craft*—domestic violence, sexual abuse, depression—and fleshes them out with empathy, delicacy, and realism, adding another layer to the allegorical nature of the witch in this context. Eve's rage is, like Nancy's, entirely justified, and here treated as legitimate. Similarly, Elzora, the "witch" is a nuanced character on her own terms, unlike Nancy. In one telling scene, when Eve arrives to pick up her spell, the older woman comes to the window of her house deep in the bayou, hair loose and floating around her head in the darkness. "Get the hell off my property before I cook you and eat you—" she hisses, until she realizes who it is, and relaxes. Elzora actively appropriates and deploys her caricatured crone status to her advantage, a strategic posture that's so effectively frightening as a control tactic that she cackles with glee. From Eve's perspective, this laughter is frightening, but the film's distanced style and layered temporality allows space for complexity. She's laughing in amusement. Elzora's true purpose is fulfilling those desires that the community's women otherwise refuse to acknowledge or act upon. In this sense, she balances Mozelle's "good magic". But the film doesn't allow for such simple delineations: when Eve approaches Mozelle about her beloved brother Louis' infidelity, she warns, "If you tell anyone, I'm gonna kill you." Elzora's justice is far more objective. Ultimately, this film's multigenerational family of magical women is complex, in many ways riven by the daily ravages and tensions of living in a man's world. But after Louis' death, the women begin to pick up the pieces, with Mozelle and her sister-in-law coming together to parent Cecily and Eve.

In this sense, the film takes a dramatically honest approach to the realities of child sexual abuse, using witchcraft not as a scapegoat, as during the Satanic Panic, but as a feminine tool for protection, retribution, and understanding. Rage, ultimately, gives way to melancholy—but both emotions are based in fierce, sisterly love. Of course, much as Rebecca Walker's plea to feminists to join in sisterhood, channel their rage, and come together in solidarity across intersectional identities went largely unheeded, so too did the lessons of the Golden Age of Black cinema. In the wake of these successes, many Black directors described experiences of being "black listed" for speaking out against the racism and misogyny of the industry, rarely receiving follow-up projects or breaking into the mainstream: "It's like they set us up to fail—all they wanted was to be able to pat themselves on the back like they did something," Darnell Martin, director, of the acclaimed 1994 indie comedy *I Like it Like That*, recalled later.[65]

Practical Magic, meanwhile, Griffin Dunne's adaptation of Alice Hoffman's 1995 magic-realist novel of the same name, tells another story of a family of witchy women on an island. This one centers on love alone,

---

65. Greenberg, 1990.

rather than rage, to build feminist community under the threat of domestic violence—though in an entirely white world. The film immediately establishes itself as a postmodern rejection of the tropes so familiar to the '80s backlash witch cycle, approaching them with humor and warmth. An intergenerational bond is established in a narrated cold-open following the attempted-hanging of a 17th-century witch, Maria (Caprice Benedetti). This scene humanizes its witch—the narration comes in the form of a dialogue between mother-figures and their daughters, learning about their family history. "For 200 years, we Owens women have been blamed for everything that goes wrong in this town," Aunt Frances (Stockard Channing) begins, contextualizing this oft-solitary archetype as a member of a family before a young Sally (Camilla Belle, eventually Sandra Bullock) chimes in. "Is that why everyone hates us?" she asks, and her Aunt Jet (Diane Keaton) replies, "They don't hate us sweetie, we just make them a little nervous." Here, an otherwise one-sided story of adultery and attempted murder is transformed, made into a gentle consciousness-raising session. Sally asks whether the townspeople wanted to hang their foremother for witchcraft. Aunt Frances takes a lightly amused tone: "Well, it didn't help that… [she] was a bit of a heartbreaker, or that her lovers' wives were members of a hanging committee… but they feared her because she had a gift." This intervention is equally pivotal—not only does this line remind viewers that witch crazes are rooted in misogynist violence, it frames her magic positively *and* sexually, while films like *The Craft* or even Diseny's *Hocus Pocus* (1993) still present their fun-loving, sexually-coded witches as deserving of their punishments. By the end of the scene, Maria breaks the hanging rope and stands, content and triumphant.

The failed murder of the pregnant witch results in her banishment to the island where the film takes place. Her sadness at her abandonment by a lover leads her to cast a spell on herself, preventing her from feeling the "agony" of love, but the spell soon turns into a curse on her line "as her bitterness grew" any man who "dared love an Owens woman" would die. The film picks up with Sally and her sister Gillian (Lora Anne Criswell, eventually Nicole Kidman) as children living with Jet and Frances after their father's death from the curse. Their upbringing is magical, full of "chocolate cake for breakfast" in their rambling Victorian mansion by the sea, with their hippie-coded Boomer aunts performing Wiccan apothecary magic for the women of the town. Still, the children of the town throw stones and chant, in unison, "Witch! Witch! You're a bitch!" at the girls (even in this romantic comedy drama, the "bitchification" of the witch is complete). Soon, Sally finds a way she believes will make falling in love impossible: she places a love spell, tossing a handful of petals out her window, binding her fate to a man who doesn't exist (with one blue eye and one green one, whose favorite shape is a star). Here, too, this poignant protective measure is presented as a bittersweet romantic ideal to keep her safe rather than a "curse", and the two sisters vow to grow old together.

When the girls grow up, beautiful and happy, Sally has a husband and children and Gillian has moved away. They keep in touch through letters. Like Gillian in *Bell, Book and Candle* (1958), Sally wants to be "normal" and doesn't practice magic, fitting in and having dance parties with her family. Meanwhile, the sultry Gillian is enjoying a sunny life of parties and having kinky sex with her hunky lover, Jimmy Angelov (Goran Visnjic), who she describes as a "Dracula-cowboy" type. Their lives, they agree, are "perfect". But soon, Sally hears the "death watch beetle", the sign of Maria's curse descending on her husband. He dies and she goes into mourning. Gillian, who has been using belladonna on Jimmy to keep his attention rapt and their sex exciting, finds that he's becoming (like Chris in *The Craft*) dangerously obsessed and possessive. She flees, returning home to care for Sally, eventually going home to be with Jimmy. In the film's most iconic sequence, Sally writes to Gillian, describing, in Alice Hoffman's poetic, folkloric prose, how she wants love to feel—looking at the moon, she describes a "dream of not wanting... I want to be seen." Love here, as her imaginary man attests, is about harmony and balance, being recognized. But Gillian's magic has gone wrong, and Jimmy has begun to beat her. Now Sally goes to Arizona to help her, only for Jimmy to take them both hostage. In a bid to escape, they accidentally dose him with too much belladonna and he dies. Panicked, they return to Massachusetts and perform a resurrection spell together, Sarah's first major spell since childhood. He returns more dangerous than before, and they kill him again. The rest of the film follows the sisters and their aunts trying to pick up the pieces as Gary (Aidan Quinn), a handsome detective with one blue eye and one green one, searches for Jimmy, whose zombified corpse stalks the house.

The plot, though, is largely secondary to the film's vignettes of sisterly love, magic and solidarity, imbuing witchcraft with warmth and pathos rather than fear, even as the film's horror elements come to the fore near the conclusion. The "investigation plot" is perfunctory, and even the detective seems to agree, like the women of *The Craft* or *Thelma & Louise*, that Jimmy deserved it. Instead, we mostly watch the women dance together, drink midnight margaritas, and air their grievances in a shower of giggles; they help Sally make inroads with the women of the local mother's "phone tree" that has spurned her as a witch; her daughters pick mint from the garden before the school bus arrives; eventually Sally "comes out of the broom closet" (a common Wiccan phrase), regaining her confidence in her magic while Joni Mitchell and Stevie Nicks play. Eventually, Gillian is possessed by Jimmy's spirit and Sally and the aunts call on the women of the town to help (through the phone tree)—despite past prejudice, they do, responding to the family's need, and all the help they've given the women in the past. Wielding brooms, they prepare the spell in an almost celebratory atmosphere. Eventually, they join, turning the 17th-century mob into a coven ("there's a little magic in every woman") and exorcize Gillian, sweeping the spirit out of the house.

Unlike *The Craft*, the film's sense of community builds into the climax. Sally and the detective slowly fall in love, though she fears, like Gillian in *Bell, Book and Candle* or Louise in *Teen Witch*, the spell she cast as a girl make his love illegitimate. But the film rejects this trope, too. In another powerful repudiation of the sexist fear of women's powers at the heart of that archetype—the concern that women are influencing men assuaged by the promise that their feminine "conscience" will prevent it—Gary tells her "I wished for you, too." We see him as a young boy on a white horse with a star painted on its side, smiling up at the shower of petals she sent from the sky. In the film's final moments, Sally concludes that she believes "our joined hands lifted Maria's curse," centering the sisterhood's impact on the love story, thus highlighting community rather than individuating the women. Gillian, the aunts, Sally and her daughters all put on a show for Halloween, standing on their roof in black pointed hats and striped tights, floating on broomsticks. They laugh, but below the town cheers, turning the witch's cackle, like Elzora's (still solitary) chuckle in *Eve's Bayou*, into a thing of joy.

Unlike *Eve's Bayou*, though, *Practical Magic* was almost universally panned in similar backlash terms to the feminism of its moment, presented as shallow, trivial, and vapid. While many critics found its blend of genres confusing, most reviews (almost all by male critics) concentrated on the film's emotional brand of overtly New Age feminism. *Entertainment Weekly*'s review called Sandra Bullock "the goddess of mopey whining."[66] The *Washington Post*'s review, meanwhile, dismissively referred to Nicole Kidman as "Mrs. Tom Cruise."[67] *Practical Magic*, complained the *Los Angeles Times*, "concentrate[s] on the emotional trappings of being a witch in the 1990s, when, God knows, there's already enough name-calling."[68] This diagnosis of the film's portrait of intergenerational solidarity recalls *Time*'s dismissal of *The Vagina Monologues* as "mindless", a tacit demand that these "whiney" witches stop talking about their problems.[69] The *Village Voice*, interestingly, complained about the film's New Ageism specifically, calling the film "the mild, Lilith-verging-on-Lifetime version" of girl power, whose "halfhearted feminism [is] further muted by an unmistakable whiff of New Age" concluding it was "basically a cross-generational female-bonding Niche-fest in supernatural drag."[70]

The film did tremendously well on DVD and VHS, though. Dunne has said that his interest in the story was inspired by his multigenerational family

---

66. Glieberman, 1998.
67. Kempley, 1998.
68. Matthews, 1998.
69. Bellafante, 1998.
70. Lim, 1998.

of "strong women", and has made repeated references to stories of talking to "women and girls in particular [who] were all so moved by it."[71] Retrospect has proven this point, even if the film's overwhelming whiteness speaks to a broader breakdown of intersectionality:

> Casually mention this film at a gathering of women who lived through the '90s, and the title alone inspires squeals of joy and devotion. (I have never met anyone who didn't like *Practical Magic*, I have only met people who haven't seen *Practical Magic*),

wrote Brianna Ashby in a twentieth anniversary retrospective. "Ostensibly a romantic comedy, it is a feminist confection that defies genre… *Practical Magic* establishes this conflation of sex and magic that's so central to its sensibility, of witchcraft as a feminist superpower shared between women."[72] But films like these were ultimately subsumed into the postfeminist atmosphere that pervaded, used to prove that feminism had already "won".

---

71. Schapiro, 2017.
72. Rehak, 2018.

Chapter Twelve

Fantasy, Franchising, Fracture, and the "Girlboss" Witch

"I decided that I was a feminist, and this seemed uncomplicated to me. But my research has shown me that feminism has become an unpopular word."
-Emma Watson, 2014[1]

This chapter will explore the way the first decade of the new millennium built on the successes *and* failures of the witch films of the '90s. In some ways, the most obvious product of the era represents the triumphant culmination of what Alexandra West called the "emboldening of white feminism" during the Clinton years. And yet, while horror itself devolved into low-budget exploitation schlock, sending the genre back into full-on disreputability, the success of the *Harry Potter* franchise simply cannot be understated.[2] Hermione Granger, whose whip-smart, driven, and confident image I myself sought to emulate (slipping into a Gryffindor robe and slapping a black pointy hat over my own frizzy curls every Halloween for about a decade), would come to symbolize the witch in general, representing the genuinely empowering possibilities of "girl power" for the young women of the aughts. At the same time, though, the failure of intersectionality and solidarity that characterized *The Craft* (1996) would continue here: Hermione, for her near-perfection as a dynamic, empowered, "strong female character", continually dismisses other, almost universally white, women throughout the series for conventionally feminine traits, the same characters most likely to be trivialized by the books and films themselves. Meanwhile, any of the archetype's darkness would be siloed, channeled into the character of wicked Bellatrix LeStrange.

In this sense, as well as in the franchise's pervasive whiteness (not to mention the personal evolution of its author's brand of TERF "feminism")[3], *Harry Potter* could be viewed as representative of the hegemonic, white, neoliberal feminism that characterized this decade—the era of what would

---

1. Emma Watson at the United Nations in 2014 as Goodwill Ambassador for U.N. Women.
2. West, 2018, 10.
3. Dec. 19, 2019, saw the first tweet on X in this regard. TERF stands for transgender exclusionary radical feminist. <https://x.com/jk_rowling/status/1207646162813100033>

become known as the "girlboss" in 2014. The utter ubiquity of *Harry Potter* would, though, also belie the broader dissolution of the archetype. Hollywood's turn to escapist fantasy in the wake of 9/11 would give rise to a wave of "fantasy" and "fairytale" witches by the decade's end, but what they looked like, how they behaved, and how they were employed in these stories varied widely, even as the misogyny of their characterization remained obvious. Where in the 1980s the bricolage of the era's witch and warlock films connoted an "epidemic of signification" after the Satanic Panic, here the postfeminist triumph of Hermione Granger served as a sort of cover for a similar set of wildly misogynistic assumptions that ran like a drumbeat throughout the decade, quickly nicknamed the "naughty aughties."[4] The highly confused results would set the stage for another reclamation of the witch—as feminists, yet again, reached a wrathful breaking point.

Like the occult revival of the 1960s, the witch craze of the 2000s began as a British import: in 1997, then-unknown British author JK Rowling released *Harry Potter and the Philosopher's Stone*, unleashing an immediate cult phenomenon that soon spread to the US. After its much-hyped American debut in the fall of 1998, the book reached the top of the *New York Times* Best Seller list in 1999 and remained there for over a year. In 2001, the American film adaptation made over a billion dollars. By the next year, elaborate, often costumed book—and-movie-release events accompanied each new installment, with lines around the block at Borders or the multiplex and merchandise flying off the shelves. The books have been credited with re-popularizing reading for children and changing the young adult publishing industry in the United States; in addition, the films' runaway success has been credited with helping create what we now know as "fandom" and sparking the wave of young adult fantasy film adaptations that led to *Twilight* (2008) and *The Hunger Games* (2012), among others. Over the course of the films' releases between 2001 and 2011, the promoters of the series took advantage of the burgeoning of the internet as we know it, (the birth of "Web 2.0") to facilitate a new kind of "fan culture": children logged onto Pottermore in 2009 to be "sorted" into their Hogwarts house with a quiz, tweens watched early viral videos on YouTube (founded in '05) like "Potter Puppet Pals: The Mysterious Ticking Noise" (the 22nd most-viewed YouTube video ever by 2013), and older fans used chat rooms and blogs to discuss the series and write fanfiction on Archive of Our Own (Ao3). Some of those writers would go on to publish the next generation of lucrative YA franchises, in a cycle that would continue with the success of *Fifty Shades of Grey* (2015) (originally *Twilight* fanfiction).

---

4. Copeland, 2000.

The cultural fervor around Harry and his "freaky friends" (as his uncle Vernon calls them) was quickly associated with a massive change in the cultural mood. In one article about the Harry Potter phenomenon, "Harry Potter and the Childish Adult", A.S. Bayatt asks with panic "But why would grown-up men and women become obsessed" by the series? Citing that contemporaneous sprawling, lore-heavy cinematic juggernaut, *Lord of the Rings* (2001-2003), as an analogous phenomenon he answers, "Comfort, I think, is part of the reason… We like to regress."[5] Lev Grossman had already made a similar argument in *Time* the year before, putting it down to the traumatic impact of 9/11.[6] Comparing the box office domination of these two franchises to the success of Tolkien's novels in a past American climate "drowning in the moral quicksand" of the Vietnam War and Watergate, he suggests that "[w]ith The Two Towers [and] the new installment of The Lord of the Rings trilogy about to storm the box office, we are seeing what might be called the enchanting of America… The future just isn't what it used to be—and the past seems to be gaining on us."[7]

Indeed, the 2000s seemed to be a return to the rampant conservatism of the '80s, this time without the tempering force of a Democratic House or Senate. Republicans regained control of all three branches of government under President George W. Bush in 2003 for the first time since 1953. The evangelical culture that set the tone for the Reagan years and continued to gain steam over the course of the '90s exploded into the dominant culture: Bush's 2004 presidential platform included language proposing a Constitutional amendment banning same-sex marriage, stating that heterosexual marriage was "the most fundamental institution of civilization."[8] [9] The sexual "purity" movement promulgated by groups like the Promise Keepers achieved major victories in pushing abstinence-only sex education, with over $100 million in federal funding going to groups that promoted this model;[10] Bush also reinstated the so-called Partial-Birth Abortion Ban Act in 2003, instating further limits on abortions in the second trimester, placed two still-sitting anti-choice justices on the Supreme Court (Justices Alito and Roberts), and declared a "National Sanctity of Life Day" during his last year in office. The statement announcing this last move explained that it was a part of the Bush administration's goal of "building a culture of life by… opposing federal

---

5. Byatt, 2003.
6. The other effects of 9/11 on the cinematic landscape could be found in the horror realm itself, alongside the only-now waning explosion of superhero films (with their world-or-city-destroying climaxes thought to be moralistic, ritual recreations of the event itself), and disaster films. "Torture porn" proliferated after the success of films like *Saw* (2004) and *Hostel* (2005), often discussed as a means of contending with the brutal images of torture that came out of the War on Terror. For more on the cinematic landscape of the 2000s, see *America in the Shadow of 9/11* by Terence McSweeney (2017).
7. Grossman, 2002.
8. Kirkpatrick, 2004.
9. Stout, 2004.
10. Du Mez, 2020, 172.

funding for abortions overseas, encouraging teen abstinence and funding crisis pregnancy programs."[11] [12]

The gleefully slut-shaming culture of the '90s (best exemplified by the universal thrashing of Monika Lewinski), meanwhile, continued apace, with a now-infamous laundry list of tabloid news cycles hounding celebrities like Brittney Spears, Lindsay Lohan, Paris Hilton, and Janet Jackson for their sexuality, behavior, and/or appearance, even as raunchy, red-meat, objectifying sexuality permeated, presented as the "empowering" result of feminism having won. The media landscape of the era (in)famously embraced this parodic new standard for women, part of what one author called the "Vulgar Wave".[13] From the ubiquitous, raucously "un-PC" comedies of the "frat pack" and others (*The Hot Chick* [2002], *The 40 Year Old Virgin* [2005], *Epic Movie* [2007], etc.), to the cartoon sexuality of advertising (eroticized ads for burgers, begun by Carl's Jr. with a skimpily-clad Paris Hilton in '05, eventually called the "Slutbuger" genre of marketing), this was the era of "bro" entertainment hegemony.[14]

The feminist movement, though, found itself trapped in the now-entrenched discourse of postfeminism, even as culture grew more conservative and overtly misogynistic. As in the '90s, anti-choice measures animated women more than ever (the March for Women's Lives after the Partial-Birth Abortion Ban Act swelled to 1.3 million participants). Feminist-run blogs, magazines, and websites like *Bustle* worked to counter the cultural tide of sexism in the media, pointing out the pervasive photoshopping of advertisements on top of covering the veritable tidal wave of anti-choice legislation. Still, the environment had changed: the riot grrrl-style activism of the '90s was swiftly redirected into the liberal anti-war movement after 9/11 and the thriving feminist blogosphere. Second Wave Wiccan authors like Starhawk (of *The Spiral Dance* [1999]) founded anti-war, pro-environmentalist groups like Pagan Cluster and Reclaiming to cast curses on the WTO or Marine Corps Recruiting Centers, but were mostly presented as ridiculous and outré, associated with the theatrical protests of Code Pink.[15] Feminist bands like The Dixie Chicks who condemned the president, faced death threats,

---

11. Barr, 2009.
12. Or in more characteristically Bushy fashion, as he put it in 2000, "families is where our nation finds hope, where wings take dream" (Watson, 2003).
13. Skallas, 2023.
14. *The Hot Chick* actually spoofs the '90s goth girl witch in a classroom scene: the only goth student is the only one to get an A on a paper about the Salem Witch Trials, to which a character poutily replies "That's not fair, she's the only one who was actually there!"
15. As a 2008 *Salon* article described the mood around Code Pink's witchy brand of performative activism: "its ruckus-raising techniques often cause me and my liberal community, who tend to agree with its politics, to regard them with distaste and embarrassment. Why did these shrieking middle-aged women in pink novelty hats believe this manner of protest was going to be effective in Congress, let alone in an almost completely co-opted media climate that seems hellbent on ignoring them?... I love peace, but why would any adult human who ever owned a nice belt want to be seen with this eyesore? Why does the peace movement have to dress and act like an irritating children's birthday party?" (Wilson, 2008).

overwhelmed by the jingoistic atmosphere of post-9/11 America that gave Bush a whopping 90% approval rating in the weeks after the attacks. "By means of the tropes of freedom and choice which are now inextricably connected with the category of 'young women'", Angela McRobbie wrote in 2007,

> feminism is decisively aged and made to seem redundant. Feminism is cast into the shadows, where at best it can expect to have some afterlife, where it might be regarded ambivalently by those young women who must in more public venues stake a distance from it, for the sake of social and sexual recognition.[16]

Indeed, even women continually distanced themselves from the label. This tendency is most clearly on display in the repeated instances of women celebrities avoiding the term throughout the decade, echoing the hackneyed notion that feminism was man-hating: Kelly Clarkson said calling herself a feminist would be "too strong. I think when people hear feminist, it's like, 'Get out of my way...' I love that I'm being taken care of and I have a man that's a leader"; Carrie Underwood rejected the label because "that can come off as a negative connotation"; Taylor Swift demurred, saying "I don't really think about things as guys versus girls"; Sarah Jessica Parker and Demi Moore separately elaborated on this last, arguing instead that they preferred the term "humanist".[17] As one interviewer quipped as late as 2012, "No interview question floors a female pop star quite like: 'Are you a feminist?'"[18] This kind of backpedaling anti-feminist rhetoric, more commonly associated with the "color-blind" attempts at anti-racism of the early-mid 2010s, was an obvious concession to the openly hostile environment for women's activism at the time.

The overt chauvinism of the culture, along with the stifling force of corporate postfeminism, led to what McRobbie called the "double-entanglement" of this phase of post-postfeminism—"family values" Christian conservatism existing in tandem with "feminism as at some level transformed into a form of Gramscian common sense, while also... almost hated... The taken into accountness permits all the more thorough dismantling of feminist politics."[19] In an article on the rise of sex toy companies called "Fun in the Naughty Aughties", this tension is on clear display. The mood for women in this environment was set this way: "Today's sexually liberated woman... [isn't] some free-lovin' hippie throwback. Her brand of sexual awareness is post-post-feminist," here centered around buying things like sex toys, even "in the

---

16. McRobbie, 2007, 255.
17. "Celebrities Who Say They Aren't Feminists", 2013.
18. Orr, 2012.
19. McRobbie, 2007, 255-6.

middle of the Bible Belt!"[20] The hyper-individualistic rhetoric of bitchified "girl power" had been reappropriated to sell "empowering" products, from dildos to diet books like *Skinny Bitch: A No-Nonsense, Tough-Love Guide for Savvy Women Who Want to Stop Eating Crap and Start Looking Fabulous!* (2005), which made it to number three on the *New York Times* paperback Best Seller list after Victoria Beckham (a.k.a "girl power godmother" Posh Spice) was photographed reading it on vacation.[21] Girl power had been fully redirected into the precise kind of eroticized diet culture riot grrrls worked to stave off—by 2012, this precise kind of rhetoric would find its way onto pro-anorexia ("pro-ana") Tumblr, where Kate Moss' infamous '09 quote, "nothing tastes as good as skinny feels", constantly made the rounds. These actively non-"feminist", "empowered women" of the aughts maintained the entrepreneurial, individualistic, and high-achieving neoliberalism of the '90s postfeminist while also being encouraged to adhere to a beauty standard sold by impossibly skinny supermodels *and* performing a particularly overt brand of "Slutburger" pornified sex-appeal (assumed, of course, to be white), barely framed as liberating (mostly embraced as openly for the guys, fugly lesbo feminazis be damned), seeming to confirm and even expand the kinds of arguments Naomi Wolfe made in *The Beauty Myth* (1990).

Enter Hermione Granger. Presented as the kind of nerdy girl who will inevitably get her glasses taken off and her hair straightened to show her hidden beauty (she does, in *Harry Potter and the Goblet of Fire* [2005]), she and the other women of the "comforting" and "escapist" *Harry Potter* series exist in a seemingly gender neutral, postfeminist world whose treatment of witchcraft is entirely secular, divorced from pagan or neo-pagan lore. In these stories, witchcraft functions as a fantasy element, not drawn from demons or devils, a natural phenomenon that simply occurs. Over the course of the *Harry Potter* series, Hermione (Emma Watson in the films) is consistently portrayed as resourceful, knowledgeable, and brave—though, often lovably irritating in her bookishness (a feminine trait in the context of this macho, anti-intellectual era).[22] Over the course of the series, Hermione, Harry, and Ron are presented, largely as equals, though Hermione's status as what Snape calls "an insufferable know-it-all" is a source of dismissal by her two stereotypically "boyish" friends (both Harry and Ron complain about studying and rely on Hermione for tests like their OWLs in *Harry Potter and the Half-Blood Prince* [2009]). Hermione, unlike Harry and Ron, also comes from the "muggle" world (her parents are dentists), and as such represents a more individualistic model for success than Ron's multigenerational

---

20. Copeland, 2000.
21. Interestingly, this vegan cookbook, full of PETA-style anti-animal cruelty invective, was framed as successful because unlike "the photos of authors on the crunchy granola books", these authors "are both drop-dead gorgeous" (Friedman and Barnouin, 2005).
22. Another classic Bushism: "Rarely is the question asked, 'is our children learning?'" (Baker, 2007).

family of wizards or Harry's unique status as a celebrity whose life has been protected and guided by the likes of Professor Dumbledore. Quite simply, she tries harder to excel at magic than everyone else (upon her introduction in *Philosopher's Stone*, before the semester starts, she's already started her homework), and is rewarded for that dedication in a meritocratic system that's presented as *gender-neutral*, pulling herself up by her witchy bootstraps. She works so hard, in fact, that in *Harry Potter and the Prisoner of Azkaban* (2004), she is given a way to literally add hours to the day: the time-turner she's given by the Hogwarts administration to take multiple classes at once seals Hermione's status as a literal "superwoman" figure. She punches bigoted bullies in the nose when they insult her, doesn't succumb to torture when captured, and helps her friends out of deadly situations in every installment of the franchise. In 2016, Hermione became the Minister of Magic in the play *Harry Potter and the Cursed Child*, breaking the ultimate magical glass ceiling.

Nevertheless, the wizarding world for women is defined by competition with each other, rarely solidarity. Hermione functions, in classic aughts fashion, as "one of the boys"—though of course, she and Ron eventually fall in love, *When Harry Met Sally*-style (1989). The witches who are presented as the most powerful are the most divorced from traditional femininity, either due to their professional status (Professor McGonagall, or Tonks who is an auror) or their no-nonsense attitude (Mrs. Weasley, a mother, whose "tough love" is celebrated). Women who fall outside the purview of these acceptably masculinized traits are presented condescendingly. In *Harry Potter and the Half-Blood Prince*, Lavender Brown (Jessie Cave) is presented as utterly ridiculous in her excessive, "girly" affection for Ron, calling him "Won-Won" in a breathy voice and pantingly drawing hearts on window panes. "Lovely," Harry quips; "I'll take your word for it," Ron replies grimly. Hermione's disdain for Lavender, who she calls a "daft dimbo", is presented as an understandable byproduct of her own secret crush on Ron. Yet it's part of a broader pattern of description in the book. Hermione rolls her eyes at the women of the French all-witch school Beauxbaton, whose "lovely ladies" arrive at Hogwarts performing a synchronized dance, punctuated by sighs, releasing butterflies into the air and, in the film, including a tight close-up of their bouncing behinds in their silk dresses. They are described as "all stunningly beautiful" (thin and white) and are received with drooling adulation from the boys.

The two most traditionally "witchy" characters in the franchise are also presented as the most ridiculous. Luna Lovegood is presented as a product of a hippie upbringing, strange for her belief in this wizarding world's equivalent of New Ageism. She reads her father's magazine, *The Quibbler*, which is marketed as the wizarding world's "Alternative Voice". She wears zany patterns, uses radishes as earrings, and is described in literally "spacey" terms. Hermione calls her "Looney" Lovegood and displays little patience for her eccentricities. Sibyll Trelawney (Emma Thompson), meanwhile, whose long shawls, beaded necklaces, enormous mane of hair, and giant, bug-eyeglasses already code her as a New Age witch, teaches divination. Hermione mocks her crystal balls openly, calling it "rubbish", imitating her voice, rolling her eyes, and mocking her predictions. This is the only class Hermione ever quits, and she does so in dramatic fashion. Though Harry befriends Luna and she, like Trelawney (whose predictions do, in fact, come true), is presented as legitimate in the end, both women's more intuitive (less "earned") forms of magical power, remain a source of ridicule for most of their time on screen, framed as a product of their feminine traits. Trelawney for her part insults Hermione back, telling her she doesn't have that most traditional of witch traits, "the inner eye": "You may be young in years, but the heart that beats beneath your bosom is as shriveled as an old maid's, your soul as dry as the pages of the books to which you so desperately cleave." This assessment speaks to another fundamental element of Hermione's magic—it's anti-sexual.

The only witch whose powers are presented as sexual is Bellatrix LeStrange (Helena Bonham Carter), with her all-black, low-cut Victorian-bodiced dresses, wild hair and iconic screeching cackle. An insane witch who revels in destruction, she laughs with delight when she sets Hagrid's house on fire in *Half Blood Prince*, dances across tables during the series' climactic battle, and is characterized by her eroticized "bloodlust" in each film, slinking up behind friends and enemies alike, whispering into their ears and stroking her cheek on their shoulders while making threats. Her status as a true villain comes from her murders of multiple protagonists' family members, and indeed, her death finally comes at the hands of the film's central mother-figure, Mrs. Weasley. When Bellatrix tries to kill Ginny, Mrs. Weasley cries, "Not my daughter, you *bitch!*", freezes her with a spell, and literally blows her up near the film's climax (a showstopping line that received an enormous cheer at my midnight premiere screening in 2011). The use of that most gendered of insults is a particular standout in the family-friendly series, which replaces swears with magical substitutes in nearly every case. The goth, bitchy witch has died, replaced with good witches like Hermione and Ginny.

Overall, of course, the women of *Harry Potter* are beloved for a reason: they are dynamic, unique, and particularly in contrast to the misogyny of the era, recognizable, empathetically drawn human women. In this charged environment, the *Harry Potter* series was the source of enormous conservative backlash, both as a backdoor entry into occultism *and* as feminist propaganda. The novels were some of the most frequently banned books of the late '90s and early aughts, taken off school shelves for their depictions of the "pagan and Satanic". Copies were even burned (alongside Ouija Boards) by Christians who called the series "a masterpiece of Satanic deception". Wrote one panicked New York parent in 2000, deploying Satanic Panic rhetoric to endorse book banning:

> You only have to open the latest Harry Potter book to see the naked evil that waits inside. Beneath the title (Azkaban) is a heraldic shield with a serpent and the motto "Draco dormiens nunquam titillandus" (never tickle a sleeping dragon). Sex, drugs, satanism. All are lurking in these words alone. It has taken too long...but in America at least, vigilant parents have mobilised to cleanse their children's soul of Potter and his twisted tales of the occult.[23]

These calls to children's safety were eminently familiar, but nevertheless powerful—"witchcraft, satanism", a father in Iowa said to his local school board, "erode the morality of our children, and therefore ultimately our society."[24] The stories were also denounced for their gender politics: "We don't believe that it's acceptable [for books]... to turn young boys into young girls," said one publisher, who charged that the books' adventures were "feminised and touchy feely."[25] Girl power in its subtlest, most "humanistic" form was still something to be condemned.

By late 2013 and early 2014, the YA and fantasy cycles of the late 2000s had largely lost steam as the *Harry Potter* and *Twilight* series released their final installments in 2011 and '12 respectively. The political and cinematic landscape had changed, too. The beginning of the Obama administration brought with it a new kind of open feminism: "The more I've spoken about feminism," Emma Watson said a speech to the United Nations in 2014 as a newly-appointed Goodwill Ambassador for U.N. Women, "the more I've realized that fighting for women's rights has... become associated with man-hating... Women are choosing not to identify as feminists.... Seen as... anti-men, unattractive even. Why has the word become such an uncomfortable one?" A 2012 TED talk by Nigerian author Chimamanda Ngozi Adichie discussing the same theme—returning to the original definition of feminism as a movement for sexual equality—was sampled in Beyoncé's 2013 song "Flawless", and turned into an influential 2014 book, *We Should All Be Feminists*, the same year Rebecca Solnit's *Men Explain Things to Me* coined the term "mansplaining". By 2016, President Obama would become the first president to refer to himself as a feminist in office.

This re-emergence of feminism as acceptable was, though, accompanied by its continued corporatization, as well as a violent backlash. Sheryl Sandberg,

---

23. Roffey, 2020.
24. *Ibid.*
25. Reynolds, 2003.

then-COO of Facebook, published *Lean In: Women, Work and the Will to Lead* in 2013, "proudly" claiming the word feminist ("I'm a pom-pom girl for feminism"), but using it to encourage the same kind of hyper-individualistic, capitalistic, cutthroat postfeminist discourse that had run through the late '90s and 2000s, suggesting that a focus on an increased number of women-CEOs (over anti-discrimination laws) would lead to trickle-down feminist gains.[26] This kind of feminist framing was solidified and named (and meme'd) when former Nasty Gal CEO Sophia Amoruso published her biography under the title *#Girlboss* in 2014. But even with the obvious gains feminism was making across the board, overtly misogynistic violence on the internet became a topic of conversation: #GamerGate, a systematic harassment campaign against female journalists and web designers by right-wing self-described incels (involuntary celibates), captured the attention of the now-fully formed internet. The harassment was extreme, with designers like Zoe Quinn, receiving a gruesome, sexual death threat and a warning, capped with: "I will write my manifesto in her spilled blood, and you will all bear witness to what feminist lies and poison have done to the men of America."[27] This incident was the first real public airing of the chilling extremism of the growing internet "manosphere", a branch of extremist "Men's rights activism". That same May, Elliot Rodger whose 141-page online anti-woman manifesto came to be a touchstone for the incel community, went on a misogynistic killing spree, stabbing women indiscriminately.

Hollywood was only just barely beginning to contend with these massive political changes. A string of what had been called "dark fairy tales" inspired by the successes of *Twilight* (and its adult-oriented analogues *True Blood* [2008-2014] and *The Vampire Diaries* [2009-2017]) were still being released, typified by *Red Riding Hood* in 2011 and *Snow White and the Huntsman* in 2012. With films like *Oz the Great and Powerful* (2013), *Beautiful Creatures* (2013), and *Hansel and Gretel: Witch Hunters* (2013), YA witches began making sporadic industry headlines as the next Hollywood trend. "Sorry, Edward Cullen. Catch you later," read one CNN article in October 2013, "after several years of success with vampires, zombies and (to a lesser extent) werewolves, Hollywood now can't seem to get enough of witches."[28] This mini-cycle, then, had nothing to do with Hermione Granger. The witches of 2013 were generally viewed as monstrous IP, a way to continue profiting off of an older trend: "Vampires are dead - and now it's the witching hour."[29] As producer Adam McKay said of director Tommy Wirkola's snarky addition to the 2013 witch microtrend, *Hansel and Gretel: Witch Hunters*, "the idea is, they've grown up and they hunt witches... We heard it and we were just

---

26. Sandberg, 2013, 158.
27. Dockterman, 2014.
28. Hanks, 2013.
29. Mottram, 2013.

like, 'That's a freakin' franchise! You could make three of those!'"[30] While no sequels appeared to this film (in which the siblings indeed hunt witches, dispatching them with pithy one-liners and guns) it was a tremendous hit. In this sense, witches become a convenient substitute for audiences grown weary of vampire or zombie lore but not ready to find something else—spawning shows like *The Originals* (2013-2018, about witches), a spin-off of *The Vampire Diaries*. Indeed, many of these witches were, either ugly, ork-like hags on brooms to be dispatched, or seductively evil queens with low necklines (*Snow White and the Huntsman*). Illustrating this, *Witch Hunters* director Wirkola went so far as to say of his orge-esque witches that he "wanted to reinvent witches as villains…. Almost like animals: dangerous, fast."[31] The suggestion that his witches are "fast" may, when looking at the witch as an archetype, feel confusing (witches are, after all, almost always just people who cast spells); in the context of a decade rife with *The Walking Dead*'s "fast" zombies (2010-2022), though, this paradigm strengthens the sense that the witch, at this point, is just another monster.

At the same time, by 2013 these filmmakers couldn't fully ignore the feminist (or pseudo-feminist, or postfeminist) valence of the witch as a cultural figure, particularly post-*Harry Potter*. Wirkola worked to distance his witches from the more traditional archetype even as he talked about them as "animals", saying "I do love *Witches of Eastwick*. We wanted to try to avoid the classical witch with the long nose stirring the pot", suggesting that the archetype had evolved away from the hag given the positive associations the '80s film (and its '90s imitators) holds in the culture.[32] He and his crew were continually asked about the relative sexism of the trope. One interviewer even asked the director whether he was "worried" about his hag witches on similar grounds: "I think some people might be kind of scared of making witches scary again… because there's this perception that it might be interpreted as sexist."[33] These questions indicate that films like *Witch Hunters* were being recognized as part of a *specifically* feminist-labeled wave of pop-fairytale films being interpreted on those terms (alongside debates around other tropes for female characters like the masculinized "Mary Sue"), however shallowly, making the tensions between Gretel's categorization as a "strong female lead" (and thus "feminist") and the witches' status as purely evil, ugly, and monstrous even more obvious. One fandom blogger (a by-then-fully-formed community, in large part thanks to *Harry Potter*) who analyzed the film, highlights the contradictory valances directly, succinctly summarizing the way feminism had been diluted in the pop culture of the early 2010s into a commercial post-feminist marketing tool:

---

30. Billington, 2009.
31. Cook, 2013.
32. *Ibid.*
33. Bibbiani, 2013.

the dark witches [in *Witch Hunters*] are eerily similar to the unfortunate popular stereotype of the 'evil feminist'... I'd love to read [it] as a playful joke about feminist stereotypes in pop culture, but... I would classify it as an example of 'popular feminism,' a work that attempts to capitalize on feminist-led social changes without embracing a fully intentional feminism.[34]

This blog post's thoughtful analysis speaks to the depth fans analyzed the media they consumed online in 2013—and indicate the direction the "witch trend" would head, beginning, for once, on television.

American Horror Story: Coven (2013-14) has been lauded since its release as a genuine attempt at a feminist entry into the canon of witch horror media. The show follows a group of nine sorceresses, descendants of the Salem witches, living in secret amongst humans. The mini-series follows the power struggle for leadership amongst this diverse group of women, divided most centrally along racial lines: though the coven has one Black member (as well as a blind witch and a witch with Down syndrome), it is largely presented as wealthy and white while their central antagonists are Black voodoo practitioners. Ultimately, the show serves as an allegorical representation of the struggle for a truly intersectional feminism, with each witch representing a different branch of discourse (neo-liberal, sex positive, radical and separatist, etc). In a notable nod to the feminist witch films of the 60s, one of the central witches, Misty Day (Lily Rabe), is an immortal hippie chick, gifted with the power of resurrection, constantly draped in colorful mismatched shawls and long strings of beads. The archetype's debt to this period is acknowledged most explicitly when Misty meets Stevie Nicks (playing herself), a white witch. Another coven member, Madison (Emma Roberts), represents individualistic "girl power" with her bubblegum pink, back-stabbing brand of irreverent, sex positive self-interest. Ultimately, the show ends on a hopeful note, with new collaborative leadership in the coven, and a large number of new women joining the group, young feminists brought into solidarity.

Where *The Craft* ultimately fails to be intersectional, *Coven*'s depiction of Black witches is more nuanced. Queenie (Gabourey Sidibe), the "white" coven's Black member joins the witch counsel, taking an influential position in the coven's future. She frequently discusses her Othered status, historicizing herself as a character within witch media directly: "I grew up on white girl shit like *Charmed* or *Sabrina* the teenage cracker; I didn't know there even were Black witches. As it turns out, I am an heir to Tituba." The shows' creators emphasized in its marketing that *Coven* would focus on the "oppression of minorities of all kinds, and within that idea, minority groups going after each other and doing the work of the larger culture... While there is a strong feminist theme that runs throughout *Coven*, there are themes of

---

34. wuscifi2014, 2014.

race and themes of oppression."[35] These corrective measures still come into tension with the fact that the major force of "black magic" is a group of Black women (led by Angela Bassett) who practice voodoo usually to cause pain and attempt to harm the "white" coven, a choice that in many ways fulfills the same set of stereotypes used in films as far back as *I Walked with a Zombie* (1943) and *Bell Book and Candle*. Nevertheless, these witches subvert this archetype, attacking the "white" coven in an attempt to reclaim power in a territory taken from them as a result of centuries of systemic racism.

This wildly successful show stood apart from the rest of the era's witch media, engaging in thoughtful feminist debate and explicitly working to turn itself into an allegory for the need for a revitalized feminist politics in America, serving as a rejoinder to non-intersectional white feminist films like *The Craft* and building on the more collectivist and positive depictions of feminine solidarity on display in *Practical Magic* (1998) and *Eve's Bayou* (1996). In some sense, no witch media to date has worked as actively to thread this complex political needle; in others, this sort of media-literate feminist critique of the archetype would saturate the landscape, becoming the narrative foundation off of which mainstream witch media would build.

The first glimpses of the explicitly feminist occult revival of the horror witch also appeared in 2013. That same October, New Queer Cinema director Kimberley Pierce directed an adaptation of De Palma's *Carrie* (1976) on similarly feminist terms. They likened the film to a "superhero origin story" for Carrie, working to give her more agency.[36] Critics criticized this choice as "'X-Men'-ish", frequently remarking that the film does little to change the story beyond references to cyber-bullying.[37] But, in an echo of the blogosphere's analysis of *Witch Hunters*, a *Wired* article pointed to the broader shift in independent horror towards its own streak of feminist revisionism, citing Carol Clover's seminal *Men Women and Chainsaws* (1992), *Jennifer's Body* (2009) and the woman-led *Evil Dead* (2013) remake to contextualize Pierce's film as a product of a broader shift: "a more self-aware protagonist [and] a more sensitive student population allow Peirce to demonstrate how women of horror, and really women of film, have evolved in the intervening years" since De Palma's version.[38] "Hopefully," the writer concludes, with the prevalence of these films "the new awareness [of feminism in horror] will seep in. If it does—then the signs that Carrie's real revenge will be coming to fruition."[39] [40] Even Disney's 2014 *Maleficent* began taking these

---

35. Etkin and Prudom, 2013.
36. Johnson, 2013.
37. Neumaier, 2013.
38. Watercutter, 2013.
39. *Ibid.*
40. This trend would continue apace in 2014. That year, polish auteur Agnieszka Holland directed a similarly "updated" yet largely faithful American television remake of *Rosemary's Baby* (with a

cues, providing the titular evil queen from *Sleeping Beauty* with a tragic and sympathetic backstory—rape by Aurora's father, the king (Sharlto Copley)—and, like *Wicked* (2024), reworking the narrative to foster solidarity between the princess (Elle Fanning) and her would-be nemesis against this patriarch. In the end, these two rule the kingdom after Maleficent's maternally loving kiss wakes Aurora from her slumber. Reviews celebrated its reimagination of the story ("long live the feminist revisionist backstory") and made puns, remarking that Maleficent waking the princess up with her motherly love constituted a new kind of "consciousness-raising."[41] [42]

A particular kind of (post)feminist witch had clearly begun to emerge from the world of television and fairytale IP—but only briefly. Though more "dark fairytale" films like *Alice Through the Looking Glass* (2016) would appear sporadically through the mid-2010s, they were already being superseded by Disney's spate of much more rigidly faithful live action remakes. The modest successes of *Carrie*, though, would in some ways prove prescient. In Part 3, I will investigate a more notable, coherent, and long-lasting explosion of the cinematic witch, one that would only truly arrive several years later, with the rise of a new horror paradigm.

---

screenplay by *American Horror Story* writer James Wong), describing it on explicitly feminist grounds in an interview with *The New York Times*: "Mr. Polanski's version was made 'before the feminist revolution, really... [Rosemary] was in some ways a victim—to the men's world, to the world of power and Satan... My Rosemary is much more willful and stronger.'" Indeed, several attempts were made to update the show, with Rosemary (Zoe Saldaña) cast as the primary breadwinner of this yuppie couple (Rosemary researches witches on an iPad). Critics largely rejected feminist analysis, describing the mini-series as generally "leaden and slack" in its stretched narrative structure and "largely true to the original" in its politics, an analysis which perhaps even overestimates the new version's "empowering" narrative bonafides. By stretching this thriller into a three-hour-long mystery, Rosemary remains ignorant and confused for almost double the length of the original, leaving the viewer with the sense of a woman even less in control of her circumstances. Nevertheless, the show speaks to the renewed interest in horror as feminist by the early-mid 2010s.
41. Taylor, 2014.
42. Hornaday, 2014.

PART THREE

Gender, Genre, Psychedelics,
and Abjection in the 2010s "Witch" Horror Cycle

Chapter Thirteen

Defining the 2010s Witch Horror Cycle

"I am a witch, and I'm hunting you."
-Lindy West, "Yes This Is a Witch Hunt"[1]

The final section of this book will investigate the image that drew me to the subject of witch horror in the first place: a witch's smile. When you picture a young woman smiling at the end of a horror film, what do you see? Perhaps by now, after almost a decade of celebrating antiheroines, villainesses, and other "unlikable female characters" you might picture the last moments of *Pearl* (2022; Pearl, grinning from ear to ear surrounded by rotting family members: "I'm so happy you're home!") or even, well, *Smile* (2022). When I began writing my undergraduate thesis in 2020, the image of a young woman smiling or laughing with abandon at the end of a horror movie had, largely as a result of the slasher cycles of the 1970s and 1980s, typically come to suggest that the Evil has been defeated—at least for now—and that the innocent victim, though scarred, will now begin her healing reincorporation into the "normal" heteropatriarchal world (think Sally in *The Texas Chainsaw Massacre*, [1974]). By 2025 though, this is no longer the case. Where once a smiling woman implied purity, over the course of the past decade or so, films like *The Witch* (2015), along with a number of other now-iconic horror movies of the 2010s such as *Midsommar* (2019) and *Suspiria* (2018) began sending up this trope, depicting a young woman in the throes of a blissful acceptance not of salvation, but of Satan. This concluding image, almost nonexistent in most horror cycles, has repeated with stark frequency in the independent horror cycle of the late 2010s (defined in large part by the indie arthouse behemoth A24 and, more recently, Neon), signaling a sea-change in the horror landscape of the 2020s in the process. The question becomes: how did we get here? What's changed? What does this enormous imagistic shift say about the state of feminism over the past decade? And where do witches fit in?

The next few chapters will explore what I will call the "2010s witch horror cycle", in relation to previous cycles, witchcraft lore, and the recent political landscape. Building on the historical analysis of the rest of this book, and using Carol Clover's *Men, Women and Chainsaws* (1992) and Julia Kristeva's *Powers of Horror* (1982) as central nodes of analysis, I

---
1. West, 2017.

will trace the representation of "demonic women" in the past decade back to older horror cycles (particularly the '60s) and demonstrate a major shift in cinematic portrayals of this archetype over time. After a brief historical investigation of the politics of the 2010s and a case study of the earliest film in this horror cycle, the rest of this section will take a very different structural approach than the previous chapters, breaking down the most iconic films of this cycle structurally and aesthetically rather than chronologically or as pure, political case studies. This is done to give a better sense of their significance as a unique, unified corpus with more narrative similarities than previous cycles, and to argue for their importance on those terms.

As the conclusion of the previous chapter indicates, by the early-mid 2010s, fans, scholars, and critics alike were regularly receiving these films as feminist objects, and feminist cultural scholars had been weighing witches explicitly on these terms since the '90s. The films I label as some of the era's most significant entries (*The Witch*, *Midsommar*, and *Suspiria*) were immediately celebrated as feminist triumphs, both in scholarly articles, in mainstream media outlets, by fans on sites like Tumblr, and with articles in *Wired* and *Marie Claire* respectively calling *The Witch* "wildly feminist" and "a high-powered feminist manifesto" upon its initial release.[2][3] *Midsommar*'s reception, though more complex, was quickly claimed as a hyper-feminine and feminist aesthetic object in articles with titles like "Monstrous Womanhood and the Unapologetic Feminism of 'midsommar'" and "Midsommar is a Scathing Takedown of Masculinity."[4][5] This film also became a meme, a shorthand for blithe, airy feminine rage—Ariana Grande tweeted that the film was her "bedtime movie", and took it as the theme for her 27th birthday party.[6] Luca Guadagnino's press tour for *Suspiria*, meanwhile, found him constantly expressing his desire to "indict the male gaze" and highlighting the film's nuanced feminist bonafides, citing anthropological studies on Goddess worship.[7] While some critics suggested these films' treatments of the monstrous feminine were fundamentally misogynist for their reflections of the fear men have of women's power, the broader trend was overwhelmingly received as "feminist" *per se*. As one writer said, and which I argue from the outset, in these films, Dani, the protagonist of *Midsommar*, "becomes an emotional anchor to the genre's perversity. She is a clear example of women establishing their unfettered and beautiful ownership of horror in all its mystique"—and therein lies women's continued fascination with them.[8] These films seem to represent a cry for help, a warning, a portent of deep

---

2. Pierce, 2016.
3. Cohen, 2016.
4. Kennedy, 2019.
5. "Midsommar Is A Scathing Takedown of Masculinity.", 2019.
6. Mauch, 2020.
7. Juzwiak, 2018.
8. "Revisiting the Addictive Feminine Pull of Midsommar.", 2019.

frustration, and a feminist howl all at once, in an era of massive, seemingly unprecedented, political upheaval.

Since the mid-2010s, there has been a surge of renewed interest in witchcraft in the United States. In 2014, a Pew poll found that 0.4 % of Americans identified as Pagan or Wicca—a percentage comparable to American Presbyterians—and estimated this number to increase over the next several decades.[9] In 2015, *Vice* posted a short documentary on "The Witches of Bushwick", an art collective who, per the documentary, posited "female bonding is near to spirituality."[10] A series of trend pieces marked the re-emergence of witchcraft as, to quote a Buzzfeed piece on the pop-phenomenon, "officially cool."[11] [12] By 2017, think pieces marveled at the "surprising" increase in visibility of magical practice among the young (rarely mentioning the "teen witch" trend of the '90s though heavily citing its pop culture), from an exponential increase in astrology and tarot, to classes on candle magic (votive candles with Ruth Bader Ginsberg's face were a common sight at bookstores). This vogue's explicitly collectivist, explicitly feminist in its orientation, recreates the Second Wave fascination—screenings of *Rosemary's Baby* (1968) once again abounded—while restoring the individualistic, consumerist impulse that drove the '90s resurgence: practitioners criticized Sephora and other brands for "witch starter kit" makeup collections, selling for $40-60.[13]

At the same time, prompted by Donald Trump's defeat of Hillary Clinton in 2016, feminism was central to the politics of the mid-late 2010s. It was characterized by the expansive #MeToo movement against sexual assault and harassment, as well as the tremendous increase in women running for elected office. The turnout for the Women's March in 2017, the day after Trump's inauguration, became the largest single-day protest in American history at that time.[14] The increase in women candidates in the 2018 midterms was so dramatic that news outlets quickly declared that year to be the second "year of the woman", accurately comparing the President's rhetorical influence on feminists to the anti-feminism and overt misogyny of the Anita Hill hearings.[15]

These two trends led to a new resurgence of the kind of occult-coded feminist activism and pop culture that bloomed in the '60s.[16] That same year,

---

9. Buder, 2019.
10. "Under the Coven: The Witches of Bushwick", 2015.
11. Paul, 2018.
12. Faife, 2017.
13. Richardson-Andrews, 2018.
14. Broomfield, 2017.
15. Dvorak, 2017.
16. *Ibid.*

the Satanic Temple was founded to protest Christian infringement on the separation of church and state in the US.[17] Since then, the group has filed numerous lawsuits working to enshrine protections for abortion access on pagan religious grounds. W.I.T.C.H's Chicago chapter was reestablished in 2015 after decades of dormancy, and Boston's remained active until at least 2020.[18] [19] Many individuals outside these covens (including noted cool-girl crooner Lana Del Rey, who covered "Season of the Witch" in 2013) performed mass hexings of politicians and public figures,[20] among them Brock Turner[21] and and Brett Kavanaugh,[22] whose confirmation to the Supreme Court was read as an eerie echo of Clarence Thomas' own less than three decades before.[23] In October 2017, in response to Woody Allen's use of the phrase "witch hunt"[24] to describe renewed scrutiny of serial sexual predation allegations against Harvey Weinstein, an op-ed by Lindy West ran in the *New York Times* unpacking the ironic political implications of this rhetoric in a manner that demonstrated how the witch's history had pervaded the era's feminism:

> Setting aside the gendered power differential inherent in real historical witch hunts (pretty sure it wasn't all the rape victims in Salem getting together to burn the mayor), and the pathetic gall of men feeling hunted after millenniums of treating women like prey, I will let you guys have this one. Sure, if you insist, it's a witch hunt. I'm a witch, and I'm hunting you.[25]

Less than a week after, a *Vulture* article entitled "Why the Witch Is the Pop-Culture Heroine We Need Right Now" described the Trump era as a "time when many truths seem to shift depending on where you stand", and suggested that that sense of doubled identity and the ontological slippage of reality is "never more true than in stories about the witch. She is either a destabilizing, dangerous villain or a powerful protagonist, and the vision you choose depends entirely on your point of view."[26] The archetype was indeed being mobilized in more ways than one—as in the '90s, Hillary Clinton was Photoshopped during her Presidential run as "the Wicked Witch of the Left" with green skin and a pointy black hat. Bringing out the multivalent subtext of this association in his typically vitriolic terms, Rush Limbaugh described Clinton "a witch with a capital 'B'," neatly linking both

---

17. For more on Satanist political activism in the mid-late 2010s, see *Hail Satan?*, 2019.
18. "W.I.T.C.H. Chicago Coven 2015-17", 2017.
19. "About", 2020.
20. See Keller and Mulvey, 2020; Wolfson, 2018; Doyle, 2019.
21. Kari, 2016.
22. Avery, 2018.
23. Siddiqui, 2018.
24. Chow, 2017.
25. West, 2017.
26. VanArendonk, 2017.

'80s witch media and chauvinism to the "bitchification" of this former First Lady in the '90s.²⁷ QAnon conspiracy theorists and the alt-right, meanwhile, promulgated accusations against prominent Democratic politicians and Hollywood celebrities like Ellen DeGeneres as well as Clinton, claiming they were Satan-worshiping pedophiles who magically extend their lifespans by cannibalizing children.²⁸ The similarity of these claims to the rhetoric of both Medieval witch hunters and proponents of Satanic Panic is clear and chilling.

Thus, as feminist witches saw it, to be a witch at this point in history, as in the 1960s, constituted "a refusal to be cowed by patriarchal structures and toxic masculine power dynamics; it's witchiness as selfhood, focused less on witchcraft as a practice and more on the witch as a feminist identity."²⁹ As one writer argued in a piece marking the late 2010s as a new "season of the witch",

> [F]or decades now, the right has spiritualized political warfare, treating it as a metaphysical contest between good and evil. It's not surprising that the rise of Trump, a person who for many represents the inversion of all decent values, would create a supernatural reaction on the left. Millennial occultists might seem silly to outsiders, but you don't have to believe in hexes, witchcraft or magic to take them seriously as a sign that many people find the present intolerable. Just under the surface of American culture, something furious is brewing.³⁰

The 2010s also marked the beginning of what has become known as the second "psychedelic renaissance" after the 1960s.³¹ Accompanying the rapid legalization of marijuana, this movement towards legalizing psychedelics increased in the cultural saliency of the drugs and their accompanying aesthetic signifiers—a turn which, in tandem with the era's fascination with witchcraft and occultism, brings the decade and its films into close conversation with the 1960s witch horror cycle. In 2014, an article in *Scientific American* called for the end of the ban on psychedelics in the name of expanding access for research. Around the same time, popular interest in this class of drugs was making a comeback: between 2015 and 2019, reports suggested that past-year usage of psychedelics among college students had increased by 47%, and by 2021, surveys found that recreational use of hallucinogens had doubled since the 2000s.³² "You're Not Tripping: LSD Is Making a Comeback" read

---

27. Schiff, 2016.
28. Roose, 2021.
29. VanArendonk, 2017.
30. Goldberg, 2017.
31. The term itself is often used to describe the '60s period of research and artistic exploration of the drugs, but as early as 2017, news outlets like PBS were reporting that psychedelics were "having a medical renaissance" (O'Brien, 2017).
32. Weleff et al., 2024.

a typical headline on the trend.[33] In 2018, Michael Pollan's bestselling book on the history of psychedelic drugs, *How to Change Your Mind*, presented a mild-mannered and thoroughly respectable account of the uses, effects, and political power of these substances for a general audience, continuing to strip some of the sordid countercultural connotations from them (these users prefer the term "entheogens" over "psychedelics" he remarked).[34] In 2019, *Goop*, Gweneth Paltrow's embattled[35] lifestyle brand, itself a hub of feminine New Age sentiment for the uber-wealthy, launched a show called *The Goop Lab*, the first episode of which featured millennial employees vomiting during their first psychedelic retreats, lauding the benefits of the emotional release.[36] "Because LSD use fell significantly in the early 2000s following a drop in availability, many college-age students haven't heard the extreme stories that circulated among earlier generations, and view LSD almost with fresh eyes," a historian of the subject reported in 2016.[37]

This last element has not been as closely associated with the new occult boom of the 2010s by the media as it was in the '60s—even as books like *Weed Witch: The Essential Guide to Cannabis for Magic and Wellness* (2023), demonstrate the overt ties between the trends. But as the case studies in this chapter will demonstrate, their roots in New Age mysticism—as well as political and ontological uncertainty—remain firmly intertwined during this period. As the decade progresses and these shifts become entrenched and culturally familiar, these threads will come together clearly. But each element was present from the beginning of the cycle, on display in a film to which I will now turn.

After a decade of evil queens and hunted witches, Rob Zombie's *The Lords of Salem* (2013) marked the beginning of a sea change for the fate of the witch on screen. The same year critics were remarking on the "return of the witch" to big budget fantasy filmmaking, the rocker-turned-director presaged many of the stylistic, generic, and thematic hallmarks of films that would define the next decade with practically zero fanfare, from psychedelic visuals to a nihilistic-yet-ecstatic ending. Set in present-day Salem, *Lords* follows Heidi (Sheri Moon Zombie), an old-school DJ and recovering heroin addict, down a narcotic spiral after she plays a record a stranger sends to her station live on air, causing an unexpected reaction in the women of the

---

33. Kruzman, 2017.
34. Pollan, 19.
35. In 2018, *Goop* was sued for "false medical advertising" specifically for claiming that one of their essential oils blends treats depression and that a vaginally-inserted jade egg boosted female sexual health. Neither claim has been backed by scientific evidence (Garcia, 2018).
36. "The Healing Trip." (2020).
37. Kruzman, 2017.

town. Self-consciously meta-referential, the film blends over-the-top '70s pastiche with a cheeky Satanic Panic frame narrative—there really *is* a subliminal Satanic message in this rock record, sent from the witches of 17th-century Salem to curse the daughters of those who burned them at the stake. The film's cold open, like the exploitation films it emulates, shows naked witches of all ages celebrating a Black Mass before being killed for their Devil's music. Margaret Morgan (Meg Foster) leads the group, and laughs during her execution. After the record plays in the present day, Heidi has psychedelically-inflected visions of witch burnings, grisly births, and torture. As in the witch films of the late-1960s, the film features exposition on the history of witchcraft from a professor-*cum*-witch hunter ('70s B-horror veteran Bruce Davison), who argues that witch crazes are "really nothing but a psychotic belief brought about by a delusional state of mind"—though he also emphasizes that "today there's a sizable Wiccan population" in Salem, explaining "it's an earth-based religion." Heidi quips, "yeah, hairy armpits and granola, I *don't* dig it," derogatorily linking modern day witches to stereotypes around aging hippie feminists. Soon, she finds herself involved with her landlady and her two sisters, who read her palm and encourage her to "make peace with your subconscious desires, the wicked thoughts burning inside your head and exploding in the juices between your legs, the darkness within your very soul, the only reason you exist," in a succinct summary of many of the tropes around female sexuality and Satanic influence.

Heidi's visions and nightmares come with an increasing sense of doom. Eventually, she succumbs to her addiction, freebasing heroin as a means of escape. Meanwhile, a concert for the "band" that supposedly sent the record (the titular Lords of Salem), is scheduled in town. The witches bring Heidi into an empty apartment, in which a huge red cross burns with neon light. Her perspective begins to fracture between the drugs and the visions, while the historian discovers that Margaret Morgan had cursed the women of those who killed her, promising that one of them would bear Satan's child. The witches kill the historian and aid Heidi to give birth, after a monstrously rapid pregnancy, while the women of the town arrive at the concert hall in a hypnotic trance. Heidi's hallucinatory visions take over and the film's climax descends into psychedelic bedlam after Heidi births a flailing, writhing, star-shaped mass on a stone altar surrounded by witches who spread her blood across their faces: step-framed shots of Heidi ecstatically riding a goat like a mechanical bull dissolve into sparkling collages of blasphemous religious imagery melting into psychedelic rainbows, while mutilated monsters flash across the screen, neon crosses are engulfed in flames, and a man's voice recites a mantra embracing Satan. Finally, Margaret Morgan looks at the camera through a red-tinted haze, and laughs. The final scene shows the three witches smiling up into an angelic white light as The Velvet Underground's "All Tomorrow's Parties" begins to play. Heidi stands, statuesque, face expressionless, draped in a silky white dress and a red shawl falling around her hair, a crown on top of her head with a brilliant godly light radiating from her like a classical religious painting. She stands atop a mountain of naked women's bodies, eyes entirely milky white, arms outstretched. The witches smile, reverent.

Ultimately, the film's depiction of witches is fundamentally conservative—the coven itself, like Polanski's, is composed of older, malevolent, and Satan-worshiping women, although Heidi herself represents many of the archetype's more aesthetic elements (more Nancy than Rosemary) and their combination in the climax is presented as awe-inspiring rather than truly frightening. Some critics noted this contradiction at the outset: "Zombie's scenario upholds all the usual notions of witchy thrillers, including that women are uniquely susceptible to demonic suggestion," reads Mark Jenkins' dismissal of the film in the *Washington Post*, "[t]hat makes 'The Lords of Salem' a weak echo of the misogyny that fueled the Salem witch trials." At the same time, Jenkins writes, seemingly not noting the tension on display, *Lords* seems "*nostalgic for a bygone era when a woman could have near-magical influence.*"[38] Taken together, these two competing impulses will become central to this cycle as male directors deliver stories of witches as abject feminine avengers, at once frightening and undeniably winning. Zombie's "nostalgia" for women's power, as feminist outrage towards Donald Trump (as in Lindy West's article) exemplifies, will come to dominate the era's horror—the A24 witch cycle builds on the same set of aesthetic signifiers and themes.

The film's aesthetic motifs, nightmarish dark-night-of-the-soul structure, and explosive concluding image—presenting the revenge of these witches upon the women of Salem as a sort of perversely triumphant inversion of Mary's coronation in Heaven or Jesus' martyrdom—represent the final piece of the puzzle that more commercial feminist witch films like *Maleficent* (2014) or empowering occult shows like *American Horror Story* (2011-2023) lack. *Lords* was almost universally panned by critics. Yet it was also recognized—like *Black Sunday* (1960) at the dawn of the *previous* recuperation of horror into the realm of prestige filmmaking in the '60s—for its "singularly unique vision in a cinematic genre too often ruled by dirt-dull sequels and imagination-free 'product'."[39] In a moment when capital-rich streamers were throwing money at an increasingly diverse array of artists to fill their digital libraries, parallels to the daring New Hollywood paradigm shift made a certain amount of sense. One *Lords* review appeared in print directly alongside a pan for *Oz the Great and Powerful* (2013) ("more like the Bland and Mediocre… the script suffers from a bad case of fan-fictionitis").[40]

---

38. Jenkins, 2013.
39. Savlov, 2013.
40. *Ibid.*

As a sort of occult music video pastiche, this burgeoning "70s-esque" cult classic (several reviews correctly predicted that "[t]heatrical play will pale beside the pic's ancillary afterlife") was nevertheless discussed for its exuberant reappropriation of "the surreal interiors of Stanley Kubrick and the blasphemous freakouts of Ken Russell" as well as homages to *Rosemary's Baby* and the post-countercultural, psychedelic horror classic *Jacob's Ladder* (1990).[41][42] In reviews on this more experimental register, shades of the reception received by most films of the '60s witch cycle can be found, like Tom Wolfe's mysto steam rising up on the margins of the new decade: in *Lords*, said one, the plot "often takes a backseat to the film's *skewed sense of the everyday* slipping into the freakishly bizarre,"[43] (recall *Sight and Sound* grappling with *Rosemary's Baby*: "mundane reality... imbued with a pointless significance"). In so doing, reviews like these acknowledge the countercultural *and* Satanic Panic roots of this heavy metal stoner film (critics note the irony of Zombie's use of "backmasking" tropes and call the witches "a trio of aging hippies" for example). The same review concludes that "The *Lords of Salem* is a head trip... just sit back and goggle."[44] Much as *American Horror Story: Coven* (2013-14) served as a compelling template for feminist witch horror in this decade politically, *Lords*, it will soon become clear, is a powerful example of the style—and the anxieties—the case studies that make up the next several chapters will embrace.

---

41. Nelson, 2012.
42. Guzman, 2013.
43. Savlov, 2013.
44. *Ibid.*

Chapter Fourteen

Genre and the 2010s "Witch Film"

As I suggest in the introduction to this book, unlike other supernatural horror films, there is no set of generic conventions that make up a "witch" film. The '60s cycle set out several different templates for future witch films to follow as it evolved, from the paranoiac stylings of *Rosemary's Baby* (1968) and *Don't Look Now* (1973), to the slasher drama of *Carrie* (1976) and *Suspiria* (1977)—though they all incorporate psychedelic imagery to some degree. These films have rarely been investigated on generic terms (as opposed to thematic ones) specifically as "witch films", more often being thematized into distinct subgenres. This chapter works to rectify this oversight. In her classic book of feminist horror theory, *Men, Women, and Chainsaws* (1993), Carol J. Clover examines one subset of the Satanic/occult horror film: what she calls the "possession film", in a chapter titled "Opening Up". She puts forward two theories about the subgenre: 1) Although the possession film is a horror subgenre uniquely focused on women and women's bodies, possession films (and occult horror more broadly) is centrally about "masculinity and male sexuality… under long and hard scrutiny." "Behind the female 'cover'" of the woman possessed, she says, "is always the story of a man in crisis", and 2) In these films, this female "cover", the grotesque and emotionally heightened body of the woman or girl possessed, serves to counter a form of homosexual panic associated with the "feminizing" emotional arcs of the men in these narratives.[1] [2] Of *The Exorcist* (1973), Clover writes that Father Karras struggles with his faith and guilt over the death of his mother, taking emotional precedent over Regan's possession, which allows him to direct his own process of "opening up" emotionally to his belief in God.[3] These same structural principles can be applied to other, non-possession witch films like *Don't Look Now*, wherein John's inability to accept his ESP is the film's central emotional arc, while his wife Laura is much more inherently open to the possibility of spirits and witchcraft. Clover ties this dichotomy to the archaic understanding of female anatomy as innately sinful: "where Satan is, in the world of horror, female genitals are likely to be nearby. The word *vulva* itself is related to *valve*—gate or entry to the body—and so it regularly serves for all manner of spirits [and

---

1. Clover, 1992, 65.
2. *Ibid*, 103.
3. *Ibid*.

Satan above all] in occult horror."[4] For Clover, women in possession films function as a point of dramatic contrast to the cosmic struggles of a man who needs to become more open, and thus stereotypically feminine.[5] With these two points in mind, she makes the argument that possession films follow two rigidly gendered emotional narrative structures: men (typically the protagonists) follow a linear progression, an "ABC" structure wherein they go from "closed" (cynical, emotionally unavailable—traditionally "masculine" traits depicted as negative in overabundance) to "open" (spiritual, or at least less cynical, more emotional) over the course of the film, while women (the victims) follow an "ABA" structure from "open" (traditionally feminine, emotionally available) to "excessively open" (possessed, hypersexual, grotesque/monstrous) and back to their normal state with no real growth or change—or end up dead.[6]

Looking specifically at witch films with this structure in mind, a pattern emerges: in the few films where the woman survives (i.e. *Don't Look Now* and *Rosemary's Baby*) the film takes pains to occlude the presence of the monstrous feminine for those characters. Some foreground a "seduction" process for women who accept black magic as in *Don't Look Now*, rendering their choices passive, while others transfer the "ABC" narrative structure onto the female protagonist as in *Rosemary's Baby*, masculinizing her in order to resolve the ending without overtly threatening the heteropatriarchy. The "ABC" structure put forth by Clover relies on an "overly closed" "masculine" baseline to conclude with a "normative" heteropatriarchally acceptable character, as opposed to something potentially "other" in its gendered and political implications, thus Rosemary is conservative and, like Carrie, struggling with her own internalized religious repression. Ultimately, as I discussed in Part 1, both movies are ambivalent, open to conservative and liberatory readings. In both cases, it's possible to read them as suggesting that the women's choices, though frightening, are not fully their own. Those interpretations would read like this: Having fought to escape and finding she could not, Rosemary, like Laura who so eagerly joins the coven to see her daughter again, succumbs to her ("natural", or feminizing and non-threatening) maternal instincts, ending the film "properly" feminine even though the context may be monstrous. The women in these two films don't quite smile in the face of their newfound powers—in fact, both films end with moments of profound tension on the part of the female characters, their pale, tired faces wavering between sadness, passive acceptance and,

---

4. Clover, 1992, 76.
5. Films like *Suspiria* that are exceptions to this rule hew more closely to the tropes of the slasher film (in the case of *Suspiria*, giallo is its own discrete slasher-esque genre in the Italian film culture) and will be significant to the 2010s cycle for that reason as it incorporates elements of the slasher such as the "final girl."
6. Clover, 1992, 103.

potentially, contentment.[7] This is a dramatic contrast to slasher films like *The Texas Chainsaw Massacre* (1974), released the same year as *Don't Look Now*, wherein Sally's hysterical whooping—involuntary laughter mingling terror and relief—borders on the ecstatic.

The witch films of the mid-late 2010s demonstrate a generic consistency markedly absent from previous witch cycles. While they employ Clover's "man in crisis" trope, they consistently subvert it by incorporating elements of the slasher, emphasizing their female protagonists' subjectivities, making them final girls. In so doing, they also heighten the failures of their male characters' attempts to control their circumstances. By refocusing on the crisis of the feminine, while still depicting a "man in crisis", these films reverse Clover's "ABC" and "ABA" structures: The male characters are so focused on maintaining their initial ("A") subject positions—often characterized not by authority and strength but passivity and rigidity—that they are emotionally broken by their failures to do so. They often die as a result, with little impact on the female character's emotional arc. Unlike *The Exorcist*, the man's death is neither heroic nor positively sacrificial and is unlikely to "save" the woman in distress. The women, for their part, begin the films in much the same way their possessed predecessors do: open. Their struggles with internalized feminine guilt and shame are central. These are heightened rather than constrained—as is the case with Rosemary or Laura—allowing them to become progressively more "open" as a male character would in prior cycles. But now they transgress "acceptable" femininity, embracing a newly unleashed form of "monstrous" femininity at the film's close: they invert the ending of a typical slasher, wherein the final girl's escape signals the evil's (likely temporary) defeat.

Ari Aster's *Midsommar* (2019) is a prototypical example of this new "witch film" in structure and narrative. Taking cues from *The Wicker Man* (1973), it follows the fracturing relationship between Dani (Florence Pugh), a young woman whose schizophrenic younger sister has recently murdered her parents and committed suicide, and Christian (Jack Reynor), her boyfriend. He struggles to decide whether to leave her—and what his doctoral thesis should be about—as the two take a trip to Sweden to observe a remote community's traditional midsummer festival. Once there, the group is encouraged to join in the celebrations, taking large doses of psychedelics. They begin to squabble as Christian steals his friend's thesis topic (the Hårga community and its midsummer traditions,) only to be slowly ritually sacrificed one by one. Christian is quickly selected by a young Hårga girl, Maja (Isabelle Grill), for reproduction and is repeatedly drugged and fed meals laced with her pubic hairs (a form of love magic). By contrast, Dani

---

7. It should also be noted that there are no films in this period wherein a man undergoes the same process. Rosemary's husband, Guy (John Cassavetes), for example, is portrayed as opportunistic in his motivations and casually, cavalierly excited about his incorporation into the coven.

is treated kindly by the community and—after winning the final game of the Midsommar celebration (a May Pole dance)—is crowned that year's May Queen. As a drugged Christian is forced to have sex with Maja while the other women of the community watch, Dani discovers him; she is finally able to express her grief at her circumstances, failing relationship, and death of her family, screaming and crying with a group of other women. The murders are eventually revealed, and Dani is told that, as the May Queen, she must select a final sacrifice: a member of the Hårga, or Christian. After a time jump, Dani, crowned in flowers, watches as Christian is burned alive along with the bodies of the other victims. A broad smile spreads across her face. While *Midsommar* is not technically a "witch film" (the Hårga don't call themselves witches), Ari Aster referred to Swedish Satanic lore in the construction of their laws and customs, from their use of an occult runic alphabet, veneficium (herbal magic) and sex magic, to the myth of the Hårga May Queen dance (that claims the Devil compelled young Hårga girls to dance until all but one died).[8] Additionally, Aster did a significant amount of occult research for his first feature, *Hereditary* (2018), and the two films share many symbols and themes, suggesting a similar frame of reference between *Hereditary*'s cult of witches and the neo-pagans of *Midsommar*.[9]

Christian, the film's central male character, is an almost perfect inversion of the men of previous cycles. Aptly named, given his eventual rejection of paganism, Christian is a passive figure, sexually frustrated and unable to emotionally support his girlfriend. Christian and his friends complain that Dani is "demanding" ("Dude she's calling you again? Seriously?") and "crazy" ("Dude, she needs a therapist"). They bemoan her lack of sexual availability, counseling him to end their relationship: "you've been wanting out of this stupid relationship for like a year now" says one friend, "and don't forget all of the beautiful Swedish women you'll meet in June!" interjects another. The film's middle passages track Christian's interest in other women and his negligence as a partner (he forgets Dani's birthday and how long they've been together). They also follow his competitive relationship with his classmate, Josh, whose thesis topic he blatantly plagiarizes. Christian lacks the motivation to break off his relationship or find an original idea. In other words, he lacks any of the basic "masculine" qualities of characters like John in *Don't Look Now*, whose expertise in his academic field is depicted as masculine, or *The Wicker Man*'s stolid Christian protagonist, Sergeant Howie, whose conviction in the law and the Lord are his ultimate downfall at the hands of another remote pagan community—like Christian, he is burned alive as a sacrifice to promote a good harvest. In *The Wicker Man*, Howie's death is depicted as pointless and tragic, yet there is still hope that he will be spiritually and legally avenged (the pagan sacrifices, it is pointed out,

---

8. Zuckerman, 2019.
9. Whalen, 2018.

have been yielding smaller harvests, and Howie's status as an investigator ensures he will be quickly missed in London). Howie ends the film with a dramatic prayer shouted above the heads of the "heathen" community who dance and sing as they set the titular "wicker man" on fire. He damns them to Hell and raises his voice in prayer until his final moments. Christian, on the other hand, is retiring, a novice even in his academic field. He seems unable to believe that women could put him in danger, continually defending what violence sees in the community as "tradition!" without question. Ultimately, he is drugged and immobilized, unable to protest as flames engulf him, a small, dull frown plastered on his slack face. In this imagistic mirroring of *The Wicker Man*'s iconic climax, *Midsommar* paints a cynical portrait of the fate of masculinity: Christian does not fight to his last breath, and it seems that no one will look for him after he is gone. His failure of masculinity is so profound that he becomes disposable.

Dani, on the other hand, is shown fraught with tension and inner conflict, desperately working to hold herself together, caught up in the paradox of womanhood. She is unmoored by the death of her family and struggles to function normally in her life, emailing her professors for extensions and wandering purposelessly from her apartment to gatherings of Christian's friends, where her lack of sex drive makes her a disruptive presence. Her anxiety is expressed in moments of self-doubt and shame: she frequently takes responsibility for Christian's failures as a partner (when he forgets her birthday, she quickly tells their friends, "It's my fault, I forgot to remind him"). Dani seems to have internalized the rhetoric of blame placed on her by Christian's friends for his interest in other women, trying to ignore his lecherous stares or recapture his attention to little avail. Like Carrie in her final moments, Dani's overwhelming emotions threaten to break her, tying her to broader stereotypes about feminine weakness and hyperemotionality used against women since Eve. The Hårga's emphasis is on emotional expression as healthy and communal, "feminine" traits that connect back to pagan constructions of womanhood as collective and positively emotional. While these were depicted as negative in the horror of the '60s, here, they allow her to heal. The debilitating anxiety attacks Dani has been forced to experience in private are channeled into this hyperconnective expression of communal, "feminized" grief. The Hårga women hold her as she cries, mirroring her facial expressions and matching her screams' pitch and volume with their own, syncing their breathing with hers until she calms. The women refer to her as their "sister", emphasizing a new belonging, vaguely Mansonoid or no, unmarred by the trauma of her past and her nuclear family.

This contrast between the positive-communal feminine and negative feminine isolation, represents a break from past witch films like *Carrie* by positing an alternative (neo-pagan) social model wherein womanhood is no longer, as Shelley Stamp says of Carrie's predicament, a subject position "impossible to occupy" due to patriarchal inhibitions, or Kristeva's internalized abjection and guilt. At the same time, the film represents this alternative, feminine space as threatening and alien—it is a horror movie after all—creating a powerful ambivalence within the text. Though the sheer contrast between the Dani's profound family tragedy and Christian's trivial personal struggles makes clear where the viewer's sympathies should lie, the film is still sympathetic to Christian's fear of the Hårga women's sexual practices (reproductively-oriented, communally-inflected sex), introducing an explicit anxiety about the collective feminine. When he finally has sex with Maja and finds they are being watched by a group of older women, the experience is depicted as strange and unnatural. The sequence is (perhaps unintentionally) comical, focusing on Christian's terrified face as the older women sing to the couple and smile at Maja encouragingly before demanding that Christian climax. The scene is hyperfeminine in its imagery (from the flowers around them, to the "strange" proliferation of female bodies). It is a male inversion of the comforting image of feminine collectivity experienced by Dani only moments later, depicting this hyperfeminine form of connection as emasculating: Maja looks to the other women not him as they have sex, and he gets no real pleasure from the encounter. The sex is then revealed to be reproductive, which affirms this interpretation of "feminine" sexuality as something threatening to the "masculine", pleasure-oriented view proffered by Christian's friends—all of whom have been sacrificed to encourage the next year's bountiful harvest at this point (a different form of reproduction). This contributes to the construction of Dani's asexual presence as a socially non-normative threat.

The film's final sequence clearly delineates the ambivalence of Dani's intimate relationship with the Hårga women. Once Dani has overcome her panic attacks and accepted her role as May Queen, she—with the encouragement of one of the Hårga women—selects Christian as the final sacrifice. Dani cries as she makes the decision, her face wavering between fear, sadness, and something that looks like hope in a slowly pushing close-up reminiscent of the final moments of *Rosemary's Baby*. But rather than explicitly showing her decision, the film cuts to older men teaching young Hårga boys how to disembowel a bear: this traditional symbol of virility is hewn with a vaginal slit in its stomach—literally emasculating it before Christian is placed inside.[10] "Mighty and dreadful beast," a man tells him, "with you we purge our most unholy affekts [sic]. We banish you now to the deepest recesses, where you may reflect on your wickedness." This final condemnation of Christian as "wicked" in the face of neo-pagan

---

10. Likely a reference to the 2006 remake of *The Wicker Man* wherein Nicholas Cage wears a bear suit to disguise himself as one of Neo-Pagan women while attempting to save a child from sacrifice. In that scene, Nicolas Cage is every bit the traditionally virile male hero, punching women to the ground to rescue the girl. He is still unsuccessful, but this contrast highlights the impotency of Christian's character.

ritual sacrifice, communal femininity and murder once more inverts the climax of *The Wicker Man*—he has indeed been depicted as an unworthy and impotent partner. It's this weak figure of masculinity, not its monstrous feminine counterpart, who is purged at the film's climax, allowing Dani to fully embrace her newfound role in the Hårga, smiling with bliss into the flames where Christian, so lacking in Sargent Howie's convictions, is symbolically damned. If in previous cycles the fear expressed by witch horror was generally emblematic of what Stamp calls the "failure of repression to contain the monstrous feminine"[11] within the woman, here the primary concern seems to be the *failure of masculinity* on the part of the man to properly maintain this repression and defeat the monstrous feminine with which he is faced as a consequence—a fear of self-inflicted emasculation in tandem with a fear of the unconstrained feminine.

Robert Eggers' 2016 film *The Witch: A New England Folktale* follows a similar pattern while going further in foregrounding female agency. *The Witch* follows a Puritan family into exile from their colony in the 1630s: William (Ralph Ineson), their patriarch, has been called a "false prophet" for refusing to strictly adhere to Puritan doctrine. The family mother, Katherine (Kate Dickie), eldest daughter Thomasin (Anya Taylor-Joy), eldest son Caleb (Harvey Scrimshaw), twins Mercy and Jonas (Ellie Grainger and Lucas Dawson), and infant son Samuel, attempt to settle anew, but, with crops plagued by an inexplicable rot, the family struggles to survive. Soon thereafter, Samuel is stolen under Thomasin's supervision, throwing the house into turmoil. A witch has kidnapped him and used his corpse to make a flying ointment. Thomasin, who has just reached reproductive age (she has recently started her period, her mother angrily tells her father), is quickly blamed.

Resentment and suspicions grow between family members over their woes, most of which are also directed at Thomasin. When Caleb too disappears in the woods, Thomasin's siblings accuse her of witchcraft. Thomasin denies this and is supported by her father until Caleb returns to the house—possessed after an encounter with the witch who seduces him before turning into a crone—and soon dies. Thomasin condemns Mercy and Jonas, who seem to hold conversations with the family goat, Black Phillip, and their father locks all three children in with the goat. In the middle of the night, their mother has visions of her dead sons who compel her to sign the Devil's Book as their father prays outside for salvation. In the morning, Mercy and Jonas have disappeared, leaving only Thomasin in the ruined shed. Black Phillip breaks loose and gores William; Katherine attacks Thomasin, forcing the girl (like Carrie) to kill her mother in defense. Thomasin approaches Black Phillip and demands he speak to her. When he does, offering her a life of boundless pleasure, she accepts and follows him through the woods to join

---

11. Stamp, 2015, 340.

a coven. She laughs with delight and abandon as she floats into the air with the other witches, finally free of repression.

In most post-'60s horror cycles, William—the father in what's essentially a haunted house film like *The Amityville Horror* (1979)—would likely have been *The Witch*'s protagonist. This is no longer the case, and his status as a failed patriarch, profoundly alters the dynamics of the film. Like Christian in *Midsommar*, William is depicted as incompetent and passive. While Christian is characterized by his utter lack of direction, William is characterized by his failure of conviction even as he attempts to strike out on his own apart from the Puritan church. It's his refusal to baptize his children (part of why he is exiled from the colony, it is implied) that ensures their damnation. When Caleb asks him directly whether Samuel is in Hell, he can't give the boy an answer. His wife blames him openly ("You've damned us all!") and, like Christian, he's incapable of comforting her in the face of the tragedies she experiences ("Think not of it"). He lacks basic pioneering skills, leaving their barn half-built and failing to harvest enough to last the family the winter.[12] William is so incapable of growing food that he is forced to sell his wife's prized possession, a silver cup, to buy traps for them to survive. When Katherine blames Thomasin for the cup's disappearance, he is too cowardly to defend her. As the film progresses, William weakens rather than rises to the challenge.

The dramatic departure of the masculine protagonist is demonstrated best through contrast. William's crisis of faith comes to a head when he prays in the final sequence, before his death. His prayer—an entreaty to God to redeem his children—is shown from behind in a wide shot at eye level, from Thomasin's perspective, prioritizing her subjectivity. This is a reversal of the more traditional high angle close-ups of faces and hands typically representative of prayer, or even the profile shots of a confessional, and implies a lack of communication, an absence of God or a refusal to hear his prayer. It also contrasts with Thomasin's confession and prayer, shot more traditionally in slowly pushing high angle close-up, where she admits she has "broken every one of Your Commandments in thought." But she begs for forgiveness before she is put in charge of Samuel moments before he is taken—a swift, condemning response to her entreaty. Together, these two scenes construct a hierarchy of piety and subjectivity wherein both characters pray to a vengeful God who is listening to only one, the daughter (though he saves neither) in the ultimate disavowal of the strength of William as a patriarchal and spiritual authority.

---

12. "Thou canst do nothing but cut wood!" Thomasin screams near the film's climax. This motif contrasts him to Jesus (a carpenter) and potentially refers back to *The Amityville Horror* wherein the patriarch's failure is also signaled by an obsessive need to cut cord after cord of wood for the fire rather than take care of his family. In that film, though, the father ultimately succeeds in rescuing his family from the demon that assails them; here though, the pile of wood collapses on William, killing him and symbolically punishing him for his hubris.

Thomasin represents a bold disavowal of the religious repression of *Carrie*. Like Dani in *Midsommar*, she struggles to meet the expectations of her loved ones. Thomasin performs all manner of household chores, from milking the cows to tending the children to fetching water from the stream. Her labors only increase after Samuel's disappearance, when her mother takes to her bed.[13] She does them all willingly but perfunctorily; she is quick-tempered and proud, prone to absentmindedness. Her mother sees her as a threat to her sovereignty over the house now that she is of mature age, the threat of incest hovering at the margins of her ire and in Caleb's prolonged stares down Thomasin's corset, later exploding into accusations. The threat of incest is inscribed onto Thomasin's newly adolescent body, like Mrs. White's self-righteous denigration of Carrie's newly pubescent body. Unlike Carrie, however, Thomasin sees and understands the scapegoating that is occurring and fights back, frequently pointing out the unfairness of her treatment.

Thomasin comes to use the tropes of witchcraft to her own advantage. At one point, she actively *performs* the role of the witch to frighten her siblings into silence as they taunt her, in what may or may not be a truthful declaration, "I am that very witch... Perchance I'll boil and bake thee, since we're a lack of food," before tackling Mercy to the ground. By assuming the role of the witch as a tool of control over her siblings, Thomasin, even more directly than Elzorah in *Eve's Bayou* (1996), usurps the condemning narrative of Christian feminine patriarchal domination for her own purposes. And when Thomasin does become a witch, she does so of her own free will. She approaches Black Phillip herself after she is forced to kill her mother. Once in the goat hutch, she commands him to speak to her, waiting with impatience and determination in an unbroken close-up of her face. Finally, when he does, asking, "What dost thou want?" she counters him by asking "What canst thou give?"—insisting on agency akin to *Belladonna of Sadness* (1973). Finally, Thomasin, like Dani, embraces her powers, fully unburdening herself of Carrie's internalized guilt. Thomasin enters a clearing to find a group of other women dancing before a bonfire. This pagan, communal, feminine, and liberatory space is like that of *Midsommar*. She laughs with delight as she sees her own body begin to float, a final departure from her previous circumstances. The film's final shot—Thomasin lit by the bonfire, laughing and floating in the posture of the crucifixion against a backdrop of trees—represents a rejection of Mrs. White's crucifixion at the end of *Carrie*. Rather than embracing the Christian doctrine that repressed her, she represents an older form of pagan reclamation: she becomes a female deity that, as Michelet says of the Black Mass, replaces the masculinized iconography of the Christian feminine with the archaic pagan feminine.

---

13. Both women are their own sort of sexual disruption. Katherine's mature age (the fact of Samuel's birth is itself somewhat uncanny) and depressive asexuality rending the rift in the family still deeper after the infant's death.

Elements of other films from the late 2010s echo the feminine gender dynamics of *The Witch* and *Midsommar*. Take Luca Guadagnino's 2018 remake of *Suspiria*. This film changes the ending of the original, with Susie (Dakota Johnson) embracing witchcraft and becoming a pagan goddess. The film follows her, the child of a Mennonite mother, to a German dance academy where girls have been disappearing—the work of a coven of witches attempting to revitalize their leader, Mother Markos (an unrecognizable Tilda Swinton), with the body of a "pure" girl. Susie is a natural dancer and is quickly chosen for this role. Eventually, after the final dance—in which the re-animated bodies of the missing girls also take part—Susie goes to Black Mass only to reveal that she is the vessel of a superior power: Mother Suspiria, one of the three demon-goddesses to whom the witches swear loyalty. Unlike Argento's protagonist, this Susie is destined to become a witch, based on psychedelically rendered prophetic dreams she had as a child. They reveal that she was rejected by her mother for her sexual expression (images of masturbation, whippings, and closets reminiscent of *Carrie* pervade), placing her with Thomasin in the tradition of the witch as sexual/pagan threat to the religious community. She finally approaches the coven and summons an elder goddess, entreating her to take possession of her body. She rips open her chest and smiles ecstatically at the sky as her still-beating heart oozes blood down her front in an inverted parody of Mary's Sacred Heart: "Death to any other mother," she croons.

Richard Stanley's 2019 psychedelic sci-fi slasher *Color Out of Space*, an adaptation of H.P. Lovecraft's short story by former warlock Richard Stanley, also focuses on a young witch. Lavinia Gardner (Madeleine Walker), one of the film's protagonists and a practicing Wiccan, is possessed by a nebulous alien "color" that invades her family's home through the water supply after a meteor lands in their backyard. While the other members of her family die one by one, Lavinia casts a spell asking Satan to save her, carving occult runes into her body with a box cutter, and, in the climax, transcending into an alternate dimension with a beneficent smile on her face, dissolving into an enormous cloud of bright white light ("I live here now," she says). Lavinia thus exists in a new dimension beyond comprehension: she overcomes the rigid family structures against which she has struggled throughout the film, namely her sexually repressive and conservative parents. Lavinia's father, Nathan Gardner (Nicolas Cage), the film's "man in crisis", shares many similarities with *The Witch*'s William. He brings his family to his deceased father's house in a remote area to start a farm, but can't take care of them. He is a terrible cook, a poor investor, and a pitiful farmer belittled by his family. He fails to rescue them from an invading evil and dies pitifully.

These narrative consistencies signal a profound departure from the loose conventions of prior witch horror cycles. Much as Tourneur's *Cat People* (1942) or De Palma's *Carrie* presented an ambivalent portrait of conventional femininity on the verge of rupture in the face of a changing social climate, these films paint a portrait of the monstrous feminine breaking loose in a new way. They focus more on the subjectivity of previously demonized figures like the witch or the possessed woman, and reverse Clover's narrative "ABC" and "ABA" structures. These films consequently highlight a reconfiguration of the anxiety at play, not merely a failure of repression in women, but a failure of masculine *repressiveness*, an impotency in the face of newly liberated, "monstrous" feminine characters. Rather than burn the witch at the stake or perform a successful exorcism, these men are themselves burned, stabbed, and exorcized, allowing witch characters—newly unburdened of the social guilt born by their cinematic predecessors—to embrace an older tradition of female power. In this new wave of horror film, a woman's smiles or laughter no longer implies safety for the normative social order which has controlled her in the past, instead suggesting a new form of freedom and safety for herself. As the witchy feminist movement of the 2010s gained traction alongside #MeToo and a wave of anti-Trump activism, these films insist to their audiences, "Yes, this is a witch hunt. I'm a witch, and I'm hunting you."[14]

---

14. West, 2017.

Chapter Fifteen

Dancing with the Devil: Psychedelics and Altered States

This shift in generic conventions and narrative structure—with its accompanying embrace of emotional excess and "monstrous" hyperfemininity—has been coupled with a renewed thematic and stylistic interest in psychedelics, reflecting the longstanding interrelation of witchcraft and altered mental states, here in the context of the so-called "psychedelic renaissance" of the 2010s. The aesthetics of the films in this analysis vary widely, some hypercomposed with linear narratives, while others employ fragmented, dreamlike nonlinearity. Each one does, however, use special effects and editing to convey the supernatural, typically precipitated by altered states of consciousness. This shift is part of a larger trend towards psychedelic horror, for example *Mandy* (2018), *Bliss* (2019) and *Climax* (2018), all of which feature elements of the occult. In witch films in particular, these stylistic elements are employed as a means of demarcating the gendered evolutions taking place between characters. They set the (monstrous) feminine apart as more in touch with the supernatural and nature. These techniques, together with the radical shift in narrative, create a sense that the power being tapped by the witches of this cycle is so divorced from the "normal" heteropatriarchal world that it—and, eventually, the women themselves—becomes impossible to contain within the diegesis of the film.

As I explained in Part 1, an understanding of herbal medicine was often a precursor for an accusation of witchcraft. And it has been theorized that witches' potions, such as flying ointment, were self-administered psychedelics that generated fantastical experiences and perceptions (the sensation of flying for example) in both "witches", many of whom were healers, and their "victims", many of whom were their patients. This connection has a long history in film as well as in myth.[1] Recall the dream-rape sequence in *Rosemary's Baby* (1968), just after Rosemary's husband drugs her into unconsciousness with her neighbor Minnie's laced "chocolate mouse". Beyond overtly depicting witches' potions, it crucially cements a style for these sorts of visions, beginning with films like Herschel Gordon Lewis' LSD-fueled *Something Weird* (1967), and on display in films throughout the occult revival, from *Rosemary's Baby* and *Carrie* (1976) (split screen, slow and reverse motion), to *Season of the Witch* (1973) and *Belladonna of Sadness* (1973). These films use their techniques to represent part of a female character's subjectivity as she goes through a radical

---

1. The original 1977 version of *Suspiria* for example was based in part on 19th century's Thomas De Quincey's "Suspiria de Profundis", an account of visions he had while under the influence of opium that provides much of the witch lore (namely the story of the three mothers) used in the film.

psychological change via supernatural (ESP) experiences, coded at that time as natural extensions of the psyche.

The films of the 2010s witch cycle employ this same sort of subjective, altered reality, beginning with extradiegetic references to both psychedelics and (neo-)pagan mythos. Though this choice was cut from the finished film, *Midsommar*'s (2019) trailer shows the traditional black crop bars replaced with white ones as a way of establishing the narrative as taking place within a space of difference.[2] *Color Out of Space* (2019) casts Tommy Chong (star and co-creator of such 1970s and '80s stoner comedies as *Up in Smoke* [1978]) as a drug-addled ageing hippie who lives on the edge of the property and incorporates the *Necronomicon*, a fictional occult spell book famously invented by Lovecraft and first printed as a real text to tremendous financial and cultural success in 1977.

Color Out of Space, *Midsommar* and *The Witch: A New-England Folktale* foreground legends, myths, and folk traditions in their narratives, to emphasize dislocation, and the supernatural through atemporality and the arcane. *Color*, set in New England, begins by quoting the Lovecraft story over panning shots of ancient woodlands dissolving into one another: "they told me the place was evil... full of witch legends. I thought the evil must be something which Grand Dames have whispered to children through centuries." *The Witch* director Robert Eggers has said that he intended the rot plaguing William's corn to be ergot, the same naturally occurring source of LSD compound famously theorized to have spurred much of the paranoia during the Salem Witch Trials, integrating psychedelic experiences into the fabric of an apparently visually conservative film.[3] [4] By deploying these extradiegetic occult and psychedelic references, the films tap into a larger history of psychedelic horror and witch lore.

These films depict "bewitched" altered states of consciousness differently but to similar liminal effect. *Color Out of Space* draws most obviously on the psychedelic stylings of predecessors like *Season of the Witch*, representing magic as a diaphanous, rainbow sheen in the air or in the water: neon rainbows frozen in the center of the ice cubes that Nathan puts in glass after glass of whiskey, or oil slick on the mugs of tea Lavinia and Ezra drink. Ezra (Tommy Chong) explains of the color, "It's not out *there*, it's in here. It's in the static, it's in the moisture, up is down, fast is slow, what's in here is out there, and what's out there is in here now," mirroring the revelatory language often used in reference to LSD trips (as well as Clover's gendered construction of being "opened" as feminizing).[5] Like the marijuana Ezra and the oldest

---

2. "MIDSOMMAR | Official Teaser Trailer HD | A24", 2019.
3. Wickman, 2016.
4. Styled as *The VVitch* in reference to early printing presses using two Vs as W during this period
5. Evidently named for the Biblical High Priest of the First Temple for his portentous, accurate declarations of alien invasion and doom much as Lavinia is likely named for the mother of the Roman Empire in reference to the role she plays in the alien invasion.

Gardner son smoke in his cabin—decorated with stained glass, windchimes, and security cameras—the color alters reality. It causes the phones and TVs to screech and emit angry purplish-rainbow static, and turns the farm into a hellish, exaggerated dreamworld. By the film's final passages, time jumps are represented by abrupt, jarring edits that, in combination with ever-present miasmic fog, destroy any sense of time. Characters are overcome with visual distortions, bodies stretching and warping with static: moving has become an impossible feat in this inhospitable cinematic space.

Suspiria (2018) depicts witches' spells and disembodied presences similarly, in addition to other special effects. Witches communicate telepathically through slight step framing. Women wake up to find shifting clouds of fragmented rainbow light above their beds, drawing them to do the coven's bidding and giving them disturbing, disjointed dreams, like the ones "sent" to Susie by Madame Blanc—rapid runs of montage, reminiscent of films like *Easy Rider* (1969) (mirrors breaking on concrete, bloodied children's underwear with worms inside them, Susie's mother with her entrails spread over her chest). The film's climax, an extravagant Grand Guignol Black Mass, departs still further from the more muted visual style of the film. This sequence employs fast motion, step framing, deep color, and rainbow aura effects for Susie's final embrace of her witchy destiny. As all the women of the school chant and dance around her in the academy's blood red basement—their bodies tangled and bent together into pentagrams and altars and stars—the pace of their movements fluctuates and warps. Susie glides forward in jerky step framed motion, chest ripped open, face esctatic, causing enemies to explode in geysers of blood with a look in their direction while the women dance frenziedly. This climactic moment, a parallel to previous dance sequences, presents the same "threatening" collective, sexual femininity as in *Midsommar* and *The Witch*. It is one of the most explicitly "Hellish" scenes in this analysis, yet its exaggerations of style and delicate musical score (sensual breathing and acoustic guitar) reframe it as beautiful and feminine. "Keep dancing," Susie insists of the bleeding, spinning girls, "it's beautiful. It's beautiful."

Midsommar, too, uses this sort of pervasive psychedelic nature imagery, though in a more subdued fashion. The students' drive from the airport into the Hårga's land signals this immediately with a shot of a welcome banner flipping upside down, flipping the world on its head as they pass beneath it. As soon as they arrive, they take magic mushrooms, collapsing their sense of time. Night does not fall in this area, adding to a sense of profound dislocation and deep uncanniness: "It can't be 9:00pm, the sky is blue!" one friend protests in a panic. "That's just how 9pm is here," another replies, an edge of anxiety under his forcedly cheerful tone: "it's like another world." Dani, who is staving off a panic attack, watches with horror as the trees around her warp, and blades of grass dig their way into her hands. She begins to cry, wandering through the forest. Behind her, the faces of her parents and sister form and reform from the leaves of the trees, growing more visible from scene to scene. As in *Color*, this feminine "other" space externalizes the characters' emotions—Dani's in particular. As she dances around the May Pole, the bodies of the other women blend and warp in slow motion, shots of different women dissolving into each other and over her face. Dani and another woman begin speaking to each other in Swedish, a language Dani doesn't know, making the previously frightening experience unifying and comforting.

The Witch's use of psychedelic visual effects is most subtle, relying more on the editing and score to convey temporal disjuncture. The film is hyper-composed, with appropriate period detail in shades of grey, green and brown, lit by candlelight and overcast skies. It begins with the family's exile, allowing still frames and long takes to convey a sense of unease, heightened by the film's teeth-grindingly discordant violin and choral score. As the tension mounts, smaller surreal details depict the danger the family faces: goats' milk turns to blood and chicks hatch, stillborn. Once the family arrives in the woods, they fall into a deep sleep on the ground, wake in the morning, and pray. A shot of the forbidding tree line slowly pushes, and the chorus of women's voices screams unbearably—before cutting sharply to black. This abrupt cut becomes one of the film's central tools of bewitchment and otherworldliness. It is continually unclear how much time passes between sleep and waking, between one scene and the next, when this cut to black is employed. Rather than extend time through a perpetual sameness and dislocation (the unnatural daylight of *Midsommar*, or perpetual twilight of *Color Out of Space*), these dramatic cuts establish time as untrustworthy through its withholding. They make sleep, too, seem unnatural and forced onto the characters.

This loss of vision motif has a basis in witch lore, wherein "sudden blindness" or "time lapse" were often reported by those claiming to have been "abducted into the other-world" implying "a symbolic death."[6] William is also literally blinded as he hunts for food in one scene, the trigger on his gun misfiring and sparking in his face. Thomasin's final game with baby Samuel is Peek-a-Boo, a more deliberate sort of temporary blindness: as the woods watch her—the first shot of the scene is a prolonged slow push onto the treeline—she covers her eyes with her hands, asking "Where is Sam?" She finds after several times that when she removes them, he *has* disappeared, a symbolic death soon to be literalized. As the film progresses, these time cuts become more pronouncedly cosmic in their inflection: after being forced to kill her mother, Thomasin goes inside, sheds her bloodied outer layers down to her shift, and abruptly lowers her head on the table, falling into a deep sleep. After a sharp cut to black, it is suddenly night. From this moment, like Lavinia and the color, Thomasin seems to understand her circumstances in

---

6. Pócs et. al., 1999, 81.

a new way, approaching Black Phillip immediately after waking up. A new sound enters the score: delicate bells and chimes, connoting enchantment.

After Samuel disappears from the grass, the film intermittently trades foreboding stillness for the gruesome symbols of classic witch myth, shockingly subverting the viewer's expectations of tone through contrast, and creating altered spaces with bewitched time. Quite suddenly, a hunched figure in a red cloak is shown hurrying through the woods, divorced from the perspective of any of the established characters. In a delayed response to Thomasin's question ("Where is Sam?"), we see a shot of Samuel lit by firelight into which a naked old woman's legs enter. Her gnarled hand strokes Samuel's body and reaches for a knife, angling it towards him before another cut to black. The music swells slowly as the witch pounds something in a giant mortar and pestle made from a hollow tree, her long hair hanging in ropes around her body. After another cut to black, she smears the bloodied pulp that was Samuel, now made into flying ointment, over her body and, in the next shot, her broomstick.[7] She rubs it between her legs and begins to rise above the ground, floating up in front of an enormous moon in a classic recreation of one of the most enduring visual representations of witches on film, here graphically literalizing the use of magic potions to induce altered states.[8] This sequence contains the greatest number of cuts to black of any in the film, affirming the connection between this type of cut and bewitched time.

The power of these films' young female protagonists is intimately linked to a history of pagan mythology and its monstrous Christian counterpart, witch lore, both of which foreground a radical gendered difference based in emotionality and interconnectedness with nature and the supernatural. All these women gain access to something incomprehensible, beyond the scope of the "normal" world, from Dani's ability to speak Swedish, to Susie's dreams, to Thomasin's flying. The films acclimatize the viewer to different visual language and codes of "comprehensibility" (i.e. the use of dream-logic, fragmented editing, slow or fashion motion) rendering the supernatural subjectively visible. As the images on screen become progressively more hallucinogenic, these characters accustom themselves and eventually grow stronger, shedding the repression (the paradox of womanhood) against which they have struggled in an explosion of emotional and visual excess—in a word, *abjection*.

---

7. Flying ointment, once obscure, has now become relatively common in film culture at this moment, used as a signal of feminized collectivity and, notably, eroticism in *Portrait of a Lady on Fire*. Additionally, a long scene in *Gretel & Hansel* (2022) is dedicated to Gretel being taught how to make flying ointment as a part of her introduction to her powers as a witch.
8. Hatsis, 2015, 171, 216.

Chapter Sixteen

Witchcraft as Abject Transcendence

> ."..she dreamed—tis a thing hard to set down in words—how a wondrous monster, the genius incarnate of life universal, was absorbed in her; she dreamed that henceforth Life and Death and all Nature were shut within her body, that at the cost of, oh! what infernal travail, she had conceived in her womb great Nature's self."
> -Jules Michelet, *Satanism and Witchcraft*[1]

As Julia Kristeva suggests in her book *Powers of Horror*, abjection is a dissolution of boundaries, a return to the pre-symbolic. It is an embrace of those antisocial elements of existence irreconcilable with the dominant order, but which "accompan[y] all religious structurings," threatening their collapse as well as the collapse of the self.[2] Building on Kristeva's notion that literature functions as a "purification of the abject through a 'descent into the foundations of the symbolic construct'... in order finally to eject the abject and redraw boundaries between the human and non-human," Barbara Creed suggests that "[a]s a form of modern defilement rite, the horror film works to separate out the symbolic order from all that threatens its stability"—particularly the monstrous, non-hegemonic feminine Kristeva describes.[3] As Stephen King points out in his construction of the horror film as fundamentally conservative, "The ritual outletting of these [abject] emotions seems to bring things back to a more stable and constructive state again."[4] Through the generic and stylistic shifts in the witch films of the 2010s horror cycle, this construction no longer seems to apply. This cycle represents a different impulse, one which examines the abject feminine, narratively embracing it while still positing its monstrosity. Barbara Creed describes horror as a defilement rite, a sort of exorcism of abjection that the society of which horror movies become the cultural id fears; however, these films seem to operate in reverse, exorcizing not the monstrous but the structures that attempt to contain it. The ruptures in the containment of the monstrous feminine found by Hollinger in Tourneur's *Cat People* (1942) and

---
1. Michelet, 1998, 76.
2. Kristeva, 1982, 17.
3. Creed, 1993, 14.
4. King, 2010, 12.

which, according to Stamp, lie at the heart of *Carrie*'s (1976) monstrosity, break loose in the films of the past half-decade. This unique response to socio-political turmoil is only sporadically present in previous cycles like that of the '60s.

Kristeva theorizes that the literature of abjection is hallucinogenic, an argument which applies well to these abject "witch" films. As an attempt to depict the pre-symbolic, she says, "abject" literature necessarily rejects much of the traditional structures at play in other forms of literature in favor of something more primal. Citing the works of writers like Kafka and Dostoyevsky, she states that in literature,

> [w]hen narrated identity is unbearable, when the boundary between subject and object is shaken, and when even the limit between inside and outside becomes uncertain, the narrative is what is challenged first. If it continues, nevertheless, its makeup changes; its linearity is shattered, it proceeds in flashes, enigmas, short cuts, incompletion, tangles and cuts… If one wished to proceed still further along the approaches to abjection, one would find neither narrative or theme but a *recasting* of syntax and vocabulary—the violence of poetry and silence.[5]

The films of the 2010s witch horror cycle—with their use of psychedelic or oneiric imagery, narrative nonlinearity, and discordant scores—follow this same trajectory, plumbing the abject feminine (which she calls "ecstatic", "edged with the sublime") and recasting the horror film in its image.[6] The reversal of the prototypical narrative structures of the horror film allows for the slow triumph of the abject over the normative, much as the witch's Black Sabbath is an inversion of God's divine rights. The cuts to black of *The Witch*, the dreams of *Suspiria* (2018), and the alien hue of *Color Out of Space* (2019) come to represent in this context a return of the repressed that goes further than many previous horror cycles, incorporating the abject into the narrative itself to the point of dissolution. This sort of literature, Kristeva continues, is replete with accounts of "Dizziness, noises, buzzings, vomitings… which make one think of drugs or epilepsy" and "madness", all cues made visual by these films in their relationship to the witch's *veneficia*.[7] The witch herself, is a figure of abjection by nature, and her presence precipitates these very forms of narrative, psychological, and physical reactions. This is clear in the cuts to black structuring her presence in *The Witch*, for example, or the chanting, panting and buzzing scores that accompany her in every film.

Most crucially, the triumph of the abject for Kristeva is signaled by an experience of *jouissance*, often characterized by *laughter*. She defines

---

5. Kristeva, 1982, 141.
6. *Ibid*, 59, 11.
7. *Ibid*, 141, 146, emphasis added.

jouissance as a violent, painful, ecstatic experience of "passion" at the point where meaning collapses and abjection overtakes normativity in "a time of oblivion and thunder, of veiled infinity and the moment when revelation bursts forth"—the ultimate embrace of abjection. Laughter as it relates to *jouissance* represents a "gushing forth of the unconscious, the repressed, the suppressed pleasure, be it sex or death… a laughing apocalypse is an apocalypse without god. Black mysticism or transcendental collapse… radical nihilism."[8] Within the mythology of the witch, the ability for the monstrous women of these films to incorporate themselves into the abject, supernatural world with which they are faced represents a uniquely gendered gesture—a triumph of the "natural" or pagan feminine over the Christian, structured masculine. By choosing to embrace their new role as a witch, Thomasin, Dani, Susie, and Lavinia refuse the guilt faced by their cinematic predecessors, in an act of *jouissance*. As Kristeva writes, "A source of evil and mingled with sin, abjection becomes the requisite for a reconciliation, in the mind, between the flesh and the law."[9] The destructive-generative acts of self-indulgence taking place in these films' final moments serve as a symbolic rejection of the Christian paradox of womanhood and as such an act of abject transcendence. Upon realizing that the rest of their loved ones are dead—and that they can go no further along a normative life trajectory—Susie, Lavinia, Dani, and Thomasin look into the chaos they have helped create, but which was also indelibly inscribed onto them by culture and circumstance. They smile and laugh with abandon, understanding, as the audience does, that their survival and power indicate a radical change. In the films of this era, they are, if only for a moment, finally free.

---

8. Kristeva, 1982, 206.
9. *Ibid*, 127-8.

Chapter Seventeen

The Tragedy of *The Love Witch*

"The reason women are obsessed with love is because that is the only insurance they have against being murdered by a man they are intimate with."
-Anna Biller, 2018[1]

"If a woman wants anything in life, she can obtain it easier through a man than another woman, despite what woman liberationists' bellows to the contrary. The truly 'liberated woman' is the complete witch, who knows both how to use and enjoy men."
-Anton LaVey, *The Satanic Witch*[2]

While the radically apocalyptic stories described in the past chapters hold a clear and powerful appeal for women, as the wave of media on witches (which this book aims to contextualize) attests, one film in the 2010s witch cycle stands out from all the others, establishing a very different, far grimmer gendered and thematic paradigm while using startlingly similar narrative and aesthetic motifs. In so doing, this film can be understood, like the most iconic films of the '60s cycle, to both embody the feminist ideals of its moment, and presage the backlash to come. *The Love Witch* (2016), directed by independent auteur Anna Biller, is perhaps the most significant example of the woman-directed witch film from this period. It made a tremendous cultural impact—particularly given its microbudget and extremely modest box office upon first release—quickly attaining cult film *and* art film status, earning Anna Biller a retrospective on the Criterion Channel.[3] Whereas the myriad examples of auteurist filmmaking by men in the previous chapter show witches transcending the heteropatriarchal matrices of their social worlds, wreaking havoc and creating alternative forms of community through their relationships with witchcraft and smiling blissfully at their conclusions, *The Love Witch* takes these same visual and structural markers (a slasher structure, Clover's ABA ABC structure, the use of psychedelics, nonlinear narrative elements etc.) and combines them with a more realistic approach

---
1. Biller, 2018.
2. LaVey, 2003, 1.
3. Weston, 2019.

to the nature of misogyny, both historically and in the present, examining how it pervades everything, from ostensibly liberatory spaces to the very minds of individual women. *The Love Witch* uses a similar structure to that of *Midsommar* (2019) or *The Witch* to present a mundane world of pervasive cruelty and casual chauvinism not even magic can overcome, leaving, for its characters, no escape in the "real world" of the film's diegesis, whether or not that diegesis includes the supernatural. While the Love Witch smiles at the conclusion of the film (that takes her chosen title for its name), her liberation is a tragic one, ending not in her salvation, but her descent into impossible fantasy—and madness.

Anna Biller, whose decades-long career as a filmmaker spans numerous short films but only two meticulously crafted features, is an auteur in the true sense: for her first feature film, *Viva* (2007), Biller starred, wrote and directed, edited, scored, produced, production designed, costumed, and even animated several sequences herself. Though she didn't act in *The Love Witch*, her breakout, she repeated all her central roles behind the camera, leaving only the cinematography to another person. This singular level of creative control makes her filmography uniquely ripe for personal analysis. Biller has said she gravitates towards the label "female filmmaker" and strives to be "brutally honest about what it's like to be a woman" in her films. Biller has also said that her crew actively fought against her during the shooting of *The Love Witch*, suggesting that it "had something to do with being a female director."[4] Soon after the film's release, she attested that the conflict continued after the shoot ended: "Fun fact: most of the crew on THE LOVE WITCH (with a few exceptions) hated what we were shooting and did not even see the movie after it was done."[5] The film's lasting adulation by young women attests to its narrative and aesthetic power as a feminist text as well as an art object, while the tension on set, which she tacitly posits as a gendered conflict between a male crew and their female director, visualizes the challenges women directors can face.

The Love Witch appropriates the tropes and visual language of an early 1970s exploitation film (down to its lovingly replicated classical lighting techniques and rich 35mm stock) as it follows Elaine (Samantha Robinson) "starting a new life" in a small California town. The film begins on Highway 1, an iconic location for classic Hollywood film noirs like *Kiss Me Deadly* (1955), and erotic art-horror like *The Mephisto Waltz* (1971). Elaine has fled San Francisco following the suspicious death of her ex-husband, Jerry (Stephen Wozniak). "They actually thought I killed him!" She laughs in voiceover, "They couldn't prove anything…" As she continues to drive, she sets the scene: "I had a nervous breakdown after he left me… they say I'm cured now… but my therapist says I'm not unusual at all—women are

---

4. Nordine, 2017.
5. Biller, 2017.

abused all over the world. Every day! *Much* worse than me, and they do fine," framing Jerry's death by poisoning as a fraught act of vigilante self-defense and a source of sublimated guilt. As she reaches for a cigarette, her tarot deck spreads itself under her fingers, revealing the three of swords—a cherry-red heart stabbed three times, dripping blood—the card of failed romances, heartbreak, and, sometimes, death. This portent follows her as she settles down, selling magical supplies to a local apothecary and looking for true love, whether men want it or not.

Elaine's world is defined by a fetishistic dedication to an extremely specific form of feminine idyll: ambiguously set in the present day (modern cars and one cell phone are the only tipoff), her witchy variations on what she calls "fairy princess fantasies" color the world around her, filling it with frilly Victorian tearooms, low-fi Renaissance fairs, and seedy burlesque clubs ripped straight from the '60s. Her conversation is similarly fanatical in its girlishness, informed by material on "how to get your man back" (she settles on witchcraft) and the idea that "we may be women but underneath we're still just little girls dreaming of being carried off by a prince on a white horse", a notion her one non-witch friend, Trish (Laura Weddell), finds outdated: "You sound like you've been brainwashed by the patriarchy! Your whole self-worth is tied up in pleasing a man!" Indeed, Elaine has been hollowed out by her husband's abuse: he verbally berated her for "unfeminine" traits like not keeping the house clean enough, eating too much, and not wearing enough makeup. After killing him, an act she can't face up to, she transforms herself into the archetype he desired, and seeks a new lover to fulfill her fantasies of romance—in exchange for her perfected performance of femininity—with the help of a coven she joins. She casts love spells desperately, using witch's ointment and hallucinogenic wine (in perfect recreations of '60s trip sequences full of kaleidoscopic visuals and rainbow colors), desperately crying out to the universe for someone, anyone: "Love me!"

Yet even with this newfound power, the men she seduces can't accept her: her lovers (who she often pictures, in flashes, as her dead husband) continue to die, not from any malice on her part, but from the depth of emotion her love potions and sex magic inspire, feelings which ironically destroy her attraction to them (she mentally calls one "a pussy", "a baby", and "just like a woman" when he cries and tells her he needs her). She turns her romantic attention to the handsome, square-jawed police officer, Griff (Gian Key) soon on her trail. Unlike her other lovers, though, Griff's masculinity is, like her femininity, too stereotypically perfect. He embodies the idealized macho script so fully that he's incapable of love. This dynamic is brilliantly encapsulated by a mock-wedding at her coven's midsummer festival: as the two feed each other grapes and make adoring expressions at each other, Elaine gushes about their love in voiceover ("when you love him, it's like fireworks and nothing else matters… the more you know him, the more you love him"), while Griff's own voiceover dismisses love on principle ("love is soft… I want an heir someday and then I would need to have a wife. But love… A man can get destroyed by things like that. It's like he's not even a man anymore"). Eventually, he becomes disgusted by her, seeing she's murdered (and, equally violently in his mind, emasculated) her other lovers, and rejects her at the burlesque club where her coven meets: "You're like a bottomless hole… you doll yourself up and do the Stepford Wife thing … but your creepy little sexy thing doesn't work on me." In response, Elaine is finally honest with a man: "All my life I've been tossed in the garbage except when men wanted to use my body, so I found my power," she cries, "Witchcraft means I take what I need from men and not the other way around!" Yet once more she's thwarted. The parodically conservative bar patrons attempt a gang rape. Griff saves her and brings her home. At her apartment, she once again tries to seduce him, but looking into his eyes, she finally realizes that he is incapable of love; a skull, the "Death" card, replaces his face. She shies away in absolute horror, and, in a final act of panic, stabs him in the heart, her prophecy fulfilled. She becomes calm again, blood dripping down her hands, her face frozen in a rapturous smile, eyes turned skyward, imagining the two of them riding off on a unicorn, a king and queen on a noble steed, very much in love. In failing to find safety or love in reality, Elaine has escaped into her fantasy for good.

The myriad aesthetic and syntactic nods to the mid-late '60s, from vintage cars to garter belts to turns of phrase, put the film in conversation with that era's witch horror cycle (its generic codes, its aesthetics, etc.) as well as the mores and politics of the occult scene of the period: Biller has said that she was inspired by the "sexy witch" on '60s paperbacks, telling a story from "her point of view, so that she's a subject and not an object" while exploring the "fraught" sexual implications of those covers "that women are evil seductresses who you hate, but you also desire."[6] Drawing inspiration from the philosophy of Church of Satan founder Anton LaVey, Elaine's self-destructive journey astutely comments on timeless gendered expectations through the foibles of the past—and present.

While the materials Elaine devours to learn "how to get your man back" are unspecified, the highly gendered approach to witchcraft she espouses hews closely to the philosophy LaVey lays out in his 1971 book, *The Satanic Witch*. Released on Valentine's Day 1971, the book, whose working title was *How to Trap a Man Through Witchcraft*, combines spellwork with self-help style advice on fashion and behavior for women based on "Witches' Workshops" LaVey held in San Francisco. The book was highly publicized in women's magazines, even making the cover of *Cosmopolitan* in November 1971. Divided into sections on appearance, behavior, and

---

6. Hadland, 2023.

philosophy, the book presents a binary system of courtship. To attract a man a woman must gauge his personality based on a combination of physical and emotional characteristics and perform the kind of femininity that will most appeal to him, sublimating her true personality in favor of a fantasy ideal, reflecting a man's desires back to him to gain power in a patriarchal system. In dress, LaVey suggests, "refer to men's magazines for her pointers in style", specifically "girlie magazines" and cartoons.[7] In conversation, a witch should copy her desired man's tone and speech patterns until "There are no longer two people talking... appearing in the guise of yourself but speaking as him... now he is the only one doing the talking."[8] This mimicry is fundamental to Elaine's strategy with her lovers—she reads them (based on their style, their profession, etc.) and reflects their desires back to them with beautiful dinners, beautiful makeup, and promises of sex she never seems to enjoy.

In the introduction to *The Satanic Witch*, Church of Satan High Priestess Peggy Nadramia positions the book within the history of Second Wave feminism, suggesting that it serves as a contemporary form of backlash intended to "[fight] against" what she termed the "societal androgyny" of the feminist movement in the late '60s and early '70s.[9] During this period, she says,

> [W]e didn't just look confused about being girls; we *were* confused... *Ms.* magazine was saying that if we let a man hold a door open for us, we were accepting a subservient and inferior role... It was great to have complete freedom over our sexuality... but we 'celebrated' our liberation by covering our curves with the same clothing and shoes guys wore and spit on them when they tried to be chivalrous.[10]

LaVey's assurances that, in Nadramia's words, "Any woman can be sexy... if she lets herself look like a woman" frames his hyper-specific paradigm of femininity as their own form of emancipation while decrying "woman liberationists" [*sic*] as being anti-woman[11], one of the many contradictions on display in the dynamics of Part 1. In some cases, the book is open in embracing harmful stereotypes, occasionally tipping into overt misogyny: For example, LaVey encourages smart women to "learn how to act stupid... I mean *stupid*... It has been said that a donkey should never be sent to college, because nobody likes a smart ass. Very few men like a woman who asserts her intelligence."[12] That said, LaVey's hyper-individualistic approach to

---

7. LaVey, 2003, 160.
8. *Ibid*, 93-4.
9. *Ibid*, 2.
10. *Ibid*, 3.
11. *Ibid*, 1, 5.
12. *Ibid*, 199-200.

sexual liberation for women through savvy manipulation and performance of archetypes (an argument that could almost evoke Judith Butler were it not so fundamentally gendered), is also clearly meant to serve as a practical, subversive set of tools for women in an overtly sexist society to the tune of *Sex and the Single Girl*. This combination produces a complex construct of witchy femininity that neatly encapsulates much of the era's perception of the malevolent Satanic witch—scheming, sexual, powerful—but covered with the aesthetics of the nouveau witch—feminine, a *Playboy* archetype; in other words, LaVey's construction both weaponizes misogynistic feminine ideals while also paradoxically embracing them, encapsulating a broader tension around sex and gendered performance for women in the process.

The Love Witch puts the nouveau witch under a microscope, then, specifically unpacking the complexities around performing sexuality for the male gaze as a way of gaining power. She brings the philosophy of the occult boom to the fore when the head of her coven, Gahan (Jared Sanford), and Elaine's witch-friend, Barbara (Jennifer Ingrum), teach new witches about the power of burlesque, watching a performer strip enthusiastically for a crowd of crowing men, taking turns explaining in a shared monologue:

> We feel that [a woman's] power lies in her sexuality. We don't view this as Satanic or anti-feminist but as a celebration, as a natural presence, an earthly body, a spiritual presence and a womb... The entire history of witchcraft is about the fear of female sexuality. They burned us at the stake because they feared the erotic feelings it elicited in them. Later they used marriage to turn us into servants and fantasy dolls... Men and women are different and their strength lies in that difference... Use perfume, wear high heels and makeup, display flesh and know what to conceal... Only then will he begin to see you as a human being... Then you may do with him what you will.

This monologue combines the same rhetoric that countless magazine articles, feminist pamphlets, and nouveau witches deployed in the '60s in a single jumble. It posits that the sexualized witchcraft of the nouveau witch can be a genuinely empowering tool as evinced by Elaine's ability to change her circumstances through her spells. It also assimilates and highlights the criticisms leveled against it, suggesting that the bioessentialist leanings of this belief system are celebratory—though still ironizing them through the fact that Elaine, it is implied through a series of uncomfortable flashbacks, felt sexually taken advantage of by Gahan during her initiation into sex magic. The coven tells its newest members that, as LaVey put it, "The 'painted woman' has been the sex symbol throughout history, so don't be afraid to use that warpaint. The real witch has always been a 'scarlet woman', despite the popular image of the old hag" and encouraging them to practice "taking advantage of men who think they're taking advantage of you"[13] arguments adopted by some sex-positive third-wave feminists—the kind of message that undergirded films like *The Mephisto Waltz*. But, in Biller's version, even with this message Elaine still finds herself ultimately stuck—this kind of sexualized hyper-femininity, when imposed from the outside (by the patriarchy) rather than from within (by taking genuine pleasure in being feminine), gets her nowhere, driven mad by the impossibility of her fantasy.[14] This tension comes through most clearly for Elaine when, during a date, Griff tells her "You're my girl and there's no one around to tell me otherwise," and she lightly replies, "except me." He pauses—"what's that supposed to mean?" to which she laughs, eyes flickering, "Nothing." They kiss.

Fundamentally, the beautiful world of *The Love Witch* is a deeply cruel and hostile one for everyone, not just Elaine, particularly to fantasies of a better life. Fantasy, specifically sexual fantasy for heterosexual men, is at the heart of LaVey's philosophy in *The Satanic Witch*; indeed, to LaVey, for a woman to be a witch she must realize that she is "simply a purveyor of fantasy—fantasy in the mind of the person you bewitch, and if you can give a man a good fantasy, you will have succeeded in throwing your spell."[15] Fantasy is Elaine's credo throughout the film, her philosophy. When she and her friend Trish first meet, she tells her that to get a man to love you, one must "give a man his *fantasy*," including sex, a tool that "unlock[s] his love potential." During sex in one scene she laughs, "I'm the love witch! I'm your ultimate fantasy!" Her fantasies of romance, though, hinge on a similar set of fetishized gendered ideals which ultimately destroy her. Early in the film, when a lover breaks down after her love spell intensifies his emotions, she berates her in her head, finding herself disgusted: "He's just like a little girl. No one was ever there for *me* when I was crying my heart out, no one ever comforted *me. No one.*" The film acknowledges that the gendered system she adopted—that necessitates this form of elaborate self-abnegation and stereotyped performance—is fundamentally emotionally broken for men as well as women (Griff's stony masculinity represented by the Death Card), but as Trish tells her at the start, to cope with this violent absence of support in the face of a chauvinist world, she attempts to game this system, and succumbs to its traps, falling in love with Griff and, as Trish puts it, "being brainwashed by the patriarchy."

As this analysis might suggest, Biller's perspective on feminism as well as femininity are complex. In her blog, she frequently criticizes feminism for what she indicts as a rejection of femininity: "for several decades now, everything feminine has been seen as retrogressive in culture, and everything

---

13. LaVey, 2003, 130, 120.
14. *Ibid*, 130, 190.
15. *Ibid*, 132.

masculine as progressive." She calls feminism a "sticky term" because of this dynamic, which she posits began with the Second Wave and the same era she deconstructs in both of her films. These feminists, she argues, "stressed equality between the genders by erasing any difference between them. Therefore, to be like a man was considered a goal of women. This idea, noble and good in its intentions, made it possible for men and women alike to disparage any image of a feminine woman."[16] In interviews, she frequently champions the "aesthetics of female pleasure" and feminine women in general, in terms that can verge on essentialist in numerous ways, suggesting without hesitation for example that to be feminine is partly "to like to be looked at by men", and to embrace the kinds of aesthetics Elaine herself seeks out, both in the sexual sphere as a vamp or a burlesque queen, and as a "princess." But, her goal is to "be brutally honest about what it's like to be a woman", which she acknowledges "means there will be lots of things that don't seem feminist at all, especially where male and female desire intersects."[17] The goal of her cinema is to celebrate feminine fantasies of the kind she suggests and that are almost always dismissed in modern filmmaking (interestingly, she has claimed to have been approached to direct *Barbie* before Greta Gerwig).[18] And thus, "Femininity" for her, she argues, "is a magic spell in that it can cast a spell on men." At the same time, though, her work is predicated on the same kind of pragmatism that shapes Elaine's cynical view of patriarchal power; *The Love Witch*, she said in an interview, springs from her feeling that

> [B]eing a woman is an experience of *fear*: you're afraid of men, you're afraid of rapists. You're afraid of being attacked, you're afraid of speaking up... And I just don't really know if that is examined much in movies. This idea that even a woman that seems so strong, she seems so together, she's still a woman, and she lives in a world with men and predators. And a world in which people are always trying to silence her. And I just want to create a feeling of reality in her world. So she does try to create her own desire and her own pleasure and she tries to make her world perfect around her, but she lives in a society. That scene in that bar, where the men all attacked her. That's not that far-fetched. Those things happen to women all the time.

The tension in *The Love Witch*, becomes a complex repudiation of the double-standards women face for performing femininity, envisioned through the lens of the '60s witch cycle. Elaine, who becomes a witch to escape domestic violence and (literally) empower herself, is trapped in a tangled web of fantasy—her *own* fantasies of love and beauty, and masculinized fantasies of sexual and social domination—both of which center on the same image

---
16. Biller, 2014.
17. Hadland, 2023.
18. Kennedy, 2023.

of the beautiful, sexy witch. She becomes the "perfect woman", stunningly beautiful, sexually available, perfectly coiffed; yet she's repeatedly punished by the people around her.

Building on this broader philosophical argument, Biller has also insisted repeatedly throughout her career that "using violence to gain power is not a viable tool for women in a patriarchal society in which they are physically weaker and in which physically assaulting others is against the law." Thus, films like those of the occult boom (she cites "60s and 70s exploitation films")

> operate almost entirely within the realm of *fantasy*. This is not to say that these films contain no agency for women, but to be feminist, a film has to make the audience aware of social inequality between men and women. So a film that contains female characters who are social equals with men, and who are physically as strong as or stronger than men, is not addressing social issues but denying they exist or pushing them under the carpet.[19]

Though here she is discussing the slasher, in this light, the tragic ending of *The Love Witch* becomes an even clearer repudiation of gendered fantasies: the 2010s witch horror cycle, as well as the films which inspired it, hinges on visions of apocalypse that, using Biller's logic, are just as unrealistic as Elaine's dreams of unicorns and princesses. For Elaine, there is no future in a world that operates so cruelly to women, and the apocalyptic rejection of heteropatriarchy on a domestic scale, i.e. killing men, is against the law whether magic is real or not. In an essay on *I Spit on Your Grave*, Biller makes a similar argument, suggesting that the kind of rape-revenge fantasy this '70s film offers is "so implausible [...] as if a frail girl like that is going to go after four men. Right.... The rape and torture feel like reality, and the revenge seems like fantasy."[20]

Released in 2016, at the beginning of the Trump era and the #MeToo movement, Biller's tortured investigation of the witch as an archetype of horror and fantasy for women in *The Love Witch* seems like a provocation, an insistence that audiences grapple with the realities of women's lives rather than simply engage with nihilistic fantasies of escape, no matter how cathartic those fantasies may be. Instead, she aligns her filmmaking with the far grimmer, more overtly political *Belladonna of Sadness* (1973), posting an anonymous woman's story of sexual abuse with stills from the film, praising its "brutality and honesty of the depiction of rape and its aftermath."[21] In these films, images of radical transcendence are shot through with the pain and suffering that undergirds them. Elaine's smile is the looking glass version of Thomasin's or Suzie's or Lavinia's, promising not freedom but

---

19. Biller, 2014.
20. Biller, 2020.
21. Biller, 2017.

imprisonment for her attempts to be a woman, suggesting that those films were the fairytales. In this context, her rebuke of these fantasies of destruction indirectly and astutely evokes Mark Fisher's famous deployment of a quote attributed to Frederic Jameson: "it's easier to imagine the end of the world than it is to imagine the end of capitalism"[22]— or here, heteropatriarchy. Biller has described this as a more honest approach, despite the stylistic artifice and focus on fantasy of her filmmaking: "the dynamics of the real world are really more like that bar [where Elaine almost gets raped]… it's not a fantasy world where women control anything"—except, sometimes, men's fantasies about them. In that sense, the film's philosophy and LaVey's own are for once completely aligned. In a later chapter of *The Satanic Witch*, he reminds his witches that creating fantasy is a delicate and dangerous thing:

> Lie and give pleasure. Lie and soothe consciences. Lie and supply the food for the ego that truth can seldom provide. Lie and become a hero, for whatever lies are popular will always win votes. Lie, but be not *yourself* deluded by your lies, lest you lose control, for he who loses control over his own motivations can never progress to a proficiency in sorcery.[23]

In simple terms, one tragedy of *The Love Witch* is that Elaine loses control of her own motivations and buys into the fantasy, a critique reminiscent of the alt-right "Trad Wives" who had only just begun to appear at the time of the film's release. This failure, though, only reveals the fundamental impossibility at the heart of the heteropatriarchal fantasy. Just moments before the attack in the bar, after Griff's rejection, Elaine smiles at him and shares one final honest thought: "A lot of women feel the way I do, only you men make us work so hard… if you would just love us for ourselves, but you *won't*." The real tragedy: without systemic feminist change, women like Elaine will be caught in this trap, waiting on men to treat them better, forever. So, where do we go from here?

---

22. Fisher, 2009, 2
23. LaVey, 2003, 199.

Epilogue

Disenchanted?

> "Renewal is inevitable"
> -Harvey, *The Substance* (2024)

Since the release of this wave of witch films, the narrative conventions and aesthetic sensibility on display within the 2010s witch horror cycle have unquestionably taken over the horror landscape. Even as films like *Suspiria* (2018) were still being released, articles like *Vanity Fair*'s "This Was the Decade Horror Got 'Elevated'" (circulated in December 2019, arguably the peak of the cycle), were already periodizing and historicizing the 2010s. This article argued that the decade was a particularly strong era for the horror genre, crediting the genre's "darkly contemplative and immersive" output with introducing a wider audience to the genre, and thus "filling more seats, giving other studios more confidence to let more directors make more weird horror flicks."[1] At the same time, dedicated horror fans took gleeful potshots at the very concept of elevated horror, asking horror maestro John Carpenter to define the term ("I have no idea what you're talking about") and calling A24's output "terror sophistry", placing "a good deal of blame" for what they termed the decade's "tedious catalogue [of] pedantry" on the studio.[2][3] This kind of pushback, like the burgeoning rejection of the cinematic occult revival in '73, speaks to both an obvious weariness with the conventions of a cycle at its saturation point, and a broader political shift as well. But the Covid-19 pandemic as well as the strikes that froze Hollywood for over six months in 2023 disrupted the film industry catastrophically, forestalling any potential shift away from this mold for several years as studios struggled to survive the rocky landscape, finding a lifeline in low-budget horror films (shot with small casts and crews to accommodate much-needed Covid-compliance guidelines or to receive SAG waivers). In 2022, I wrote an article predicting that the A24 elevated horror cycle had entered its decline, using Joel Coen's suitably witchy *Macbeth* (2021) as a point of entry. Below, an extract from article is quoted to give a sense of the atmosphere that pervaded the US immediately post-pandemic:

---

1. Bradley, 2019.
2. Hughes, 2022.
3. Knight, 2018.

It's unsurprising that folk horror as a subgenre has captivated our cultural consciousness and our fears in the decade of the #MeToo movement, the Trump presidency, and the increasing climate crisis. In *Woodlands Dark and Days Bewitched...*(2021) folk horror is described in part as a representation of "ancient wisdoms ... that have long been repressed and forgotten [that] rise up again—often to the consternation of a complacent modern man..."[4]

So-called elevated horror, has become so ubiquitous that more commercial horror films have incorporated its themes of sublimated communal trauma and cultural myth-making without fully delving into the implications of this choice. *Scream* (2022), the newest entry in the *Scream* franchise, begins with its Gen-Z final-girl-to-be explaining what "elevated horror" is to Ghostface: "you know, it's scary but with complex emotional and thematic underpinnings, not just some schlocky cheeseball nonsense with wall-to-wall jumpscares." When Ghostface dismisses *The Babadook* (2014) as "boring" and "fancy pants" and asks her a slasher trivia question, she tearfully entreats him to ask her about movies she does know: "ask me about *It Follows*! Ask me about *Hereditary*! Ask me about *The Witch*!" Tellingly, this theme, once acknowledged in the film's cold open, is dropped throughout the rest of the slasher film.

As "elevated horror" and its aesthetic sensibilities become omnipresent, the anxieties at the heart of the folk horror cycle lose their meaning. *The Green Knight* (2021) and *Macbeth* feature many of the same stylistic flourishes characteristic of the A24's catalog—psychedelic imagery and references, superimpositions, and jarring time cuts—and even many of the same actors. For example, both films feature actors from *The Witch*: Ralph Ineson, in *Macbeth*, and Kate Dickie in *The Green Knight*. Both films are by filmmakers with a pre-established, recognizable style. David Lowry's credits include conventionally shot, softly-lit rural dramas, such as *Ain't Them Bodies Saints* (2013), a film bearing little to no stylistic similarity to the smooth lateral tracking shots, symmetrical framing, slow dissolves, and chapter-based structure in *The Green Knight*. Similarly, Joel Coen's classic films like *The Big Lebowski* (1998) share little visual DNA with the stark cinematography, 4:3 aspect ratio, and highly-stylized, symmetrical gothic frames of *Macbeth*. Both films have more in common with Robert Eggers's *The Lighthouse* (2019). As Eggers and Ari Aster shift away from the horror genre into action and comedy respectively [this was before Eggers' *Nosferatu*, though the point remains]... the style they brought to A24 is passed on through the work of other filmmakers whose own styles are overshadowed by the trends of the moment.

As the political climate has shifted in the wake of President Biden's election, so too has the representation of witches. A reversal away from the youthful abandon and rage of Thomasin and Dani at the height of #MeToo and back towards the old hags and crones who have long stalked young innocents, eaten children (a frighteningly familiar theme for today's QAnon conspiracists)[5],

---

4. *Woodlands Dark and Days Bewitched: A History of Folk Horror*. Directed by Kier-La Janisse (2021).
5. Roose, 2021.

and spoiled crops can be seen in the critically and commercially successful horror films of the past year, from *Macbeth* to *The Conjuring: The Devil Made Me Do It* (2021). In films like *The Unholy* (2021) as well as *The Conjuring*, a paternal male authority figure can subdue the witch, rescue his female co-star, and restore order. The decline of elevated horror can be seen in this progressively more commonplace rejection of non-normativity, in favor of a return to the conservative narrative conventions films like *The Wizard of Oz* (1939): rather than smile, the witches burn—or melt. At the same time, a lack of thematic significance in favor of the raw aesthetics Ghostface describes as "fancy pants" is on display in films like *Lamb* (2021), *The Green Knight*, and *Macbeth*. Where the new *Scream*'s final girl describes *The Babadook* as "an amazing meditation on motherhood and grief", *Lamb*'s attempt to explore the same dynamics concludes with startlingly little emotional or thematic payoff. These recent films and their more commercial counterparts feign what Ghostface's victim calls "complex emotional and thematic underpinnings", yet, with horror cycles like the creature features of the Cold War fifties or the paranoid horror-thrillers of the post-Watergate seventies, the cycles ultimately peter out into an echo chamber of visual derivation and empty narrative allusion. Finding his success empty of meaning, *Macbeth* stands on the stairs, his life "full of sound and fury, signifying nothing."[6]

While much of the core argument in the above excerpted article remains true, since its publication the elevated horror cycle hasn't completely collapsed (at least not yet), as the '60s witch horror cycle did, into comedy horror and parody (although the *Scream* franchise has remained consistently profitable). Indeed, the increasingly tumultuous political landscape—which continues to shift in directions that Americans of almost every stripe find alarming for their own reasons—continues to inject fresh anxiety and rage into the horror films of this second wave of the 60s-and-70s-inflected second occult boom, now curdling into conservative "conspirituality". Beginning in 2020 with the pandemic, as in the mid-1960s, concerns around American "nihilism" have pervaded the American consciousness. At the same time Americans mobilized politically on an unprecedented scale: even as the massive wave of Black Lives Matter demonstrations in the wake of the murder of George Floyd by police became the largest protest in US history, anti-mask and anti-shutdown conspiracists (unified by a conspiritualistic coalition of alt-right and New Age influencers), who had already staged armed protests at numerous state capitols, joined forces with other branches of the MAGA right on January 6th in an attempt to violently overturn the presidential election. Articles with titles like "Our Summer of American Nihilism: How did 'If I die, I die' become this country's mantra?" began to circulate.[7] Buzzy documentaries like *This Place Rules!* (2022), as well as

---

6. McCarty-Simas, *Brooklyn Rail*, 2022.
7. Martin, 2020.

countless think pieces discussing the ways in which internet (counter)culture has turned our national politics into a polarized spectator sport, proliferated.[8]

By 2024, this sentiment, originally leveled largely at the far right, had become broader. *The Atlantic* published an article in February delving into the pervasive conspiracism of our culture which argued that a highly visible element in American politics was a public indulging in "the need for chaos": people seemed to be expressing the sense that, as a researcher quoted in the piece put it, "We cannot fix the problems in our social institutions, we need to tear them down and start over."[9] In 2023, Noah Smith made a similar set of connections, arguing that while the 2010s (~2014-2021) represented a return to the '60s, replete with political ferment, protest, and

> cultural shifts over gender, religion, and national identity… the 2020s are the new 1970s—a decade of exhaustion, confusion, and retrenchment that follows an explosion of unrest… On the intellectual side of things too… data sources show that the anger and intellectual ferment that characterized the 2010s is beginning to ebb…There are still bitter fights over trans issues and abortion, but overall the 2020s culture war feels more like what Americans have become used to.[10]

He goes on to cite the inverse phenomenon to America's vengeful nihilism—a so-called "vibecession", or a sense of broad reaching pessimism that makes "Jimmy Carter's famous "malaise" speech from 1979… [seem] somewhat applicable to the national mood of 2023."[11] This "vibes"-based comparison to Carter, whose "soft" masculinity came under fire at the beginning of the backlash era, then, could easily be applied to critiques leveled at President Biden, whose age became the ruinous focal point of his campaign before his unprecedented choice to drop out in July in favor of his female VP, Kamala Harris—who Trump quickly labeled "Laffin' Kamala",[12] an indirect replication of Hillary Clinton being labeled a witch[13]—at the top of the ticket. In retrospect, Smith's analysis in many ways feels eminently correct, particularly when paired with his assertion that "[I]n [early] 2020s America, as in the 1970s… we've just been through great changes, but we aren't yet sure what the new social and political equilibrium will look like."[14] After Donald Trump won the presidency in both the electoral college *and* the popular vote, though,—the first Republican to do so since George W. Bush's paternalistic, evangelical-coded run in 2004—and the MAGA-fied

---

8. *This Place Rules*. Directed by Andrew Callaghan (2021).
9. Thompson, 2024.
10. Smith, 2023.
11. *Ibid.*
12. Schiff, 2016.
13. Mulholland, 2024.
14. Smith, 2023.

Republican party won both the House and the Senate, it becomes clear what direction that equilibrium is headed. In the still-ongoing aftermath, *Time*'s 1984 cover story cheerfully recounting "talk of pendulum swings, matters coming full circle and a psychic return to prerevolutionary days," with its concluding declaration that "[w]e are in a '50s period again"[15] feels, in some ways, right at home in 2025.

Still, while Smith's diagnosis of a sort of return to the socially conservative mean proved prescient, like my assessment that the feminist elevated horror cycle was on the verge of collapse in 2022, these analyses will no doubt be complicated by the tremendous legal empowerment of the chauvinistic conservative movement and the inevitable thermostatic effect it will have on feminist activism. In 2020, Susan Faludi republished *Backlash* with a new introduction, arguing that Donald Trump's election in 2016 marked the beginning of a nationwide backlash even worse than the '80s. She called Trump "the most flagrantly misogynist president in history," and wrote that "If anything, Backlash written in 2020 would be *direr* in many respects… [Reagan] never… suggested locking women up if they had an abortion."[16] The religious right's freshly enlivened campaign to regulate women's and queer people's bodies added fuel to a cycle which could have likely otherwise declined, as the first occult boom did, on the heels of a slow erosion of feminist gains. In June 2022, the newly Trump-stacked Supreme Court's *Dobbs* decision to overturn *Roe v Wade*, alongside extreme anti-choice regulation in states across the country, have frequently cited overtly religious, openly misogynistic doctrine. In *Dobbs*, Justice Alito cited Sir Matthew Hale, a 17th-century judge credited with the first "marital rape exemption". Hale also presided over several witch trials that served as a model for Salem's own witch craze.[17] Trump for his part continued to court the religious right, assuring one anti-choice group which has called abortion "child sacrifice" that he would stand "side by side" with them on religious issues.[18] Speaker of the House Mike Johnson brought these overtures to organized religion to the forefront, making the suggestion that the very notion of the separation of church and state was itself a "misnomer".[19]

Trump's 2024 presidential campaign was similarly characterized by an overtly vulgar, hyper-misogynist, Christian-coded tone that should by now feel unfortunately familiar: Tucker Carlson suggested that abortions (which he also called "human sacrifice") cause hurricanes;[20] advertisements called Harris a "a big ole c-word";[21] at Trump's MSG rally, David Rem called the

---

15. Leo, 1984.
16. Faludi, 2020, i.
17. Armstrong, 2022.
18. Wang, 2024.
19. Shabad, 2023.
20. Cameron, 2024.
21. Kinnard, 2024.

then-Vice President "the Devil" and "the Antichrist";[22] at a "Get Out the Worship" rally, evangelical preacher Lance Wallnau, suggested that Harris used "witchcraft" to "look presidential."[23] After the 2024 election, Democrats reported a profound feeling of deflation. Articles with titles like "Resist or Retreat? Democratic Voters Are Torn About Whether to Keep Fighting" proliferated (reminiscent of mid-70s "Will Feminism Survive?" headlines), suggesting the energy of 2016 wasn't forthcoming. As one Democratic poll worker put it in that same article, "It feels so much more definitive this time."[24] Like Reagan's tidal wave of triumph over Carter, America answered its "vibecession" with a candidate who presented himself as the virile, masculine alternative to a liberalism viewed as excessively "feminine" (first embodied by "soft" President Biden, then by Kamala Harris herself)—a shift with immediate, obvious, and monumental implications for women's and queer people's rights. The conservative manosphere wasted no time after Harris defeat to revel in the political significance of its victory. Media outlets reported a slew of #Gamergate-style posts and comments from men, that read "your body, my choice."[25] President Trump assured women that he was going to "protect" them… "whether they like it or not."[26]

These and other examples of chauvinistic Christian Nationalism's political ascendency have already become a focal point for feminist activism and filmmaking, buoying the significance of the previous decade's occult-inflected feminism in the process, but clearly demonstrating the uphill battle at hand as the President and his advisors have begun systematically dismantling the social safety net[27], rolling back women's[28] and queer people's civil liberties and bodily autonomy[29], and stifling free speech[30]. The Satanic Temple has continued its own form of political action, and its membership has more than doubled since 2021, founding the "Samuel Alito's Mom's Satanic Abortion Clinic" in 2023.[31] The Satanic Temple's Boston headquarters, meanwhile, have faced repeated bombing-attempts in recent years. One pipe-bomb left on the organization's doorstep in 2024, came with a scrawled note warning members to "REPENT".[32] Near the end of the 2024 campaign, the Christian Broadcasting Network ran an article highlighting the contrast with 2016 on

---

22. Jones, 2024.
23. "That's the seduction of what I would say is witchcraft. That's the manipulation of imagery that creates an impression contrary to the truth, but it seduces you into seeing it. So that spirit, that occult spirit, I believe is operating on her and through her" (Hixenbaugh and Marquez, 2024).
24. Mazzei and Russell, 2024.
25. Spencer-Elliot, 2024.
26. Hubbard, 2024.
27. Mandavilli, Sanger-Katz, and Hoffman, 2025.
28. Vagianos, 2025; National Women's Law Center, 2025.
29. Reed, 2025.
30. Raymond, 2025.
31. Domb, 2023.
32. US Attorney's Office, District of Massachusetts, 2024.

this score: "Witches Report Their Spells Against Trump Aren't Working" the headline read, "He Has a Shield."[33]

It is unsurprising, then, that the witch remains prevalent in pop culture. The Satanic Panic has regained popular cultural attention since the mainstreaming of QAnon and related conspiracist ideology, explored narrative horror films like *Late Night with the Devil* (2024) and *MaXXXine* (2024). As in the early '70s, films with supernatural and Satanic subject matter are almost inescapable, often folding in different facets of the occult genre and its history: over the past year or so, for example, Satanists and witches have haunted the innocent in films like *Tarot* (2023) and *Longlegs* (2024). As the examples in my 2022 article indicate, it is clearly true and unsurprising that a more conservative strain of witch film is returning alongside Trump's conservative wave (the demonic hand in *Talk to Me* (2023) belonged to an evil witch for example—elisions reminiscent of both *The Exorcist* [1973] and *Ghostbusters* [1984]), and Christian-coded films like *God is a Bullet* (2023) occasionally conjure up evil, as well as overtly queer-coded Satanists, in a gesture to the wave of social conservatism on display. That said, in an interesting shift, the genre's current, universal association with "elevation" seems to come with a liberal inflection that keeps this trend largely below the surface—at least for now.

The feminist witch, for her part, is perhaps more visible than ever. Since 2020, videos about witches have taken off on TikTok ("WitchTok")—as of 2022, videos with the "#witch hashtag have received nearly 20 billion views, #witchtiktok has nearly two billion views, and #babywitch, a hashtag for those new to the craft, has more than 600 million views" according to the BBC.[34] The reason? As one practitioner put it: "Witchcraft, paganism, it all gives you a bit of control back, you can live your life how you want… It gives people a real sense of individuality and power."[35] Cinematically, the witch has continued to proliferate in horror as well—*The Devil's Bath* (2024) tells a story very similar to *The Witch*, taking "Satan's influence" as a metaphor for mental illness, while two separate occult horror films about pregnant nuns, *Immaculate* and *The First Omen* were released in a single weekend in March 2024. Both films channel anxieties about the rising wave of anti-choice Christian nationalism. In the former, Sister Cecilia (Sydney Sweeney), a novice in an Italian convent, finds herself immaculately pregnant. It is eventually revealed that it isn't Satan who impregnated her, but a deranged priest who hopes to bring about the Messiah through DNA taken off a nail used in Jesus' crucifixion. Cecelia flees this Christian coven and, once she gives birth, crushes her baby's head with a rock. Meanwhile, in Arkasha Stevenson's prequel to *The Omen*, *The First Omen*, a novitiate named Margaret arrives in Rome in 1971 and, like Sister Cecelia, becomes

---

33. Gill, 2024.
34. Jones, 2022.
35. *Ibid.*

pregnant. It eventually becomes clear that while she herself is the daughter of Satan, she has been forcibly impregnated by the church, desperate to fight religious decline. In this telling, her daughter (she has twins), the result of an incestuous coupling between Satan's daughter and Satan himself, could become the anti-antichrist, positing a matriarchal line of Satanic women bent on combating the now-evilly-coded clerical patriarchy.

As in the '70s, this feminist witch horror boom has matured enough to include its own meta-commentary: documentaries like *Woodlands Dark and Days Bewitched* and, more recently, Elizabeth Sankey's *Witches* (2024) explore the political implications of the folk horror genre, indicating that the cycle has, without question, reached its saturation point, entering an almost meta space in the culture. Interestingly, though, as happened in the early '70s when the occult revival began to wane, critics have expressed boredom with the subject. *Witches*, for example, was called "trivial pop feminist pseudo-history" in the *Hollywood Reporter*, whose critic suggested (rather sourly) that there was nothing new to add on the subject:

> [Sankey] unravels witch tropes we've all heard unraveled many times before, once again linking witches to forbidden power and a divine feminine that patriarchy has apparently attempted to quash time and time again… She even trots out that old yarn about how the burgeoning male medical establishment of early modern Europe conspiratorially persecuted midwives and healer women as witches to oust their competition.[36]

This deep familiarity with the genre's tropes has led to an interesting sort of collapse in narrative cohesion relative to the clear thematic unity of the 2010s cycle itself alongside the rightward drag of the 2020s vibecession. Even as A24 imitators with overtly radical feminist themes continue to appear, as in the 2000s after the '90s teen horror cycle, the witch is being pulled into the realm of YA, fantasy, and (as in the 80s,) comedy once more—though her status as a feminist symbol is being incorporated into this shift, to mixed results. Enough time has passed since the hyper-liberal mid-2010s that pendulum swings are on display in feminism itself: as the yuppie returns to the top of the cultural pile, a return to the kind of individualized, corporatized feminism of the 1980s and 2000s is somewhat visible among young people. Much as ex-hippies expressed enthusiasm for business as the '70s dawned ("like, wow!"), witchcraft has become corporate, thoroughly branded, packaged and sold by a generation that no longer treats being a "sellout" like an insult, dominated by a masculinist wave of conservative "counterculture" helmed by online figures like Joe Rogan. Thus, in the mid-2020s, the witch can no longer truly be presented as countercultural—i.e. the continuing gestures towards the goth witches of the '90s, (Sankey's

---

36. Barh, 2024.

documentary was also denigrated as "goth-lite"), the use of psychedelic imagery taken from its original context (the psychedelic movement has itself become mainstream, once more a product of Silicon Valley)—rather she is for the moment broadly empowering, but, as in the 1980s, *safe*. In this sense, even as films like *The First Omen* maintain an edge of genuine feminist rage, my 2022 assessment has been proven largely correct—the witch has taken on *so many meanings*, that she once more becomes a solipsism.

There is ample evidence that the feminist witch has reached her cultural zenith by the mid-2020s, reappropriated and stripped of her rough edges. As of the end of 2024, *Wednesday* (2022-), Netflix's *Addams Family* spin-off (that turns its title character into a witch), remains the streamer's most watched show of all time even three years after its release, followed by *Stranger Things* (2016-2025), a show that takes the Satanic Panic as a central historical event.[37] *The Mayfair Witches* became AMC+'s largest premiere ever in 2023 and continues to draw large audiences.[38] Pop culturally, the angry female character more broadly, had taken over to the point where microtrends abounded in 2022, with TikTokers promoting "feral girl summer", while *Pearl* (2022) and the self-consciously feminist update of *Fatal Attraction* (1987) spawned think pieces on "female rage", celebrating violent women as "the brutal new icons of film and TV."[39] Since then, the hallmarks of the 2010s witch horror cycle as I've defined it, have pervaded the atmosphere in the US, with films like *The Substance* and *I Saw the TV Glow* (2024) reappropriating some of those iconic final shots to newfound potency, while satanic conspiracies appear over and over again in films like *Longlegs* and *MaXXXine*. Yet the witch herself cannot always fit comfortably within the positive ideological construction she has been assigned at present, her rage bumping up against the respectability of these new tropes.

Of course, the notion that the feminist witch has gone mainstream enough to proliferate media for women and girls is likely a net good, reflective of the fact that even amidst backlash, feminism pushes forward, expanding the bounds of acceptability for femininity. Unlike the backlash witch films of the '80s, the "good" witches of women-directed films like Netflix's *Fear Street* (2021), *Hocus Pocus 2* (2022), or Sophia Takal's *Black Christmas* (2019), are allowed to be, at least on the surface, nuanced. They're allowed to be queer. They're allowed to be Black. And yes, in many ways, they are allowed to express their rage at the patriarchy as the archetype demands they be. In 2024, the first of two big budget installments of *Wicked* was released in

---

37. "Top 10 Most Popular TV (English)", 2024.
38. Maas, 2023.
39. Blanaescu, 2022.

December, starring Ariana Grande and Cynthia Erivo as Glinda and Elphaba. Perhaps the most classic example of a meta-narrative deconstruction of witch-tropes, this YA musical's positive message of self-acceptance and feel good ending (the Wicked Witch lives and her name is cleared) clearly indicates the apotheosis of the witch's recuperation as a symbol of, capital E, Empowerment—here, Elphaba is presented not as evil, but as misunderstood, driven to her anger by a biased and corrupt system that turns on her for her differences. She and Glinda will eventually come together to resist the patriarchal Wizard, satisfying once more the desire for feminine solidarity that's so central to the genre. Nel Noddings tells us that the ultimate path out of the paradox of womanhood can be resolved "with the realization that the dichotomous view of woman as evil (because of her attraction to matters of the flesh) and good (because of her compassion and nurturing) served as a means of control."[40] As the current wave of solipsistic and upbeat witch representation shows us, feminists over the past decade have brought this message home with enormous force.

At the same time, though, whenever the witch is brought out of the horror realm and into fantasy—whenever her actions are shown as not only justified and sympathetic, but pure and simply "*good*", caused by a series of unfortunate and easily understood circumstances stacked against her, she loses some of her strength as a symbol of nonconformist femininity. The power of the witch, as over fifty years of cinema history has shown, is the power to frighten, to harness the anxieties of men and women alike, channeling them into a vessel of unholy (if often wholly justified) retribution and rage. She is wrathful, a hungry ghost, reminding us of the injustices women have faced. She herself is a complex representation of how those injustices can curdle into hatred. She's, well, *scary*. Thomasin's life in *The Witch* may have driven her to the Devil, but she chose the moniker "witch" *beforehand*, mocking her siblings and reveling in their discomfort, reveling in her ability to control her circumstances in a deeply flawed way. Nancy Downs didn't put her stepfather in prison, or magically make him nicer, *she killed him*. That isn't to say that this need for female villains isn't being fulfilled elsewhere in the culture—indeed, as I've said before, the "unlikable female character" is an insistent presence across genres in the mid-2020s and, as I've shown, the witch has helped put her there. At the time of writing this book, a remake of *Possession* (1981) is in the works, alongside a *Carrie* remake and another recent prequel to *Rosemary's Baby* (1968), *Apartment 7A* (2024), spurred per the studio by a wave of heightened interest from Gen Z. Films like *The Substance* and *I Saw the TV Glow* take up the tropes of the 2010s witch horror cycle, triumphantly pushing the boundaries of feminist filmmaking, the witch visible in their margins.

---

40. Noddings, 1989, 3.

Yet, although as Anna Bogutskaya puts it in her book on this now-omnipresent trend, *Unlikeable Female Characters*, "we are now living in a cultural reckoning of the stories we had accepted as canon… finally asking ourselves the question: *Why* do I consider [a female character] unlikeable?"[41] The domestication of the witch highlights the fact that simple recuperation of this kind of role is not always an escape from sexist representation. The book—which addresses a wave of discourse on the subject that feminist theorist Andrea Long Chu has called "an imaginary debate that has dribbled like a chronic nosebleed down the internet's face since 2013, when the novelist Claire Messud upbraided an interviewer for asking if she would want to be "friends" with her rage-filled female narrator"[42]—replicates many of the discourse's problems: only a sentence before pondering the valorization of a woman's relative "likability", Bogutskaya suggests that, in previous decades, "only a woman's intense suffering [could] justify her unlikeability."[43] What are movies like *Wicked* doing if not exactly that? Will the next generation of witches be allowed to misbehave? One thing's for certain: we'll love them less if they aren't.

Where the witch goes from here depends, as history has demonstrated, on where the American political landscape takes us in the next few years; as of now, writing in the continually "historically unprecedented" summer and fall of 2024, that trajectory is largely unclear, if clearly frightening. As Susan Faludi put it in her new introduction to *Backlash*, "depending on how you turn the kaleidoscope, the current situation for American women is a budding rose garden or a thicket of noxious weeds."[44] Going into 2025, the kaleidoscope is spinning at a genuinely dizzying pace. From this vertigo-inducing vantage, it appears that, at least for now, the witch remains a fractured signifier, constantly on the verge of transformation. It is entirely possible, even likely, that the witch film will continue her run as a symbol of women's empowerment in the broadest sense (as evinced by the recently announced *Practical Magic 2*); it's also possible that, given the new political landscape, she could return to her degraded Reaganite status as the butt of a backlash-era joke (as evinced by the recently announced *Witchboard* [1986] remake); and it is equally plausible that the same conservatism which spurred that impulse will bring her back into the realm of the crone or the hag (as evinced by a recently announced *Blair Witch* sequel and hag movies like *The Substance*). These three poles continue to coexist in tension, proliferating the culture. But no matter what happens in the next year, or four, or ten, as she has since the beginning of cinema history, the witch will continue to haunt American screens big and small. Feminists will continue to resist and the

---

41. Bogutskaya, 2023, 5.
42. Long Chu, 2022.
43. Bogustkaya, 2023, 5.
44. Faludi, 2020, ii.

pull of this iconic female villain will continue to draw, her seductive reply to the Devil's question "what do you want to do?" casting its spell over and over again: "Anything" she murmurs, "so long as it's bad."

Acknowledgements

This book has taken the better part of five years to complete, and so many people have helped me along the way.

To begin, I am deeply grateful for the consideration and support of my agent, Stacey Kondla and my editor Francesca Barbini, as well as well as Meg Hafdahl and Kelly Florence. The four of you took me on fresh out of college and gave me the tools to get this horror show on the road. You were the first people who suggested I could actually make this project happen—and because of you, it did.

I would also like to thank my academic advisors, Professors Ron Gregg and Rob King, as well as the entire film and media studies faculty at Columbia University. Without their insight and enthusiasm (thoughtfully offered over the course of two advanced degrees, a handful of massive world events, and lots of Zoom coffee breaks) this book would not have been possible.

Without my family and friends, this project would never have come to pass. I thank them all for their unflagging encouragement, kindness, patience, and good cheer (or much needed snark as the case may be) as I watched the hundreds of films I write about here. Thank you to my queer family—to AJ, for sticking with me through the movie marathons, and to Madi, Nick, Sean, and Cecina in particular as non-horror fans. I couldn't ask for a better set of movie-watching buds. Thank you to my avós, who kept me grounded (and well fed) through the marathon research sessions during lockdown. Thank you to my parents, Shauna and David, for believing in me. To my sister and partner in crime, Rowan Jane—thanks for the memes, the love, and the phone calls.

Finally, to my partner, Ben Cooper, thank you for your steadfast companionship, your critical mind, and your trust in my work. You've read every word of this book with such love and curiosity. You're my sun, my moon, and all my stars.

Works Cited

W.I.T.C.H. Boston. "About." *W.I.T.C.H. Boston*. Accessed June 9, 2024, <https://www.witchboston.org/about>.

Adams, Marjory. "'Rosemary's Baby' good horror story." *Boston Globe*, June 21, 1968. Columbia University *Proquest*, accessed April 22, 2024. <http://ezproxy.cul.columbia.edu/login?url=https://www.proquest.com/historical-newspapers/rosemarys-baby-good-horror-story/docview/366867793/se-2>.

Adler, Renata. "'Rosemary's Baby,' a Story of Fantasy and Horror." *New York Times*, June 13, 1968. <https://timesmachine.nytimes.com/timesmachine/1968/06/13/90035075.html?pageNumber=57>.

Alexander, Shana. "The Ping is the Thing." *The Feminine Eye, Life* p. 3, February 17, 1967. *Google Books*, accessed April 22, 2024. <https://books.google.com/books?id=XlYEAAAAMBAJ&lpg=PA3&dq=%E2%80%9CThe%20Ping%20is%20The%20Thing%2C%E2%80%9D%201967&pg=PA3#v=onepage&q=%E2%80%9CThe%20Ping%20is%20The%20Thing,%E2%80%9D%201967&f=false>.

Allison, Peter Ray. "The great 1980s Dungeons & Dragons panic." *BBC*, April 11, 2014. Accessed August 28, 2024. <https://www.bbc.com/news/magazine-26328105>.

"The Alternative Jesus: Psychedelic Christ." *Time*, June 21, 1971. Accessed June 22, 2024. <https://content.time.com/time/subscriber/article/0,33009,905202,00.html>.

"Amid Ruins of an Empire, a New Hollywood Arises." *Life*, pp. 146-7, 150, 152, 155-6, 158-9, 163-4, 166. June 10, 1957. Google Books, accessed June 22, 2024. <https://books.google.com/books?id=Nz8EAAAAMBAJ&pg=PA146#v=twopage&q&f=false>.

"An Epidemic of 'Acid Heads'." *Time*. Vol. 87(10) (1966), pp. 44-46. Columbia University *ProQuest*, accessed April 22, 2024. <https://web-p-ebscohost-com.ezproxy.cul.columbia.edu/ehost/detail/detail?vid=0&sid=9ca3d473-2bf4-4cb3-a058-258409bb7587%40redis&bdata=JkF1dGhUeXBlPWlwJnNpdGU9ZWhvc3QtbGl2ZSZzY29wZT1zaXRl#AN=54033344&db=tma>.

Anapol, Avery. "Brooklyn witches planning to publicly hex Brett Kavanaugh." *The Hill*, October 15, 2018. Accessed March 31, 2025. <https://thehill.com/blogs/blog-briefing-room/news/411449-witches-planning-to-publicly-hex-brett-kavanaugh/>.

"Anton LaVey on the Joe Pyne Show." Youtube, uploaded by Rev. Draconis Blackthorne, May 10, 2012. Accessed February 24, 2025. <https://youtu.be/Kqb54soKU8M?si=vAWzQ4-C2BgvXq_S>.

AP. "Robertson Letter Attacks Feminists." *New York Times*, August 26, 1992. <https://www.nytimes.com/1992/08/26/us/robertson-letter-attacks-feminists.html>.

Armstrong, Ken. "Draft Overturning Roe v. Wade Quotes Infamous Witch Trial Judge with Long-Discredited Ideas on Rape." *ProPublica*, May 6, 2022. Accessed June 22, 2024. <https://www.propublica.org/article/abortion-roe-wade-alito-scotus-hale/>.

Asimov, Isaac. "Husbands Beware!" *TV Guide*, March 22, 1969. *Bewitched Collector*, accessed June 22, 2024. <https://bewitchedcollector.tripod.com/cgi-bin/TVGuideMar690001.pdf>.

Atwood, Margaret. "Stephen King's First Book Is 50 Years Old, and Still Horrifyingly Relevant." *New York Times*, March 25, 2024. <https://www.nytimes.com/2024/03/25/books/review/stephen-king-carrie-50-anniversary.html>.

Bahr, Robyn. 'Witches' Review: Self-Serious Doc Links Women's Mental Health With the Ethereal." *The Hollywood Reporter*, June 11, 2024. Accessed June 11, 2024. <https://www.hollywoodreporter.com/movies/movie-reviews/witches-review-elizabeth-sankey-1235918084/>.

Baker, Peter. "Bush stumbles while asserting progress in education." *Seattle Times*, September 27, 2007. Accessed June 28, 2024. <https://www.seattletimes.com/seattle-news/politics/bush-stumbles-while-asserting-progress-in-education/>.

Bansak, Edmund G. *Fearing the Dark: The Val Lewton Career*. Jefferson, NC: Macfarland, 2003.

Bareket, O., Kahalon, R., Shnabel, N. et al. "The Madonna-Whore Dichotomy: Men Who Perceive Women's Nurturance and Sexuality as Mutually Exclusive Endorse Patriarchy and Show Lower Relationship Satisfaction." *Sex Roles* no. 79 (2018), pp. 519—532. Accessed June 5, 2023. <https://doi.org/10.1007/s11199-018-0895-7>.

Barr, Andy. "Bush: 'sanctity of Human Life Day.'" *Politico*, January 15, 2009. Accessed June 24, 2024. <https://www.politico.com/story/2009/01/bush-sanctity-of-human-life-day-017494>.

Baxter, John. *Stanley Kubrick*. New York, NY: Carroll & Graf Publishers, 1997.

Beard, Drew. "Horror Movies at Home: Supernatural Horror, Delivery Systems and 1980s Satanic Panic." *Horror Studies*, vol. 6(2) (2015), pp. 211-223. Accessed November 20, 2023. <http://doi.org/10.1386/host.6.2.211_1>.

Beauparlant, Bonnie. "To be in film: Merrill transformed into Devonsville." *Wausau Daily Herald*, October 6, 1982. *Newspapers.com*, accessed August 28, 2024. https://www.newspapers.com/article/wausau-daily-herald/120065866/.

Beck, Richard. *We Believe the Children: A Moral Panic in the 1980's*. New York, NY: PublicAffairs, 2015.

Beckley, Paul V. "The New Movie: 'Black Sunday.'" *New York Herald Tribune*, n.d. 1961, p. 15. Columbia University *Proquest*, accessed June 21, 2024. <http://ezproxy.cul.columbia.edu/login?url=https://www.proquest.com/historical-newspapers/new-movie/docview/1336939344/se-2>.

Bellafante, Gina. "Is Feminism Dead?" *Time*, June 29, 1998. Accessed June 20, 2024. <https://time.com/archive/6733024/feminism-its-all-about-me/>.

Benton, Robert and Newman, David. "The New Sentimentality." *Esquire*, July 1, 1964. Accessed June 22, 2024. <https://classic.esquire.com/article/1964/7/1/the-new-sentimentality>.

Best, Joel and Horuichi, Gerald. "The Razor Blade in the Apple: The Social Construction of Urban Legends." *Social Problems*, vol. 32(5) (1985), pp. 488-499. Accessed November 10, 2023. <https://doi.org/10.2307/800777>.

"Bewitching Hostess." *Ladies Home Journal*, n.d. 1969.

"Bewitching Tale About Witches: *Bell, Book and Candle* Makes an Eerie Film." *Life*, November 24, 1958, pp. 66-101. *Google Books*, accessed June 22, 2024. <https://books.google.com/books?id=aD8EAAAAMBAJ&q=bewitching#v=snippet&q=bewitching&f=false/>.

Bibbiani, William. (2013). "Extreme Version: Tommy Wirkola on Hansel & Gretel: Witch Hunters." *Crave Online*, May 14, 2013. *Internet Archive*, accessed May 27, 2024. <https://web.archive.org/web/20130514004947/http:/www.craveonline.com/film/interviews/204185-extreme-version-tommy-wirkola-on-hansel-a-gretel-witch-hunters>.

Biller, Anna. "Fun Fact." *Twitter*, December 7, 2017. Accessed August 24, 2023. <https://x.com/missannabiller/status/938829359456051200>.

Biller, Anna. "The Misogyny of the Modern Slasher." *Anna Biller's Blog*, January 19, 2014. Accessed August 24, 2023. <http://annabillersblog.blogspot.com/2014/01/the-misogyny-of-modern-slasher-film.html>.

Biller, Anna. "Notes on I SPIT ON YOUR GRAVE." *Anna Biller's Blog*, December 30, 2020. Accessed August 24, 2023. <http://annabillersblog.blogspot.com/2020/12/notes-on-i-spit-on-your-grave.html>.

Biller, Anna. "Obsessed with love." *Twitter*, March 18, 2018. Accessed August 24, 2023. <https://x.com/missannabiller/status/975446485209825280>.

Biller, Anna. "A Rape Story for the Trump Era." *Anna Biller's Blog*, October 7, 2017. Accessed August 24, 2023. <http://annabillersblog.blogspot.com/2017/10/a-rape-story-for-trump-era.html>.

Billington, Alex. "Tommy Wirkola Tackling Hansel and Gretel: Witch Hunters." Firstshowing.net, March 4, 2009. *Internet Archive*, accessed May 27, 2024. <https://web.archive.org/web/20101009120856/http://www.firstshowing.net/2009/04/30/tommy-wirkola-tackling-hansel-and-gretel-witch-hunters-next/>.

Black, Eric. "Ferraro rejoins Mondale to ponder history." *Star Tribune*, 2004. Columbia University *ProQuest*, accessed June 26, 2024. <http://ezproxy.cul.columbia.edu/login?url=https://www.proquest.com/newspapers/ferraro-rejoins-mondale-ponder-history-former/docview/427614609/se-2?accountid=10226>.

Blatty, William Peter. *The Exorcist*. United Kingdom: HarperCollins, 1994.

Blumenthal, Ralph. "'Hard-core' grows fashionable—and very profitable." *New York Times*, January 21, 1973. <https://www.nytimes.com/1973/01/21/archives/pornochic-hardcore-grows-fashionableand-very-profitable.html>.

Boeth, Richard. "HOODOO VOODOO AND YOU!" *Cosmopolitan*, July 1970, pp. 126-129, 133. Columbia University *ProQuest*, accessed June 22, 2024. <http://ezproxy.cul.columbia.edu/login?url=https://www.proquest.com/magazines/hoodoo-uoodoo-you/docview/1843867241/se-2>.

Bogutskaya, Anna. *Unlikeable Female Characters: The Women Pop Culture Wants You to Hate*. New York, NY: Sourcebooks, 2023.

Boucher, Anthony. "Criminals At Large." *New York Times*, January 3, 1964. <https://www.nytimes.com/1964/03/01/archives/criminals-at-large.html>.

Bradley, Laura. "This Was the Decade Horror Got 'Elevated.'" *Vanity Fair*, December 17, 2019. Accessed June 26, 2024. <https://www.vanityfair.com/hollywood/2019/12/rise-of-elevated-horror-decade-2010s>.

Brackett, Paul. "Satan, Subliminals, and Suicide: The Formation and Development of an Antirock Discourse in the United States during the 1980s." *American Music*, vol. 36(3) (2018), 271-302. <https://www.jstor.org/stable/10.5406/americanmusic.36.3.0271>.

Briggs, Ken. "Can the Devil Make Us Do It: A look at some of the knotty questions raised by the popularity of 'The Exorcist.'" *Newsday*, p. 6. Columbia University *ProQuest*, accessed April 22, 2024. <http://ezproxy.cul.columbia.edu/login?url=https://www.proquest.com/historical-newspapers/can-devil-make-us-do/docview/920931986/se-2>.

Brit. "Elvira, Mistress Of The Dark." *Variety*, September 28 1988. Columbia University *ProQuest*, accessed April 22, 2024. <https://www.proquest.com/docview/1438506042?accountid=10226&parentSessionId=ualfbpVrxyh%2BkagnbtTsDkVUwTlfIyeRMcPPFoMxMA8%3D&imgSeq=1>.

Britton, Andrew. "Blissing Out: The Politics of Reaganite Entertainment." *Britton on Film: The Complete Film Criticism of Andrew Britton*, edited by Barry Keith Grant. Detroit, MI: Wayne State University Press, 2009.

"Broken Vertebra Caused Kim Novak to Quit Movie." *The Sun*, 1965. Columbia University *ProQuest*, accessed, May 25, 2024. <http://ezproxy.cul.columbia.edu/login?url=https://www.proquest.com/historical-newspapers/broken-vertebra-caused-kim-novak-quit-movie/docview/539510782/se-2>.

Broomfield, Matt. "Women's March against Donald Trump is the largest day of protests in US history, say political scientists." *Independent*, January 23, 2017. <https://www.independent.co.uk/news/world/americas/womens-march-anti-donald-trump-womens-rights-largest-protest-demonstration-us-history-political-scientists-a7541081.html>.

Brown, Connie E. "Monumental Music Hall: THE EXORCIST." *Afro-American*, February 9, 1974 p. 11. Columbia University *ProQuest*, accessed May 21, 2024. <http://ezproxy.cul.columbia.edu/login?url=https://www.proquest.com/historical-newspapers/monumental-music-hall/docview/532508756/se-2>.

Brundson, Charlotte. "Post-feminism and shopping films." *Screen Tastes*, p. 83-103. London, ENG: Routledge, 1997. <https://www.taylorfrancis.com/chapters/mono/10.4324/9780203993002-18/post-feminism-shopping-films-charlotte-brunsdon>.

Buder, Emily. "Inside Paganism: The Many Faces of the Occult." *The Atlantic*, December 23, 2019. <https://www.theatlantic.com/video/index/604084/pagans/>.

Buchanan, Pat. "1992 Republican National Convention Speech." *Patrick J. Buchanan Official Website*, August 17, 1992. Accessed June 20, 2024. <https://buchanan.org/blog/1992-republican-national-convention-speech-148?doing_wp_cron=1738776266.0916969776153564453125>.

Buckland, Raymond. *Here is the Occult*. New York, NY: House of Collectibles, Inc, 1974.

"Bush's Wife Assails Ferraro, But Apologizes." *The New York Times*, October 9, 1984. <https://www.nytimes.com/1984/10/09/us/bush-s-wife-assails-ferraro-but-apologizes.html>.

Buursma, Bruce. "TV Religion Ratings Are Sky-High." *Chicago Tribune*, August 9, 2021. <https://www.chicagotribune.com/news/ct-xpm-1985-10-26-8503130362-story.html>.

Byatt, A.S. "Harry Potter and the Childish Adult." *New York Times*, July 7, 2003. <https://www.nytimes.com/2003/07/07/opinion/harry-potter-and-the-childish-adult.html?mcubz=0>.

Callow, John. *The Last Witches of England: A Tragedy of Sorcery and Superstition*. New York, NY: Bloomsbury Academic, 2021.

Canby, Vincent. "'The Exorcist II: The Heretic' Is Heavy Stuff." *New York Times*, June 18, 1977. <https://www.nytimes.com/1977/06/18/archives/film-exorcist-ii-the-heretic-is-heavy-stuff.html>.

Canfield, David. "Confessions of a Creature Feature Preacher: or How I Learned to Stop Worrying About Satanism and Love Mike Warnke." *Satanic Panic: Pop-Cultural Paranoia in the 1980*, pp. 263-275, edited by Janisse, Kier-La & Croupe, Paul, FAB Press, 2016.

Capua, Michelangelo. *Deborah Kerr: A Biography*. Jefferson, NC: McFarland & Company. Google Books, Accessed May 27, 2024. <https://books.google.com/books?id=pTP06LksISkC&q=sharon+tate#v=snippet&q=sharon%20tate&f=false>.

Casta, Nicole. "Falwell called NOW "the National Order of Witches." *Media Matters*, November 23, 2004. <https://www.mediamatters.org/jerry-falwell/falwell-called-now-national-order-witches>.

Champlin, Charles. "CRITIC AT LARGE: PRIEST PLAYS PRIEST IN 'THE EXORCIST.'" *Los Angeles Times*, August 25, 1972, pp. 1-g1. Columbia University *ProQuest*, accessed April 22, 2024. <http://ezproxy.cul.columbia.edu/login?url=https://www.proquest.com/historical-newspapers/critic-at-large/docview/157140463/se-2>.

Champlin, Charles. "'Mephisto' make-Believe." *Los Angeles Times*, February 1971, pp. 1-e27. Columbia University *ProQuest*, accessed April 22, 2024. <http://ezproxy.cul.columbia.edu/login?url=https://www.proquest.com/historical-newspapers/mephisto-make-believe/docview/156704454/se-2>.

Chaturvedi, Richa. "A closer look at the gender gap in presidential voting." *Pew Research Center*, July 28, 2016. Accessed June 22, 2024. <https://www.pewresearch.org/short-reads/2016/07/28/a-closer-look-at-the-gender-gap-in-presidential-voting/>.

"Cher's Raciest Interview Yet." *Playboy*, December 1988.

Chow, Andrew R. "Woody Allen warns of "witch hunt" after allegations against Harvey Weinstein." The Boston Globe, October 15, 2017. Accessed April 31, 2025. < https://www.bostonglobe.com/arts/movies/2017/10/15/woody-allen-warns-of-witch-hunt-after-weinstein-allegations/fgyeVOJPW6lb9qo63MojwN/story.html>.

Cameron, Chris. "Tucker Carlson Says Abortions Cause Hurricanes in Election Eve Broadcast." *New York Times*, November 11, 2024. <https://www.nytimes.com/2024/11/04/us/politics/tucker-carlson-hurricanes-abortion-demonic-nuclear-weapons.html>.

Clifford, Terry. "'Rosemary's Baby' Mixture of Obstetrics, Occult." *Chicago Tribune*, July 28, 1968, pp. 1-e7. Columbia University *ProQuest*, accessed April 22, 2024. <http://ezproxy.cul.columbia.edu/login?url=https://www.proquest.com/historical-newspapers/rosemarys-baby-mixture-obstetrics-occult/docview/175812620/se-2>.

Clover, Carol J. *Men, Women, and Chainsaws*. London, ENG: British Film Institute, 1992.

Cockburn, Alexander. "The Mcmartin case: indict the children, jail the parents." *Wall Street Journal*, February 8, 1990.

Cohen, Richard. "A New Stereotype The Crazy Career Woman." *The Washington Post*, October 5, 1987. Accessed November 12, 2023. <https://www.washingtonpost.com/archive/opinions/1987/10/06/a-new-stereotype-the-crazy-career-woman/d34fa844-1a10-466e-b148-be25df57e3f5/>.

Cohen, Scott. "The Witch' Isn't a Horror Flick—It's a High-Powered Feminist Manifesto." *Marie Claire*, March 17, 2016. Accessed June 22, 2024. <https://www.marieclaire.com/culture/a19362/the-witch-review/>.

"Condemned Rating by NCO To 'Rosemary's Baby.'" (1968). *Boxoffice*, vol. 93(10) (1968), p. 16. Columbia University *ProQuest*, accessed April 22, 2024. <http://ezproxy.cul.columbia.edu/login?url=https://www.proquest.com/magazines/condemned-rating-nco-rosemarys-baby/docview/1476027722/se-2>.

Conley, WM. "The Tracking of Evil: Home Video and the Proliferation of the Satanic Panic" *Satanic Panic: Pop-Cultural Paranoia in the 1980*, pp. 231-247, edited by Janisse, Kier-La & Croupe, Paul, FAB Press, 2016.

Cook, Tommy. "Director Tommy Wirkola Talk HANSEL AND GRETEL: WITCH HUNTERS." *Collider*, January 13, 2013. Accessed June 22, 2024. <https://collider.com/tommy-wirkola-hansel-gretel-witch-hunters-interview/#more-226342>.

Copeland, Libby. "Fun in the Naughty Aughties." *Washington Post*, January 27, 2000. Accessed June 22, 2024. <https://www.washingtonpost.com/archive/lifestyle/2000/01/27/fun-in-the-naughty-aughties/62c781e9-e799-4b41-992e-4a1543d41e23/>.

Coppins, McKay. "The Man Who Broke Politics." *The Atlantic*, November 2018. <https://www.theatlantic.com/magazine/archive/2018/11/newt-gingrich-says-youre-welcome/570832/>.

Costigan, Ken. "Wicked witchcraft to sell 'Rosemary's Baby.'" *Kine Weekly*, vol. 620(3202) (1969), pp. 30. Columbia University *ProQuest*, accessed April 22, 2024. <http://ezproxy.cul.columbia.edu/login?url=https://www.proquest.com/trade-journals/wicked-witchcraft-sell-rosemarys-baby/docview/2600942441/se-2>.

Cotter, Robert Michael. *Vampira and Her Daughters: Women Horror Movie Hosts from the 1950s into the Internet Era*. New York, NY: McFarland & Company, 2017.

"The Coven of One's Choice." *Time Magazine*, April 27, 1970, pp. 96-98. Accessed April 22, 2024. <https://time.com/archive/6843010/books-the-coven-of-ones-choice/>.

Cowan, Belita H. "Salem Witch Trials." *Her-Self*, vol. 1(5) (1972), p. 6-7. *Archives of Sexuality and Gender, JSTOR*, accessed June 22, 2024. <https://www.jstor.org/stable/community.28038331>.

Creed, Barbara. "Horror and the Monstrous-Feminine: An Imaginary Abjection." *Feminist Film Theory: A Reader*, pp. 251-267, edited by Sue Thornham. Edinburgh University Press, Edinburgh, 1999. <http://www.jstor.org/stable/10.3366/j.ctvxcrtm8.26>.

Creed, Barbara. *The Monstrous-Feminine: Film, Feminism, Psychoanalysis*. New York, NY: Routledge, 1993.

C-Span. "Senator Orrin Hatch Reads 'The Exorcist' at Thomas Hearing." *New York Times*, September 20, 2018. <https://www.nytimes.com/video/us/politics/100000006118721/orrin-hatch-the-exorcist-clarence-thomas.html>.

"The Cult of the Occult." *Newsweek*, April 13, 1970. Columbia University *ProQuest*, accessed April 22, 2024. <https://cas.columbia.edu/cas/login?service=https%3a%2f%2fwww1.columbia.edu%2fsec-cgi-bin%2fcul%2fprox%2fezproxy-authcgi%3furl%3dezp.2aHR0cHM6Ly93d3cucHJvcXVlc3QuY29tL21hZ2F6aW5lcy9jdWx0LW9mLW9jY3VsdC9kb2N2aWV3LzE4NjMyMTAvc2UtMj9hY2NvdW50aWQ9MTAyMjY>.

Curtiss, Thomas Quinn. "Venice Fete Cancels Public Showing of 'The Devils.'" *New York Times*, August 29, 1971. <https://timesmachine.nytimes.com/timesmachine/1971/08/29/79688739.html?pageNumber=55>.

Cush, Denise. "Consumer witchcraft: are teenage witches a creation of commercial interests?" *Journal of Beliefs & Values*, vol. 28(1) (2007), pp. 45-53. Columbia University *ProQuest*, accessed June 22, 2024. <https://www.proquest.com/docview/2081634?accountid=10226&parentSessionId=61e2UJAuq1gT4cdxtpMERO14QQ5nUa7rCenjVG10mis%3D&pq-origsite=summon&sourcetype=Scholarly%20Journals>

"Dear Cosmopolitan." *Cosmopolitan*, March 1968, p. 194. Columbia University *ProQuest*, accessed April 22, 2024. <http://ezproxy.cul.columbia.edu/login?url=https://www.proquest.com/magazines/rosemarys-baby/docview/1824572748/se-2>.

deAtley, Richard. "VCRs put entertainment industry into fast-forward frenzy." *The Free Lance-Star*, September 7, 1985. Internet Archive, accessed November 10, 2023. <https://web.archive.org/web/20200404235716/https://news.google.com/newspapers?id=lc8vAAAAIBAJ&sjid=1Y0DAAAAIBAJ&pg=5630%2C870934>.

De Hon, Jackie. "A Feminist's Response to Time's 1998 Cover Story, 'Is Feminism Dead?'" *Huffington Post*, June 28, 1998. Accessed June 22, 2024. <https://www.huffpost.com/entry/a-feminists-response-to-t_b_9768224>.

Deighan, Samm. "Trick or Treat: Heavy Metal and Devil Worship in '80s Cult Cinema." *Satanic Panic: Pop-Cultural Paranoia in the 1980*, pp. 201-217, edited by Janisse, Kier-La & Croupe, Paul, Toronto, CN: FAB Press, 2016.

D'Emilio John and Freedman, Estelle. *Intimate Matters: A History of Sexuality in America*. Third ed.. Chicago, IL: University of Chicago Press, 2012.

"The Demon of Death Valley." *Time*, December 12, 1969. Accessed November 15, 2023. <https://time.com/vault/issue/1969-12-12/page/24/>.

Dempsey, Michael "The World of Ken Russell." *Film Quarterly*, vol. 25(3) (1972), pp. 14, 1. Columbia University *ProQuest*, accessed June 22, 2024. <http://ezproxy.cul.columbia.edu/login?url=https://www.proquest.com/scholarly-journals/world-ken-russell/docview/223109691/se-2>.

De Quincey, Thomas. "Suspiria de Profundis." *Suspiria de Profundis and Other Writings*, pp. 9-70. Digireads Publishing, 2011.

Dewell, Marsha J. "Defending 'The Exorcist': There is truth in its ugliness." *Chicago Tribune*, February 12, 1974, p. 14. Columbia University *ProQuest*, accessed April 22, 2024. <http://ezproxy.cul.columbia.edu/login?url=https://www.proquest.com/historical-newspapers/defending-exorcist/docview/171090176/se-2>.

Dickey, Colin. "Why the United States Government Embraced the Occult." *The New Republic*, April 26, 2017. Accessed April 22, 2024. <https://newrepublic.com/article/142268/united-states-government-embraced-occult>.

Didion, Joan. *The White Album*. FSG Classics ed. New York, NY: Farrar, Straus and Giroux, 2008.

"Directing The Craft: An Interview with Andrew Fleming." *The Craft* [Blur-ray]. Shout Factory, 2019.

Dixon, Wheeler Winston. "'I Do Not Believe': Night of the Eagle (Sidney Hayers, 1962)." *Senses of Cinema*, March 2019. Accessed April 22, 2024. <https://www.sensesofcinema.com/2019/cteq/night-of-the-eagle-sidney-hayers-1962/>.

Dockterman, Elena. "What Is #GamerGate and Why Are Women Being Threatened About Video Games?" *Time*, October 16, 2014. Accessed June 22, 2024. <https://time.com/3510381/gamergate-faq/>.

Doherty, Maggie. "The Forgotten Feminists of the Backlash Decade." *New Republic*, September 24, 2020. Accessed November 10, 2023. <https://newrepublic.com/article/159234/history-forgotten-feminists-1990s-levenstein-book-review/>.

Domb, Arielle. "The Satanic Abortion Clinic That's Pissed Off Pretty Much Everyone...and Might Beat the Bans Anyway." *Cosmopolitan*, November 14, 2023. Accessed November 14, 2023. <https://www.cosmopolitan.com/lifestyle/a45613416/satanic-group-abortion-clinic-samuel-alito-mom/>.

Donovan, Barna William. *Conspiracy Films: A Tour of Dark Places in the American Consciousness*. New York, NY: McFarland & Company, 2011.

Dowd, Maureen. "Other Side of 'Gender Gap': Reagan Seen as Man's Man." *New York Times*, September 17, 1984. Accessed November 10, 2023. <https://www.nytimes.com/1984/09/17/us/other-side-of-gender-gap-reagan-seen-as-man-s-man.html?searchResultPosition=1>.

Doyle, Sady. "Monsters, men and magic: why feminists turned to witchcraft to oppose Trump." *The Guardian*, August 7, 2019. Accessed June 22, 2024. <https://www.theguardian.com/lifeandstyle/2019/aug/07/monsters-men-magic-trump-awoke-angry-feminist-witches>.

Dr. Cyclops. "Wicked Stepmother." "The Video Eye of Dr. Cyclops" *Fangoria* #94 (July 1990), p. 30.

Du Mez, Kristin Kobes. *Jesus and John Wayne: How White Evangelicals Corrupted a Faith and Fractured a Nation*. New York, NY: Liveright, 2020.

Dvorak, Petula. "2017: The Unexpected (and inspiring) Year of the Woman." *Washington Post*, December 28, 2017. Accessed June 22, 2024. <https://www.washingtonpost.com/local/2017-the-unexpected-and-inspiring-year-of-the-woman/2017/12/28/8e13611a-ebd6-11e7-8a6a-80acf0774e64_story.html>.

Ebert, Roger. "The Witches of Eastwick." *Chicago Sun-Times*, June 12, 1987. Accessed November 10, 2023. <https://www.rogerebert.com/reviews/the-witches-of-eastwick-1987>.

Echols, Alice. *Daring to Be Bad: Radical Feminism in America 1967-1975*. Thirtieth Anniversary ed. Minneapolis, MN: University of Minnesota Press, 2019.

Edsall, Thomas B. "GOP's Volatile Mix: Mainstream Activists and Evangelical Right." *The Washington Post*, January 17, 1993. Accessed June 26, 2024. <https://www.washingtonpost.com/archive/politics/1993/01/18/gops-volatile-mix-mainstream-activists-and-evangelical-right/7da6c00d-0cc5-4b6e-9f9a-19747b2e09aa/>.

Edwards, Catherine. "Wicca Casts a Spell on Teen-Age Girls." *Insight on the News*, October 9, 1999, pp. 22-25. Columbia University ProQuest, accessed June 25, 2024. <http://ezproxy.cul.columbia.edu/login?url=https://www.proquest.com/magazines/wicca-casts-spell-on-teen-age-girls/docview/205887042/se-2>.

Ehrenreich, Barbara and English, Deirdre. *Witches, Midwives, & Nurses: A History of Women Healers*. 2nd ed. New York, NY: Feminist Press, 1973.

Eichelbaum, Stanley. "Slavic Vampires on Rampage." *The San Francisco Examiner*, 1961. Columbia University *ProQuest*, accessed April 22, 2024. <http://ezproxy.cul.columbia.edu/login?url=https://www.proquest.com/historical-newspapers/february-24-1961-page-26-60/docview/2163483110/se-2>.

"Eiichi Yamamoto Interview." *Belladonna of Sadness* [Blu-ray]. Cinelicious, 2016.

Ellis, Bill. *Raising the Devil: Satanism, New Religions, and the Media*. Lexington, KY: University Press of Kentucky, 2000. Google Books, accessed April 22, 2024. <https://books.google.com/books?id=oLcqlypMCe8C&q=Sharon+tate+#v=snippet&q=Sharon%20tate&f=true>.

Ellis, Janey. "The Mysterious Horror Hostess that Reportedly Cursed James Dean." *Atomic Redhead*, October 18, 2018. Accessed November 15, 2023. <https://atomicredhead.com/2018/10/18/the-mysterious-horror-hostess-that-reportedly-cursed-james-dean/>.

Elson, John T. "Is God Dead?" *Time*, April 8, 1966. Accessed April 22, 2024. <https://time.com/archive/6629149/is-god-dead/>.

Etkin, Jaimie and Prudom, Laura. "'American Horror Story: Coven': Marie Laveau Played By Angela Bassett; Sarah Paulson Will Play Jessica Lange's Daughter." *Huffington Post*, August 2, 2013. Accessed June 22, 2024. <https://www.huffpost.com/entry/american-horror-story-coven-marie-laveau_n_3697960>.

Faife, Corin. "How Witchcraft Became a Brand" *Buzzfeed News*, July 26, 2017. Accessed June 22, 2024. <https://www.buzzfeednews.com/article/corinfaife/how-witchcraft-became-a-brand#.vhpqaYq0w>.

Faludi, Susan. *Backlash: The Undeclared War Against American Women*. Broadway Books Trade Paperback ed. New York, NY: Broadway Books, 2020.

Farber, Stephen. "The Devils' Finds An Advocate." *New York Times*, August 15, 1971. Accessed April 22, 2024. <https://timesmachine.nytimes.com/timesmachine/1971/08/15/90686619.html?pageNumber=143>.

Farber, Stephen. "'Don't Look Now' Will Scare You-Subtly." *New York Times*, December 23, 1973. Accessed April 22, 2024. <https://timesmachine.nytimes.com/timesmachine/1973/12/23/91063745.html?pageNumber=67>.

Faxneld, Per. *Satanic Feminism: Lucifer as the Liberator of Woman in Nineteenth-Century Culture*. Oxford, ENG: Oxford University Press, 2014.

Feasey, Rebecca. "Watching 'Charmed': Why Teen Television Appeals to Women." *Journal of Popular Film & Television*, vol. 34(1) (2006).

"FEATURE REVIEWS: Eye of the Devil." *Boxoffice*, vol. 91(21) (1967), pp. a11, a12. Columbia University *ProQuest*, accessed April 22, 2024. <http://ezproxy.cul.columbia.edu/login?url=https://www.proquest.com/magazines/feature-reviews-eye-devil/docview/1705124545/se-2>.

"FEATURE REVIEWS: THE MEPHISTO WALTZ." *Boxoffice*, February 15, 1971. Columbia University *ProQuest*, accessed April 22, 2024. <http://ezproxy.cul.columbia.edu/login?url=https://www.proquest.com/magazines/feature-reviews-mephisto-waltz/docview/1476039786/se-2>.

Ferguson, Kevin L. "Devil on the Line: Technology and the Satanic Film." *Satanic Panic: Pop-Cultural Paranoia in the 1980*, pp. 97-127, edited by Janisse, Kier-La & Croupe, Paul. Toronto, CN: FAB Press, 2016.

Fisher, Mark. *Capitalist Realism*. Ropely, UK: 0 Books, 2009.

Fleming, Thomas. "BE A WITCH!" *Cosmopolitan*, July 1972, pp. 136-137, 148-150. Columbia University *ProQuest*, accessed April 22, 2024. <http://ezproxy.cul.columbia.edu/login?url=https://www.proquest.com/magazines/be-witch/docview/1866037392/se-2>.

"For Its Own Sake." *Time*, September 15, 1961, pp. 25-25. <https://content.time.com/time/subscriber/article/0,33009,938731,00.html>.

Ford, Christopher. "The Devils in London: Christopher Ford reports on the production of Penderecki's opera 'The Devils of Loudun.'" *The Guardian*, p. 10. Columbia University *ProQuest*, <http://ezproxy.cul.columbia.edu/login?url=https://www.proquest.com/historical-newspapers/devils-london/docview/185720386/se-2>.

Federici, Silvia. *Witches, Witch-Hunting, and Women*. Binghamton, NY: PM Press, 2018.

Freedman, Rory and Barnouin, Kim. *Skinny Bitch: A No-Nonsense, Tough-Love Guide for Savvy Women Who Want to Stop Eating Crap and Start Looking Fabulous!*, New York, NY: Hachette Press, 2005.

Fremont-Smith, Eliot. "Books of The Times; What Witches? Where?" *New York Times*, April 7, 1967, p. 35. Accessed April 22, 2024. <https://www.nytimes.com/1967/04/07/archives/books-of-the-times-what-witches-where.html>.

Friedan, Betty. *The Feminine Mystique*. 1997 ed. New York, NY: W. W. Norton & Company, 1997.

Friedan, Betty. "Television and the Feminine Mystique." *It Changed My Life: Writings on the Women's Movement*, pp. 59-71. New York, NY: Harvard University Press, 1998.

Galloway, Stephen. "Sherry Lansing Book Excerpt: Screaming Matches and Tears on 'Fatal Attraction' Set (Exclusive)." *The Hollywood Reporter*, March 29, 2017. Accessed November 10, 2023. <https://www.hollywoodreporter.com/movies/movie-features/sherry-lansing-biography-fatal-attraction-book-excerpt-989565/>.

Garcia, Sandra E.. "Goop Agrees to PaY $145,000 for 'Unsubstantiated' Claims About Vaginal Eggs." *New York Times*, September 5, 2018. Accessed March 27, 2022. <https://www.nytimes.com/2018/09/05/business/goop-vaginal-egg-settlement.html>.

Gardner, R. H. "New Stage For The Classic Horror Film: William Castle Turns Gimmick To Technique In 'Rosemary's Baby.'" *The Sun*, June 30, 1968, p. 1. Columbia University *ProQuest*, accessed April 22, 2024. <http://ezproxy.cul.columbia.edu/login?url=https://www.proquest.com/historical-newspapers/new-stage-classic-horror-film/docview/539359401/se-2>.

Gehnis, Joseph. "'THE EXORCIST': A CASE OF AN AUDIENCE POSSESSED." *Newsday*, February 10, 1974. Columbia University *ProQuest*, accessed April 22, 2024. <http://ezproxy.cul.columbia.edu/login?url=https://www.proquest.com/historical-newspapers/exorcist/docview/919497730/se-2>.

Gelmis, Joseph. "'Rosemary's Baby' Is a 1st-Grade Nail-Biter." *Newsday*, June 13, 1968, p. 1. Columbia University *ProQuest*, accessed April 22, 2024. <http://ezproxy.cul.columbia.edu/login?url=https://www.proquest.com/historical-newspapers/rosemarys-baby-is-1st-grade-nail-biter/docview/922683507/se-2>.

Geringer, Dan. "FOR CHER, LIFE's BEEN A WITCH: 'EASTWICK' STAR'S HAD HER BATTLES WITH PRESS." *Philadelphia Daily News*, June 11, 1987. Columbia University *ProQuest*, accessed August 28, 2024. <https://www.proquest.com/docview/1831241013/1547767C27EB4F09PQ/19?accountid=10226>.

Gill, Benjamin. "Witches Report Their Spells Against Trump Aren't Working: 'He Has a Shield.'" *CBN*, October 28, 2024. Accessed June 23, 2024. <https://cbn.com/news/us/witches-report-their-spells-against-trump-arent-working-he-has-shield>.

Glieberman, Owen. "Practical Magic." *EW*, October 16, 1998. *Internet Archive*, accessed June 24, 2024. <https://web.archive.org/web/20120112150837/http:/www.ew.com/ew/article/0,,63751,00.html>.

"Graduates and Jobs: A Grave New World." *Time*, May 24, 1971. Accessed April 22, 2024. <https://content.time.com/time/subscriber/article/0,33009,905096-11,00.html>.

Graham, Joshua Benjamin. "Masters of the Imagination: Fundamentalist Readings of the Occult in Cartoons of the 1980s." *Satanic Panic: Pop-Cultural Paranoia in the 1980*, pp. 83-87, edited by Janisse, Kier-La & Croupe, Paul. FAB Press, 2016.

Grammary, Ann. *The Witch's Workbook*. New York, NY: Pocket Book, 1973.

Grant, Barry K. "Science fiction double feature: Ideology in the cult film." *The Cult Film Reader*, pp.76-87, edited by Mathjis, Ernest and Mendik, Xavier, 2008.

Greenberg, James. "In Hollywood, Black Is In." *New York Times*, March 4, 1990. Accessed June 22, 2024. <https://www.nytimes.com/1990/03/04/movies/in-hollywood-black-is-in.html>.

Greene, R.H. "The real Maleficent: The Surprising Human Face Behind the 'Sleeping Beauty' Villain." *Salon*, February 15, 2014. Accessed June 24, 2024. <https://www.salon.com/2014/02/15/the_real_maleficent_the_surprising_human_face_behind_the_sleeping_beauty_villain/#:~:text=A%20wider%20exploration%20of%20Disney's,pivotal%20contribution%20to%20the%20character>.

Greenspun, Roger. "CARRIE, AND SALLY AND LEATHERFACE AMONG THE FILM BUFFS." *Film Comment*, vol. 13(1) (1977), pp. 14-17, 64. Columbia University *ProQuest*, accessed April 22, 2024. <http://ezproxy.cul.columbia.edu/login?url=https://www.proquest.com/scholarly-journals/carrie-sally-leatherface-among-film-buffs/docview/210267083/se-2>.

Griffin, Nancy. "The 'Thriller' Diaries." *Variety*, June 24, 2010. Accessed November 13, 2023. <https://www.vanityfair.com/culture/2010/07/michael-jackson-thriller-201007>.

Griffith, EV. "The Sabbats of Satan." *Playboy*, July 1963.

Groer, Ann. "George Bush Celebrates Locking Up Nomination." *Orlando Sentinel*, 1988. Columbia University *ProQuest*, accessed June 22, 2024. <https://www.proquest.com/docview/277326357/42371262F6E84CD0PQ/1?accountid=10226>.

Grossman, Lev. "Feeding On Fantasy." *Time*, December 2, 2002. Accessed June 26, 2024. <https://time.com/archive/6667771/feeding-on-fantasy/>.

"God Is A Woman." *The Devonsville Terror* [DVD]. Vinegar Syndrome, 2016.

Goldberg, Michelle. "Season of the Witch." *New York Times*, November 3, 2017. Accessed June 24, 2024. <https://www.nytimes.com/2017/11/03/opinion/witches-occult-comeback.html>.

Goldberg, Reid. "The Original Script for 'Ghostbusters' Was Much More Grim." *Collider*, March 23, 2024. <Accessed June 22, 2024. https://collider.com/ghostbusters-original-script/>.

Golden, Susan Giber. "A Therapist's View of the Occult." *Her-Self*, vol. 1(5) (1972), pp. 6-7. *Archives of Sexuality and Gender. JSTOR*, accessed April 22, 2024. <https://www.jstor.org/stable/community.28038331>.

Goldstein, Jacob. "The Long Life of Yuppie Scum." *New York Times*, June 2, 2024. <https://www.nytimes.com/2024/06/02/books/review/triumph-of-the-yuppies-tom-mcgrath.html>.

Goodman, Mike. "'THE EXORCIST': FAINTING AND FLEEING: 'EXORCIST.'" *Los Angeles Times*, January 6, 1974, p. 3. Columbia University *ProQuest*, accessed June 22, 2024. <http://ezproxy.cul.columbia.edu/login?url=https://www.proquest.com/historical-newspapers/exorcist-fainting-fleeing/docview/157299450/se-2>.

Guzman, Rafer. "'The Lords of Salem.'" *Newsday*, April 9, 2013. Columbia University *ProQuest*, accessed May 15, 2024. <http://ezproxy.cul.columbia.edu/login?url=https://www.proquest.com/newspapers/lords-salem/docview/1328522596/se-2>.

Haberski, Raymond J. "Critics and the Sex Scene." *Sex Scene: Media and the Sexual Revolution*, March 2014. Accessed April 22, 2024. <https://read.dukeupress.edu/books/book/281/chapter/113489/Critics-and-the-Sex-Scene>.

Hadland, Gracie. "An interview with filmmaker Anna Biller." *Metrograph Journal*, February 2023. Accessed June 22, 2024. <https://metrograph.com/anna-biller/>.

"Halloween Horror Film Weekend" [Advertisement]. *The Daily Times*, October 27, 1983. *Newspapers.com*, accessed November 2023. <https://www.newspapers.com/article/the-daily-times/53974816/>.

Hamilton, Doug. "MOVIES REVIEW 'The Craft' ** ½." *The Atlanta Journal the Atlanta Constitution*, May 3, 1996. Columbia University *ProQuest*, accessed June 24, 2024. http://ezproxy.cul.columbia.edu/login?url=https://www.proquest.com/newspapers/movies-review-craft-1-2-starring-robin-tunney/docview/293195888/se-2.

Hanish, Carol. "Introduction." Notes from the Second Year: Women's Liberation, edited by Shulamith Firestone and Anne Koedt, New York NY: Radical Feminism, 2006.

Hanks, Henry. "Witches Casting a Spell over Hollywood." *CNN*, October 9, 2013. Accessed June 24, 2024. <https://www.cnn.com/2013/10/09/showbiz/witch-trend/index.html>.

Hanna, Kathleen. "RIOT GRRRL MANIFESTO" [Zine], 1992. *History is a Weapon*, accessed June 24, 2024. <https://www.historyisaweapon.com/defcon1/riotgrrrlmanifesto.html>.

Har. "Satanis, The Devil's Mass." *Variety*, March 11, 1970, p. 22. Columbia University *ProQuest*, accessed April 22, 2024. <http://ezproxy.cul.columbia.edu/login?url=https://www.proquest.com/magazines/pictures-satanis-devils-mass/docview/1017173756/se-2>.

Harmetz, Aljean. *The Making of The Wizard of Oz*. Chicago, IL: Independent Publishers Group, 2013.

Haskell, Molly. *From Reverence to Rape: The Treatment of Women in the Movies*, Third ed. Chicago, IL: University of Chicago Press, 2016.

Hatsis, Thomas. *The Witches' Ointment: the Secret History of Psychedelic Magic*. New York, NY: Park Street Press, 2014.

Hayden Casey, and King, Mary. "A Kind of Memo" [Pamphlet]. N.d. 1965. *Freedom Archives*, accessed June 22, 2024. <https://www.freedomarchives.org/Documents/Finder/Black%20Liberation%20Disk/Black%20Power!/SugahData/Essays/Hayden.S.pdf>.

Heffernan, Nick. "No Parents, No Church, No Authorities in Our Films: Exploitation Movies, the Youth Audience, and Roger Corman's Counterculture Trilogy." *Journal of Film and Video*, pp. 3-20, Vol. 67(2) (2015). <https://www.jstor.org/stable/10.5406/jfilmvideo.67.2.0003>.

Hefner, Hugh. "The Playboy Philosophy: Part 9." *Playboy*, August 1963.

Heriot, John and Newton Abbott. *Teaching Yourself White Magic and How to Try It Out*. ENG: David & Charles Publishing, 1973.

Hertz, Gary. "The Secret Life of Jack's Wife: Interview with Jan White." *Season of the Witch* [DVD]. Anchor Bay Films, 2005.

Hilderbrand, Lucas. *Inherent Vice: Bootleg Histories of Video and Copyright*. Durham, NC: Duke University Press, 2009.

Hirsch, Foster. "Mapping the Route." *Detours and Lost Highways: A Map of Neo-noir*. New York, NY: Limelight Editions, 1999.

Hixenbaugh, Mike and Marquez, Alexandra. "Vance to attend event with evangelist who said Harris used 'witchcraft.'" *NBC News*, September 27, 2024. <https://www.nbcnews.com/politics/2024-election/jd-vance-event-evangelist-kamala-harris-witchcraft-rcna173020>.

Hoberman, J. *The Dream Life: Movies, Media, And the Mythology Of The Sixties*. New York, NY: The New Press, 2005.

Hoberman, J. *Make My Day: Movie Culture in the Age of Reagan*. New York, NY: The New Press, 2019.

Hoberman, J. "Michael Douglas: Victim Victorious." *Village Voice*, March 7, 1995. Accessed November 15, 2023. <https://www.villagevoice.com/michael-douglas-victim-victorious/>.

Hollinger, Karen. "The Monster as Woman: Two Generations of Cat People." *The Dread of Difference: Gender and the Horror Film*, pp. 346-358, ed. Austin, TX: University of Texas Press, 2015.

Hornaday, Ann. "Angelina Jolie stars in 'maleficent,' a feminist-revisionist take on Sleeping Beauty." *Washington Post*, May 29, 2014. Accessed June 25, 2024. <https://www.washingtonpost.com/goingoutguide/movies/angelina-jolie-stars-in-maleficent-a-feminist-revisionist-take-on-sleeping-beauty/2014/05/29/86dc9ec8-e75e-11e3-afc6-a1dd9407abcf_story.html>.

Houston and Kinder. "Rosemary's Baby." *Sight and Sound*, vol. 38(1) (Winter 1968), p. 17. *ProQuest*, accessed April 22, 2024. <http://ezproxy.cul.columbia.edu/login?url=https://www.proquest.com/magazines/rosemarys-baby/docview/1305507397/se-2>.

"How Groups Voted in 1976." *Roper Center for Public Opinion Research at Cornell University*. Accessed June 22, 2024. <https://ropercenter.cornell.edu/how-groups-voted-1976>.

Howard, Alan R. "The Exorcist." *The Hollywood Reporter* vol. 229(23) (1973), pp. 3, 7. Columbia University *ProQuest*, accessed June 22, 2024. <http://ezproxy.cul.columbia.edu/login?url=https://www.proquest.com/trade-journals/exorcist/docview/2931995412/se-2>.

Hubbard, Kaia. "Trump says "whether the women like it or not, I'm going to protect them" at Wisconsin rally." *CBS News*, October 31, 2024. Accessed June 26, 2024. <https://www.cbsnews.com/news/trump-protecting-women-whether-they-like-it-or-not-wisconsin/>.

Hughes, Sarah. "American Monsters: Tabloid Media and the Satanic Panic, 1970-2000." *Journal of American Studies*, vol. 51(3) (2017). pp. 691-719. Accessed Novemer 15, 2023. <https://www.jstor.org/stable/10.2307/26803447>.

Hughes, William. "John Carpenter talks us through his favorite video games of 2022, plus scoring Halloween Ends." *AV Club*, October 11, 2022. Accessed June 24, 2024. <https://www.avclub.com/john-carpenter-video-games-interview-halloween-ends-1849641145>.

"Interview with Ulli Lommel." *The Devonsville Terror* [DVD]. Vinegar Syndrome, 2016.

"Introduction to Something Weird with Herschel Gordon Lewis." *Something Weird* [DVD]. Arrow Video, 2020.

Jacobs, Matthew, and Brucculieri, Julia. "Relax, It's Only Magic: An Oral History of The Craft." *Huffington Post*, May 20, 2016. Accessed June 24, 2024. <https://www.huffpost.com/entry/the-craft-oral-history_n_5734f7c9e4b060aa7819d362>.

Jacobsen, Annie. *Phenomena: The Secret History of the U.S. Government's Investigations into Extrasensory Perception and Psychokinesis*. Boston, MA: Little, Brown and Company, 2017.

Jagr. "Film review: The Witches Of Eastwick." *Variety*, June 10, 1987. Columbia University *ProQuest*, accessed June 22, 2024. <https://www.proquest.com/docview/1438468442/fulltext/E182D5F22B8F42C6PQ/1?accountid=10226>.

Jamieson and Gabbatt. "'You don't fit the image': Hillary Clinton's decades-long push against a sexist press." *The Guardian*, September 15, 2016. Accessed June 24, 2024. <https://www.theguardian.com/us-news/2016/sep/15/hillary-clinton-press-sexism-media-interviews>.

Jeffords, Susan. *Hard Bodies: Hollywood Masculinity in the Reagan Era*. New Brunswick, NJ: Rutgers University Press, 1994.

Jenkins, Mark. *Convergence Culture: Where Old and New Media Collide*. New York, NY: New York University Press, 2006.

Jenkins, Mark. "'The Lords of Salem' movie review." *The Washington Post*, April 19, 2013. Columbia University *ProQuest*, accessed June 22, 2024. <http://ezproxy.cul.columbia.edu/login?url=https://www.proquest.com/blogs-podcasts-websites/lords-salem-movie-review-posted-2013-04-19-16-15/docview/1330815914/se-2>.

Johnson, Kevin C. "Director likens 'Carrie' to a superhero origin story." *St. Louis Post-Dispatch*, October 7, 2013. Accessed June 25, 2024. <https://www.stltoday.com/life-entertainment/local/movies-tv/director-likens-carrie-to-a-superhero-origin-story/article_98b433ed-0468-5745-b4c9-ee27d5a291bf.html>.

Johnson, Sydney. "The San Franciscans who pioneered safe and legal abortions." *San Francisco Examiner*, October 27, 2022. Accessed April 22, 2024. <https://www.sfexaminer.com/archives/the-san-franciscans-who-pioneered-safe-and-legal-abortions/article_4aed5427-93f5-5fef-b396-24579e575c42.html>.

Jones, Claire. "WitchTok: The witchcraft videos with billions of views." *BBC*, October 31, 2022. Accessed June 23, 2024. https://www.bbc.com/news/newsbeat-63403467.

Jones, Sarah. "Why Did Trump's MSG Rally Call Kamala Harris the Antichrist?" *New York Magazine*, October 28, 2024. Accessed October 28, 2024. <https://nymag.com/intelligencer/article/david-rem-antichrist-kamala-harris-trump-madison-square-garden.html>.

Jong, Erica. "Ally McBeal and Time Magazine Can't Keep the Good Women Down." *Observer*, July 13, 1998. Accessed June 23, 2024. <https://observer.com/1998/07/ally-mcbeal-and-time-magazine-cant-keep-the-good-women-down>.

Juzwiak, Eric. "Director Luca Guadagnino on Assaulting the Senses and Indicting Patriarchy in Suspiria." *Jezebel*, October 25, 2018. Accessed June 25, 2024. <https://www.jezebel.com/director-luca-guadagnino-on-assaulting-the-senses-and-i-1829994124>.

Kael, Pauline. "The Feminine Mystique in Eighties Film." *The New Yorker*, October 11, 1987. Accessed November 15, 2024. <https://www.newyorker.com/magazine/1987/10/19/pauline-kael-fatal-attraction-review-the-feminine-mystique>.

Karlsen, Carol F. *The Devil in the Shape of a Woman: Witchcraft in Colonial New England*. New York, NY: W.W. Norton & Co, 1998.

Kehr, Dave. "FOR A GOOD TIME CALL ON THE 'WITCHES OF EASTWICK.'" *Chicago Tribune*, June 1987. Columbia University *ProQuest*, accessed June 11, 2024. <http://ezproxy.cul.columbia.edu/login?url=https://www.proquest.com/newspapers/good-time-call-on-witches-eastwick/docview/291026651/se-2?accountid=10226>.

Keller, Jessalynn and Mulvey Alora Paulsen. "Salem Witches Are Casting Spells to Defeat Trump." *US News & World Report*, October 30, 2020. Accessed June 25, 2024. <https://www.usnews.com/news/cities/articles/2020-10-30/witches-in-salem-massachusetts-are-casting-spells-to-defeat-trump>.

Kelly, Kevin. "WEEKEND: MOVIES 'THE EXORCIST' CASTS A SPELL." *Boston Globe*, January 4, 1974, p. 29. Columbia University *ProQuest*, accessed April 22, 2024. <http://ezproxy.cul.columbia.edu/login?url=https://www.proquest.com/historical-newspapers/weekend/docview/612872035/se-2>.

Kempley, Rita. "'Practical Magic,' Nearly Beguiling: [FINAL Edition]." *The Washington Post*, October 16, 1998, p. D05. Columbia University *ProQuest*, accessed June 11, 2024. <http://ezproxy.cul.columbia.edu/login?url=https://www.proquest.com/newspapers/practical-magic-nearly-beguiling/docview/408414525/se-2>.

Kennedy, Caitlin. "Monstrous Womanhood and the Unapologetic Feminism of 'midsommar.'" *Screen Queens*, June 13, 2019. Accessed June 23, 2024. <https://screenqueens.wordpress.com/2019/07/13/monstrous-womanhood-and-the-unapologetic-feminism-of-midsommar/>.

Kennedy, Cory. "Anna Biller calls out corporate feminism in Hollywood." *ONTD*, July 25, 2023. Accessed June 24, 2024. <https://ohnotheydidnt.livejournal.com/126479863.html>.

Kersh, Gerald. "The powers of darkness at work: Rosemary's Baby." *Chicago Tribune*, May 7, 1967, pp. 1-m3. Columbia University *ProQuest*, accessed April 22, 2024. <http://ezproxy.cul.columbia.edu/login?url=https://www.proquest.com/historical-newspapers/powers-darkness-at-work/docview/179206097/se-2>.

King, Stephen. *Carrie*. Mass-Market ed., New York, NY: Anchor Books. 2011.

King, Stephen. *Danse Macabre*. Gallery Books ed. New York, NY: Gallery Books, 2010.

Kinnard, Meg. "Musk's pro-Trump super PAC uses vulgarity demeaning women to describe Harris." *AP News*, October 29, 2024. Accessed October 29, 2024. <https://apnews.com/article/election-2024-trump-harris-elon-musk-vulgarity-d9bc9fabb2f9c17de54a31da7c2874c2>.

Kirkpatrick, David D. "THE 2004 CAMPAIGN: THE REPUBLICAN PLATFORM; Committee Adopts Draft; Some Grumble." *New York Times*, August 8, 2004. Accessed June 23, 2024. <https://www.nytimes.com/2004/08/27/us/the-2004-campaign-the-republican-platform-committee-adopts-draft-some-grumble.html>.

Kleno, Larry. *Kim Novak on Camera*. San Diego, CA: A.S. Barnes, 1980.

Knight, Jacob. "There's No Such Thing as An 'Elevated Horror Movie' (And Yes, 'Hereditary' Is A Horror Movie)." SlashFilm, June 8, 2018. Accessed June 22, 2024. <https://www.slashfilm.com/558818/elevated-horror/>.

Knopf, Christina M. "Zany Zombies, Grinning Ghosts, Silly Scientists, and Nasty Nazis: Comedy Horror at the Threshold of World War II." *The Laughing Dead: The Horror-Comedy Film from Bride of Frankenstein to Zombieland*, pp. 30-39, edited by Miller, Cynthia & Van Riper, Bowdoin A. Rowman & Littlefield Publishers. 2016.

Koteki, Rob. "When Beauty Is the Beast: The Carnal Pleasures of Black Sunday." *VHS Revival*, October 27, 2021. Accessed April 22, 2024. <https://vhsrevival.com/2021/10/27/when-beauty-is-the-beast-the-carnal-pleasures-of-black-sunday/>.

Krassner, Paul. "'60s live again, minus the LSD." *Los Angeles Times*, January 28, 2007. <https://www.latimes.com/archives/la-xpm-2007-jan-28-ca-yippies28-story.html>.

Kreimer, Heinrich and Sprenger, James. *Malleus Maleficarum*, New York, NY: Dover Publications Inc, 1971.

Kristeva Julia. *Powers of Horror*. New York, NY: Columbia University Press, 1982.

Kruzman, Diana. "You're not tripping: LSD is making a comeback." *9news*, July 27, 2017. Accessed June 25, 2024. <https://www.9news.com/article/news/health/youre-not-tripping-lsd-is-making-a-comeback/73-459883560>.

"Kuni Fukai Interview" *Belladonna of Sadness* [Blu-ray]. Cinelicious, 2016.

Lambe, Stacey. "'Like a Prayer' 30 Years Later: How the Controversial Music Video Barely Made It to Air." *Entertainment Weekly*, March 7, 2019. Accessed November 15, 2023. <https://www.etonline.com/like-a-prayer-30-years-later-how-the-controversial-music-video-barely-made-it-to-air-121023>.

Lanning, Kenneth. "United States, U.S. Department of Investigations, Federal Bureau of Investigation, National Center For the Analysis of Violent Crime." *Investigator's Guide to Allegations of 'Ritual' Child Abuse*, 1992. U.S. Department of Justice, Office of Justice Programs, accessed June 11, 2024. <https://www.ojp.gov/ncjrs/virtual-library/abstracts/investigators-guide-allegations-ritual-child-abuse>.

Lattman, Peter. "The Origins of Justice Stewart's 'I Know It When I See It.'" *Wall Street Journal*, September 27, 2007. Accessed February 24, 2025. <https://www.wsj.com/articles/BL-LB-4558>.

LaVey, Anton. *The Satanic Witch*. Port Townsend, WA: Feral House, 2003.

Leak, Sibyl. *The Complete Art of Witchcraft: Penetrating the Secrets of White Magic*. New York, NY: Signet, 1973.

Lear, Martha Weinman. "The Second Feminist Wave." *New York Times*, March 10, 1968. <https://timesmachine.nytimes.com/timesmachine/1968/03/10/90032407.html?pageNumber=323>.

Leiber, Fritz. *Conjure Wife*. ACE Books ed. New York, NY: ACE Books, 1977.

Leo, John. "The Revolution Is Over." *Time*, April 9, 1984. Accessed November 15, 2024. <https://content.time.com/time/subscriber/article/0,33009,1714248,00.html>.

Levin, Ira. *Rosemary's Baby*. New Dell edition, New York, NY: Dell Publishing, 1967.

Levin, Ira. "'Stuck with Satan': Ira Levin on the Origins of Rosemary's Baby." *Current*, November 5, 2012. Accessed April 22, 2024. <https://www.criterion.com/current/posts/2541-stuck-with-satan-ira-levin-on-the-origins-of-rosemarys-baby>.

Lewis, Jon. *Hollywood v. Hard Core: How the Struggle Over Censorship Created the Modern Film Industry*. New York, NY: NYU Press, 2002.

Lewis, Jon. *Road Trip to Nowhere: Hollywood Encounters the Counterculture*. Berkeley, CA: University of California Press, 2022.

Lim, Dennis. "Practical Magic." *The Village Voice*, October 27, 1998, p. 135. Columbia University *ProQuest*, accessed June 22, 2024. <http://ezproxy.cul.columbia.edu/login?url=https://www.proquest.com/newspapers/practical-magic/docview/232271878/se-2>.

Long Chu, Andrea. "Ottessa Moshfegh Is Praying for Us." *Vulture*, June 2022. Accessed June 25, 2024. <https://www.vulture.com/article/ottessa-moshfegh-lapvona-review.html>.

Longworth, Karina. "Prologue: Porn, Feminism, & the folly of NC-17." *You Must Remember This* [podcast], March 2023. Accessed March 12, 2023. < https://podcasts.apple.com/us/podcast/you-must-remember-this/id858124601?i=1000606226509>.

Longworth, Karina. "Thelma & Louise." *You Must Remember This* [podcast], April, 2023. Accessed April 14, 2023. <https://podcasts.apple.com/us/podcast/you-must-remember-this/id858124601?i=1000609421632>.

Lor. "Witches' Brew." *Variety*, January 30, 1985. Columbia University *ProQuest*, accessed April 11, 2024. <https://www.proquest.com/docview/1438433812/1E9009ED1AF243EEPQ/2?accountid=10226>.

"LSD." *Time*, vol. 81(13) (1963), p72-74.

Lucas, Tim. *Mario Bava - All the Colors of the Dark*, 2nd ed. Cincinnati, OH: Video Watchdog, 2013.

Baker, Luther G. "The Rising Furor over Sex Education." *The Family Coordinator*, vol. 18(3) (1969). pp. 210—17. *JSTOR*, accessed April 22, 2024. <https://doi.org/10.2307/581979>.

Lynn, Rick. "DID ROSEMARY's BABY REALLY TELL IT LIKE IT IS?" *Cinéaste*, vol. 2(2) (1968), p19. *JSTOR*, accessed April 22, 2024. <http://www.jstor.org/stable/43240817>.

Maas, Jennifer. "Mayfair Witches' Tops 'Interview With the Vampire' as AMC+'s Biggest Series Premiere." *Variety*, January 13, 2023. Accessed June 23, 2024. <https://variety.com/2023/tv/news/mayfair-witches-premiere-ratings-amc-plus-alexandra-daddario-1235488888/>.

Maddin, Guy. "I Married a Witch: It's Such an Ancient Pitch." *Current*, October 7, 2017. <https://www.criterion.com/current/posts/2924-i-married-a-witch-its-such-an-ancient-pitch>.

Mandavilli, Apoorva, Sanger-Katz, Margot and Hoffman, Jan. "Trump Administration Abruptly Cuts Billions From State Health Services." *New York Times*, March 26, 2025. Accessed March 27, 2025. <https://www.nytimes.com/2025/03/26/health/trump-state-health-grants-cuts.html>.

Mann, Judy. (1998). "An Unfair Assessment of Feminism." *Washington Post*, June 26, 1998. Accessed November 15, 2023. <https://www.washingtonpost.com/archive/local/1998/06/26/an-unfair-assessment-of-feminism/27821ccf-2c92-451b-8819-72ad16aa99f1/>.

Manoy, Lauren, and Apostolides, Yan. *Where to Park Your Broomstick: A Teen's Guide to Witchcraft*. New York, NY: Atria Books, 2002.

"March 5, 1970." *The San Francisco Examiner*, March 5, 1970, p. 26. Columbia University *ProQuest*, accessed June 22, 2024. < http://ezproxy.cul.columbia.edu/login?url=https://www.proquest.com/historical-newspapers/march-5-1970-page-26-56/docview/2164601592/se-2>.

Markham-Cantor, Alice. "What Trump Really Means When He Cries, 'Witch Hunt.'" *The Nation*, October 28, 2019. Accessed June 26, 2024. <https://www.thenation.com/article/archive/trump-witch-hunt/>.

Martello, Luis. "Some rambling reviews." *Other Scenes*, 1971.

Martin, Nick. "Our Summer of American Nihilism." *The New Republic*, September 4, 2020. Accessed September 4, 2020. <https://newrepublic.com/article/159202/summer-american-nihilism>.

Matthews, Jack. "Big Stars Just Can't Conjure 'magic': 'Practical Magic.'" *Los Angeles Times*, October 16, 1998. Columbia University *ProQuest*, accessed June 11, 2024. <http://ezproxy.cul.columbia.edu/login?url=https://www.proquest.com/historical-newspapers/big-stars-just-cant-conjure-magic/docview/2100808976/se-2>.

Mauch, Ally. "Ariana Grande Celebrated Her Birthday with a Midsommar - Themed Party—and Florence Pugh Approved!" *Yahoo! News*, June 27, 2020. Accessed June 23, 2024. <https://ca.news.yahoo.com/ariana-grande-celebrated-her-birthday-150020950.html#:~:text="I%20love%20uuuuuu%2C"%20Grande%20posted%20in%20response.&text=The%20"thank%20u%2C%20next",should%20I%20seek%20help%20immediately>.

Mazzei, Patricia, and Russell, Jenna. "Resist or Retreat? Democratic Voters Are Torn About Whether to Keep Fighting." *New York Times*, June 11, 2024. <https://www.nytimes.com/2024/11/06/us/democrats-election-activism.html>.

McCarty-Simas, Payton. "Acid Flashbacks: The Psychedelic Horror Film Post-1979." *Horror Studies*, Vol. 15(1) (April 2024). <https://intellectdiscover.com/content/journals/10.1386/host_00080_1>.

McCarty-Simas, Payton. "A24's Folk Horror Boom and Bust." *The Brooklyn Rail*, April 2022. <https://brooklynrail.org/2022/04/film/A24s-Folk-Horror-Boom-and-Bust>.

McCarty-Simas, Payton. "Becoming a 'Horrifying Woman': Belladonna of Sadness at Fifty." *The Brooklyn Rail*, July, 2023. <https://brooklynrail.org/2023/07/film/Eiichi-Yamamotos-Belladonna-of-Sadness>.

McCarty-Simas, Payton. "Season of the Witch: Looking Back on George Romero's Psychedelic Feminist Should-Be Classic." *Film Inquiry*, August 2, 2022. <https://www.filminquiry.com/season-of-the-witch-looking-back/>.

McCarty-Simas, Payton. "'Single White Female' at Thirty: The Legacy of the Women Stalkers of the 1990s." *Film Daze*, August 14, 2022. <https://filmdaze.net/single-white-female-at-thirty-the-legacy-of-the-women-stalkers-of-the-1990s/>.

McLellan, Dennis. "Sol Saks dies at 100; creator of 'Bewitched." *Los Angeles Times*, April 21, 2011. Accessed April 22, 2024. <https://www.latimes.com/entertainment/la-xpm-2011-apr-21-la-me-sol-saks-20110421-story.html>.

McLeod, Hugh. *The Religious Crisis of the 1960s*. Oxford, ENG: Oxford University Press, 2007.

McRobbie, Angela. "Post-Feminism and Popular Culture." *Feminist Media Studies*, 4(3) (2007), pp. 255—264. <https://doi.org/10.1080/1468077042000309937>.

McSweeney, Terence. *America in the Shadow of 9/11*, Edinburgh, Scotl.: Edinburgh University Press, 2017.

Meacham, Roy. "How Did 'The Exorcist' Escape an X Rating?" *New York Times*, February 3, 1974. Accessed April 22, 2024. <https://timesmachine.nytimes.com/timesmachine/1974/02/03/148779212.html?pageNumber=109>.

Metz, Walter. *Bewitched*. Detroit, MI: Wayne State University Press, 2007.

Michelet, Jules. *Satanism and Witchcraft*, New York, NY: Kensington Publishing Corp, 1998.

"Midsommar Is A Scathing Takedown of Masculinity." *Feminist Film Reviews*, July 5, 2019. Accessed June 23, 2024. <https://feministfilmreviews.com/2019/07/05/midsommar/>.

Miller, Cynthia and Van Riper, Bowdoin A. "Introduction." *The Laughing Dead: The Horror-Comedy Film from Bride of Frankenstein to Zombieland*, pp. xiii-xxiii, edited by Miller, Cynthia and Van Riper, Bowdoin A. Rowman & Littlefield Publishers, 2016.

Mills, Nancy. "The women's vroom." *The Guardian*, October 17, 1987. Columbia University *ProQuest*, accessed June 11, 2024. <https://www.proquest.com/docview/186765458/1547767C27EB4F09PQ/12?accountid=10226>.

Mistress Nancy. "The First Female Horror Host: A History of Vampira." *Slug Mag*, October 31, 2023. Accessed November 15, 2023. <https://www.slugmag.com/music/interviews/music-interviews/the-first-female-horror-host-a-history-of-vampira-by-ashes-fallen/>.

Morgan, Robin. *Going Too Far: The Personal Chronicle of a Feminist*, 2014 ed. New York, NY: Open Road Media, 2014.

Morrison, Toni. *Race-ing Justice, En-gendering Power: Essays on Anita Hill, Clarence Thomas, and the Construction of Social Reality*. New York, NY: Pantheon Books, 1992.

Mottram, James. "Season of the witches - Hollywood's new villains meet match in 'Hansel and Gretel.'" *South China Morning Post*, January 20, 2013. Accessed June 22, 2024. <https://www.scmp.com/lifestyle/arts-culture/article/1130966/season-witches-hollywoods-new-villains-meet-match-hansel-and>.

Mulholland, James. "How Trump Plotted to Be Ready for 'Laffin' Kamala' Harris." *The Daily Beast*, July 21, 2024. Accessed June 23, 2024. <https://www.thedailybeast.com/how-trump-plotted-to-be-ready-for-laffin-kamala-harris/>.

Munn, James. *This Is No Dream: Making Rosemary's Baby*. New York, NY: Reel Art Press. 2018.

"NBC's Obscene Masquerade." *The New York Times*, October 28, 1988. Accessed November 15, 2023. <https://www.nytimes.com/1988/10/28/opinion/topics-of-the-times-nbc-s-obscene-masquerade.html?searchResultPosition=2>.

Nelson, Rob. "The Lords of Salem." *Variety*, vol. 428(7) (2012), p. 96. Columbia University, accessed April 22, 2024. <http://ezproxy.cul.columbia.edu/login?url=https://www.proquest.com/magazines/lords-salem/docview/1095783649/se-2>.

Neumaier, J. "Carrie." *New York Daily News*, October 17, 2013. Accessed April 22, 2024. <https://web.archive.org/web/20131017184108/http:/www.nydailynews.com/entertainment/tv-movies/carrie-movie-review-article-1.1488761>.

"Night of the Eagle." *Kine Weekly*, vol. 538, (1962), p. 16. Columbia University *ProQuest*, accessed April 22, 2024. <http://ezproxy.cul.columbia.edu/login?url=https://www.proquest.com/trade-journals/night-eagle/docview/2600910255/se-2>.

"NIGHT OF THE EAGLE." *Monthly Film Bulletin*, vol. 29(336), (1962), p. 82. Columbia University *ProQuest*, accessed April 22, 2024. <http://ezproxy.cul.columbia.edu/login?url=https://www.proquest.com/magazines/night-eagle/docview/1305823165/se-2>.

Noddings, Nel. *Women and Evil*. Berkeley, CA: University of California Press, 1989.

Nordine, Michael. "'The Love Witch' Director Anna Biller: Most of the Film's Crew 'Hated What We Were Shooting' and Never Even Saw the Movie." *IndieWire*, December 7, 2017. Accessed June 24, 2024. <https://www.indiewire.com/features/general/the-love-witch-anna-biller-crew-1201904994/>.

Norma, Lee B. (1968). "Trial of Sirhan or of a Ghost?" *Chicago Tribune*, August 23, 1968, pp. 1-b10. Columbia University *ProQuest*, accessed April 22, 2024. <http://ezproxy.cul.columbia.edu/login?url=https://www.proquest.com/historical-newspapers/trial-sirhan-ghost/docview/168782731/se-2>.

Nowell, Richard. "'There's More Than One Way to Lose Your Heart': The American Film Industry, Early Teen Slasher Films, and Female Youth." *Cinema Journal* 51(1) (2011). JSTOR, accessed June 22, 2024. <https://www.jstor.org/stable/41342285>.

O'Brien, Miles. "Why psychedelic drugs are having a medical renaissance." *PBS News*, January 25, 2017. Accessed June 23, 2024. <https://www.pbs.org/newshour/show/psychedelic-drugs-medical-renaissance>.

"The Occult Revival: A Substitute Faith." *Time*, June 19, 1972. Accessed April 22, 2024. <https://content.time.com/time/subscriber/article/0,33009,877779-10,00.html>.

Oldfield, Barney. "Campus Cinema: ABC To 'R' And 'X.'" *Variety*, January 6, 1971, vol. 261(8), p. 26. Columbia University *ProQuest*, accessed April 22, 2024. <http://ezproxy.cul.columbia.edu/login?url=https://www.proquest.com/magazines/campus-cinema-abc-r-x/docview/964091305/se-2.ield>.

Satan—Official. "The Oprah Winfrey Show - Satanic Worship!" [Advertisement]. *Channel 7*, 1989. *Reddit*, accessed November 18, 2023. <https://www.reddit.com/r/pics/comments/15l0rwi/oprah_used_to_promote_satanic_panic/>.

Orr, Gillian. "Feminism: It's Not A Dirty Word." *Independent*, October 24, 2012. <https://www.independent.co.uk/news/people/news/feminism-it-s-not-a-dirty-word-8223712.html>.

Park, Ed. "Rosemary's Baby: It's Alive." *Current*, October 30, 2012. Accessed April 22, 2024. <https://www.criterion.com/current/posts/2535-rosemarys-baby-its-alive>.

Pau, Kari. "Hundreds of Witches Just Hexed Stanford Rapist Brock Turner." *Vice*, June 9, 2016. Accessed March 31, 2025. <https://www.vice.com/en/article/hundreds-witches-hex-spell-stanford-rapist-brock-turner/>.

Paul, Kari. "Why millennials are ditching religion for witchcraft and astrology." *Market Watch*, October 31, 2018. Accessed June 23, 2024. <https://www.marketwatch.com/story/why-millennials-are-ditching-religion-for-witchcraft-and-astrology-2017-10-20>.

Peterson, Cassandra. *Yours Cruelly, Elvira: Memoirs of the Mistress of the Dark*. New York, NY: Hachette Books, 2023.

Pevere, Geof. "Elvira plunges lower than her neckline." *Toronto Star*, September 30, 2018. Columbia University *ProQuest*, accessed June 22, 2024. <http://ezproxy.cul.columbia.edu/login?url=https://www.proquest.com/newspapers/elvira-plunges-lower-than-her-neckline/docview/435771444/se-2?accountid=10226>.

"Pictures: 'nice, unwashed, pot-smoking kids' will go for 'fantasia'— predicts NGT." *Variety*, November 18, 1970, pp. 261, 7. Columbia University *ProQuest*, accessed April 22, 2024. <http://ezproxy.cul.columbia.edu/login?url=https://www.proquest.com/magazines/pictures-nice-unwashed-pot-smoking-kids-will-go/docview/1014861380/se-2>.

Pierce, Scott. "The Witch Is Sinister, Smart, and Wildly Feminist." *Wired*, February 19, 2016. <https://www.wired.com/2016/02/the-witch-demonization-women/>.

Plath, Sylvia. *The Bell Jar*, Modern Classics, ed. New York, NY: Harper Perennial Modern Classics, 2005.

Pócs, Éva, Szilvia Rédey, and Michael Webb. "The Alternative World of the Witches' Sabbat." *In Between the Living and the Dead: A Perspective on Witches and Seers in the Early Modern Age*, pp. 73-105. Budapest: Central European University Press, 1999. *JSTOR*, accessed December 23, 2020. <http://www.jstor.org/stable/10.7829/j.ctt1cgf83g.8>.

Pollan, Michael. *How to Change Your Mind*. New York, NY: Penguin Press, 2018.

Poole, W. Scott. "A brief history of poisoned Halloween candy panic." *CNNHealth*, October 30, 2019. Accessed November 15, 2023. <https://www.cnn.com/2019/10/30/health/halloween-candy-panic-conversation-wellness/index.html>.

Pope Paul VI. *Humanae Vitae*. Vatican City, VC: Ignatius Press, 1968.

Powers, James. "ITALIAN 'BLACK SUNDAY' A SERIOUS HORROR STORY: VAMPIRE DRAMA IN OLD TRADITION." *The Hollywood Reporter*, vol. 164(3) (1961). Columbia University *ProQuest*, accessed April 22, 2024. <http://ezproxy.cul.columbia.edu/login?url=https://www.proquest.com/trade-journals/italian-black-sunday-serious-horror-story/docview/2338347762/se-2>.

Prasch, Thomas. "'Oy, Have You Got the Wrong Vampire': Dislocation, Comic Distancing, and Political Critique in Roman Polanski's The Fearless Vampire Killers (1967)." *The Laughing Dead: The Horror-Comedy Film from Bride of Frankenstein to Zombieland*, edited by Miller, Cynthia & Van Riper, Bowdoin A., pp. 3-25. Rowman & Littlefield Publishers, 2016.

Press, Joy. "How the First Abortion Speak-Out Revolutionized Activism." *Vanity Fair*, October 19, 2022. Accessed June 22, 2024. <https://www.vanityfair.com/news/2022/10/abortion-stories-speakout>.

"A Prevalence of Witches." *IME Magazine*. Vol. 82(26) (1963), pp. 53-53. Columbia University *ProQuest*, accessed April 22, 2024. https://web-p-ebscohost-com.ezproxy.cul.columbia.edu/ehost/detail/

detail?vid=0&sid=f706ef91-b4b8-4acf-8ceeb48074a9ffb3%40redis&bdata=JkF1dGhUeXBlPWlwJnNp dGU9ZWhvc3QtbGl2ZSZzY29wZT1zaXRl#AN=54214038&db=tma.

"Producing The Craft: An Interview with Douglas Wick." *The Craft* [Blur-ray]. Shout Factory, 2019.

"The Psyche in 3-D." *Time*, March 28, 1960, pp. 83-85. Accessed April 22, 2024. <https://time.com/archive/6622315/medicine-the-psyche-in-3-d/>.

"The Rape Corroboration Requirement: Repeal Not Reform." *The Yale Law Journal*, vol. 81, no. 7, June 1972, pp. 1365-91. *JSTOR*, accessed June 22, 2024. <https://doi.org/10.2307/795246>.

RavenWolf. *Teen Witch: Wicca for a New Generation*. Woodbury, NY: Llewellyn Publications, 1998.

Raymond, Nate. "Trump administration detains Turkish student at Tufts, revokes visa." *Reuters*, March 27, 2025. Accessed March 27, 2025. <https://www.reuters.com/world/us/tufts-says-international-student-taken-into-us-custody-visa-revoked-2025-03-26/>.

Real, Evan. "Cher Recalls the Time Jack Nicholson Called Her 'Too Old, Not Sexy.'" *The Hollywood Reporter*, August 20, 2018. Accessed November 15, 2023. <https://www.hollywoodreporter.com/news/music-news/cher-jack-nicholson-he-called-me-old-not-sexy-1135992/>.

Reed, Erin. "Anti-Trans National Risk Assessment Map: March Edition." *Erin in the Morning*, March 25, 2025. Accessed March 27, 2025. <https://www.erininthemorning.com/p/anti-trans-national-risk-assessment>.

Rehak, Hope. "The Sisters We Want to Be: The Feminist Seductions of Practical Magic." *Bright Wall/Dark Room*, Issue 64 (October 2018). Accessed June 24, 2024. <https://www.brightwalldarkroom.com/2018/10/30/feminist-seductions-practical-magic/>.

"Revisiting the Addictive Feminine Pull of Midsommar." *Unpublished Magazine*, August 24, 2020. Accessed June 25, 2024. <https://www.unpublishedzine.com/film/revisiting-the-addictive-feminine-pull-of-midsommar-2019nbsp>.

Reynolds, Nigel. "Forget the namby-pamby girly stuff, here are ripping yarns for real chaps. Rattling good tales have been sacrificed on the altar of feminism." *The Daily Telegraph*, 2003. Columbia University *ProQuest*, accessed April 22, 2024. <http://ezproxy.cul.columbia.edu/login?url=https://www.proquest.com/newspapers/forget-namby-pamby-girly-stuff-here-are-ripping/docview/317766661/se-2>.

Richardson-Andrews, Charlotte. "Witches are speaking out about big brands commodifying their craft." *Dazed*, September 14, 2018. Accessed June 22, 2024. <https://www.dazeddigital.com/life-culture/article/41355/1/witches-speak-out-brands-sephora-pinrose-commodifying-witchcraft>.

Rickler, Mordecai. "Witches' Brew." *Playboy*, July 1974.

Riva, Anna. *The Modern Witch's Spellbook*. International Imports, 1973.

"Rock Demons." In "Forum Newsfront" pp. 53-54. *Playboy*, September 1982.

Rock, Gail. "Arts & Pleasures: Flicks: 'The Mephisto Waltz.'" *Women's Wear Daily*, vol. 122(70) (1971), p. 12. Columbia University *ProQuest*, accessed April 22, 2024. <http://ezproxy.cul.columbia.edu/login?url=https://www.proquest.com/trade-journals/arts-pleasures-flicks-mephisto-waltz/docview/1523599915/se-2>.

Roeder, Eric. "Freedom Fighters." *Playboy*, August 1981, pp. 100-102. Accessed November 20, 2023. <https://www.iplayboy.com/issue/19810801>.

Roffey, Hallam. "Obscenity: Harry Potter and the Corruption of Kids." *Medium*, April 1, 2020. Accessed June 22, 2024. <https://medium.com/@hallamroffey/obscenity-harry-potter-and-the-corruption-of-kids-20a04c5ce270>.

Roose, Kevin. "What Is QAnon, the Viral Pro-Trump Conspiracy Theory?" *New York Times*, September 3, 2021. Accessed June 24, 2024. <https://www.nytimes.com/article/what-is-qanon.html>.

"'Rosemary's Baby' Buggy." *Boxoffice*, August 12, 1968. Columbia University *ProQuest*, accessed April 22, 2024. <http://ezproxy.cul.columbia.edu/login?url=https://www.proquest.com/magazines/rosemarys-baby-buggy/docview/1476012932/se-2>.

Rusnack, Stacy. "Scapegoat of a Nation: the Demonization of MTV and the Music Video." *Satanic Panic: Pop-Cultural Paranoia in the 1980*, pp. 173-201, edited by Janisse, Kier-La & Croupe, Paul. FAB Press, 2016.

Sandberg, Sheryl. *Lean In: Women, Work, and the Will to Lead*, New York, NY: Knopf Doubleday Publishing Group, 2013.

Sanderson, Mark. *Don't Look Now*. BFI Modern Classics, London, ENG: British Film Institute, 1996.

Savlov, Marc. "THE LORDS OF SALEM." *Monterey County Weekly*, April 25, 2013, p. 50. Columbia University *ProQuest*, accessed April 22, 2024. <http://ezproxy.cul.columbia.edu/login?url=https://www.proquest.com/newspapers/lords-salem/docview/1419397869/se-2>.

Schapiro, Lila. "Practical Magic Got Cursed by an Actual Witch. Is That Why It Bombed?" *Vulture*, October 26, 2017. Accessed June 22, 2024. <https://www.vulture.com/2017/10/practical-magic-griffin-dunne-witch-curse.html>.

Schettino, Allyson. "The Salem Witch Trials: The Real History Behind One of the Most Terrifying Events in Colonial History." *New-York Historical Society*, October 25, 2019. Accessed June 22, 2024. <https://www.nyhistory.org/blogs/salem-witch-trials>.

Scheuer, Philip K. "Shocker Pioneers Tell How to Make Monsters: Want to Make a Monster? Experts Tell How It's Done." *Los Angeles Times*, September 21, 1958. Columbia University *ProQuest*, accessed June 22, 2024. <http://ezproxy.cul.columbia.edu/login?url=https://www.proquest.com/historical-newspapers/shocker-pioneers-tell-how-make-monsters/docview/167287343/se-2>.

Schiff, Stacy. "Witchcraft on the Campaign Trail." *New York Times*, October 30, 2016. Accessed June 23, 2024. <https://www.nytimes.com/2016/10/31/opinion/witchcraft-on-the-campaign-trail.html>.

Schimmelpfennig, Annette. "Chaos Reigns: Women as Witches in Contemporary Film and the Tales of the Brothers Grimm." *Gender Forum*, no. 44 (2013).

Schmidtt, William E. "For Jim and Tammy Bakker, Excess Wiped Out a Rapid Climb to Success." *New York Times*, May 16, 1987. Accessed November 15, 2023. <https://timesmachine.nytimes.com/timesmachine/1987/05/16/398487.html?pageNumber=8>.

Scott, Jay. "THE WITCHES OF EASTWICK Witches of Eastwick is a baroque look at the battle of the sexes Faust meets the Feminine Mystique." *The Globe and Mail*, June 12, 1987. Columbia University *ProQuest*, accessed June 22, 2024. <http://ezproxy.cul.columbia.edu/login?url=https://www.proquest.com/newspapers/witches-eastwick-is-baroque-look-at-battle-sexes/docview/386197495/se-2?accountid=10226>.

Shabad, Rebecca. "Speaker Mike Johnson says separation of church and state is a 'misnomer.' *NBC News*, November 14, 2023. Accessed June 22, 2024. <https://www.nbcnews.com/politics/congress/speaker-mike-johnson-says-separation-church-state-misnomer-rcna125181>.

"Showmandiser: Para. Phone Stunt Set Up For 'Rosemary's Baby.'" *Boxoffice*, June 24, 1968. Columbia University *ProQuest*, accessed April 22, 2024. <http://ezproxy.cul.columbia.edu/login?url=https://www.proquest.com/magazines/showmandiser-para-phone-stunt-set-up-rosemarys/docview/1476027935/se-2>.

Simpson, Jacqueline. "Margaret Murray: Who Believed Her, and Why?" *Folklore*, vol. 105, (1994). Accessed June 22, 2024. <http://www.jstor.org/stable/1260633>.

Siddiqui, Sabrina. "Kavanaugh hearing recalls Clarence Thomas case: will history repeat itself?" *The Guardian*, September 27, 2018. Accessed March 31, 2025. <https://www.theguardian.com/us-news/2018/sep/27/brett-kavanaugh-clarence-thomas-anita-hill-hearings>.

Siskel, Gene. "Friedkin's 'The Exorcist': Brutal in its brilliance." *Chicago Tribune*, December 28, 1973, pp. 1-a1. Columbia University *ProQuest*, accessed April 22, 2024. <http://ezproxy.cul.columbia.edu/login?url=https://www.proquest.com/historical-newspapers/movie-review/docview/171028775/se-2>.

Skallas, Paul. "The Vulgar Wave." *The Lindy Newsletter*, May 15, 2023. Accessed June 23, 2024. <https://lindynewsletter.beehiiv.com/p/vulgar-wave>.

Smith, Noah. "The New 1970s." *Noahpinion*, July 4, 2023. Accessed June 23, 2024. <https://www.noahpinion.blog/p/the-new-1970s>.

Smith, Peter, and Stanley, Lisa. "Bible-quoting Alabama chief justice sparks church-state debate in embryo ruling." *PBS*, February 23, 2024. Accessed June 23, 2024. <https://www.pbs.org/newshour/nation/bible-quoting-alabama-chief-justice-sparks-church-state-debate-in-embryo-ruling#:~:text=Human%20life%2C%20Parker%20wrote%2C%20",frozen%20embryos%20were%20accidentally%20destroyed>.

Sobchack, Vivian. "Bringing It All Back Home: Family Economy and Generic Exchange." *The Dread of Difference: Gender and the Horror Film*, pp. 171-192, edited by Barry Keith Grant. Austin, TX: University of Texas Press, 2015.

Spain, Tom. "Stepmother's Wicked Irony." *The Washington Post*, October 19, 1989. Columbia University *ProQuest*, accessed June 22, 2024. <http://ezproxy.cul.columbia.edu/login?url=https://www.proquest.com/newspapers/stepmothers-wicked-irony/docview/307189672/se-2?accountid=10226>.

Spencer-Elliot, Lydia. "'Your body, my choice': Women report rise in online misogyny following Donald Trump's victory." *Independent*, November 8, 2024. Accessed June 23, 2024. <https://www.independent.co.uk/life-style/trump-misogyny-tiktok-reproductive-rights-us-election-b2643207.html>.

Sragow, Michael. "Bell, Book and Candle." *The New Yorker*, August 20, 2012. Accessed April 22, 2024. https://www.newyorker.com/goings-on-about-town/movies/bell-book-and-candle.

Stamp, Shelley. "Horror, Femininity, and Carrie's Monstrous Puberty." *Dread of Difference: Gender and the Horror Film*, pp. 329-245, ed. 2, edited by Barry Keith Grant. Austin, TX: Univ Of Texas Press, 2015.

Starhawk. *The Spiral Dance*. Twentieth Anniversary ed., San Francisco, CA: Harper San Francisco. 1999.

Stell, John. *Sickos! Psychos! Sequels! Horror Films of the 1980s*. Kirby Lithographic Press, 1998.

Stephens, Jay. *Storming Heaven: LSD and the American Dream*, New York, NY: Grove Press, 1987.

Sterle, Lisa. "The Modern Tarot Deck." *Lisa Sterle*, 2019.

Stern, Leslie, and Strachan, Hallie. "Interview with Maleva the Witch." *Her-Self* vol. 1(5) (1972). *JSTOR*, accessed April 22, 2024. <https://www.jstor.org/stable/community.28038331>.

Sterritt, David. "Why those box-office lines for 'The Exorcist'— a faddish guided tour through demonology?" *The Christian Science Monitor*, February 21, 1974, p. 1. Columbia University *ProQuest*, accessed April 22, 2024. <http://ezproxy.cul.columbia.edu/login?url=https://www.proquest.com/historical-newspapers/why-those-box-office-lines-exorcist-faddish/docview/511607888/se-2>.

Sterritt, David. "'The Witches of Eastwick' brought to screen." *The Christian Science Monitor*, June 12, 1987. Columbia University *ProQuest*, accessed June 22, 2024. <http://ezproxy.cul.columbia.edu/login?url=https://www.proquest.com/newspapers/witches-eastwick-brought-screen/docview/1034924889/se-2?accountid=10226>.

Stone, Merlin. *When God Was a Woman*. New York, NY: Houghton Mifflin Harcourt Publishing Company, 1976.

Stout, David. "Bush Backs Ban in Constitution on Gay Marriage." *New York Times*, February 24, 2004. Accessed June 22, 2024. <https://www.nytimes.com/2004/02/24/politics/bush-backs-ban-in-constitution-on-gay-marriage.html>.

Stratford, Jennifer Juniper. "Off Hollywood - Joshua John Miller." *Vice*, March 20, 2013. Accessed April 22, 2024. <https://www.vice.com/en/article/jmv37g/off-hollywood--joshua-john-miller.>

Swann, Christopher. "That's exactly what I meant to say CAMPAIGN BITES." *Financial Times*, 2004. Columbia University *ProQuest*, accessed June 22, 2024. <http://ezproxy.cul.columbia.edu/login?url=https://www.proquest.com/newspapers/thats-exactly-what-i-meant-say-campaign-bites/docview/249439267/se-2?accountid=10226>.

Taggart, Patrick. "Carrie leavens horror with humor." *The Austin American*, November 24, 1976. Columbia University *ProQuest*, accessed April 22, 2024. <http://ezproxy.cul.columbia.edu/login?url=https://www.proquest.com/historical-newspapers/carrie-leavens-horror-with-humor/docview/1671829955/se-2>.

Taubin, Amy. "The Craft." *The Village Voice*, May 14, 1996, p. 65. Columbia University *ProQuest*, accessed June 22, 2024. <http://ezproxy.cul.columbia.edu/login?url=https://www.proquest.com/newspapers/film-craft/docview/232241243/se-2>.

Taylor, Kate. "Why Angelina Jolie's Maleficent is magnificent." *Globe and Mail*, May 29, 2014. Accessed June 23, 2024. <https://www.theglobeandmail.com/arts/film/film-reviews/why-angelina-jolies-maleficent-is-magnificent/article18915980/>.

Taylor, Trudy. "Witchcraft Offers Reward of Supernatural Now." *LA Free Press*, October 26, 1973. JSTOR, accessed April 22, 2024. <https://www.jstor.org/stable/community.28040061>.

Tepperman, Jean. "Witch." *Ann Arbor Argus*, October 29, 1970. *JSTOR*, accessed April 22, 2024. <https://www.jstor.org/stable/community.28032592>.

"The Trump Administration's First Actions in 2025 Targeting Patients, Providers, and Reproductive Healthcare Access." National Women's Law Center, February 25, 2025. Accessed March 27, 2025. <https://nwlc.org/resource/the-trump-administrations-first-actions-in-2025-targeting-patients-providers-and-reproductive-health-care-access/>.

Thomas, Kevin. "'Eye of the Devil' Playing Citywide." *Los Angeles Times*, 1967. Columbia University *ProQuest*, accessed April 22, 2024. <http://ezproxy.cul.columbia.edu/login?url=https://www.proquest.com/historical-newspapers/eye-devil-playing-citywide/docview/155768961/se-2>.

Thomas, Kevin. "'Gruesome' Screening Citywide." *Los Angeles Times*, 1968, pp. 1-c7. Columbia University *ProQuest*, accessed April 22, 2024. <http://ezproxy.cul.columbia.edu/login?url=https://www.proquest.com/historical-newspapers/gruesome-screening-citywide/docview/155952343/se-2>.

Thomas, Kevin. "Pity, Terror and Wit in 'Carrie." *Los Angeles Times*, November 17, 1976, pp. 1-f23. Columbia University *ProQuest*, accessed April 22, 2024. <http://ezproxy.cul.columbia.edu/login?url=https://www.proquest.com/historical-newspapers/pity-terror-wit-carrie/docview/158181244/se-2>.

Thompson, Derek. "The Americans Who Need Chaos." *The Atlantic*, February 23, 2024. Accessed June 23, 2024. <https://www.theatlantic.com/ideas/archive/2024/02/need-for-chaos-political-science-concept/677536/>.

Thompson, Howard. "The Mephisto Waltz." *New York Times*, April 10, 1971. Accessed April 22, 2024. <https://timesmachine.nytimes.com/timesmachine/1971/04/10/81937025.html?pageNumber=10>.

Thompson, Howard. "Supernatural Thriller Is on Double Bill." *New York Times*, July 5, 1962. Accessed April 22, 2024. <https:www.nytimes.com/1962/07/05/archives/supernatural-thriller-is-on-double-bill.html>.

Thompson, Hunter, S. *Generation of Swine: Tales of Shame and Degradation in the '80's*. First Vintage Books ed., New York, NY: Random House Vintage Books, 1989.

Tinee, Mae. "Here's a Movie that's Bizarre and Beguiling." *Chicago Daily Tribune*, January 15, 1943. Columbia University *ProQuest*, accessed August 28, 2024. <http://ezproxy.cul.columbia.edu/login?url=https://www.proquest.com/historical-newspapers/heres-movie-thats-bizarre-beguiling/docview/176885868/se-2>.

Todd, Derek. "The Thing that Goes Bump in the Night." *Kine Weekly*, 1966. Columbia University *ProQuest*, accessed April 22, 2024. <http://ezproxy.cul.columbia.edu/login?url=https://www.proquest.com/trade-journals/thing-that-goes-bump-night/docview/2600942696/se-2>.

"Top 10 Most Popular TV (English)." *Netflix*, January 2024. Accessed June 24, 2024. <https://www.netflix.com/tudum/top10/most-popular/tv>.

Treichler, Paula A. "AIDS, Homophobia, and Biomedical Discourse: An Epidemic of Signification." *How to Have Theory in an Epidemic: Cultural Chronicles of AIDS*. Durham, NC: Duke University Press, 1999.

Truzzi, Marcello. "The Occult Revival as Popular Culture: Some Random Observations on the Old and the Nouveau Witch." *The Sociological Quarterly*, Vol. 13(1), (1971). *JSTOR*, accessed April 22, 2024. https://www.jstor.org/stable/4105818.

Tube. "Film Review: Black Sunday." *Variety*, vol. 221(13), (1961), p. 6. Columbia University *ProQuest*, accessed April 22, 2024. <http://ezproxy.cul.columbia.edu/login?url=https://www.proquest.com/magazines/film-review-black-sunday/docview/1032432216/se-2>.

Turk, Katherine. *The Women of NOW: How Feminists Built an Organization That Transformed America.* New York, NY: Farrar, Straus and Giroux, 2023.

Turner, Fred. *From Counterculture to Cyberculture: Stewart Brand, the Whole Earth Network, and the Rise of Digital Utopianism.* Chicago, IL: University of Chicago Press, 2006.

unkle lancifer. "Burned at the Stake (1981)." *Kindertrauma*, April 23, 2023. Accessed November 15, 2023. <https://www.kindertrauma.com/burned-at-the-stake-1981/>.

U.S. Attorney's Office, District of Massachusetts. "Press Release: Oklahoma Man Arrested for Allegedly Throwing Pipe Bomb at Satanic Temple in Salem, Mass." *US Department of Justice*, April 17, 2024. Accessed June 23, 2024. <https://www.justice.gov/usao-ma/pr/oklahoma-man-arrested-allegedly-throwing-pipe-bomb-satanic-temple-salem-mass>.

"Using Technology to Address Gender Bias in Film." *Google*, 24 Feb. 2017. Accessed June 22, 2024. <https://about.google/main/gender-equality-films/>.

Vagianos, Alanna. "Trump Makes Moves Toward Defunding Planned Parenthood." *Huffington Post*, March 26, 2025. Accessed March 27, 2025. <https://www.huffpost.com/entry/trump-makes-moves-toward-defunding-planned-parenthood_n_67e45fc3e4b052ce9096cd92>.

Valerius, Karyn. "'Rosemary's Baby,' Gothic Pregnancy, and Fetal Subjects." *College Literature*, vol. 32(3), 2005, pp. 116-35. *JSTOR*, accessed April 22, 2024. <http://www.jstor.org/stable/25115290>.

VanArendonk, Kathryn. "Why the Witch is the Pop-Culture Heroine We Need Right Now." *Vulture*, October 25, 2017. Accessed June 23, 2024. <https://www.vulture.com/2017/10/why-the-witch-is-the-pop-culture-heroine-we-need-right-now.html>.

Variety Staff. "Anton Szandor LaVey." *Variety*, November 19, 1997. Accessed April 22, 2024. <https://variety.com/1997/scene/people-news/anton-szandor-lavey-1116674361/>.

Yohalem, John Brightshadow. "An Interview with Pat Devlin, Consultant for 'The Craft.'" *Castle Between the Worlds*, March 1998. Accessed June 22, 2024. <http://wychwoodacastlebetweentheworlds.com/interviewWithPatDevin.htm>.

Young, Charles, M. "Skank or Die." *Playboy*, May 1984, pp. 190-196.

Walker, Martin. "Barbara Bush Stands By Her Man." *The Guardian*, 1992. Columbia University *ProQuest*, accessed June 22, 2024. <http://ezproxy.cul.columbia.edu/login?url=https://www.proquest.com/historical-newspapers/barbara-bush-stands-her-man/docview/187289994/se-2?accountid=10226>.

Walker, Rebecca. "Becoming the 3rd Wave." *Miss Magazine* reprint, vol. 12(2) (2002), pp 86-7.

Wang, Amy. "Trump vows to be 'side by side' with group that wants abortion 'eradicated.'" *Washington Post*, June 10, 2024. Accessed June 10, 2024. <https://www.washingtonpost.com/politics/2024/06/10/trump-speech-danbury-institute-abortion/>.

Warnke, Mike. *The Satan-Seller*, Logos International, 1972.

Watercutter, Angela. "Carrie Remake Shows Women in Horror Are More Than Pretty Victims." *Wired*, October 22, 2013. Accessed June 23, 2024. https://www.wired.com/2013/10/carrie-women-horror-movies/.

Watson, Beccah. "Where Wings Take Dream." *Harvard Crimson*, November 14, 2003. Accessed June 24, 2024. https://www.thecrimson.com/article/2003/11/14/where-wings-take-dream-on-a/.

Weaver, Tom. "Herbert L. Strock." *Return of the B Science Fiction and Horror Heroes: The Mutant Melding of Two Volumes of Classic Interviews.* 329-30. New York, NY: Mcfarland Publishing, 1999.

"Weirdsville." *Something Weird* [DVD]. Arrow Video, 2020.

Weldon, Michael. "Burn, Witch, Burn." *The Psychotronic Encyclopedia of Film*, New York, NY: Ballantin, 1983.

Weleff, Jeremy, Anand, Akhil, Dewey, Elizabeth N., and Barnett, Brian S. "LSD use in the United States: Examining user demographics and their evolution from 2015—2019." *Journal of*

Psychedelic Studies (published online ahead of print 2024). Accessed June 20, 2024. <https://doi.org/10.1556/2054.2024.00309>.

West, Alexandra. *The 1990s Teen Horror Cycle: Final Girls and a New Hollywood Formula*. New York, NY: McFarland & Company, 2018.

West, Lindy. "Yes This Is a Witch Hunt. I'm a Witch and I'm Hunting You." *New York Times*, October 17, 2017. Accessed June 22, 2024. <https://www.nytimes.com/2017/10/17/opinion/columnists/weinstein-harassment-witchunt.html>.

Westbrook, Bruce. (1989). "'Teen Witch' casts innocent spell." *Houston Chronicle*, April 26, 1989. Columbia University *ProQuest*, accessed April 22, 2024. <http://ezproxy.cul.columbia.edu/login?url=https://www.proquest.com/newspapers/teen-witch-casts-innocent-spell/docview/295516386/se-2?accountid=10226>.

Weston, Hillary. "Anna Biller's Pleasure Principles." *Current*, May 29, 2019. Accessed June 25, 2024. <https://www.criterion.com/current/posts/6400-anna-billers-pleasure-principles>.

Whalen, Andrew. "'Hereditary' Director Ari Aster Describes Disturbing Occult Research and His Horror Movie's Original Pitch." *Thrillist*, June 8, 2018. Accessed June 22, 2024. <https://www.newsweek.com/hereditary-director-ari-aster-interview-horror-movie-occult-967869>.

Wickman, Forrest. "All The Witch's Most WTF Moments, Explained: A Spoiler-Filled Interview With the Director." *Slate*, February 23, 2016. Accessed June 23, 2024. <https://slate.com/culture/2016/02/the-witch-director-robert-eggers-on-the-real-history-behind-the-movies-most-wtf-scenes.html>.

Williams, Tony. "Jack's Wife." *The Cinema of George A. Romero: Knight of the Living Dead*, online ed. New York, NY: Columbia Scholarship Online, 2015. Accessed August 28, 2023. <https://doi.org/10.7312/columbia/9780231173551.001.0001>.

Williams, Tony. "Trying to Survive on the Darker Side: 1980s Family Horror." *The Dread of Difference: Gender and the Horror Film*, pp. 192-209, edited by Grant, Barry Keith. Austin, TX: University of Texas Press, 2015.

Williams, Zoe. "Feminazi: the go-to term for trolls out to silence women." *The Guardian*, September 15, 2015. <https://www.theguardian.com/world/2015/sep/15/feminazi-go-to-term-for-trolls-out-to-silence-women-charlotte-proudman>.

Williamson, Bruce. "Sex in Cinema." *Playboy*, November 1987, pp. 140-146.

Williamson, Bruce. "Witches of Eastwick." *Playboy*, September 1987, p. 25.

Willis, Ellen. "Dept. of Public Health Hearing." *The New Yorker*, February 22, 1969. Accessed April 22, 2024. <https://www.newyorker.com/magazine/1969/02/22/hearing>.

Wilmington, Michael. "Nothing bewitching about 'The Craft's' tale of student sorcerers." *Chicago Tribune*, May 3, 1996. Columbia University *ProQuest*, accessed April 22, 2024. <http://ezproxy.cul.columbia.edu/login?url=https://www.proquest.com/historical-newspapers/nothing-bewitching-about-crafts-tale-student/docview/2195044202/se-2>.

Wilson, Cintra. "Cracking Code Pink." *Salon*, July 17, 2008. Accessed June 24, 2024. <https://www.salon.com/2008/07/17/code_pink/>.

W.I.T.C.H. "W.I.T.C.H. Manifesto." *Ann Arbor Argus*, November 12, 1970. *JSTOR*, accessed November 12, 2023. <https://www.jstor.org/stable/community.28032592>.

"W.I.T.C.H. Chicago Coven 2015-17." *Witch Chicago*, 2017. Accessed April 22, 2024. <https://witchchicago.tumblr.com>.

"Witches' Curse." "Special witch edition." *The Spectator*, July 29, 1969. Accessed April 22, 2024. <https://www.jstor.org/stable/community.28045127>.

Wolfe, Tom. *The Electric Kool-Aid Acid Test*. New York, NY: Picador. 1968.

Wolfe, Tom. "The 'Me' Decade and the Third Great Awakening." *New York Magazine*, August 23, 1976. Accessed April 22, 2024. <https://nymag.com/article/tom-wolfe-me-decade-third-great-awakening.html>.

Wolfson, Sam. "Cursed: witches are planning a public hexing of Brett Kavanaugh." *The Guardian*, October 16, 2018. Accessed June 23, 2024. <https://www.theguardian.com/us-news/2018/oct/15/witches-public-hexing-brett-kavanaugh>.

Wood, Robin. "American Nightmare: Hollywood in the 70s." *Hollywood from Vietnam to Reagan... and Beyond*, A Revised and Expanded Edition of the Classic Text. New York, NY: Columbia University Press, 2003.

Wurtzel, Elizabeth. *Bitch: In Praise of Difficult Women*, Anchor Books ed. New York, NY: Anchor Books, 1999.

wuscifi2014. "Welcome to the (Feminist?) Witch Hunt—Hansel & Gretel: Witch Hunters (2013)." *Time Lords, Super Heroes, and Brave New Worlds*, November 21, 2014. Accessed June 23, 2024. <https://tlshbnw.wordpress.com/2014/11/21/welcome-to-the-feminist-witch-hunt-hansel-gretel-witch-hunters-2013/>.

"WWDeadline." *Women's Wear Daily*, vol. 117(75) (1968), p. 20. Columbia University *ProQuest*, accessed April 22, 2024. Accessed April 22, 2024. <http://ezproxy.cul.columbia.edu/login?url=https://www.proquest.com/trade-journals/wwdeadline/docview/1565410036/se-2>.

Zuckerman, Esther. "The Real Places, People, and Art That Inspired the Horrifying Village in 'Midsommar.'" *Thrillist*, July 12, 2019. Accessed June 23, 2024. <https://www.thrillist.com/entertainment/nation/midsommar-is-harga-real>.

"10 Celebrities Who Say They Aren't Feminists." *Huffington Post*, December 17, 2013. Accessed June 24, 2024. <https://www.huffpost.com/entry/feminist-celebrities_n_4460416>.

"THE 2004 POLITICAL LANDSCAPE - Part 8: Religion in American Life." *Pew Research Center*, November 5, 2003. Accessed June 23, 2024. <https://www.pewresearch.org/politics/2003/11/05/part-8-religion-in-american-life/>.

Film/Mediography

The Age of Curiosity. (1963). Gerald Weiler. Vavin Inc.
A Nightmare on Elm Street. (1984). Directed by Wes Craven. New Line Cinema.
A Star is Born. (1976). Directed by Frank Pierson. Warner Bros.
A Woman Under the Infuence. (1974). Directed by John Cassavetes. Faces Distribution.
Ain't Them Bodies Saints. (2013). Directed by David Lowery. IFC Films.
Alice Doesn't Live Here Anymore. (1974). Directed by Martin Scorsese. Warner Bros.
Alice Through the Looking Glass. (2016). Direcrted by James Bobin. Walt Disney Studios Motion Pictures.
All Eyes on Sharon Tate. (1966). MGM.
All of Me. (1984). Dircted by Carl Reiner. Universal Pictures.
Amazing Colossal Man, The. (1957). Directed by Bert I. Gordon. American International Pictures.
American Horror Story: Coven. (2013-14). Created by Ryan Murphy and Brad Falchu. FX.
Amityville Horror, The. (1979). Directed by Stuart Rosenberg. American International Pictures.
Amityville II: The Possession. (1982). Directed by Damiano Damiani. Orion Pictures.
Apartment 7A. (2024). Directed by Natalie Erika James. Paramount Pictures.
Astounding She-Monster, The. (1958). Directed by Ronnie Ashcroft. American International Pictures.
Attack of the Crab Monsters. (1957). Directed by Roger Corman. Allied Artists.
Babadook, The. (2014). Directed by Jennifer Kent. Umbrella Entertainment.
Back to the Future. (1985). Directed by Robert Zemeckis. Universal Pictures.
Barbie. (2023). Directed by Greta Gerwig. Warner Bros.
Basic Instinct. (1992). Directed by Paul Verhoeven. TriStar Pictures.
Beautiful Creatures. (2013). Directed by Richard LaGravenese. Warner Bros.
Belladonna of Sadness. (1973). Directed by Eiichi Yamamoto. Nippon Herald Films.
Bell, Book and Candle. (1958). Directed by Richard Quine. Columbia Pictures.
Beware! The Blob. (1972). Directed by Harry Hagman. Jack H. Harris Enterprises, Inc..
Bewitched. (1964-1972). ABC.
Beyond the Valley of the Dolls. (1970). Directed by Russ Meyer. 20th Century Studios.
Big Lebowski, The. (1998). Directed by Joel and Ethan Coen. PolyGram.
Black Christmas (1974). Directed by Bob Clark. Warner Bros.
Black Christmas. (2019). Directed by Sophia Takal. Blumhouse Productions.
Black Sunday. (1960). Directed by Mario Bava. AIP.
Blair Witch Project, The. (1999). Directed by Eduardo Sánchez and Daniel Myrick. Summit Entertainment.
Bliss. (2019). Directed by Joe Begos. MPI Media Group.
Blood on Satan's Claw. (1971). Directed by Piers Haggard. Tigon Pictures.
Blow-Up. (1966). Directed by Michelangelo Antonioni. Metro-Goldwyn-Mayer.
Blue Velvet. (1986). Directed by David Lynch. De Laurentiis Entertainment Group.
Body Heat. (1981). Directed by Lawrence Kasdan. Warner Bros.
Bonnie and Clyde. (1967). Directed by Arthur Penn. Warner Bros.-Seven arts.
Boy Friend, The. Directed by Ken Russell. Metro-Goldwyn-Mayer.
Brady Bunch Movie, The. (1995). Directed by Betty Thomas. Paramount Pictures.
Buffy the Vampire Slayer. (1997-2003). Created by Joss Whedon. The WB.
Cage aux Folles, La. (1978). Directed by Edouard Molinaro. United Artists.
Carrie. (1976). Directed by Brian De Palma. Metro-Goldwyn-Mayer.
Carrie. (2013). Directed by Kimberley Pierce. Sony Pictures.
"Case of the Meddling Medium, The." (1961). *Perry Mason.* October 21. Directed by Arthur Marks. CBS.
Cat Girl. (1957). Directed by Alfred Shaughnessy. Anglo Amalgamated Film Distributers.
Cat People. (1942). Directed by Jaques Tourneur. RKO Radio Pictures.
Cat People.(1982). Directed by Paul Schrader. Universal Pictures.
Cat Women of the Moon. Directed by Arthur Hilton. Astor Pictures.
Charmed. (1998-2006). Created by Constance M. Burge. The WB.
Chinatown. (1974). Directed by Roman Polanski. Paramount Pictures.
Cisco Pike. (1972). Directed by Bil L. Norton. Columbia Pictures.
Cleopatra. (1963). Directed by Joseph L. Mankiewicz. 20th Century Studios.
Climax. (2018). Directed by Gaspar Noé. Wild Bunch.
Close Encounters of the Third Kind. (1977). Directed by Steven Spielberg. Columbia Pictures.
Clueless. (1995). Directed by Amy Heckerling. Paramount Pictures.
Craft, The. (1996). Directed by Andrew Fleming. Columbia Pictures.
Crawling Hand, The. (1963). Directed by Herbert L. Strock. Donald J. Hanson Enterprises.

Color Out of Space. (2019). Directed by Richard Stanley. SpectreVision.
Coming, The. (1981). Directed by Bert I. Gordon. International Film Market.
Commando. (1985). Directed by Mark L. Lester. 20th Century Fox.
Conjuring: The Devil Made Me Do It, The. (2021). Directed by Michael Chaves. Blumhouse Productions.
Damien: Omen II. (1978). Directed by Don Taylor. 20th Century Studios.
Daughters of Satan. (1972). Directed by Hollingsworth Morse. United Artists.
Deadly Eyes. (1982). Directed by Robert Clouse. Warner Bros.
Deep Throat. (1972). Directed by Jerry Gerard. Bryanston Distributing Company.
Devil and Father Amorth, The. (2017). Directed by William Friedkin. The Orchard.
Devil's Wedding Night, The. (1973). Directed by Luigi Batzella and Joe D'Amato. Variety Distribtion.
"Devil Worship: Exposing Satan's Underground" *The Geraldo Rivera Show*. (1988). Investigative News Group, October 22.
Devil Worship: The Rise of Satanism. (1989). Directed by Patrick Matrisciana & Caryl Matrisciana. Jeremiah Films.
"Devil Worshippers, The" (1985). *20/20*. ABC News Productions.
Devils, The. (1971). Directed by Ken Russell. Warner Bros.
Devil's Bath, The. (2024). Directed by Veronika Franz and Severin Fiala. Filmladen.
Devonsville Terror, The. (1983). Directed by Ulli Lommel. Embassy Pictures.
Die Hard. (1988). Directed by John McTiernan. 20th Century Fox.
Die Hard with a Vengeance. (1995). Directed by John McTiernan. 20th Century Fox.
Dirty Harry. (1971). Directed by Don Siegal. Warner Bros.
Disappearance of Shere Hite, The. (2023). Directed by Nicole Newnham. IFC Films.
Do You Know the Muffin Man? (1989) Directed by Gilbert Cates. CBS.
Don't Look Now. (1973). Directed by Nicholas Roeg. British Lion Films.
Dracula. (1931). Directed by Tod Browning. Universal Pictures.
Easy Rider. (1969). Directed by Dennis Hopper. Pando Company Inc. and Raybert Productions.
Elvira, Mistress of the Dark. (1988). Directed by James Signorelli. New World Pictures.
Emmanuelle. (1974). Directed by Just Jaeckin. Columbia Pictures.
Empire of the Ants. (1977). Directed by Bert I. Gordon. American International Pictures.
Epic Movie. (2007). Directed by Jason Friedberg and Aaron Seltzer. 20th Century Fox.
E.T.. (1982). Directed by Stephen Speilberg. Universal Pictures.
Eve's Bayou. (1996). Directed by Casi Lemons. Trimark Pictures.
Evil Dead. (2013). Directed by Fede Álvarez. TriStar Pictures.
Exorcist, The. (1973). Directed by William Friedkin. Warner Bros.
Exorcist II: The Heretic. (1977). Directed by John Boorman. Warner Bros.
Eye of the Devil. (1966). Directed by J. Lee Thompson. MGM.
Fantasia. (1940). Directed by Ben Sharpsteen, James Algar, Bill Roberts, David D. Hand, Wilfred Jackson, Paul Satterfield, Hamilton Luske, Jim Hadley, Ford Beebe, T. Hee, and Norman Ferguson.
Fatal Attraction. (1987). Directed by Adrian Lyne. Paramount Pictures.
Fear Street Part One: 1994. (2021). Directed by Leigh Janaik. Netflix.
Fear Street Part Two: 1978. (2021). Directed by Leigh Janaik. Netflix.
Fear Street Part Three: 1666. (2021). Directed by Leigh Janaik. Netflix.
Fearless Vampire Killers, The. (1967). Directed by Roman Polanski. Metro-Goldwyn-Mayer.
Fifty Shades of Grey. (2015). Directed by Sam Taylor-Johnson. Universal Pictures.
First Blood. (1982). Directed by Ted Kotcheff. Orion Pictures.
First Omen, The. (2024). Directed by Arkasha Stevenson. 20th Century Studios.
Flatliners. (1990). Directed by Joel Schumacher. Columbia Pictures.
Friday the 13th. (1980). Directed by Sean S. Cunningham. Paramount Pictures.
Friday the 13th. (2009). Directed by Marcus Nispel. New Line Cinema.
Friday the 13th Part II (1981). Directed by Steve Miner. Paramount Pictures.
Ghostbusters. (1984). Directed by Ivan Reitman. Columbia Pictures.
God is a Bullet. (2023). Directed by Nick Cassavetes. WayWard Entertainment.
Green Knight, The. (2021). Directed by David Lowery. A24.
Gretel & Hansel. (2002). Directed by Oz Perkins. Orion Pictures.
Graduate, The. (1967). Directed by Mike Nichols. United Artists.
Gruesome Twosome, The. (1967). Directed by Herschell Gordon Lewis. Hur-Lew Productions.
Hail Satan? (2019). Directed by Penny Lane. Magnolia Pictures.
Halloween. (1978). Directed by John Carpenter. Compass International Pictures.
Hansel and Gretel: Witch Hunters. (2013). Tommy Wirkola. Paramount Pictures.
Harry Potter and the Chamber of Secrets. (2002). Directed by Chris Columbua. Warner Bros.
Harry Potter and the Deathly Hallows: Part 1. (2010). Directed by David Yates. Warner Bros.
Harry Potter and the Deathly Hallows: Part 2. (2011). Directed by David Yates. Warner Bros.

Harry Potter and the Goblet of Fire. (2005). Directed by Mike Newell. Warner Bros.
Harry Potter and the Half-Blood Prince. (2009). Directed by David Yates. Warner Bros.
Harry Potter and the Order of the Phoenix. (2007). Directed by David Yates.
Harry Potter and the Prisoner of Azkaban. (2004). Directed by Alfonso Cuarón. Warner Bros.
Harry Potter and the Philosopher's Stone. (2001). Directed by Chris Columbus. Warner Bros.
Häxan. (1922). Directed by Benjamin Christensen. AB Svensk Filmindustri.
"Healing Trip, The" (2020). *The Goop Lab*, 1(1). Netflix.
Head. (1968). Directed by Rob Rafelson. Columbia Pictures.
Heaven's Gate. (1980). Directed by Michael Cimino. United Artists.
Hereditary. (2018). Directed by Ari Aster. A24.
Hocus Pocus. (1993). Directed by Kenny Ortega. Buena Vista Pictures Distribution.
Hocus Pocus 2. (2022). Directed by Anne Fletcher. Disney+.
Hot Chick, The. (2002). Directed by Tom Brady. Touchstone Pictures.
Hostel. (2005). Directed by Eli Roth. Sony Pictures Releasing.
House of Usher, The. (1960). Directed by Roger Corman. American International Pictures.
Hunger Games, The. (2012). Directed by Gary Ross. Lionsgate.
I Know What You Did Last Summer. (1997). Directed by Jim Gillespie. Columbia Pictures.
I Like It Like That. (1994). Directed by Darnell Martin. Columbia Pictures.
I Love Lucy. (1951-1957). CBS.
I Married a Witch. (1942). Directed by René Clair. Paramount Pictures.
I Saw the TV Glow. (2024). Directed by Jane Schoenbrun. A24.
I Spit on Your Grave. (1978). Directed by Steven R. Munroe. Anchor Bay Entertainment.
I Walked with a Zombie. (1943). Directed by Jaques Tourneur. RKO Radio Pictures.
I Was a Teenage Frankenstein. (1957). Directed by Herbert L. Strock. American International Pictures.
Immaculate. (2024). Directed by Michael Mohan. Neon.
Indictment: The McMartin Trial.(1995). Directed by Mick Jackson. HBO.
Jacob's Ladder. (1990). Directed by Adrian Lyne. TriStar Pictures.
Jennifer's Body. (2009). Directed by Karyn Kusama. 20th Century Studios.
Kiss Me Deadly. (1955). Directed by Robert Aldrich. United Artists.
Lamb. (2021). Directed by Valdimar Jóhannsson. A24.
Last Tango in Paris. (1972). Directed by Bernardo Bertolucci. United Artists.
Late Night with the Devil. (2024). Directed by Cameron Cairnes and Colin Cairnes. Shudder.
Lighthouse, The. (2019). Directed by Robert Eggers. A24.
Longlegs. (2024). Directed by Osgood Perkins. Neon.
Look What's Happened to Rosemary's Baby. (1976). Directed by Sam O'steen. ABC.
Lord of the Rings, The: The Fellowship of the Ring. (2001). Directed by Peter Jackson. New Line Cinema.
Lords of Salem, The. (2012). Directed by Rob Zombie. 20th Century Studios.
Love Witch, The. (2016). Directed by Anna Biller. Oscilloscope Laboratories.
Macbeth. (2021). Directed by Joel Coen. A24.
Maleficent. (2014). Directed by Robert Stromberg. Walt Disney Pictures.
Mandy. (2018). Directed by Cosmos Panatos. SpectreVision.
Manoir du Diable, Le. (1896). Directed by George Méliès.
Mark of the Devil. (1970). Directed by Michael Armstrong. Hallmark Releasing.
Mark of the Witch. (1970). Directed by Tom Moore. Lone Star Productions.
Masque of the Red Death, The. (1964). Directed by Roger Corman. American International Pictures.
MaXXXine. (2024). Directed by Ti West. A24.
Mayfair Witches, The. (2023-). Created by Michelle Ashford and Esta Spalding. AMC.
Mephisto Waltz, The. (1971). Directed by Paul Wendkos. 20th Century Studios.
Mia and Roman. (1968). Directed by Shahrokh Hatami. Paramount Pictures.
Midsommar. (2019). Directed by Ari Aster. A24.
"MIDSOMMAR | Official Teaser Trailer HD | A24." (2019). [Youtube video]. Posted by "A24."
Miracle Worker, The. (1962). Directed by Arthur Penn. United Artists.
Mutiny on the Bounty. (1962). Directed by Lewis Milestone, Carol Reed, and George Seaton. Metro-Goldwyn-Mayer.
Near Dark. (1987). Directed by Kathryn Bigelow. De Laurentiis Entertainment Group.
Night of the Eagle. (1962). Directed by Paul Frees. AIP.
Night of the Living Dead. (1968). George A. Romero. Continental Distributing.
Omen, The. (1976). Directed by Richard Donner. 20th Century-Fox.
Originals, The. (2013-2018). The CW.
Oz the Great and Powerful. (2013). Directed by Sam Raimi. Walt Disney Studios.
Pawnbroker, The. (1964). Directed by Sidney Lumet. American International Pictures.
Pearl. (2022). Directed by Ti West. A24.

Peyton Place. (1964-1969). ABC.
Pit and the Pendulum, The. (1961). Directed by Roger Corman. American International Pictures.
Poltergeist. (1982). Directed by Tobe Hooper. Metro-Goldwyn-Mayer.
Possession. (1981). Directed by Adrzej Zulawski. Gaumont.
Power of the Witch, The: Real or Imaginary?. (1971). BBC.
Practical Magic. (1998). Directed by Griffin Dunne. Warner Bros.
Predator. (1987). Directed by John McTiernan. 20th Century Fox.
Premature Burial, The. (1962). Directed by Roger Corman. American International Pictures.
Pretty Woman. (1990). Directed by Garry Marshall. Buena Vista Pictures Distribution.
Psycho. (1960). Directed by Alfred Hitchcock. Paramount Pictures.
Pulp Fiction. (1994). Directed by Quentin Tarantino. Miramax Films.
Rage, The: Carrie 2. (1999). Katt Shea. Metro-Goldwyn-Mayer.
Reality Bites. (1994). Directed by Ben Stiller. Universal Pictures.
Rebecca. (1940). Directed by Alfred Hitchcock. United Artists.
Red Riding Hood. (2011). Directed by Catherine Hardwicke. Warner Bros.
Red Shoe Diaries, The. (1992-1997). Showtime.
Ricky 6. (2000). Directed by Peter Filardi. Image Group Entertainment.
Rocky. (1976). Directed by John G. Avildsen. United Artists.
Rocky Horror Picture Show, The. (1975). Directed by Jim Sharman. 20th Century Studios.
Rollover. (1981). Directed by Alan J. Pakula. Warner Bros.
"Roman Polanski on Rosemary's Baby" (2012). *Vice.*
Rosemary's Baby. (1968). Directed by Roman Polanski. Paramount Pictures.
Rosemary's Baby. (2014). Directed by Agnieszka Holland. NBC.
Sabrina the Teenage Witch. (1996-2003). Created by Nell Scovell. ABC.
Satan Wants You. (2023). Directed by Steve Adams & Sean Horlor. Nootka St. Film Company.
"Satanic Worship!" *The Oprah Winfrey Show.* (1989). Harpo Productions, May 1.
Satanis: The Devil's Mass. (1971). Directed by Ray Laurent. Sherpix.
Saw. (2004). Directed by James Wan. Lionsgate Films.
Scooby Doo and the Witch's Ghost. (1999). Directed by Jim Stenstrum. Warner Bros.
Scream. (1996). Directed by Wes Craven. Dimension Films.
Scream. (2022). Directed by Matt Bettinelli-Olpin and Tyler Gillett. Paramount Pictures.
Season of the Witch. (1973). Directed by George Romero. Anchor Bay Entertainment.
Seventh Victim, The. (1943). Direcred by Val Lewton. RKO Pictures.
Sex and the Single Girl. (1964). Richard Quine. Warner Bros. Pictures.
Shaft. (1971). Directed by Gordon Parks. Metro-Goldwyn-Mayer.
Silence of the Lambs, The. (1991). Directed by Jonathan Demme. Orion Pictures.
Smile. (2022). Directed by Parker Finn. Paramount Pictures.
Snow White and the Huntsman. (2012). Directed by Rupert Sanders. Universal Pictures.
Something Weird. (1967). Herschell Gordon Lewis. Hur-Lew Productions.
Son of Dracula. (1974). Directed by Freddie Francis. Cinemation Industries.
Stepford Wives, The. (1975). Directed by Bryan Forbes. Columbia Pictures.
Substance, The. (2024). Directed by Coralie Fargeat. Mubi.
Sugar Hill. (1974). Directed by Paul Maslansky. AIP.
Suspiria. (1977). Directed by Dario Argento. Produzioni Atlas Consorziate.
Suspiria. (2018). Directed by Luca Guadagnino. Amazon Studios.
Stranger Things. (2016-2025). Created by the Duffer Brothers. Netflix.
Sweet Sweetback's Baadasssss Song. (1971). Directed by Melvin Van Peebles. Cinemation Industries.
Talk to Me. (2023). Directed by Danny Philippou and Michael Philippou. A24.
Tarot. (2024). Directed by Anna Halberg and Spenser Cohen. Sony Pictures Releasing.
Teen Witch. (1989). Directed by Dorian Walker. Metro-Goldwyn-Mayer.
Texas Chainsaw Massacre, The. (1974). Directed by Tobe Hooper. Vortex.
Thelma & Louise. (1991). Directed by Ridley Scott. MGM.
This Place Rules! (2022). Directed by Andrew Callaghan. A24.
Tootsie. (1982). Directed by Sydney Pollack. Columbia Pictures.
Trip, The. (1967). Directed by Roger Corman. American International Pictures.
Twilight. (2008). Directed by Catherine Hardwicke. Summit Entertainment.
"Under the Coven: The Witches of Bushwick" (2015). *Girl Gangs.* Directed by Pippa Bianco. Vice.
Up in Smoke. (1978). Directed by Tommy Chong and Lou Adler. Paramount Pictures.
Wednesday. (2022-). Created by Alfred Gough and Miles Millar. Netflix.
Valley of the Dolls. (1967). Mark Robson. 20th Century Studios.
Vampire Diaries, The. (2009-2017). The CW.
Viva. (2007). Directed by Anna Biller. Cult Epics.

Walking Dead, The. (2010-2022). AMC.
Wasp Woman, The. (1959). Directed by Roger Corman. Allied Artists.
When Harry Met Sally. (1989). Directed by Rob Reiner. Columbia Pictures.
Who's Afraid of Virginia Woolf? (1966). Directed by Mike Nichols. Warner Bros.
Wicked: Part One. (2024). Directed by Jon M. Chu. Universal Pictures.
Wicked Stepmother. (1989). Directed by Larry Cohen. Metro-Goldwyn-Mayer.
Wicker Man, The. (1973). Directed by Robin Hardy. British Lion Films.
Wicker Man, The. (2006). Directed by Neil Labute. Alcon Entertainment.
Witch, The. (2015). Directed by Robert Eggers. A24.
Witchboard. (1986). Directed by Kevin Tenney. Paragon Arts Entertainment.
Witchcraft '70. (1970). Directed by Luigi Scattini. Caravel.
Witchhammer. (1970). Directed by Otakar. Vávra. Filmové studio Barrandov.
Witches. (2024). Directed by Elizabeth Sankey. Ardimages UK.
Witches' Brew. (1980). Directed by Herbert L. Strock & Richard Shorr. United Artists.
Witches of Eastwick, The. (1987). Directed by George Miller. Warner Bros.
Wizard of Oz, The. (1939). Directed by Victor Fleming. Metro-Goldwyn-Mayer.
Woodlands Dark and Days Bewitched: A History of Folk Horror. (2021). Directed by Kier-La Janisse. Severin Films.
Yellow Submarine. (1968). Directed by George Dunning. United Artists.
10 Things I Hate About You. (1999). Directed by Gil Junger. Touchstone Pictures.
2001: A Space Odyssey. (1968). Directed by Stanley Kubrick. Warner Bros.
3 Women. (1977). Directed by Robert Altman. 20th Century-Fox.
40-Year-Old Virgin, The. (2005). Directed by Judd Apatow. Universal Pictures.
9 to 5. (1980). Directed by Colin Higgins. 20th Century Fox.

www.ingramcontent.com/pod-product-compliance
Lightning Source LLC
Chambersburg PA
CBHW061214070526
44584CB00029B/3830